By the same author:

REPUTATION FOR A SONG

THE HASTENING WIND

FAR MORNING

THE SECOND MAN

THE CAPTAIN GENERAL (John P. Stevenson)

STORM BIRD: The Strange Life of Georgina Weldon

DARK TORRENT OF GLENCOE

THE MASSINGHAM AFFAIR

A CRIME OF ONE'S OWN

THE FATAL INHERITANCE

The Fatal Inheritance

PHILIP II AND THE SPANISH NETHERLANDS

Edward Grierson

GARDEN CITY, NEW YORK

Doubleday & Company, Inc.

1969

The Crossroads of World History Series

EDITED BY ORVILLE PRESCOTT

Library of Congress Catalog Card Number 69–12199

*To my wife, who shared the burdens and
pleasures of this book.*

INTRODUCTION

This is a remarkable book on many counts. Far more a narrative history than it is a work of exposition, *The Fatal Inheritance* tells a great story marvelously well. Edward Grierson is a writer with a sense of style as well as of the past. His urbane prose is marked by flights of formal elegance, by ironic humor and by penetrating insights into individual minds and also into the tragic drama which is so much of history.

Objective in his judgments without being dryly aloof, sympathetic in his understanding of conflicting points of view, impeccable in his scholarship, Mr. Grierson never neglects the reasons for opinions and actions, the psychological, religious, political and economic forces which always mold men and events. But such matters do not obscure the dramatic impact of personality or the fierce drive of his story.

It is, of course, a terrible story and a heroic one, a story of fanaticism, cruelty, terror, torture, battle and massacre. But always amid the slaughter, the ruin and hatred were the courageous deeds of individual men, men of patience, persistence and unceasing valor.

The cast is large, the parts wonderfully various. But the play is dominated by three men of major stature: Philip II, the bigoted idealist whose every decision and every deed were the result of his passionate dedication to his religious faith; the Duke of Alva, the greatest soldier of his time, whose ruthless use of terror anticipated events in our own bloody century; and William of Nassau, Prince of Orange, astute, ambiguous, subtle and devious, a cautious politician who became a great statesman and a national hero.

Edward Grierson's approach to the rebellion in the Netherlands against the tyranny of Spain, one of the most extraordinary and probably the most prolonged rebellion in history, is fresh and original. He is not only concerned with epochal events in the Netherlands, but also with the rebellion's crucial significance as perhaps the most important cause for the decline of the imperial power of the greatest state in Europe. Empires always decline as well as rise. Why they decline is a perennially interesting question. Seldom can a historian demonstrate as clearly as has Mr. Grierson how one cause helped precipitate such a decline. The rebellious people of the Netherlands were indeed Spain's fatal inheritance.

For several generations readers whose imaginations have been intrigued by references to the drama and melodrama of the Netherlands rebellion have had to turn to the stirring pages of John Lothrop Motley's *The Rise of the Dutch Republic,* which was published more than one hundred years ago. But modern scholarship has unearthed much that Motley never knew and modern historians strive for an objectivity to which Motley never aspired. Therefore the publication of *The Fatal Inheritance* is all the more welcome. It presents a grand panorama of politics and war, intrigue and religious controversy. It is solidly packed with information.

Reading *The Fatal Inheritance* is an intellectually stimulating experience. It is also an immensely enjoyable one. With this book Edward Grierson joins the exclusive company of writers whose works of history are also works of literature.

ORVILLE PRESCOTT

CONTENTS

INTRODUCTION by Orville Prescott.   ix

AUTHOR'S NOTE.   xiii

1. PRELUDE. THE EMPEROR. 1555.   1

2. SPAIN.   10

3. PHILIP II. HIS POLICIES. THE FINANCES.   17

4. WAR WITH THE PAPACY AND FRANCE. 1556–59.   25

5. THE SPANISH NETHERLANDS. 1559.   39

6. REGIME OF THE DUCHESS MARGARET. 1559–67.   51

7. THE GOVERNMENT AND ECONOMY OF SPAIN.
   COUNCILS, CHURCH AND INQUISITION.   87

8. THE NETHERLANDS. REGIME OF THE DUKE
   OF ALVA. 1567–73.   105

9. PHILIP IN MIDDLE AGE. DON CARLOS. 1568.
   THE GRAND COMMANDER. SIEGE OF
   LEYDEN. TURNING OF THE TIDE.
   1573–74.   139

10. THE PRINCE OF ORANGE. MUTINIES.
    THE SPANISH FURY. 1574–76.   161

11. PACIFICATION OF GHENT. SUMMIT OF
    PATRIOT FORTUNES. ORANGE AT
    BRUSSELS. 1576–77.   172

12. ARCHDUKE MATTHIAS. GOVERNMENT AND
    DEATH OF DON JOHN. 1577–78.   182

13. SPAIN AND THE INDIES. NEW TRENDS IN
    SPANISH POLICY. 1579. THE CONQUEST
    OF PORTUGAL. 1580.   195

14. ALEXANDER OF PARMA. UNIONS OF ARRAS
    AND UTRECHT. THE PROVINCES DIVIDE.
    ANJOU. DEATH OF ORANGE. 1578–84.   212

15. ADVANCE OF PARMA. FALL OF ANTWERP.
    1584–85.   234

16. INTERVENTION OF ELIZABETH. 1585.   243

17. THE ARMADA. 1585–88.   247

18. THE PROBLEM OF FRANCE. 1588–89.   284

19. PARMA'S LAST CAMPAIGN. 1589–92.   288

20. FAILURE IN FRANCE. REGIMES OF MANSFIELD,
    THE ARCHDUKE ERNEST AND FUENTES.
    1593–96.   319

21. TROUBLES IN ARAGON. 1590–92.
    THE DARKENING SCENE. FINANCIAL
    PROBLEMS. THE SETTLEMENT. 1595–98.   334

22. THE BREACH MADE FINAL. DEATH OF PHILIP.
    1598.   348

    APPENDIX.   364

    SOURCES OF QUOTATIONS.   366

    BIBLIOGRAPHICAL NOTE.   371

    INDEX.   375

AUTHOR'S NOTE

This book is an attempt to assess the rebellion of Spain's Netherlands provinces during the reign of Philip II and to measure its importance in the much wider setting of Spanish imperialism and "decline." Our concern is therefore not wholly with the Netherlands —for we must consider also Spain herself, her government, social and religious structure and empire—but these provinces are nevertheless central to our theme: and here any writer of the period must start with John Lothrop Motley, whose *Rise of the Dutch Republic* is not only required but compulsive reading.

Let us enter a *caveat* at this point. Modern research, under the inspiration of another great writer and scholar, Dr. Pieter Geyl, has established that Motley is not the most trustworthy of guides through the labyrinth of the social, political and religious problems of the age, for in fact he misunderstood many of them completely, and by a reading of sixteenth-century Europe in terms of nineteenth-century liberalism came to some very odd and sometimes comical conclusions.

But in the field of action and portraiture he shines. In the painting of great canvases he excels. No one will understand what the Netherlands rebellion was about by sticking too closely to Motley's opinions or even to many of his "facts." But no one will *visualize* it at all without the benefit at least of glimpses into this brilliant and exciting book. I have shamelessly quarried from it. I can think of no better way of breathing back life into one of the most heroic and engrossing eras in history.

THE FATAL INHERITANCE

1

PRELUDE. THE EMPEROR. 1555.

Midway through the seventeenth century it began to dawn on thinking minds that the leadership of Europe had passed out of Spanish hands, where everyone had assumed it had lain at least since the battle of Lepanto in 1571. Spain's manners and modes were still widely copied; the prestige of her literature and art was at its height. But at Rocroi in 1643 her once invincible infantry had been crushed; by the Treaty of Munster, after eighty years of struggle, she had been forced to recognize the independence of her rebellious Netherlands provinces; and at the Peace of the Pyrenees she tacitly acknowledged French supremacy in Europe.

This profound change in the status and structure of a nation obviously had not happened overnight but had its roots much further back in Spanish history. The pacifism of the reign of Philip III at the beginning of the seventeenth century and the belligerence of Olivares which succeeded it were both reactions of people in search of remedies for a condition which was already felt to be mortal. That these were also the periods which saw the greatest flowering of Spanish culture is either an agreeable irony or else proof that nations like individuals often compensate for emotional deprivations by outbursts of creative genius in the arts. For everyone was conscious that somewhere on the way something had been irretrievably lost.

Don Quixote, which appeared between 1605 and 1615, illustrates these problems and trends. Its great popular success was due to the affection people still felt for the chivalry books, for those tales of giants and sorcerers in whom they half believed. But for the educated, for the intellectuals, it was a parable, and a bitter one. Through their eyes, and with the experience of our own time to guide us, we discern a society that has begun to be impatient with heroics and its imperial past. The knight in his rusty armor who dreams great dreams is mad. Sancho, who believes in the easy life, is sane—until he too catches the infection of grandeur. On this level *Don Quixote* is the forerunner of the modern anti-heroic novel which looks back in anger on attitudes which its author resents and may subconsciously envy; not that Cervantes himself—no intellectual—envied anyone anything except money and position in the world. Nevertheless, like all great artists, he was the expression of his age and could not help reflecting its mixture of contempt and admiration for the Spain of the past, the Spain of Philip II, for the "good old days" which had left such a legacy of trouble.

But at what precise point did trouble start? How far back had one to go—has one to go—to detect the first symptoms of decline? To the state bankruptcies, the first of which occurred in 1557, the year after Philip's accession in the peninsula? To the failure of the great Armada or intervention in the French religious wars? But both these arose out of the rebellion in the Netherlands which was central to almost all the King's problems, even the financial ones. And that rebellion itself stemmed from the unnatural association of Spain and the Low Countries under one ruler which had come about as a result of dynastic accident long before Philip's birth and had been perpetuated by his father's disposal of his inheritance. If the disposition of this property had been better ordered, who can doubt that the futures of both Spain and the Low Countries would have been radically different?

To draw dividing lines in history is an exercise full of danger, but great movements on the world stage nonetheless have a time and a place of beginning if only we can isolate them, as perhaps we can here, by focusing on an event which was judged extraordinary in its own age and seems in retrospect to have been arranged by those cruelly dispassionate Immortals whom Hardy imagined as watching over men's affairs. The scene was certainly worthy of them—a late October day in 1555 in the palace of the dukes of Brabant in Brussels. The occasion: the abdication by the Emperor Charles V of his patrimonial provinces in Burgundy and the Netherlands in favor of his son.

For the details of the ceremony one should go to Motley's classic *Rise of the Dutch Republic*. Profoundly out of sympathy though he was with the Catholic Emperor and the son whose tyranny forms one of the twin themes of his book, the Protestant historian of the Netherlands could no more forgo the pageantry and poignancy of the scene than he could curb himself from moralizing about it in splendidly biased prose.

In Motley's pages it is all there: the brilliant assembly of the States General and knights of the order of the Golden Fleece; the solemn entrance of "Caesar," as contemporaries called him, leaning on the shoulder of that same Prince of Orange who was to thwart the ambitions of his son; the oration of Councilor Philippe de Bruxelles; the Emperor's reply with its inventory of his journeys on the business of empire over a period of forty years; to its moving end, in which he begged forgiveness of his hearers for any wrongs he might have done them in the past. "And here," wrote an English eyewitness of the scene, "he broke into a weeping, whereunto, besides the dolefulness of the matter, I think he was much provoked by seeing the whole company do the like before, [there] being in my opinion, not one man in the whole assembly, stranger or other, that during the time of a good piece of his oration poured not out abundantly tears, some more, some less."

The grief was almost certainly genuine: not even Motley suggests otherwise. Though he had taxed them heavily throughout his reign to pay for adventures elsewhere, had persecuted the growing heretical minority with ferocious edicts and spent only a small fraction of his reign on their soil, Charles had never lost the love and admiration of the Netherlanders among whom he had been born and had lived in the formative years before other cares drew him away.

This liking, which was a matter of race and heart, Charles fully returned—he thought of his Burgundian inheritance as *nuestra patria.*" Yet the seventeen provinces governed from Brussels by a Vicereine formed a minute part of his realms, and the ceremony itself was only a stage in a phased withdrawal from power unparalleled since the time of Diocletian, which would end with the handing over of territories from Sicily to Peru and titles as diverse as titular King of Jerusalem and Holy Roman Emperor.

The acquisition of this world empire which Charles was in the process of laying down is one of the romances of history and a remarkable tribute to the matrimonial expertise of the Hapsburg family, which always very sensibly preferred marrying territories to running the risks of conquering them.

The young and impoverished Archduke Maximilian of Austria had had the good fortune to marry Mary of Burgundy, heiress of Charles the Bold, whose attempts to make a reality of the "middle kingdom" between France and the German states had revived an old European dream. The Burgundian dukes, a cadet branch of the reigning French house of Valois, had made some inroads into their suzerain's territories along the Moselle, but with Charles the Bold's death in battle under the walls of Nancy the dream had faded; the duchy, which was the heart of Burgundy, was reabsorbed into France; and the heiress of what remained, the Duchess Mary, could count herself fortunate to keep the Franche Comté, Luxemburg and various provinces in the Netherlands which had been acquired piecemeal by her ancestors and now formed the nub of her inheritance, just large enough to tempt a Hapsburg into marriage.

Nothing might have come of this, and indeed Mary herself was soon dead in a hunting accident. But a son had been born—Philip the Fair—who was destined to attract no mere duchess, however well endowed, but a Spanish princess, Joanna, second daughter of Ferdinand of Aragon and Isabella of Castile, the "Catholic Kings," the most celebrated rulers of their time, the patrons of Columbus.

Of this union the future emperor Charles V was born in Ghent in 1500.

His astonishing future would not have been immediately evident to contemporaries: Joanna's dead elder sister had had a son, Don Miguel, who stood between the Burgundian branch and the Castilian crown. Even when this matter was resolved by Don Miguel's death in infancy, Charles's claim to Aragon, the other half of Spain, remained tenuous, being dependent on the good will and future childlessness of Ferdinand the Catholic, Isabella's Machiavellian partner, who was to waste little time in marrying again after the great Queen's death. Besides, Charles's parents were still young; he could expect a long wait before inheriting the Netherlands and the Austrian lands along the Danube ruled by his Hapsburg grandfather, now the Emperor Maximilian.

But in the result everything fell to Charles in the perverse way in which fate can deal even the winning cards. He was only a few months old when his mother Joanna became heiress to Castile and to its enormous territories in Mexico, Peru, the Isthmus and the Caribbean islands which had been carved out by the *Conquistadores:* with the death of Isabella in 1504 she was queen, and the prospects of world empire were opening for her son. Two years later Philip the Fair was dead and the nine-year-old Charles found himself Duke of Burgundy and doubly bereaved by the loss of a father and of a mother driven hopelessly insane by the shock of this event. In 1516 died Ferdinand the Catholic, without living heir of his second marriage, and the crown of Aragon, with Catalonia, Valencia, the Balearics and the dependencies in Naples and Sicily were Charles's also.

The boy—he was still only sixteen—was proclaimed in Brussels as sovereign of the Spains jointly with his mother, who however was never fit to rule and lived out her days in the castle of Tordesillas for nearly forty years. Charles always showed her a filial respect and visited her when he could—which by the nature of things could not be often. For in 1519 the Emperor Maximilian died and the Hapsburg lands, including Austria, Styria, Tyrol and Carinthia, fell to the nineteen-year-old prince, who in the following year was elected King of the Romans and Emperor Designate of the Holy Roman Empire—the overlordship of Germany. It only remained for him to be crowned by the Pope a decade later and to annex the duchy of Milan to round out an empire greater than that of Charlemagne, supported by the rising military power of Spain, the Genoese fleets under Andrea Doria, and the silver of the Indies which gave promises of undreamed-of wealth.

Fortune, as Charles himself remarked in a bitter hour, is a strumpet who gives her favors to the young. He might have added that even then she acts equivocally; indeed it is one of the major ironies of history that all these abundant gifts, which seemed to point to the creation of a unified Catholic, autocratic Europe, had been given to a man perfectly equipped to rule it, at precisely the moment when the spiritual unity of Christendom had cracked forever.

For when Charles was nine years old John Calvin was born at Noyon; he was twelve when Luther took the chair of theology at Wittenberg; seventeen when the famous theses were nailed to the door of its castle church; he had been Emperor-elect for less than two years when Luther was summoned before the imperial Diet at Worms and the great rift of the Reformation opened up before the startled eyes of the people and their rulers.

Charles was a devoted Catholic who drew much strength from his religion and believed wholeheartedly in its sanctions. In the lands where his power was absolute he persecuted the "Reformed" sects with the utmost ruthlessness. The first Lutheran martyrs were burned at the stake in Brussels when he was twenty-three, and right at the end of his life the news that Protestant cells had been discovered in that most orthodox country, Castile itself, drove him to a frenzy of exhortation to his successors to destroy the heretical tree, root and branch.

Yet he was no mere bigoted enthusiast but a statesman of acute insight, a realist who understood the limitations of power and was always prepared to make concessions where his intelligence found them to be necessary and his faith permitted them. Throughout his life he pursued two ideals: the advancement of his family and Catholic supremacy in Europe. He himself would have seen nothing irreconcilable in these aims, in pursuit of which he was ready to use every weapon to hand: force when the situation was ripe for it, or conciliation. Thus after the first crude attempts to silence Luther were seen to lead only to a hardening of resistance among the Protestant north German princes, he did his utmost to come to a compromise with them, and might even have succeeded in achieving religious peace if the political blindness of the Papacy and the ambitions of the Catholic south German rulers had not been matched by an increasing radicalism on the Protestant side, leaving the Emperor and his Lutheran alter ego, Melancthon, high and dry, as is the fate of most moderates in ages of faith.

It was a traumatic experience. After the failure of the Regensburg diet in 1541 Charles no longer tried to tame the whirlwind; he rode it. At the battle of Muhlberg, rising from a sickbed, he smote his enemies hip and thigh, as he had smoked out the Moslem pirate lair of Tunis and beaten back the Turks from the gates of Vienna, almost unaided. He was Catholicism's only true champion, just as he was Europe's: the last of the medievalists, for whom the two conceptions were one and the same.

This made him a lonely figure. Few great men have had more dangerous and persistent rivals in so many fields. To have been born to dispute in theological terms with Luther and in battle with the Ottoman sultan Suleiman the Magnificent at the height of his formidable power was a heritage scarcely to be envied. The French king, Francis of Valois, he had always with him—

the irreconcilable rival who had disputed the imperial crown in 1520 and all the visions of one Hapsburg-dominated European polity which had stemmed from it. Captured at Pavia, brought ignominiously a prisoner to Spain, Francis had still managed to emerge unscathed: the eternal gadfly whose intrigues and wars called out the loans at ruinous rates of interest which the Emperor was forced time and again to raise from his German and Genoese bankers, till even the flow of treasure from the New World was swallowed up before it left the Isthmus of Panama.

This financial crisis, hidden from the vast bulk of the Emperor's subjects if not from his creditors in the banking houses of the Fuggers and Welsers, is the key to the last years of Charles's reign and to most of Philip's. The humiliating end to the struggle against the north German princes, when the aging Emperor had been forced to flee bag and baggage across the Brenner Pass from Maurice of Saxony's raiders, could well have been reversed, given the funds and the armies one hired with them. Even his failure to recover the imperial city of Metz, which these same German princes had handed over to the French, was an event which Charles could bear with fortitude, though it was on this occasion that he expressed himself on the whorish inconstancy of fortune. But money was crucial, even in an age which reflected the last gleams of the medieval spirit. Without money the mercenaries could not be paid; the court with its horde of bureaucrats and expensive hangers-on could not function; the Emperor, crippled with gout and increasingly a prey to melancholia, the legacy of his unfortunate mother, could not even be sure of raising the fleet which would take him to retirement in Spain.

The people of his time marveled at his abdication: posterity quite simply understands it. He was in a rage to be gone if only he could go with honor. In a sense he had been abdicating for years. Thus as early as 1521, at the outset of his reign, he had handed over his Austrian possessions to his brother Ferdinand, destined as his successor in the empire. This had been partly an administrative convenience and partly a sop to ensure the loyalty of a man who could have made trouble for him; but whatever the motive, it had meant a shedding of power, and he had followed it up in 1540 by creating his own son Philip Duke of Milan and giving him the kingdom of Naples on the occasion of the "English marriage" to Mary Tudor.

Now at the end of his reign he shed the rest of a now intolerable burden. Three days before the abdication of the Netherlands in Brussels he had stepped down in Philip's favor from sovereignty of the famous Burgundian order of the Golden Fleece, founded by his great-great-grandfather, Philip the Good. A little less than three months later, in the course of a ceremony in his private apartments attended by only a small circle of his family and high officials, he surrendered his powers over the crowns of Castile, Leon, Aragon, Sicily, the Indies and the islands, together with the masterships of the three orders of Santiago, Calatrava and Alcantara. Lastly, after a much longer delay, the imperial crown itself was sent to Ferdinand.*

Throughout his active life Charles had remained a Burgundian at heart, a prince of the middle lands along the Rhine which formed the core of western Europe. Most of his time between journeyings had been spent there, not in Italy or Spain. His tastes were Burgundian, even to his appetite, which was enormous, and his sense of the common touch which never deserted him. Blessed with a son who was his antithesis and entirely Castilian in cold reserve of manner, he had nevertheless tried to introduce him into the wider European spheres which were governed from Brussels and Vienna. Toward the end of his reign, repenting of the way he had handed over ancestral possessions to the now thoroughly Germanized Ferdinand, he had even tried to reverse the irreversible and insert Philip into the imperial succession either ahead of Ferdinand or at least as a kind of sandwich between Ferdinand and *his* son, another Maximilian.

This, as it proved, was no longer a practical proposition. Taken at its face value, the attempt would seem to point both to a refusal to recognize realities and to a desire to inflict on Philip the cares of an empire too vast for one man to govern.

Deep down, however, Charles had understood the dangers and also perhaps the limitations of his son. In retrospect, the "family compact" by which he tried to impose his will on Ferdinand has a halfhearted look, and it is significant that Philip himself never pressed the matter seriously either in his father's lifetime or after his death. Far more to the point is the English marriage of Philip with Mary Tudor which formed the focal point of Charles's

* The imperial Electors delayed their choice for another eighteen months. The Papacy for years refused to ratify.

diplomacy in the years immediately preceding his abdication. The heir of this union was to succeed to a joint kingdom of England and the Netherlands, while Philip's son by his first marriage, Don Carlos, was to succeed in Spain. The aim was clear—to turn the Netherlands into a viable unit by giving it a base of support across the English Channel and to take this part of the old Burgundian inheritance *away* from Spain into the position of an allied but independent power.

With Mary Tudor's death, childless, this imaginative idea was stillborn. But one may perhaps see an echo of it in Charles's choice of Brussels for the one ceremonial abdication he allowed himself— a public farewell to an arena which had been his birthplace but which he foresaw might have less happy associations for his successor. Finally, by choosing to return to die in Castile, a country which had not engaged his youthful sympathies but which he had come to respect, the Emperor was making the same declaration in another form. His choice of a grave on Castilian soil is symbolic of his knowledge that it was *here* that the future lay for his successors and that Spain had become the powerhouse of the world.

2

SPAIN.

Physically, Spain is a poor country. Nine tenths of its surface lies at over fifteen hundred feet; a quarter, over three thousand feet; a tenth of it is bare rock. It is a geological and meteorological curiosity unmatched anywhere else in Europe: a Siberia in the sun, with extremes of heat and cold that make nonsense of theories that lands surrounded by oceans should be climatically equable and *douce*.

In fact Spain is a paradox: not an entity but a series of divisions. In the north and west it is Atlantic country of high rainfall, with hills and green valleys and almost Norwegian-style fjords. In parts of the south it is little better than a desert companion to the Sahara across the Gibraltar straits. Along the Mediterranean shore and in parts of Andalusia the soil is rich; indeed the Valencian strip is one of the most fertile in the world. But at least as much of the land is mountainous. The Pyrenees cut off the whole peninsula from the rest of Europe. The Cantabrian Mountains divide the northern coastal belt of Galicia and Asturias from Castile. In a broad arc the Iberian range isolates the fertile Ebro plain. In the south, the Sierra Morena and the much higher Cordilleras and Sierra Nevada surround the coastal lands around Alicante and Malaga. The real heart of Spain, occupying perhaps half of its mass, is the great central plateau of the Meseta, where the local saying has it that life is nine months winter and three months hell—a country of thin soil and winds off the sierra, where sheep-rearing is the soul of husbandry. And even here there are mountains to cut off Leon and Old Castile in the north from New Castile and the plain of La Mancha where Don Quixote rode.

These divisions of the land itself were reflected in the sixteenth century (as to some degree today) in political and racial divisions. In the west of the peninsula Portugal was an independent kingdom, with its own language and jealously guarded identity. But even the Spanish remainder had no unity. In the northeast the territories

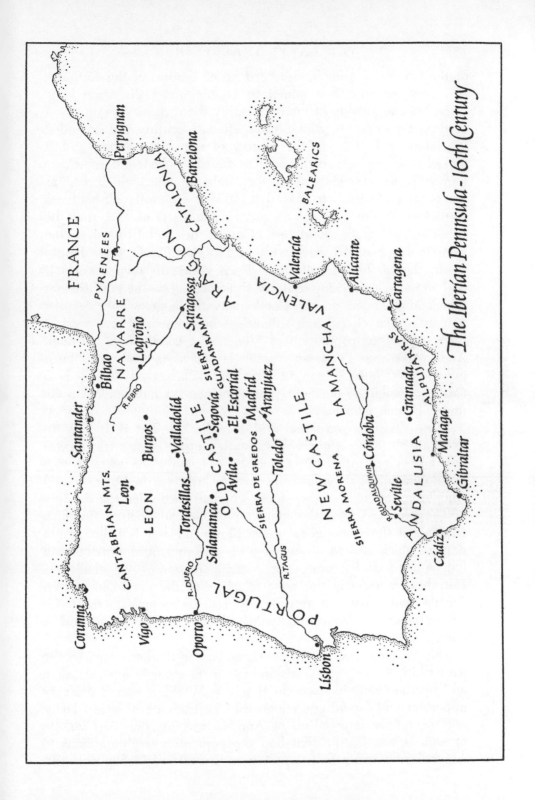

The Iberian Peninsula - 16th Century

of the Crown of Aragon, the heritage of Ferdinand the Catholic, had only recently been joined to Castile under the same king. There was no identity of interest—rather the reverse. Aragon was a Mediterranean power, which in the fifteenth century had expanded into Italy and Sicily to the disgust of successive Popes, and it looked eastward, not to the west as Castile looked: indeed it was barely Spanish—certainly not in its Catalan province which remains markedly un-Spanish to this day. It was an exotic offshoot: so suspicious, so grudging, privilege-loving and stiff-necked, that the subsidies which its assemblies (*Cortes*) deigned to vote to the ruler it happened to share with neighboring Castile were hardly worth the trouble of collection. Even within its own borders it had no unity, comprising as it did three provinces—the northeastern tableland of Aragon proper; Catalonia, with the great but declining seaport of Barcelona; and Valencia, where the land was worked by a submerged population of Moors in a condition of serfdom. And on the west Pyrenean frontier lay Navarre, which had been incorporated into Aragon in 1512 but which now belonged to Castile, though its northern half remained an independent state under French influence.

These divisions were real and ineradicable. But it is easy to overstate their importance to sixteenth-century Spain. Aragon was only a sleeping partner in the business of empire. The presence of a large unassimilated population of non-Christians in Valencia and Andalusia, the relics of the Moors who had once ruled the Emirate of Córdoba and later the kingdom of Granada before the final triumph of the *reconquista* under Ferdinand and Isabella, was a danger which was to obsess Spanish governments for more than half a century to come, not without reason as we shall see. But these were only the poor relations of the dominant power, Castile, which had outgrown all its sister kingdoms to the point where the words Castile and Spain were synonymous in the world's eyes.

This pre-eminence, which had been earned the hard way, by the leadership of medieval Christendom in its struggle against Islam and by the *Conquistadores* in the New World, was to have very important and fateful consequences. The tradition of great deeds, not the milder imperialism of Aragon, was the one that was to prevail. It was Castile that had the population—eight millions to Aragon's one and a half. Apart from Barcelona, Lisbon and Saragossa, the great cities of the peninsula were Castilian: Valladolid, where Philip was born, Toledo, Salamanca, Burgos, Granada, Segovia, above all Seville, the entrepôt of the Indies trade, which was rapidly becoming one of the largest of European towns. Even industrially, Castile was not to be despised. Toledo and Segovia had developed flourishing trades in arms, leather goods and woolen fabrics; Granada, with its memories of luxurious emirs, dealt profitably in silks; Seville was a banking center and clearinghouse for the *Carrera de Indias,* the world's most envied trade. It was Castile that had conquered the Indies, with the exception of Brazil. The silver of the Peruvian mines was hers. The ships that carried it across the Atlantic were hers and they put in at her ports. Here was affluence. Yet, paradoxically enough, Castile's main industry was wool—raw wool—controlled by the great sheep breeders' guild of the *Mesta:* aristocratic, reactionary, hostile to every interest, even agricultural, that conflicted with the primitive economy of the wool clip carried on the backs of its flocks as they moved between grazing grounds and markets across the breadth of Spain.

The *Mesta* is typical of Castile, both of its economy and its people, as we find marvelously preserved for us in the pages of *Don Quixote.* In this book, the most representative work of the Spanish genius, one finds the high and the low in excellent humor with one another. Here, in the delicious dialogues between knight and squire, is democracy at its most fundamental, its most felicitous —but it is a meeting of extremes. There are few middlemen in the story, few traces of a bourgeois class. Such a class existed, particularly around Seville and in the towns of Old Castile, but in general the merchant had long been the object of scorn. Hidalgos —small gentry—would not soil their hands with trade. Such middle class as had begun to raise its head was mostly Jewish, and this had been progressively destroyed, first by pogrom and expulsion of the hard core of the race under Ferdinand and Isabella, then by forced baptism of those who remained (the *conversos* as they were called) and the later pitiless persecution launched by the Inquisition against the backsliding and secret "Judaizing" of these reluctant converts, many of them men of great ability who had reached the highest posts.

In the capitalist world then dawning this absence of a substantial middle class with opportunities for advancement and ambitions to match was a severe loss to Spain and in the end was one of the causes of her decline. Much of the specie brought from Peru in the treasure fleets escaped into the hands of foreign entre-preneurs and was not used productively to prime the Castilian economy. Its ultimate effect was adverse, by tempting rulers into adventures beyond their means and helping to bring about an inflation which the authorities could neither understand nor check.

Nevertheless the silver imports, even allowing for the leakage abroad, were substantial and gave Spain a significant margin over her rivals in days of rudimentary finance. These imports rose from an annual average of 195,000 ducats* in the five-year period of 1506–10, to 2,367,000 for the period 1551–55, reaching their height in 1591–95 at 8,444,000 ducats. Conversion of these figures into modern money is unrealistic, given the inflationary spiral of our age, but by the standards of the times they were enormous sums—far larger than the entire revenue of most of Spain's com-petitors. And even the anti-commercial spirit of Castile, though ultimately ruinous, had its short-term advantages. Most Castilians were poor, if we except the few grandees whose vast estates and imposing titles became legendary. The small gentry, their depend-ents and the peasants of the Meseta resembled them only in that they came of the same basic stock—the men who had conquered empires in the Indies with a handful of foot soldiers and a few horses. Too poor to work their small holdings with advantage, many of them deeply in debt to moneylenders, they took naturally to arms, if only in the hope of pillage and fat ransom money to be won. In the realms of adventure they set themselves no limits: indeed the conquests of Mexico and Peru would be incredible if they had not actually happened.

This spirit of imperialism was not confined to one class but embraced a whole people, from magnates like the Duke of Alva to the humblest "Old Christian" in his armies. The national crusade against the Moors had created it and nurtured it. Military ob-servers were to note the frugality and toughness of the Spanish soldier. From the days of the "Great Captain," Gonzalo de Córdoba,

---

* The gold ducat, modeled on the Venetian ducat, was introduced in 1497. It equaled 375 maravedis. As a coin in general use it was replaced in 1537 by the escudo, which equaled 350 maravedis. The ducat continued as a unit of account. The escudo was ac-cepted and circulated for a hundred years without change of content. The silver real was equivalent to 34 maravedis. The *real de a ocho*, the famous "Piece of Eight" of pirate tales, was the silver peso of 8 reals or 272 maravedis. One might roughly equate the dollar today with two and a half ducats.

in Isabella's time, no Spanish army was to be defeated in a
pitched battle for a century, till Turnhout in 1597 and the larger
affair at Nieuport in 1600, when Europe held its breath at the
incredible event. This superiority was not only proved in action
but in the long haul of a campaign, for even physically Spanish
armies were more enduring than others and less subject to the
ravages of fever and disease.

Nor was this entirely due to the fact that those who could
survive the Meseta in winter and its caldron of a summer could
endure anything. There was a dynamic behind it. The long traditions of the *reconquista* had given Castilians the certainty that
God was on their side. Their ancestors had driven the Moors from
Spain; they themselves were to face and turn back another wave
of Islamic expansion in the destruction of the Ottoman fleets in
the gulf of Lepanto. And heretics in Castilian eyes were as godless
as Moors. The exploits of Philip's troops in the Netherlands and
on the "Enterprise of England"—the great Armada—were prompted
by just the same passionate devotion to a country and a faith.
Cervantes was wounded at Lepanto, and he remembered it as
the great event of his life. Lope de Vega was aboard the fleet so
disastrously defeated in '88. There was a great sense of national
purpose.

And the Church supported it. No student of sixteenth-century
Spain can even begin to understand its golden age without some
knowledge of what the Catholic religion meant to its peoples. It
was an all-pervasive Church, a Church militant, even a revolutionary Church imbued with a passion for reform. Its scholars were
among the most learned in Europe; certainly it included in its
ranks the most mystical and visionary—St. Teresa to begin with,
a prodigy among women. As to its virtues and vices, opinions will
always differ. To Protestants, the era of the Inquisition must always
appear as the dark night of the human spirit, and so in a very
real sense it was. Men died and died horribly in the flames of
its *braseros*, though far fewer than mythology remembers and at
a time when the annals of most European countries, including
Protestant ones, were stained with deeds just as cruel and nearly
as widespread.

Whatever its demerits, the Inquisition was by no means unpopular in Spain. Its absolutism matched the national mood with
its dislike of compromise. This brought solid advantages to Spain

in an age when Europe was plagued by religious strife, either just submerged, as in Tudor England, or erupting into savage civil war of the kind which tore France apart throughout our period and in the next century almost destroyed Germany and Bohemia in the ghastly horrors of the Thirty Years War.

All this Spain escaped, because if she had many provinces, she had only one religion. Perhaps in retrospect, with those wars in mind, the Inquisition seems a little less of an evil. Certainly it ensured unity of belief and was a solvent of discord. Together with the absolutism of the King, it provided a sense of direction and purpose in an age of changing values when the fundamental beliefs of centuries were everywhere being questioned or overthrown. And this gave the nation its special strength. Spain was not the most populous country in Europe; its economy was not the soundest-based; its people in the mass were far from the richest. But it held the New World. It had the best armies, increasingly effective fleets, a system of government that suited it and a living faith to inspire it. At the date of Philip's accession no one doubted that it was the most formidable power in Christendom, rivaled only by the Ottomans and by distant unknown empires in China and the Ganges plain.

3

PHILIP II. HIS POLICIES. THE FINANCES.

The inheritor of this power and of these vast resources was not yet the "Prudent King" of Spanish tradition, still less the bogeyman of Protestant mythology, but a young man of twenty-eight, already once widowed and now the husband of an ailing wife thirteen years his senior.

Philip had been born at Valladolid in 1527 to the Empress Isabella, a Portuguese princess whom Charles, for all his many absences from her side, came to love devotedly. After her death he never thought of marrying again. This thoroughly dynastic union was part of a pattern, for the royal families of Spain, Portugal and Austria had been intermarrying for years and were to continue to do so for over a century. The mothers of Charles the Bold and the first Maximilian had both been Portuguese. Philip's father, as we have seen, had married into Portugal; so had his aunt; another aunt on the Burgundian side had married into Castile. It was an ancestry interbred to a pitch that would have satisfied the Pharaohs, and Philip's own matrimonies, like those of both his sisters, kept up the family tradition. His first wife had been a Portuguese cousin; his second, Mary Tudor, was the daughter of his great-aunt, Catherine of Aragon; his fourth was his own niece. Such a heredity and such tastes in themselves suggest a closed society, inward-looking, self-sufficient, proud, exclusive. Philip was its perfect and natural exemplar. Small-boned, delicately made, with pale complexion and blue eyes, he had a gravity of manner, a cold reserve, that impressed itself on all beholders. Few of them— and certainly not the Italians—found it easy to enthuse over his appearance. "*Statura piccolo et membri minuti . . . flammatica et malenconica . . . infirmo et valetudinario . . . naturalmente debile, et persone di poca . . . Di complessione delicatissime et di statura minore, chi mediocre*"—it all has a slighting sound. In face and figure a reflection of his father whose ugliness had been legendary until the brush of Titian ennobled it, Philip had the thick lower lip and projecting jaw of his Burgundian ancestors which can still be glimpsed beneath the trim beard and moustaches of the portraits dating from this time.

From any comparison of the characters of the two men Philip must emerge as by far the less sympathetic and fitted to rule a polyglot empire.

The Emperor, whose very mixed heredity was mirrored in his tastes, was at home everywhere; he had to be. In a touchingly boastful passage in his abdication speech he numbered off his journeys up and down Europe—nine to Germany, six to Spain, seven to Italy, four to France, two to England, ten to the Nether-lands (where he was speaking: a typically artful claim on his listeners' affections)—and though these descents had sometimes been abrupt there can be no doubt that on the whole they were popular, like Elizabeth's "progresses" through England, and helped to further the very desirable image of Charles as father figure. In this matter of projection the Emperor was usually fortunate: he had a good press in his own lifetime, and for all the comical tales of gluttony and funeral caperings at Yuste he has fallen mostly into the hands of respectful biographers, willing to show him off with his virtues and faults as a recognizable figure of flesh and blood.

Philip by contrast is always seen through the distorting lens of prejudice of one kind or another. "His body," says Cabrera, "was a human cage, however brief and narrow, in which lived a soul for whose flight the illimitable expanse of heaven was too small." Cabrera was a favorable critic and has been much quoted by Catholic biographers. Within the space of three pages the Prot-estant champion Motley, supported by an array of footnotes culled from contemporary sources, contrives to accuse his subject of ti-midity, sickliness, cowardice, cruelty, mediocrity of mind, inflex-ibility, flatulence, religious bigotry and gross licentiousness—this last on the strength of alleged roisterings in Brussels at the age of nineteen which hardly seem to match the rest of the indictment with the neatness a committed historian would wish.

No doubt much of this was propaganda, conceived in anger and perpetuated in bile. But behind it we may glimpse, however

indistinctly, the outlines of a man still young but already set
in his ways, intransigent, opinionated, devout: a bigot in the making.
Excessive piety, of which many contemporary witnesses complain,
squares with all we know of the later man and seems already
to have become a dominant strain in his nature; so does pride,
of which everyone accused him and which the portraits confirm;
also fastidiousness and a certain lack of animal spirits, of robustness,
which made the popular courtly amusements of feasting and joust-
ing profoundly uncongenial to him.

These characteristics of his son and the dangers that might
attach to them had certainly not escaped the Emperor, a shrewd
judge of men and their opinions. Something of a Polonius in his
way and always prodigal of fatherly advice, he had long since
taken steps to put Philip through his princely paces in a ceremonial
progress through the Low Countries and Italy, in the course of
which the youth was induced to break lances in the lists at Brussels
along with the most experienced competitors of the day, winning
golden opinions at least from those whose duty it was to record
them. Alas! outside their ranks the results were less encouraging.
"Disagreeable to the Italians," noted the Venetian envoy Soriano,
"detestable to the Flemings, odious to the Germans"—again we
meet the oddly shrill and venomous response to Philip: and this
seven years before his accession, nineteen before he sent Alva to
the Netherlands, exactly forty before the Armada, from the envoy
of a nation whom he never harmed.

The reaction is interesting precisely because it is so unfair: like
the blame the English thrust on him for the Marian persecution
of heretics which in fact he had done his utmost to prevent. The
brilliant wedding celebrations at which he had appeared dressed
from head to toe in white, distributing purses to all bribable magnates—of whom there were a great many—left as their legacy only
a hatred which nothing could overcome. Obviously one is encountering here something organic: a complete withdrawal of sympathy which seems to have no basis in logic but to be instinctive:
a repugnance which was in part due to the changing allegiances
of Englishmen, moving uneasily between Rome and the Reformation
away from the traditional alliance with Spain, but more distinctly
personal—perhaps a knowledge that these gracious actions of a
"clement, benign and debonair prince," to use the phraseology of

the time, were not heartfelt but assumed, and assumed reluctantly by a man whose nature altogether rejected them.

If these were indeed the feelings of Philip's critics, they were acute. Benevolence was not the key to his nature, nor did he care for display for display's sake. To judge him as coldhearted, however, would be far from the mark. His very compliance with the Emperor's wishes over the English marriage, which can hardly have been personally agreeable to him, was just one proof of filial piety and devotion to his father. He was by no means incapable of love, as his delightful letters to his daughters were one day to show. But he loved within a very narrow range. Outside the small circle of his family and intimates he seems to have had little affection to spare for anyone. He lacked warmth, bonhomie, the power to charm, perhaps even the desire to charm.

These were not disadvantages in Spain, where gravity was admired and where Charles himself, a Fleming by birth, was only fully accepted when he had come to Yuste to die. The Spanish people, and particularly the Castilians among whom he had been brought up, loved and revered Philip because they saw in him a reflection of their own attitudes to life and death. No man—except on another plane Don Quixote—was ever more truly their representative. But in the Netherlands, where the general prosperity had bred a numerous and rising middle class, this proud reserve was as deeply resented as his foreignness, the inability to speak Flemish or even tolerable French (the language of the Burgundian court) which had become painfully evident in the very first moments of the reign, at the abdication scene itself, when the new ruler of the Netherlands had had to employ a Church dignitary to read his speech to the assembly.

Problems of this kind were not insoluble, as the Emperor himself had proved when as a young man he had gone to his Spanish inheritance without a word of its language and with a retinue of grasping foreign courtiers at his back. Patience and suppleness had turned him (who had never been out of the Netherlands) into an acceptable Spaniard and his brother Ferdinand (who had as a boy never been out of Spain) into a model Austrian.

Unfortunately Philip, unlike his more flexible father and uncle, was never anything but his own intransigent self. There was nothing pliant in his nature. He believed in solutions, not compromises. And by an unhappy chance the Fates had provided him in the

Netherlands with an insoluble problem and opponents who shared his state of mind. In a very real sense Philip deserved the Calvinists. Perhaps they deserved each other.

The concerns of a world power are surprisingly constant; they vary very little from one generation to another. The Netherlands apart, Philip's problems at his accession mirrored with an extraordinary fidelity those that had faced his father forty years earlier, when in the same town of Brussels he had heard himself proclaimed King of Spain and the Indies. A hostile Pope busily engaged in plots to expel the Spaniards from Naples and Milan with French help; a young French king easily lured into adventures; England a lukewarm ally; the menacing Ottoman power poised to thrust deeper into Europe; the Moslem corsairs on the Barbary Coast—the comparison was very exact.

In some respects Philip's situation was less troubled than his father's because his obligations were smaller and more manageable. The defense of the Danube frontier against the Turk and of Catholicism in Germany against its Lutheran princes were no concern of his, nor was he exercised to find money to bribe his way to an imperial throne now firmly vested in the Austrian branch of his house. And this was just as well. For if other problems had receded, a crucial one had grown, and bankruptcy, if by a politer name, was already stalking the Spanish treasury which Charles had so woefully mismanaged.

How this came about is not strictly part of our story. Most of the details are obscure, even now that the records of Charles's finance council, the *Consejo de la Hacienda,* are available to economists who care to burrow their way through the archives. There is even a school of thought with very distinguished advocates prepared to argue that Charles's wars did no financial harm to Spain, though this might well have surprised the Emperor's bankers in Augsburg and Genoa as they waited with what fortitude they could muster for the repayment of interest years overdue. That Charles at the outset of his reign plunged half a million ducats into debt to raise bribes for the imperial Electors is hardly to be disputed. That Philip at the beginning of *his* was trying to borrow at 40 per cent interest and finding no takers provides a piquant commentary on the inflationary nature of debts.

In between had stretched a lifetime of strenuous effort, most for worthy causes, which bore down heavily on the Emperor and all his dominions. The Netherlands, which in 1541 were voting subsidies to their ruler to the tune of one million gold florins, had been screwed up to nearly seven times that sum by 1556. Naturally there were complaints: a growing reluctance to pay for the imperial connection and its all-consuming wars. In Spain, in 1551, Philip, his father's regent at the time, was reporting an estimated deficiency of nearly a million ducats for the year. In 1552, treasure from the Indies, a major source of wealth, yielded two million ducats; this was almost exactly the sum that Charles spent on one single military operation, his disastrous siege of Metz, his borrowings for that year being four million. Two years earlier, the two million ducats which the Emperor's special envoy, Legazpa, had fetched back from the Peruvian mines were to everyone's astonishment swallowed up in a matter of months.

In his notes for a book published after his death under the title of *The Emperor Charles V*, Royall Tyler estimates that imperial expenditure in the last decade of Charles's reign was running at several times receipts. Basing himself on the researches of Carande, Tyler has reckoned that by 1554 the annual deficit was over four million ducats, even after receipts from the next six years had been anticipated and spent in advance. Here was a sad recession from the early halcyon days of the Emperor's life when a world of plenty had seemed only just round the corner; indeed if we accept Tyler's figures and his deductions from them we are faced with a classic case of the borrower who falls steadily deeper in the toils till in the end he lives entirely on his debts, only surviving because his creditors have an interest in keeping him afloat, if only by clinging like shipwrecked mariners to the last raft of his solvency.

Charles, a man of sound common sense, had not been without some conception of his dangers. Very early in his reign he had been warned in a state paper, couched in the most solemn terms, of bankruptcy ahead, and he had done his best to set his house in order by creating a finance council to keep some check on receipts and expenditure. The results, if not sensational, at least sealed up the drain at one level by stopping the enormous peculations of the nobility who had been raiding the treasury for years; moreover the chosen secretary of the council, Los Cobos,

was not personally as rapacious as Charles's earlier mentor, the
Burgundian Chièvres, of whom the pleasant ditty was sung:

> *Norabuena venistes, doblón de a dos;*
> *Que Monsieur de Chièvres no topó con vos.*

(Lucky double doubloon that M. de Chièvres
didn't spot you.)

Unfortunately he was not much better versed in economics.

To contemporaries, apart from those who were actually lending
the Emperor money or expecting to be paid their debts, all this
was of course hidden; they saw only the brilliant façade of power
that could draw on the revenues of the Netherlands, the wealthiest
provinces in Europe, vast dependencies in Italy, a docile Spain
and the silver of Peru that was to cause Drake to tell his men
before the gates of Nombre de Dios that he had brought them to
the treasure house of the world.

All this existed—almost as glamorously as a dazzled Europe believed. The Netherlands *were* wealthy, with the solid base that
comes from a merchant society prepared to work for its money.
The capacity of the mine of Potosí could hardly be exaggerated—
from the proceeds of one successful raid on a treasure convoy
Drake paid his expenses, enriched himself and his crew and had
a surplus that was actually large enough—marvel of marvels!—to
satisfy his backers and the Queen.

Such advantages, such enormous receipts of treasure, should have
been more than sufficient to prime the Spanish economy to a
level unmatched anywhere else in Europe. The Netherlanders, the
French, the English (already a nation of shopkeepers in embryo),
Italians of any state, even Papal, or the Jews—certainly the Jews—
would have known how to use this specie to their own and the
national advantage in investment, banking, trade. The Castilians,
who had deprived themselves of all their brighter mercantile minds,
could not even keep it physically in Castile, in spite of laws for-
bidding its export, which they had crassly qualified by exempting
the Crown from their provisions. The Emperor, though well-meaning, had availed himself of this loophole, of which he had solemnly
promised not to take advantage. Desperate to pay for his wars,
he had granted Crown licenses for the export of specie from

Spain. Large quantities had gone abroad into German and Italian pockets. Little of the rest was put to productive use. There resulted what Tyler has called "a brutal pumping of specie" through the primitive Castilian economy, helping on an inflation which no one understood, least of all the Emperor, who was so lost to economic sense that he had bartered away Spain's share in the spice trade as part of the marriage settlement with his Portuguese bride, in return for a dowry which was of course promptly swallowed up in military costs.

Prices, which had been rising throughout Europe, in Spain began to shoot up much more steeply. The authorities, becoming thoroughly alarmed, applied remedies—or what they thought were remedies. They pegged the prices of necessities. Producers in the basic industries naturally turned elsewhere for profits: to the luxury trades. These were promptly checked by sumptuary laws aimed at preventing too much investment in industries which were regarded as unhealthy and damaging to the economy. By these actions the legislators effectively depressed home industries, both luxury and basic. They had by no means done with remedies. Observing shortages at home, they forbade exports. Suspecting from high prices that exorbitant profits were being made by manufacturers in Spain, they encouraged imports from abroad.

Here are phenomena recognizable today in an age more familiar with economic ills. A well-meaning government, actively urged on by its provincial assemblies and local chambers of trade, was discouraging all those forces that would have brought in money, and aiding and abetting the flight of specie abroad. A permanent adverse balance of trade was being created—and created ironically enough with the very tools of wealth.

In fact, as we can now see, it was a recipe for disaster, however long delayed in its effects. Of Philip's two great problems, religious and economic, the second was by no means the less intractable. It was to prove as damaging to him as all the heresies of Europe.

4

WAR WITH THE PAPACY AND FRANCE. 1556–59.

We stand at the beginning of a reign. Ahead lie the famous battles, the sieges of rebellious towns, the invasions of foreign lands.

Yet the reign began in peace. Peace was its watchword if only because war was beyond its means. One of the Emperor's last official acts had been to ratify the truce of Vaucelles with France: giving at least a respite from the struggle which had been tearing Europe apart for over half a century.

In these wars the Emperor had been at one time the aggressor: he had coveted his lost Burgundian lands at least as hungrily as his rival Francis had yearned to hold Milan. But this aggression had soon been tempered by experience, by the increasing burdens of his life, even by a genuine idealism which had tried to win Francis to a new crusade against the Turks. In fact imperial policy by the middle of the reign had gone over to the strategic defensive, whatever its tactical moves might be. Perhaps in essence it had always borne this character which was inherent in the very structure of the empire—disparate parts, as opposed to the centrally placed nucleus for expansion that was France. And with Philip, the realism which had brought Charles at the end of his life to an acceptance of peace was reinforced by a nature that was pacific.

That this very evident truth should have a controversial sound in modern ears is proof of the power of hindsight and folklore. Whatever Philip was to become—saint, or monster, or fallible human being whose fate it was to be involved in many wars—in 1556 he had given proof only of docility. This was very generally recognized by contemporaries. The Venetian Badovaro had found him timid; Soriano, more disposed to idleness than to labor; Michele had judged that by nature he abhorred war; and these opinions are the more acceptable because they come from critics by no means inclined to say favorable things.

In fact Philip's whole life very largely bears out the judgments of these shrewd and observant men whose duty as envoys and ambassadors of a foreign power was to weigh and balance the King's character. Unlike his father, who had been rated as a "great captain"—admittedly on somewhat slender evidence—Philip had no aptitude for war. Only twice in a long life was he involved even distantly in action. He never commanded an army in battle. He saw the effects of campaigning in one captured town and it seems to have brought from him a gesture of humanity. In 1556 he certainly desired only peace and a Catholic Europe. And it was from precisely the most Catholic quarter, from the Papacy itself, that the first challenge came.

Giovanni Pietro Caraffa, Pope Paul IV, is certainly one of the most remarkable figures ever to sit on the throne of St. Peter. A Neapolitan of distinguished birth, founder of the monastic order of the Theatines which had tried to reconcile the contemplative and active sides of religious life, he had bounded at the age of seventy-nine onto the center of the European stage at almost the same moment that the Emperor, a mere stripling in years compared with him, had abandoned it forever. Few historians have been able to resist the ironical contrast of these events—Pope and Emperor exchanging places in the limelight like figures on some mechanical clock wound up by destiny.

Paul IV was an enthusiast. He wanted obedience in Christendom and an end to the ignoble tolerance (as he saw it) which the Peace of Augsburg had extended to Protestantism in Germany. More rationally he desired the advancement of his family, and this he sensationally achieved. The great American historian Prescott, in a passage full of Gibbonian irony, records how after making his eldest nephew a duke the worthy Pontiff made the next a cardinal—"a dignity," noted Prescott, "for which he was indifferently qualified by his former profession, which was that of a soldier, and still less fitted by his life, which was that of a libertine."

These were understandable excesses, nepotism not being unknown in Rome. But the Pope had a third passion: he loved Italy, if only in the vengeful sense of burning to drive out its foreign despoilers. No doubt there was self-interest involved in this too, and we should beware of seeing his patriotism in modern terms, but the words he addressed to the Venetian ambassador Navagero are not without grandeur and go far to redeem actions which brought much suffering in their train. "Whatever others may feel," he said, "I at least will have some care for my country. If no one listens, at least it will be some comfort for me to know that I have spoken for such a cause, and that one day it will be said that an old Italian, very near to death, who might have had nothing better to do than to rest and regret his sins, had this great design at heart."

This care for Italy, expressed by many Italians, furthered by few, was estimable and good. What Machiavelli preached, Paul practiced after his fashion. But this carried important and indeed inexorable consequences. For to love Italy was by definition to hate Spain, the major power controlling the Italian peninsula.

For Spain the Pope's hatred was absolute and lifelong. Personal factors had sharpened it. Dismissed for his pro-French leanings from the royal council of Naples, he had only succeeded to its archbishopric over the Emperor's strenuous objections, and to the Papacy itself because of gross Spanish blunders at the conclave which had been expected to exclude him. None of this had sweetened the temper of a naturally irascible man. It drove him to new heights of invective. For him Spaniards were "a race accursed of God, the spawn of Jews and Moors, the dregs of the earth." "Idle vapourings," Prescott dubs these outbursts of octogenarian rage, forgetting perhaps the boasted fetish of the monarchy and nobility of Spain for *limpieza de sangre** (pure Aryan descent as racists might say today) and the whisper in Europe which credited the whole hierarchy of Castile with copious strains of Jewish and Moslem blood. This was no vaporing. It was propaganda of a recognizably modern kind: a desirable preliminary to action by the Pope against the throne on which the Papacy itself had conferred the title of "Most Catholic," in the alliance with the

* In a fair-skinned person the veins show up more clearly. Hence the similar phrase "blue blood." In England it was never more than a phrase, indeed a meaningless one. In Spain the myth of racial purity was jealously guarded and carried advantages protected by law. Even Sancho Panza boasts of being an "Old Christian" with no strain of Jew or Moor in him. The rumors that royal and noble blood was impure in this sense were substantially true. Spaniards, Jews and Moors had coexisted for centuries and much intermarriage and interbreeding had taken place at the highest levels.

"Most Christian" king, the King of France, signatory of a solemn truce with Spain on which the ink was barely dry, and in hopeful expectation of assistance from the Turks!

Cynicism, it might be thought, could go no further, though there were helpful precedents from the time of Francis I. The inducements used were perfectly in keeping. Papal diplomacy could even offer absolution in advance, in case the French king had scruples and was so blind to his best interests as to resist the bribe of Naples and the duchy of Milan. This from a self-declared Italian patriot! Perhaps the measure of that patriotism is best seen in those clauses in the treaty of alliance which provided for large extensions of Papal territory after the victory and patrimonies for all the deserving nephews of the Caraffa clan.

But the project itself is even more revealing of the state of informed opinion about the new ruler of Spain. Faced with Milan and Naples firmly in Spanish hands, an actively pro-Spanish Genoa, a hostile Tuscany, and with a near-bankrupt France for ally, Paul had not hesitated to dare what no predecessor had attempted since the days of Julius II. He must have had great faith in the pusillanimity and impotence of the man whom he was challenging. He did not even pay him the compliment of trying to deceive him with the diplomatic lies customary on such occasions, but on the contrary waged a full-scale diplomatic offensive, insulting Spanish representatives in Rome, inciting the Roman Inquisition to start excommunication proceedings against both King and Emperor, and even talking of a Bull of Dethronement.

This was a misjudgment both of the situation and the man, though perhaps the most interesting thing about it is that it should ever have been made. Philip on his side had approached the crisis much more cautiously. It was none of his seeking. The sack of Rome by the imperialists in his father's time, news of which had cut short the celebrations at his own birth, had cast long shadows after it and made him deeply reluctant to risk the odium of a repetition of that most Pyrrhic of victories. Nevertheless plans were well in hand to deal with the coming storm. The Duke of Alva, Spain's foremost general, had already been dispatched to Naples as viceroy. A panel of Spanish churchmen and jurists was assembled and polled as to the legality of defensive war against the Pope, the possible confiscation of Papal revenues in Spain and other measures likely to be disturbing to Roman nerves, always highly sensitive on this front. There remained the matter of financing the war.

In fact neither side was in any condition to begin one; they had all but run out of credit—and this was an age when military costs had soared beyond the dreams of practitioners at the beginning of the century. Warfare had become infinitely more professional, arms and drills more complex and beyond the scope of half-trained or part-time troops. In face of increased specialization the day of the feudal levy and the town militia was over. That of the citizen army, the nation in arms of French Revolutionary times, had not yet dawned; or perhaps it might be truer to say that its traditions dating from classical Greek and Roman times had long since been forgotten.

In the cavalry—always the aristocratic arm—and on the staffs, there was a good supply of volunteers from the ranks of the nobility and gentry in search of experience, adventure, patronage and fat ransom fees from captives, but essentially this was the heyday of the mercenary fighting for the best money he could get, no matter from whom. Thus the Papal infantry that faced Alva's Catholic levies was composed of German Lutherans. No one thought this odd. It was an accepted fact of life. These German *Landsknechts,* forming the central core of armies with their massed antennae of pikes that decorate the battle pictures of the time, were among the most feared infantry in Europe, greatly in demand on both sides. The mainstay of the Vatican and the kings of France and Spain, they would have served the Sultan or sacked St. Peter's with equal thoroughness. The Spanish *tercios,** destined to surpass them in fame, were mercenaries too, though intensely national in spirit and vastly more bigoted. Even the bulk of the cavalry engaged were mercenaries—the German *Schwartzreiters* (pistoleers) and the Flemish companies of the "Bands of Ordonnance" which Charles the Bold had created in his military reorganization and still formed the frontier defense of the Netherlands against the French. Mercenaries again were the arquebusiers and their successors, the musketeers, who served alongside the infantry; and the gunners of the field and siege artillery. All had to be paid

* *Tercios* were units of 3000 men divided into 12 companies. Weapons were the pike, the shorter javelin and the arquebus, later succeeded by the musket. With cavalry and guns they made up the Spanish field armies. All personnel were Spanish. *Tercios* were named after the areas where they were quartered. They ruled the battlefield from 1534 till Rocroi in 1643.

for, either by wages or by loot in captured towns. Failure was apt to be infinitely more painful to employers than any activity by the enemy. Loyalties counted for nothing, the paymaster for everything—this was the first principle of war which kept these brutalized, anarchic armies marching.

Philip's appreciation of this fact provides his one claim to military virtue. Given a breathing space by Alva's brilliant campaign in the Papal states in the autumn of 1556, he had set himself with the new year to a last urgent search for funds. Even the Emperor was brought into play from his retreat at Yuste to beg half a million ducats from the Spanish Church, perhaps the one organism in Europe which still had cash to spare. Since even this windfall was insufficient to meet costs until the arrival of the treasure fleet from the Isthmus in midsummer, Philip applied still more desperate remedies, and in March 1557 crossed to England for his second (and as it proved last) visit to his neglected wife.

He wanted money, troops, a declaration of war on France: the small change of an alliance which in its design had been dynastic and intended to tie England into the Spanish system through an heir. Every hope had been disappointed. The unfortunate queen had not even been spared the pathetic delusions of a pregnancy that never came. She remains a tragic figure. Loving her country, she lost it its most prized possession: Calais. Her love for her religion has more abiding memorials: the cross let into the pavement on the spot where Latimer and Ridley burned, near where the cars now park in Oxford's "Broad," and the hideous Gothic pinnacle in the shade of Balliol College which provides a nursery slope for the university's night climbers. Above all else she loved her husband: and he spent seventeen reluctant months with her—three on this last visit, which was just long enough (thanks to French meddling in English affairs) to get the alliance he had come for. She had no other charms for him.

By July he was back again in Brussels for the concentration of the army which he was forming under command of his cousin the Duke of Savoy, a tough exponent of the warfare school of Charles V and a recent suitor for the hand of Elizabeth Tudor. Up to this point the war which the Pope's ambitions had loosed on Europe had lasted for nearly a year and had been marked by little beyond atrocities in Italian towns and wary maneuverings in the Roman Campagna between two highly professional commanders, whose point of view is best exemplified by the Duke of Alva's remark that he was not prepared to stake the kingdom of Naples against the embroidered coat of his opponent, the Duke of Guise. Since M. de Guise was equally sensible and the Pope could not hope to survive without his aid, the way was open for the Papacy and Naples to make peace with one another, as happened early in September in a solemn mummery of reconciliation.

War in Italy, in fact, had proved a farce to all but the unfortunates who had been raped and butchered indiscriminately in captured towns. But on the borders of the Netherlands, in the debatable lands which have seen many of the world's most savage battles, very much larger armies had been assembled at a cost that demanded action. With Guise still away in Italy, the French had concentrated a force of approximately 24,000 men, most German *Landsknechts* but with excellent Gascon infantry in support. Philip's army was considerably larger, now that the treasure ships had reached the Guadalquivir and his agents had seized not only the royal "fifth" but almost every bar of specie aboard. De Thou, whose figures both Prescott and Motley accept, puts the infantry, including the ubiquitous Germans, at 35,000, the cavalry at 12,000, with 8000 English in support: a total of 55,000 men—odds therefore of more than two to one. France had begun the war. But by July, when Philip returned to the Netherlands from London, the initiative was firmly in his hands and it remained only to decide at which point to strike along the thinly held French fortress line. St. Quentin was selected, and at the end of the month the Duke of Savoy's army, with its banners and tents reminiscent of some expensive fair, suddenly appeared before its walls and invested it with all the pomps of sixteenth-century war.

France's commander in Picardy was her Constable—Montmorency —a picturesque figure who might have sprung straight out of Shakespeare's histories. Brantôme, always full of good anecdotes, has a splendid one about this paragon of piety and jovial brutality, relating how in wartime he would sometimes break off from his prayers to call out instructions to his guards to hang or quarter captives, mutineers or others who had incurred his displeasure. Consistent in all things, he had earnestly besought his royal master Henry II to hang the English herald who had brought Mary Tudor's declaration of war—a very lame one which certainly justified the Constable's excellent advice on this occasion.

St. Quentin, on the main trade route between the Netherlands and Paris, was a town of great strategic importance whose fortifications had been allowed to decay. Both these facts were appreciated by the French command only when the Spanish investment of the city was complete and it became a matter of urgency to reinforce the garrison. Gaspard de Coligny, Admiral of France, future victim of the massacre of St. Bartholomew, managed to throw himself and a small force into the town, which he found in a ruinous condition, though naturally strong, with two sides protected by swamps and the river Somme.

The Admiral, like the Constable, was a man of decisive character. Finding part of the suburbs in Spanish hands, he mounted a well-timed assault and burned it to the ground, clearing a glacis between himself and the enemy. The population was another problem, but by expelling all but the able-bodied and locking the women and children into the church, where their lamentations were less distracting, he managed to sustain the morale of the garrison and the bread ration.

Meanwhile Montmorency had fixed his headquarters in nearby La Fère. There was communication between the city and the French camp in spite of the besieging Spanish army, and on the tenth of August the Constable advanced to the relief, with the aim of passing reinforcements into St. Quentin by boat and across fords through the swamps which Coligny had reconnoitered.

Ancient battles defeat much reading. The war diaries which illuminate the actions of our fortunate century (at least for the commanders when they come to write their memoirs) were absent from these more primitive times. Commentators were free to express their own views of what they thought had happened, without fear of contradiction except from other commentators expressing *their* views. Agreement was rare. But this much at least is clear from the somewhat confused accounts of St. Quentin. The Constable, in spite of his initial advantage of surprise, succeeded in passing only a handful of men across the treacherous swamps into the city. And he lingered much too long over the attempt, ignoring warnings from subordinates who saw more clearly the dangers of the position into which he had ventured.

These materialized with terrifying suddenness. The Spanish vanguard, moving rapidly from its camp across the river by a ford which allowed the passage of far greater numbers than the Constable had reckoned on, gained the high ground along the line of his retreat, and when he turned at bay his cavalry was swept from the field by a furious charge of the Netherlands horse under Count Egmont, leaving the stubborn Gascon infantry to be broken up by a combination of *Schwartzreiters* and light artillery as Savoy's main army came on the scene. Not since Pavia had France suffered such a disaster, and perhaps the more exact comparison is with Agincourt. Fully a quarter of her army was captured, including the wounded Constable, the dukes of Montpensier and Langueville, the Marshal St. André and six hundred men of rank; three thousand on the lowest estimate were killed—other accounts say twice as many and the figure may well have been still higher. On the Spanish side the loss were perhaps a thousand, though de Thou puts it as low as fifty.

Next day the triumphant Philip, armed cap-à-pie for the occasion like his father in Titian's famous Muhlberg portrait, entered the Spanish camp to accept the surrender of the prisoners and review the captured flags and guns, while the wreck of the French army under Nevers and the Prince of Condé took refuge in La Fère. A fortnight later, after a desperate defense, St. Quentin itself was stormed amidst scenes of carnage which, in the words of an English onlooker, the Earl of Bedford, "would grieve any Christian heart." What also incensed the good Earl was the rapacity of the German "schwartzrotters" (as he called them in a letter to Mr. Secretary Cecil) who had formed the bulk of the assault force and now snatched most of the booty from their allies, so that "none could enjoy nothing but themselves." "They have showed such cruelty," he complained, "as the like hath not been seen for greediness: the town by them was set afire and a great piece of it burnt."

This last, by common consent, was wasteful. King Philip, entering the captured city in the wake of its tormentors, seems to have taken prompt steps to put out the flames and forbid the massacre of non-combatants, sending many of them under guard to safety. Prescott pays a tribute to his humanity. Motley denies it him altogether, citing in derision the tender removal to the royal tent of Church relics, including the bones of St. Quentin himself and the head of "the glorious St. Gregory"—"whoever," adds Motley, "that glorious individual may have been in life"—at a moment when the living who had escaped butchery were hiding in cellars in the last extremities of fear. "Within the sacred enclosure," Motley goes on with furious relish, "many masses were said daily while all this devil's work was going on without. The saint who had been buried for centuries was comfortably housed and guarded by the monarch, while the dogs were gnawing the carcases of the freshly slain men of St. Quentin, and troopers were driving into perpetual exile its desolate and mutilated women."

Whatever its condition, the town was now in Spanish hands and the road into France open to a repetition of the English invasion under Henry V a century and a half earlier. That dreams of conquest were in the air is clear from the advice of a council of war held after the battle of August 10 favoring an immediate march on Paris; and indeed Brantôme, always better at stories than with facts, has Charles at Yuste querulously asking whether Philip had yet arrived there—a good tale which ignores the central fact known to the Emperor if not to the bravoes in Philip's camp in Picardy.

For of course there was no money to go on. The proceeds of the treasure fleet, of the exactions from the Church and the shameless sale of offices had all been spent and the great army on the frontier was already beginning to melt away. Just as the victory of Pavia had brought Charles nothing except the mirage of a conquest never achieved, so St. Quentin remained barren, except in the sense that Philip's gratitude to St. Lawrence, on whose name day it was fought, was to lead in time on a Spanish hillside to a great building in the shape of the gridiron on which the saint suffered martyrdom—the monastery-palace of the Escurial where the King still lies in his marble tomb.

In fact as so often happens in war the initiative had shifted, as though there really were a god of battles throwing the dice. While Philip's army retired into winter quarters from its capture of a few minor fortresses, and its German mercenaries changed sides in the ill-founded belief that there were still solvent paymasters to be found in Europe, the Duke of Guise returned from Italy and fell with dramatic suddenness not on the Spanish army, but on the territory of its English ally, the city of Calais which for two hundred years, since the heroic times of Crécy and Poitiers, had nourished the national thirst for glory.

Of one thing the English have always been assured in France: a perfect French understanding of their foibles: and on this subject Brantôme is a splendid witness for the prosecution. The islanders, he says, "were so vainglorious, as comes naturally to them, that they wrote above the walls of Calais the inscription that when the French besieged it lead and iron would float."

This great possession and sally-port into France, the last relic of the conquests of Edward III, the Black Prince and Henry V and for that reason more cherished than any other piece of English soil, fell to the Duke of Guise's cannon in a week. Edward III had spent a year in capturing it. The shock in England was traumatic. Every schoolboy knows Queen Mary's anguished thought on the event. Calais might well be written on her heart: she knew her people, then rightly judged the most volatile and ungovernable in Europe. The Spanish representative in London, Feria, reported that attendance at the mass dropped by two thirds as a result, though the governor of the town, the Earl of Wentworth, had actually been a Protestant. There was a desperate search for scapegoats, accusations of treason and bitter declamations against the Spanish alliance which was held to blame for dragging England into war, though in fact Philip had done his utmost to warn his wife's government of the sorry state of the town's defenses and had even offered to reinforce the garrison—a prime cause for suspicion in itself!

In the strangely interwoven histories of France and England the loss of Calais was a great event, the end of a long and bloody chapter. But in the context of the Hapsburg-Valois duel it was only an irrelevance, and worse, an embarrassment when it came to peacemaking. The balance of the war, which had tilted France's way with Guise's coup, speedily reversed itself and the summer of 1558 saw a defeat at Gravelines—at the hands of that same Count Egmont who had led the cavalry at St. Quentin—which ended any hope of further advances eastward and may have finally broken the French will to resist. In August and September of that year very large armies, paid for with the last rags of credit, faced one another again along the disputed border, with the rival kings in nominal command, but though no battles resulted, the viruses of defeat and victory had already done their work and decided the shape of the coming peace.

When the delegations met in October at the abbey of Cercamps near Cambrai it was soon clear that the French had accepted the decision of a war which had been lost more in their imagination than in fact. Before the Emperor's truce of Vaucelles they had made substantial gains in Italy and Savoy and since that time had occupied stretches of the Netherlands: all these they were prepared to cede in return for the much smaller territories in Picardy which Philip's troops had overrun. But they would not give back Calais to the English. Two hundred years of history cried out against it. Two centuries in pride of possession lay behind England's demand for its return.

Here was material for a new judgment of Solomon, but alas! not mothers but nations in arms were in dispute and King Philip himself was a party as England's ally and husband of its Queen. His temptations to make a settlement must have been very strong. Nothing divided him from a triumph over France as great as any his father had achieved in a lifetime of effort except this stiff-necked refusal of his partner to look facts in the face and end a war which neither of them had the means of continuing. He was already in debt to his mercenaries alone to the extent of a million ducats. Yet he never hesitated to instruct his plenipoten-tiaries at Cercamps to support the English claim to Calais to the hilt. There was nothing in the least provident or diplomatic in this; it was due entirely to Castilian punctilio and a loyalty very ill-requited by Englishmen then and since.

From this trap of his own making he was rescued by a death as pitiful as it was providential, since it removed the sick and unhappy wife to whom he was bound. Once Mary Tudor was gone and he was no longer even titular king of a nation that rejected him, the field for diplomacy had widened. Yet—and here is one of the comedies of history—he was so far from taking ad-vantage of this fact that he tried to plunge straight back into the maelstrom by proposing to her successor, Queen Elizabeth!

What a marriage it would have been! No Armada. No Tilbury Speech. No Drake on the "Main"—certainly not as a pirate. Perhaps even a son or a daughter to succeed to a joint Anglo-Dutch kingdom instead of the Anglo-Scottish one of James the First and Sixth. No Gunpowder Plot: or it might have *had* to succeed. The possibilities are incalculable.

Could it have happened? Elizabeth was young: by no means yet the formidable virtuoso in ruffs and farthingale of the portraits and legends. Two years earlier the sharp eyes of the Venetian ambassador had noted her large and well-made figure, fine eyes and delicate hands—a countenance, he wrote, "rather pleasing from its expression than beautiful." One sees in passing that it is always the Venetian ambassadors who report the worth-while things. Now at the age of twenty-five, a crowned queen, we see her through the eyes of an English witness, Sir Robert Naunton. "She was of person tall, of hair and complexion fair, and therewithal well-favoured, but high-nosed; of limb and feature neat, and, which added to the lustre of these external graces, of a stately and majestic comportment . . ." This we may believe.

That Philip desired this paragon for a wife seems evident in spite of his difficulties at Cercamps. England was a prize worth holding. Elizabeth must turn Catholic of course, if not Catholic already, a matter open to some doubt. That he wanted her as a woman is distinctly possible; his partiality for her in the dangerous days when she had been heiress to the throne had certainly been sufficient to arouse Queen Mary's jealousy and was later to supply a possible argument to the nimble mind of the Spanish ambassador, Count Feria, when he came to commend his master's proposal to the lady. Philip forbade him to use it. He was a gentleman.

As for her partiality for him . . . ? With Elizabeth one never knows. That she can have dreamed of carrying things as far as marriage is in the last degree unlikely. In the state of Protestant feeling in England such a course would have been unwise, perhaps suicidal, even if she had had marriage in mind at all—and it is significant here that within a few days of her accession, at her very first Parliament, she was already speaking of her wish to reign and die a virgin. Yet out of gratitude, respect, or something warmer, she kept his portrait in her cabinet throughout the years of bitter rivalry ahead and showed decided signs of pique on learning of his marriage on the rebound to her namesake of France. "Your master," she scolded Feria, "must have been much in love with me not to be able to wait four months." And when the ambassador protested that it was all her fault, "I gave your master no decided answer," she replied. Here is the true, the basic Elizabeth who kept poor Robert Dudley waiting for a lifetime and raised procrastination to an art, even a method of government.

But these were early days for her. The technique was as yet imperfect; the strings were not in her hands, as later, when she had much of Europe dancing to her tune. Philip seems to have accepted rejection with some fortitude. But he was determined

to make peace, with or without her. Either the English must continue the war as an active ally, contributing troops and money,
in which case he would stand by their claim to Calais, or they
must accept a face-saving compromise which his diplomats had
managed to work out—a veritable masterpiece of sixteenth-century
double-think, calculated to appeal to the Queen's tortuous mind
and absolute need of peace.*

Once this nettle was grasped and the realities of power and
national bankruptcy had been digested by the high contracting
parties, everything else followed without difficulty, and on the
second and third of April 1559, at Câteau-Cambrésis, treaties
were signed which not only matched the results of the recent trial
of strength, but foreshadowed the future with a rare accuracy.
Elizabeth got peace and with it a freedom from old entanglements.
The French got Calais, a rampantly Catholic house of Guise in
the ascendant and the return from imprisonment of Coligny, now
turned Calvinist—a whole row of dragons' teeth. Philip had the
rest: lost territories returned, prestige, a chastened Papacy, even
a wife in the fourteen-year-old daughter of the French king who
was now converted from enemy into potential ally against the
threat of heresy spreading throughout Europe.

Câteau-Cambrésis marked the apex of Philip's fortunes. He was
to win great victories and add new territories to his crowns, but
never again did he reach the same position of equipoise that was
his on the morrow of this triumph of firmness and good management which set the bells ringing in Spain and the Spanish Netherlands. Only one thing was lacking—the Emperor's applause. For
Charles had died at Yuste in the previous summer and the "Prudent King" was now alone with his problems.

* Calais or its cash equivalent of half a million crowns was to be returned to England within eight years unless either party broke the peace or contravened the
treaty, in which case the offending party forfeited its rights to the town. Calais
remained French. No one was surprised, least of all Elizabeth. She would have
liked her 500,000 crowns. She never got them.

5

THE SPANISH NETHERLANDS. 1559.

In history there are no barren years; some are simply more fruitful than others; a few are climactic, and 1559, the year of Câteau-Cambrésis, was certainly one of these.

The peace itself, which was the most decisive and durable of an age of chronic unrest, marks the watershed between Charles's wars in central Europe and the struggle about to break out in the west where the new dynamic forces were springing to life: the balance was about to shift decisively toward the maritime powers of Spain, England and the northern Netherlands, and away from Germany (for three centuries) and France (for three decades).

Philip's return from the Low Countries to the peninsula, which he was never again to leave, marks one stage of this westward drift; the death that July of the French king Henry II in an accident in the lists at a tournament to celebrate his daughter's wedding to Philip was to prove even more fateful, since it left France to a succession of weak kings and petticoat rule in a time of bitter political and religious faction when the nation was visibly drifting toward civil war between Catholic north and Huguenot south.

Everywhere in western Europe the lines of religion were hardening. The year 1559 saw a new pro-Spanish Pope in Rome—Giovanni Angelo Medici, Pius IV, whose aims were reformative and not national as those of the Caraffa, Paul IV, had been. The Counter-Reformation was soon to be on its way and the works of the moderate Erasmus were already on the Index of forbidden books. A few months earlier, in England, the Anglican Church had been given shape by the Acts of Supremacy and Uniformity which were among the first fruits of Elizabeth's first Parliament. This was the year in which John Knox landed in Scotland; the year that Calvin founded his Protestant academy at Geneva under Theodore Beza

The Spanish Netherlands
Before the Rebellion

NORTH
SEA

Groningen

FRIESLAND

Enkhuizen

ZUIDER
Hoorn ZEE

Alkmaar

OVERYSSEL

RYSSEL

Deventer

Zutphen

Amsterdam
Haarlem

HOLLAND

Leyden

GELDERLAND

The Hague
Delft

Utrecht

UTRECHT

Gouda

R. NEDER RIJN

Arnhem

Rotterdam

Nymegen

R. RHINE

Brill

Dordt

R. WAAL

ZEELAND

Geertruidenberg

R. MEUSE

Zeirickzee

Breda

Middelburg
Flushing

Goes

Roermond

EMPIRE

Sluys

Antwerp

Cologne

Ostend

Bruges

Ghent

R. SCHELDT

Mechlin

BRABANT

Maastricht

Nieuport
Dunkirk
Gravelines

FLANDERS

Brussels

Louvain

BISHOPRIC OF LIÈGE

Liège

Ypres

BR

Gembloux

WALLOON

Tournai
Mons

Namur

Douai

STATES

Valenciennes

Arras

Cambrai

LUXEMBURG

FRANCE

Luxemburg

and in which appeared the definitive edition of his *Institutes of the Christian Religion*. And pre-eminently, from the point of view of our story, it was the year in which Philip's troubles in the Netherlands began.

At once one encounters an enigma, an oddity on the map of Europe. To appreciate what the Netherlands were, we must bear constantly in mind what they were *not*.

Geologically they formed an expanse of very flat land laid down over countless centuries by the silt of rivers flowing from the highlands of central Europe into the shallows of the North Sea, with fringes of more broken ground to the east and south and an appendix of hill country in Luxemburg.

But there the usefulness of positive definition comes to an end. The Netherlands were not—nor ever have become—a nation. Three associated but independent states have been carved from them. In 1559 there were seventeen—drawn together in subjection to the old duchy of Burgundy which had been inherited by the Spanish Crown. Ruled by a king, the Netherlands were not a kingdom. Nor were any of the component parts kingdoms. In none of them was Philip crowned. He was a duke in Brabant, a count in Flanders, only a lord in Utrecht and Groningen—as such he ruled each of his sovereign territories: *if* they were sovereign and not fiefs of the Holy Roman Empire as some believed. In this area, only a sixth the size of France, there was no ancestry or tradition that was common to all, no common language. A racial and linguistic barrier had formed itself along the line of mass settlement by invading Germanic tribes in the sixth century, and this line, running from just north of Liège, through Tournai to the sea near Dunkirk, divided, as it still divides, the French-speaking "Walloon" south of what is now Belgium from the Flemings to the north and the Dutch of present-day Holland, both of low-German speech.*

By 1559 these fragments, born of invasions long past, of family aggrandizements and of recent conquests in Charles's wars, had been brought together into a kind of federation without a center, an untidy union of states, some rich, some poor, some industrialized, some pastoral, some maritime, whose common denominator was a watchful suspicion of their ruler. Such community of interest as

* Brussels, north of the line, is however largely French-speaking.

existed was overlaid by deep divisions, racial and political if not yet religious. The Walloon south, with French affinities, felt a deep cultural difference from its Dutch-speaking sisters, among whom the most recent additions on the German fringe in the northeast were themselves resentful of the shotgun wedding into which they had been forced with neighbors to the west who were admittedly Germanic but not of the same tribe.

These divisions were passionately felt on every level. It may seem sufficiently absurd that Flanders, a Flemish-speaking state, should have shown a yearning toward France, which for centuries had bullied it and tried to gobble it up; that near neighbors in Friesland and Groningen should have felt a murderous antipathy for one another, and that bishops in Utrecht lusted to possess a share in Gelderland; but such trends can be seen in the early histories of almost every national state, from twelfth-century England and thirteenth-century France to the America of Lincoln and the African nations of our own time.

In fortunate England, in France, in the United States, strong rulers, acting nationally for what was felt to be the general good, managed to create out of the caldron of petty jealousies and parochial ambitions a central unity with the power and the state machinery to survive. In the Netherlands the ruling Burgundian dukes had been alien Frenchmen, and by a singular misfortune the only two of their line who might have become truly national figures—Philip the Handsome and his son Charles V—were removed from the scene, the first by an early death, the second by responsibilities in Europe which took him far from Brussels and its Lilliputian problems.

In spite of this, these alien rulers had introduced—if only for their own convenience—some of the means that might have made for Netherlands unity. Immensely desirous of getting money for their wars, they had prevailed on the provincial assemblies (or "States" as they were called) to send delegates to a national States General which it was hoped would prove a docile subsidy-voting body. Thus, quite by accident, they provided the Netherlands with a voice—a very muted one, often servile and timorous, but nevertheless a voice, and one which came increasingly to be heard as the years went by and the need for money grew. Nor was the States General the regime's sole gift toward unity. The dukes and their descendants were great modernizers. Faced with a maze of archaic feudal rights and liberties in every warring province, they had rushed in with a tidy despotism of their own: creating stadt-holders, their personal representatives, in each state or group of states; captains general to command their local levies; provincial courts to administer their laws; a supreme appellate court at Mech-lin; new royal councils at the center; oligarchical bodies in each town to curb the power of the guilds—indeed there was no end to these busy and necessary innovations or to the fury they aroused in libertarian breasts.

In Charles's time the pace had grown hotter, for this last of the medieval emperors was in his homeland the most formidable modernizer of all. By an ordinance of 1531 he reorganized the royal council into three branches: the Council of State which dealt with matters of high policy; the Privy Council, staffed with jurists, the "men of the long robe"; and the Finance Council, most necessary of organs. In 1534 he had gone further and submitted through his Regent a scheme for closer integration of the prov-inces and fixed-scale subsidies for the maintenance of a standing army; worse still, he tried to codify the laws, whose anomalies would have horrified Roman jurists of a millennium earlier.

These last attempts had failed. The Netherlands were not to be led by the nose into the new age. And it was not the least of Charles's virtues as a ruler that he appreciated if not the charms, at least the realities of a system which laid it down that no order of the central government was valid unless the individual states approved, and made it possible for a single village in one of seventeen provinces to withhold its quota of the tax the ruler was demanding and get away with it. Before his abdication the Emperor had gone out of his way to warn his son of the dangers of pressing this remarkable organism too far. He had played very expertly on it for thirty years, getting a lot of money for his pains, besides credit for his democratic acceptance of its ab-surdities, and he knew its weakness and its strength.

In fact the country he had handed over was the prodigy of the age. We can forgive Motley's rapturous praise for "three mil-lions of people, the most industrious, the most prosperous, perhaps the most intelligent under the sun"; for cattle "perhaps the finest in Europe"; the boldest navigators, most enterprising merchants, most artistic and cultivated citizens; for 208 walled and "stately" cities; 150 chartered towns; and 6300 villages "with their watch-

towers and steeples." Motley was a committed writer: so committed that he was prepared to vouch not only for the beauty of
the women of the Netherlands but even for their moral purity,
basing himself apparently on the Florentine Guiccardini, a contemporary witness of this happy state of affairs. We may smile
at some of this. It remains true that this comparatively small area,
politically so backward and torn with internal jealousies, was also
the most advanced trading society in Europe and contained within
itself the seeds of an extraordinary expansion.

Not all the seventeen provinces were equally prosperous. Some
were agricultural and earned their living in the sober wintry landscape soon to be immortalized in the canvases of Peter Breughel.
Flanders, for centuries the leading Netherlands state, was actually
in decline, like its once dominant port of Bruges whose access
to the sea was silting up beyond repair. It was a resilient state,
however, and though its famous wool trade was only a shadow of
its former self in the face of English competition, "new drapery"
centers had sprung into life and there was also a flourishing trade
in tapestries and linen. Flanders therefore was still rich—immensely so by standards ruling elsewhere. Brabant was growing
richer. Brussels, where the royal court had settled, was Brabantine,
its glories preserved for us in one of Motley's most charming
passages:

A wide expanse of living verdure, cultivated gardens, shady groves,
fertile corn-fields, flowed round it like a sea. The foot of the town was
washed by the little river Senne, while the irregular but picturesque
streets rose up the steep sides of the hill like the semicircles and
stairways of an amphitheatre. Nearly in the heart of the place rose
the audacious and exquisitely embroidered tower of the town-house,
three hundred and sixty six feet in height, a miracle of needlework
in stone, rivalling in its intricate carving the cobweb tracery of that
lace which has for centuries been synonymous with the city, and rearing
itself above a facade of profusely decorated and brocaded architecture.
The crest of the elevation was crowned by the towers of the old
ducal palace of Brabant, with its extensive and thickly-wooded park
on the left, and by the stately mansions of Orange, Egmont, Aremberg,
Culemberg, and other grandees on the right. The great forest of Soignies,
dotted with monasteries and convents, swarming with every variety of
game, whither the citizens made their summer pilgrimages, and where
the nobles chased the wild boar and the stag, extended within a

quarter of a mile of the city walls. The population, as thrifty, as intelligent, as prosperous as that of any city of Europe . . . the tapestry workers, whose gorgeous fabrics were the wonders of the world . . .

Motley was not the only one to use superlatives. The cities of the Netherlands were just as much objects of veneration for contemporary writers like Guiccardini; and indeed some of the buildings they marveled at are still there for us to see and judge for ourselves. Brussels, so brilliantly described, was not even the chief glory of Brabant. That honor belonged to Antwerp. Again there is no avoiding Motley.

Placed upon a plain along the banks of the Scheldt, shaped like a bent bow with the river for its string, it enclosed within its walls some of the most splendid edifices in Christendom. The world-renowned church of Notre Dame, the stately Exchange where five thousand merchants daily congregated . . . the capacious mole and port where twenty-five hundred vessels were often seen at once, and where five hundred made their daily entrance or departure, were all establishments which it would have been difficult to rival in any other part of the world.

Even in Venice, apparently, to judge from the sad lament of a visitor from the *Serenissima* that in Antwerp he had seen his city surpassed.

At the head of road and river routes from Germany and near the strategic center of the narrow seas, where the trade from Russia and the Baltic crossed that of Portugal and Spain in spices and precious metals, Antwerp was the natural mart for the wide-ranging forces of western Europe. Prescott likens her to nineteenth-century London and in many ways this is just, for there had grown up within her walls all the machinery of the new capitalism —banking and credit facilities; a great Exchange. Yet there were flaws in this brilliant picture. Though a port of perhaps a hundred thousand people, one of the largest in the Western hemisphere, she had no fleets of her own and surprisingly little trade actually in her own hands. The town was full of foreign business houses: indeed one might say that the comparison with London is inexact

and that nineteenth-century Shanghai or Canton, with their colonies
of European merchants, provide much the closer parallel. Also her
life line to the sea was long and tenuous and was commanded by
the territory of another state.

To the north of her, in the county of Holland, another city,
still allied but potentially her rival, had been steadily gaining
ground—Amsterdam, with still only half her wealth but with the
fortunes of the future in her lap and a great merchant fleet which
was already pre-eminent along the Baltic coasts. About Holland,
Guiccardini grows lyrical, quite in Motley's manner, no doubt in
astonishment at finding in that small and supposedly backward
province the orderly graciousness of towns whose names, still
strange to him, were to become as familiar as that of his native
Florence—Haarlem, Alkmaar, The Hague, Delft, Leyden, Rotterdam.

These Flemish- or Dutch-speaking states along the coast—Flanders, Brabant, Holland—with the addition of Zeeland, a congeries
of islands lying across the estuary of the Scheldt, were the most
prosperous of the seventeen. The French-speaking Walloon provinces of the south were not commercially as viable, but culturally
they had begun to rule the roost: it was their nobility that held
most of the stadtholderates, their language that was the language
of the court and government. Perhaps it is misleading to make
distinctions. There were pockets of depression in the strange tangle
of states between the Rhine, the Channel and the Zuider Zee,
but socially the Netherlands formed one reasonably affluent world:
well ordered, invincibly middle class in inspiration. Nowhere else
were there to be found burghers so well fed, so well clothed,
so handsomely housed, so self-satisfied. Even the peasants—the
"boors," as they still figure in catalogues of "old master" paintings
at the best sales in London and New York—enjoyed comforts
unknown to their kind elsewhere. As for the great nobles of the
order of the Golden Fleece, their tastes were bourgeois also. Hearty
guzzlers, enormous drinkers, lovers of buffoonery and display, they
belong in spirit with the cheerful hedonists of Frans Hals a few
generations later and with those aspiring magnates of the town
guard who turned their back on Rembrandt in the end because
he chose to see them as they were and not as they had contracted
to be seen, at so much per square foot of paint.

Like other affluent worlds, in fact, it was not one much given to refinement. It had all the machinery of culture: artistic schools, chambers of rhetoric, a great university at Louvain, printing presses by the score—indeed the Netherlands disputed with Germany the invention of movable type. Yet apart from Erasmus, who wrote in Latin and spent most of his life abroad, and Peter Breughel, it produced no cultural figure of the very first rank. It was coarse-grained. To say that it was an entirely Philistine society would be absurd in the face of Thomas à Kempis, Hieronymus Bosch in painting, the passionately Catholic verse of Anna Bijns, musicians of the stature of Orlando Lasso (de Lattre) and Gombert—indeed in the words of another Venetian, Cavallo, the Netherlands was a "fountain of music"—but these are not names to ring like a clarion call down forgetful centuries. Memling and Jan van Eyck were dead; the great artists whose canvases line the walls of the Rijks-museum and the Mauritshuis were not yet born; and in the interim there were pageants, gorgeous ones, mounted with every luxury that money could buy: the "Land Jubilees" staged by chambers of rhetoric in each aspiring town to astonish rivals and the ground-lings.

It was in sum a mediocre age. Kindhearted after their fashion, opinionated, hedonistic, great sticklers for their rights, pigheaded, boisterous, fecund, the audiences which delighted in these quaint precursors of vaudeville and Mardi gras formed one of the most solid and least aesthetic civilizations that have ever existed. A spark set it alight and by some alchemy transformed it.

The spark was religion. The incendiary was the King.

Lutheran doctrines had early made their way into the Nether-lands from the German states along the eastern border, and these in the fullness of time had been reinforced and largely replaced by the social ferment of Anabaptism, essentially a creed for the manic and the deprived. The royal government in Brussels had from the start set its face against these heresies. The first Lutheran martyrs had gone to the stake soon after Charles V's accession, and the challenge as it developed had been met by a series of edicts, culminating in the Emperor's so-called "Edict of Blood" in 1550 which provided remedies, by fire, sword and burial alive, perhaps as draconic as man has ever devised for the aberrations of his neighbor's conscience. Sensational figures were banded about by Protestant propagandists as to the number of unfortunates who died from these decrees—thirty thousand was widely credited: an absurdly inflated tally. Yet certainly a substantial number suffered—mostly Anabaptists, whose crimes were as much social as religious and whose deaths were therefore acceptable to an age which was shocked by their polygamous and leveling tendencies.

On his accession Philip had hastened to ratify his father's edicts, being careful to make it plain that he was merely reissuing them and not indulging in any lawmaking of his own. By then, a far more important force than Anabaptism was beginning to seep into the southern Netherlands: the doctrines of Calvin which had found a sure theocratic base in the city of Geneva and were on the march throughout Europe, not least in France, the country that was nearest to the contagion.

This increasing wave of heresy, which threatened both warring parties equally, was one of the main causes of the Hapsburg-Valois *rapprochement* at Câteau-Cambrésis. Protestant observers were quick to see in this a joint design on the part of both monarchs to exterminate Protestantism root and branch; and indeed many years later the Prince of Orange was to declare in his *Apologia* that at the time of Câteau-Cambrésis the French king had actually revealed to him the existence of a plan for a general massacre of heretics. For some reason this accusation, which rests on one man's word alone and appears in a document riddled with inaccuracies and patently propagandist in its intent, has been taken seriously by some historians, though it merely echoes other tales of Papist plots which have long since been exploded, and indeed flies in the face of Philip's whole record as a man of temporizing and cautious nature with an almost pathological distrust of other human beings and of common action with anyone. There was no need for a plot or for any such extravagant undertaking. There was need only for peace, to free the hands of the parties for their own internal problems; and that heresy was among the foremost of those problems may readily be believed.

In fact the situation in the Netherlands, once the first rejoicings at victory were over, was becoming every day more grave. There was no check on the spread of the new doctrines. Only three bishoprics existed in the seventeen states, vast areas of which were subject to sees in France and Germany over which Philip had no control. For this reason he had planned to carry out and

enlarge a scheme of his father's for a complete ecclesiastical reorganization of the Netherlands, by the creation of three arch-
bishoprics: at Cambrai for the Walloon country, with four sub-
ordinate sees; at Mechlin for the central area up to the line of
the Rhine, with six sees; and at Utrecht for the north with five;
Mechlin having the primacy over the whole. This proposed measure,
in many respects wise and timely, suffered from one grave disadvantage: it was bound to incur the united opposition, not only
of the Protestant sects, but also of the Catholic abbots and nobles
whose comfortable pickings in ecclesiastical livings for themselves
and their relations alike seemed threatened by a reform which
aimed to provide men of scholarship and piety for the chief posts
in the Church—a gross invasion of established rights! For this
reason the project was meant to be shrouded in deepest secrecy
while the necessary bulls to set it up were being obtained in
Rome. Nevertheless the news leaked out and added to the sim-
mering discontent of the country.

Aware of this, Philip proceeded with caution. In a still semi-feudal
society the great nobles were of paramount importance, and he
therefore set himself to win them over by appointing their leaders
to the much-prized honor of the Golden Fleece and to stadtholderates in those provinces where they happened to own least
land. Egmont, of whom most could be hoped, was given Flanders
and Artois; Count Aremberg, a fervent loyalist, got Friesland,
Groningen and Overyssel on the vulnerable northeastern frontier;
Orange, already marked out as potentially the most dangerous,
had Holland, Zeeland and Utrecht. Brabant, containing as it did
the seat of government, had no stadtholder; but with gracious tact
the King appointed as Regent his Netherlands-born half sister,
Duchess Margaret of Parma, daughter of Charles V by one of
his romantic first loves in the days before his marriage.

This last appointment was applauded; it was deemed an honor
to the country and a renewal of the fortunate system by which
the King's great-aunt and aunt in turn had ruled the provinces,
and ruled them well. The stadtholderates and the appointments
to the collar of the Fleece were also well received by the grandees.
But there the gratitude stopped. The nobility, like the burghers
and artisans, were in a restless mood. Possessing money, they
desired power, not the appearance of power, with which they felt
they were being fobbed off by a regime both weaker and fussier

than the rule of the Emperor, which no one except the incorrigible city of Ghent had thought of challenging. The States General, a notoriously tentative body, had caused astonishment in 1558 by quibbling over the customary nine-year subsidy to its ruler. Summoned in the summer of 1559—to Ghent of all places!—to hear the King's plan for the provinces before his imminent departure for Spain, it went further and demanded the recall of the three thousand Spanish troops who garrisoned the strategic centers for the Crown.

According to eyewitnesses the King greeted this unparalleled demand with anger and petulance. But on reflection he kept his politic sense. Soft answers were returned. Promises were made for a future withdrawal of the troops, and in the interim the King disarmingly engaged to pay for their upkeep himself and appointed Count Egmont and the Prince of Orange to command them.

These conciliatory measures had some effect. The crisis passed. The King took his ceremonial leave of the Netherlands which he was never again to visit, and for a brief while at the embarkation port of Flushing the flags flew, the notables paraded in a last gleam of medieval chivalry such as Henry VIII had brought to the Field of the Cloth of Gold. But the die had been cast; the shape of future conflicts had been marked out. Philip was not to forgive the provinces for the humiliation which had been forced on him by the free talking of free men. According to one story, while he was waiting to embark he bitterly reproached the Prince of Orange for being the author of the opposition to his plans, and when the Prince protested that all had been done in due accord with the States General's undoubted rights, seized hold of him, crying: *"No los estados mas vos, vos, vos"*—"Not the Estates but *you, you, you.*"

Once again it is a questionable story depending on the chronicle of a man who got it from his father, who had it from a friend of Orange who was allegedly present at the scene. That it sounds so splendidly in character, so *true*, is no proof of its truth but only of the way future generations were to seek back and try with every art to unravel and personalize the beginnings of the epic struggle which had been in the making ever since Luther took the chair of theology at Wittenberg.

6

REGIME OF THE DUCHESS MARGARET. 1559–67.

The Papal bull agreeing to the creation of the new bishoprics had reached Philip just before his embarkation at Flushing. The final details of the plan were not in fact published until another two years had passed, yet the secret was out and he must have known as his fleet beat up the Channel homeward that the storm clouds were gathering in the country he had just left and that he might well be repeating the mistake his father had made in 1520 in sailing from Corunna, after his first visit to Spain, with the Germania revolt already blazing in Valencia and the whole of Castile about to break into flames behind him.

In one respect Philip had been more provident than his father, whose selection of a Regent for Spain had been inept. Duchess Margaret of Parma was by contrast an excellent choice to govern provinces which traditionally had thrived under princesses of the ruling house. She was a competent, rather masculine woman of good presence, twice married, imperial if only on one side of the family, a *bon viveur*, as proved (if chroniclers are to be believed) by a tendency toward the gout; most importantly, she was Netherlands-born. Her substitution in fact for the objectionably foreign King was a positive advantage to the government and seemed to promise a lowering of the political temperature.

To assist her, she had been provided with three councils, two of them (Privy and Finance) presided over by Netherlanders, the third (the State Council) liberally staffed with the high nobility whose friendship or at least tolerance was of such crucial importance. On these bodies there was not one Spaniard. Unfortunately, as it proved, there was one Burgundian from the Franche Comté: Antony Perrenot, Bishop of Arras (soon to be more widely known under the name of Granvelle), whose presidency of the Council of State was bound to be resented by the native-born magnates—the more so because his father had been one of Charles's most trusted ministers and a deep family commitment was assured. Nor was this all. For by a secret instruction to his half sister Philip had laid it down that in all important matters—and that meant religion—she was not to consult her advisers as a group but only a cabal of them, or *Consulta* as it was called, composed of the presidents of the three councils: Viglius van Aytta, an able lawyer but politically a lightweight; Count Berlaymont, a timeserver deeply committed to Spain; and Granvelle, whose force and intellect were outstanding and whose channel of correspondence directly with the King made him in effect the real ruler of the Netherlands.

This Spain-directed junta was now called upon to rule seventeen provinces rife with discontent and dislike of all things Spanish, particularly the religious edicts on which the King had laid such stress. Persecution was brisk, but we must beware of exaggerating its extent. The picture that is sometimes drawn of a Protestant nation writhing in the toils of religious tyranny belongs more to propaganda than to fact. The country was by no means Protestant. The vast mass of its people in all provinces were Catholic and conformist. The edicts which carried away numbers of Anabaptists from their midst caused them no more than mild revulsion, since like most majorities they were lethargic. Their care for their neighbors was lukewarm, but so was their Catholicism. The vigorous current of the Counter-Reformation had not yet reached them. Any government faced with so biddable and lumpen a proletariat might have been forgiven for thinking that it was not of the stuff of which revolutionaries were made. And the government would have been quite right. The danger was to come from the few— from the Protestant activists, full of fire and the Word.

When we turn the people to their natural leaders, the nobility of the Netherlands, we see the same situation again writ large. The majority were Catholic. They had no love of religious persecution, which provided spectacles distressing to lovers of the easy life, but they did not feel themselves personally involved. As great seigneurs, semi-independent princes on their vast estates, they disliked despotic and modernizing government, but they might still hope for pickings even from that. Immensely rich and self-satisfied, having great possessions, they were by nature opposed to change, and were hardly likely to feel much affinity with artisans and weavers practicing heresies which contained a strong leaven of democratic thinking. In any crisis their inclination was to trim and then to look around for some personal advantage that might be gained, now from one side, now from the other. Prosperity had fattened them—not all of course. Among their number were Protestants, some of whom had made the pilgrimage to the fountain-head of Calvinism in Geneva. These were of tougher breed: soldiers and thinkers like the two Marnixes and Count Louis of Nassau; though they included also self-seeking adventurers and wild men such as Brederode, a born extremist in search of a cause.

In this gallery two men stood out far above the rest by character and reputation: Egmont and the Prince of Orange.

Lamoral, Count Egmont, Prince of Gavre, was the Rupert of his times, but a sadly muddled one. Beethoven's splendid overture reflects the heroism but certainly not the doubts and perplexities of the living man whose talents were for the battlefield, not for the dangerous game of politics. By race a Hollander, but with large possessions in the south, stadtholder of Flanders and Artois, knight of the Golden Fleece, victor of Gravelines and St. Quentin, his was the most glittering figure in the provinces: a hero indeed, but perhaps a costume hero with something already archaic about him: a relic of a less complicated age.

William of Nassau, Prince of Orange, was by contrast very much a man of his own time. The title of "the Silent" by which he is so often remembered is a misnomer. In fact it comes from a translation of the Latin *taciturnus*, itself a mistranslation of the Dutch word *schluwe*—"sly"—originally applied to him by his enemies. William the Silent, the Taciturn, he certainly was not, but a man of en-gaging manners and charm, German by race but French by culture, owing his title to his small principality of Orange on the Rhone which was a fief of the French king. William the Sly is better—it well suggests the devious, clever, diplomatic side of his nature which helped him to read his opponents' minds and find his way through the political jungle of his times—but it too is a misnomer. If he was sly, he had slyness thrust upon him. It was the price one paid for survival, as Egmont should have learned, not the real nature of the man which was essentially consistent and of one piece. Only the chiaroscuro was baffling.

Baffling indeed it was. On the face of it few more unlikely champions of Protestant revolt against the house of Hapsburg could have been looked for. The boy, born of Lutheran parents, had been brought up a Catholic at the court of Charles V. His tutor had been a Perrenot, in fact a brother of his future antagonist Gran-velle, the leading light of the *Consulta*. The Emperor, kindly by nature, had taken a great liking to the young man, to the extent of promoting him at an early age to important commands in the army and even finding him a rich wife. It was on William of Orange's shoulder, as we have seen, that the Emperor leaned at his ceremonial abdication; it was William who carried the imperial crown to Charles's brother and successor; and it was he who pro-claimed the death of his benefactor with solemn pageantry in the church of St. Gudule. Nor was Philip disinclined in his turn to use this gilded young man of wealth and talent. On the birth of the Prince's eldest son, the Count of Buren, the King graciously agreed to act as godfather and permitted his own name to be given to the child, who was christened Philip William—a piquant incident, though perhaps surpassed by the really desperate embassy on which the King next sent his councilor: to borrow money for the Crown from the merchants of Antwerp!

William himself was fabulously rich. In her biography of him Veronica Wedgwood tells us that he owned, besides his principality of Orange, fully a quarter of Brabant, portions of Luxemburg, Flanders and the Franche Comté, baronies in Italy and three hundred smaller estates—also a number of debts, but debts were in fashion. His table, served by an army of cooks and menials, was famous throughout Europe. His family had once provided a Holy Roman Emperor, and one could hardly hope to be grander than that. This was the man who was to die in a simple house in the small town of Delft with hardly a florin to his name and only a rebel nation to mourn him; but at twenty-six, his age when the King sailed for Spain, he was more a byword for magnificence than for the virtues that usually go to make a national leader. So little did he appear a friend to the Protestant sects, that we shall soon find him engaged in putting down heresy in his principality of Orange and explaining his orthodox intentions to the Pope. In Spanish circles there were already doubts of him however. He was a man to be watched.

And very soon, in the year of the King's departure, came the first proof of the Prince's disaffection and of the powerful position in which he stood: the matter concerned the Spanish troops, whose presence in the Netherlands was a constant irritant and one which seemed all too likely to continue in spite of the King's promise to recall them. Acting together, Orange and Egmont now threw up their commands and wrote to Philip threatening to withdraw from the State Council unless promises were kept and the troops removed. Even Granvelle felt driven by the pressure of public opinion to urge the need for surrender on this point, and in January 1561 the troops finally set sail from Zeeland amidst general rejoicing.

It was a triumph, but short-lived. They had been gone only two months when the detailed plans for the new bishoprics were published in a Papal bull and the hated system was actually in being on Netherlands soil.

At once a tremendous outcry arose. The very brilliance and logic of the plan condemned it. It offended everyone, every interest, aristocratic and popular, lay and clerical. It was judged to be a breach and indeed a defiance of the ancient charters of the provinces and particularly that of Brabant, the most admired of all, which provided against any change of the religious status quo without consultation with all parties concerned.

This in itself would have been quite sufficient to damn the measure as despotic, even if it had not in fact contained provisions for the appointment of prebendaries in each diocese, two of whom were to be Inquisitors. These were loaded words. They had only to be uttered for the specter of the Spanish Inquisition to spring fully armed into the popular mind with all its power to disgust and terrify. The reaction was universal throughout the country: yet this in retrospect seems particularly odd, since a full-fledged Inquisition, if on the Papal and not Spanish model, had been operating in the provinces for years.* These fears were in any case quite groundless. The Regent and Granvelle were altogether adverse to importing something for which they had a perfectly good substitute already: one which the new reform of the bishoprics would merely rationalize. The King himself was of one mind with them. He went further. The Inquisition of the Netherlands, as he remarked in mild surprise when acquainted with these phobias, was more pitiless than that of Spain. Indeed one can question some of Motley's hair-raising accounts of the activities of the Netherlands Inquisitors, whom he pictures more as demons than as creatures of flesh and blood, and still agree with him that here was

* Not however in Brabant.

an institution of singular horror which tried men for their beliefs and secret thoughts and reaped a ghastly harvest of suffering.

This native Inquisition had been endured. It was a devil the people knew, but they had no intention of accepting the devil they did not know. The unfortunate bishops—many of them men of learning and compassion—were seen as so many Herods. They were resented everywhere. Some provinces refused point-blank to admit them. The great town of Antwerp petitioned the King with the utmost urgency to revoke the honor he had in mind for them. The Antwerpers, hosts to large colonies of foreigners, many of them heretics, felt with some reason that a bishop with inquisitorial powers would be the ruin of their trade, and astonishingly this argument succeeded, more from the forces of inertia that Philip's rule engendered than from anything else.

Antwerp, with its vast commercial prestige, was a special case. Most, though not all, of the provinces had to accept the King's *Diktat*. But they did it with a reluctance that boded no good. Granvelle—now a cardinal, by grace of the Regent who had made interest for him in Rome—entered his own archbishopric of Mechlin in a sullen silence, without even a claque to cheer him. All the odium of the new measures had fallen on his shoulders—most unfairly, for he was not their author, as the King himself bore witness. But no one believed this, and the Cardinal was never to stop lamenting the unfortunate scheme which he kept assuring everyone had brought him neither honor nor profit. "Would to God," he exclaimed feelingly, "that the matter of these new sees had never been thought of! Amen! Amen!"

Much of Granvelle's correspondence has this rather self-pitying sound. In letter after letter to the King he recounts the slurs that his devotion to the well-being of the provinces and to the true religion bring down on his innocent head. Never did anyone so persistently turn the other cheek to those who persecuted and maligned him. Meanwhile he settled down in his palace of Brussels and his charming countryseat outside its walls to govern the Regent and the provinces with the adroitness and natural delight in ruling that mark the born man of affairs. He was in no doubt about his difficulties. Neither with that "wicked animal the people," as he dubbed them, nor with the great nobles, could any stranger to the Netherlands (and a parvenu at that) hope to be popular. He had a very clear notion that disorders were lurking only just below the

surface and that the country could on the least provocation
collapse into civil war. Nevertheless he had his followers among the
more timeserving magnates and gentry and held all the levers of
power through his primacy of the Netherlands Church, his position
at the head of the *Consulta* and above all in the confidence of the
King, who listened to him alone. The Regent was entirely docile.
And by a singular chance the man he most feared and who
could have been his rival for the King's attention was out of the
country that summer, engaged in compromising himself beyond
hope of redemption by marriage to a German princess.

This second, the Saxon, marriage of William of Orange is one
of the choicest minor mysteries of the age. Left early a widower,
the Prince had naturally looked around for eligible and preferably
rich brides. Highly aspiring, he had even set his cap at Mary
Queen of Scots, but this prize had eluded him, as had also the
daughter of the Duchess of Lorraine—though the girl's mother had
shown herself considerably more willing. His final choice however
was the Princess Anna of Saxony. She was a Lutheran. All her
relatives were Lutherans and most of them regarded the bridegroom with aversion as a Papist and socially beneath them. Anna
herself was an enthusiastic hoyden of sixteen with a limp and slight
curvature of the spine; as the future was to show, she was also
lecherous and ungovernable. But, worst of all, she happened to be
the daughter of that same Elector Maurice of Saxony, the Protestant
champion, who had chased Charles V over the Alps in 1552 and
ruined all his hopes of an imposed religious settlement in Germany.
This was unforgivable to a man of filial piety like Philip. When told
of the projected match, "I don't know," he wrote pathetically to
Granvelle, "how the Prince could dream of marrying the daughter
of a man who treated his late Majesty, now in glory, as Duke
Maurice did."

What the Prince hoped to gain by this union is not immediately
apparent—it can hardly have been Anna's charms, though the
appeal of any very young and very amorous woman should never
be discounted altogether. The need for money was somewhere at
the back of it, for the Princess was reckoned to be one of the richest
heiresses in Europe; but no doubt the overriding aim was diplomatic
and military insurance against the chance of a Netherlands civil
war by the attachment of Protestant allies in Germany—a maneuver very typical of a man of whom Granvelle wrote that he was

Catholic, Calvinist or Lutheran according to the particular needs and aims of the moment. Equally typical was the caution the Prince showed in assuring Philip that his wife would have to worship "Catholically" and would not be allowed the free and open practice of her religion—double indemnity in fact.

For the details of the wedding celebrations Motley is the indispensable guide: no other writer has described with so much *élan* the pompous mummery of the event, with its cavalcades of knights riding into Leipsic—four thousand to support the bride, a mere thousand for the bridegroom—the banquets and masques, the religious rites, the public bedding in the gilded four-poster.

It was St. Bartholomew's Day, on which eleven years later the bells were set ringing throughout the Catholic world for celebrations of another kind, and already the ferment of the strife that was to bring the Huguenot nobles, among hosts of others, to their doom was working throughout northern Europe in books, and the sermons of itinerant preachers, and Calvinist cells which grew and multiplied with astonishing rapidity until they became synods and consistories with agreed forms of worship and fierce proselytizing zeal. In this same year of the Prince's marriage, one Guy de Bray drew up a "Confession" of faith for a "Reformed" Netherlands Church and threw an open letter to King Philip over the ramparts of Tournai castle in the Walloon country just south of the language line. The place is significant. De Bray's pamphlet was translated into Flemish and speedily distributed northward across the great rivers into territory that was to prove the most fruitful soil of all, but the origin of the ferment was Walloon. The language in which the new doctrines spread was chiefly French. And it was in France that Calvinism first challenged the authority of a great European power.

In the spring of 1562, not long after Orange's return with his bride to his Brabant estates, France erupted into religious civil war. Perhaps the strangest thing about the outbreak is that it had been delayed so long, for Calvin had been settled in Geneva for twenty years and the infection of his doctrines, spreading outward from his city into Provence and Gascony, had been widespread and virulent.

In the time of Henry II, a strongly national king, this spiritual invasion had been contained—not without difficulty, for as we have seen, his surrender to Spanish interests at Câteau-Cambrésis had been largely dictated by the need he felt for smiting his own heretics. But Henry had died in the immediate aftermath of that peace. His successors were two sickly boys: the first—Francis II —a tool of the ultra-Catholic faction of the Guises; the second— Charles IX—under the domination of the Queen Mother, Catherine de Medici, one of history's most enigmatic figures.

Chiefly remembered as a byword for treachery and murderous hatred of Protestants, Catherine's is still a name to conjure with. The guides who to this day marshal their captive bands of tourists into her rooms in the castle of Blois know their business, if not the woman they malign. The Beefeaters on Tower Green, where Anne Boleyn and Raleigh suffered, do no better by the public. With grave *empressement* the hidden spring is pressed to reveal the secret "poison cabinet" of the Queen to an accompaniment of marveling gasps and a few titters from the young. How abominable a monster! A few of the guides, more informed, more daring, go on sometimes to tell of Catherine's other machinations: of the *"Escadrille Volant,"* her flying squadron of frail and beautiful young ladies whom she used as a kind of prophylactic to calm the bloodier political passions of her time. "Poor woman," remarked the most famous of her victims, her son-in-law Henry of Navarre, many years later when he was King of France, "what could she do with a husband dead, and five small children to bring up, and two families scheming to seize the throne—our own and the Guises? I only marvel she didn't do even worse." Perhaps this is an epitaph which Catherine herself would have accepted. She knew her limitations; she had been taught them as orphan, as neglected wife, as mother of a degenerate brood. Another Elizabeth Tudor, with the same crafty, skeptical turn of mind but without the dignity or the vast prestige—poor woman indeed, she had good aims: reconciliation, religious peace and the advancement of her children. They merely happened to be impracticable.

Under her well-intentioned but weak government the country fell apart. Both the extremist parties were to blame. In 1560, during the brief reign of her eldest son, the Calvinist (Huguenot) nobles had been the first to appeal to force in an attempt to get possession of the King. Alarmed by this, the Queen Mother had made overtures toward the new faith, and after the succession to the crown of the ten-year-old Charles IX she had developed this conciliatory role by the famous Colloquy of Passy, a kind of religious "teach-in" which led to an increase in open Calvinist worship and a complete estrangement of the Catholics, who still formed by far the stronger of the forces that were preparing to tear France apart.

When the day of reckoning came, Catherine showed her realism by joining the Catholic side. After all, she was the niece of a Pope, and the court normally resided in Touraine, which was Catholic, or in Paris, which was fanatically so. Her distrust of the. Guises undoubtedly checked her enthusiasm for any cause they might support, yet she had no choice but to conform and act against the Huguenot enemy who had called in the heretic Queen of England and had actually ceded French territory—the seaport of Havre— as security for English expenses.

The counter, of course, was an appeal to Spain. The pattern of a whole series of future conflicts was being set. Across the Netherlands border Cardinal Granvelle had already discerned the menacing nature of the times and the need for supporting the government in Paris, since there were many in the Low Countries who wished ill to the Catholic faith and would cheerfully walk the same heretical road. "None of our like-minded magnates," he wrote, not naming Orange, "have declared themselves as yet, but only God can preserve us from a similar catastrophe if they do."

This was preaching to the converted. Philip was at least as Catholic as his minister, and his response to the danger was immediately to order a force of two thousand Netherlands cavalry to be dispatched to France to deal with it at its source. This in effect was a mobilization of the "Bands of Ordonnance" which had come to be regarded purely in the light of a frontier defense force, and, as might have been expected, the reaction in the provinces to this inept attempt to send it adventuring far from the borders of the Netherlands—and on such an errand—was outspoken and intense. Even the Regent Margaret, being a Netherlander herself, understood the national mood and looked around in desperation for a middle way between the King's impossible demands and the increasing turbulence of the people and nobles who were demanding the summoning of a States General, a body she had been instructed by Philip on no account to call.

Acting on Orange's advice, she opted to convene a chapter of the order of the Golden Fleece, and this duly assembled in Brussels in May 1562. Since some kind of a safety valve for the popular discontent had become a necessity, the choice of this aristocratic body was the wisest the Duchess could have made; and indeed it soon found a face-saving formula to get over the awkward matter of the cavalry by commuting their services for a money payment which Philip grudgingly accepted. The person who gained most from the assembly of the knights of the Fleece, however, was the Prince of Orange, who at a series of private meetings, in the absence of the Regent and Granvelle, pressed on his fellow magnates the need for the removal of the hated minister and for a complete change in the King's religious policy which was causing widespread emigration and threatening the economic life of the provinces. At a second formal session of the Fleece it was agreed with the Regent that a delegate should be sent to Spain to set the full facts of the situation before the King; and Count Montigny, a Catholic moderate likely to prove acceptable to Philip, was selected for this task over his own heartfelt objections. "It had been written in his destiny," says Motley in a chilling passage, "that he should go twice into the angry lion's den, and that he should come forth once alive."

Battle was now squarely joined between the dissident nobles under the guidance of Orange on one side and Granvelle, supported by the Regent, on the other. It was by no means a one-sided contest. The Cardinal was a man of high abilities and courage, a worthy opponent for Orange, with whom he had once been on terms of considerable intimacy if not genuine affection. "Though the Prince pretends to be friendly," he informed Philip, "when he is apart from me he is full of disaffection." The Cardinal was too astute a diplomat however to feed the King with too many direct attacks on his enemy; he preferred more oblique methods—a hint here, a half-truth there, with many a reference to his own saintly acceptance of insults and contumely. "I bear these things patiently," he wrote. "God will reward those who suffer for religion and justice." The rumor then current that he had urged the cutting off of a few noble and traitorous heads filled him with concern, and both he and the Regent besought the King to deny this calumny in the most forthright way. "It is untrue," the King replied, "that Granvelle ever pressed me to cut off half a dozen heads. It might be quite a good idea however."

If this half-joking sentence presages the regime of the Duke of Alva, who was to carry it out with interest, Philip's policy in the main was still cautious and pacific. Well briefed by Granvelle, he was aware that nothing less than his own royal authority was being challenged, and challenged openly by the leading seignors, but he still hoped by fair words and a few small concessions to neutralize the more dangerous and to detach the weaker brethren by the payment of certain awards from the treasury which were not exactly bribes. Egmont, whom the Regent and Granvelle both judged the most biddable of the magnates, received the lion's share of these handouts (*mercedes*); while the Duke of Aerschot, in whom love of pre-eminence was a disease, was chosen instead of the Prince of Orange to represent the provinces at the Frankfurt Diet at which Philip's cousin, the Archduke Maximilian, was to be elected King of the Romans. Like most half measures these had only limited success, and when Montigny returned from Spain that December bearing little beyond the King's assurance that the Inquisition in its Spanish form would not be introduced into the provinces, popular fury broke out afresh in disturbances and savage lampoons of the Cardinal, now generally regarded as the source of every evil.

Hated, mocked, ostracized, in danger of his life, Granvelle continued to forgive his enemies with a truly Christian and maddening humility. He would serve them, he told Philip, whether they liked it or not. He had no fear of them. "If they kill me," he is reported to have said, "then in God's name I shall be quit of living and they of a very good friend whom they will mourn one day." Such a man could not easily be edged out of office. When he was still seen to be entrenched there in the spring of 1563, three months after Montigny's return from Spain, Orange, Egmont and Count Horn (Montigny's brother), acting for a consortium of the high nobility, signed a letter of protest to the King, coupled with a plea to be allowed to leave the Council of State.

Another three months passed—a normal period for any dealing with the incredibly dilatory Spanish court—before the King's reply reached the seignors, blandly side-stepping their complaints—quite in the style of the Cardinal, who in fact had got wind of what was afoot and had more or less dictated the contents in advance. Perhaps he had underestimated the resolution and persistence of his enemies, who responded with detailed charges against him and with plain speaking that was no longer wrapped up in the double-talk of the times. "It is no longer a question," wrote the seignors, "of censuring the said cardinal, but of dismissing him from an office for which he is not only ill fitted but which he can no longer hold without danger of grave embarrassment and strife."

This second letter dated July 29 and signed as before by Orange, Egmont and Horn is worthy of Granvelle himself. The signatories declare their artless, bucolic nature and their preference for deeds, not words. This from Orange, the subtlest diplomat of the age! The message was clear enough however: the three magnates, on behalf of a wide consensus of opinion among the nobility, were serving notice that the Cardinal must go. They could no longer guarantee public order if he stayed. And in earnest of this—having sent the letter and drawn up a "Remonstrance" for the Regent—the signatories withdrew from the State Council on which, as they explained, they had become "but shadows."

The Regent, Margaret of Parma, had accepted and indeed promoted the dominance of the Cardinal, whose red hat she had busied herself to get from Rome. She was no cipher however but a woman whom Granvelle had taken a little too much for granted in the course of his intimate dialogue with the King. Left alone with the Cardinal and his puppets of the *Consulta* and deprived of the support of the seignors, her fellow countrymen and traditionally the props of her rule, she began to develop hesitations, then doubts, then a covert resistance to the master hand. That August, becoming bolder, she sent her secretary Armenteros to Spain with a personal letter for the King, in which she set out in diplomatic language both the brilliant qualities of the Cardinal and the end to which his policies seemed to be leading: "great inconveniences and even a popular rising in the country." The wording of this letter may owe something to Armenteros himself—"Argenteros," as the people called him for his propensity to make money out of his position: a sly and unscrupulous creature who hated Granvelle—but the sentiments were nonetheless deserving of respect and represented a basic truth which the King would ignore at his peril.

In Spain the arrival of the letter and of Armenteros himself, with the glosses he was able to give to it, were received with dismay and a sense of outrage. But even the Duke of Alva, the King's most forthright adviser, whose belief in the virtue of cutting off heretic heads was sincere and uninhibited, felt that the occasion called for temporizing measures, a policy of divide and rule, by supporting Egmont and the moderates against the Orangists until the whole gallery could be brought to the block. And this climate of opinion which seemed to favor compromise at the Cardinal's expense was undoubtedly sensed in the Netherlands also, so that the unfortunate minister, no longer basking in the Regent's approval, soon found himself deserted by his timeserving friends and almost alone except for a small remnant of the faithful.

In this crisis, which as he told the King's secretary, Pérez, had turned his hair so gray that he was barely recognizable, Granvelle behaved with a dignity and courage that command respect. Surrounded by danger on every side, he was resigned to live as long as God allowed him and hoped that those who took his life would fail to profit by it. In the meantime he did not neglect to supply the King with facts and rumors about his enemies, particularly the Prince of Orange, whom he drew in vivid colors as a dangerous man, "subtle, full of finesse," a man of "profound views, very difficult to handle and unchangeable in his opinions."

Granvelle was right. He also had a policy: the King must come to the Netherlands in person. Weeks, months, passed without reply. The Cardinal complained that if he had been living in the Indies he could not have been worse informed as to the royal intentions. And all the time he had to face the growing insolence of enemies: broadsheets; caricatures; lampoons; finally the creation of a burlesque costume in coarse gray cloth with fools' caps and bells embroidered on it—designed by the supposedly loyal Egmont of all people!—which caught the popular fancy to such a degree that every nobleman in Brussels clamored to have himself and his retainers dressed in this parody of the Cardinal's ostentatious style.

It was all very heartfelt and rather ridiculous, like the language of protest in any age. Granvelle, an adult among adolescents, could no doubt have put up with any amount of symbolism so long as the King stayed staunch. But the King was in a mood to temporize. In this context Granvelle was expendable. The Regent had said it in so many words; and indeed the Cardinal himself had expressed his humble desire to go if his going would serve the general welfare and his master's convenience.

By January 1564, after a four-month delay, the King had made up his mind and sent Armenteros back to Brussels with secret instructions for Granvelle.

I have reflected much on all that you have written me during these last few months, concerning the ill-will borne you by certain personages. I notice also your suspicion that if a revolt breaks out, they will commence with your person, thus taking occasion to proceed from that point to the accomplishment of their ulterior designs . . . All of which has given me much anxiety, as well from my desire for the preservation of your life, in which my service is so deeply interested, as for the possible results if anything should happen to you, which God forbid. I have thought, therefore, that it would be well, in order to give time and breathing space to the hatred and rancour which those persons entertain towards you, and in order to see what course they will take in preparing the necessary remedy for the provinces, for you to leave the country for some days, in order to visit your mother, and this with the knowledge of the Duchess my sister and with her permission, which you will request, and which I have written to her that she must give, without allowing it to appear that you have received orders to that effect from me. You will also beg her to write to me requesting my approbation of what she is to do. By taking this course neither my authority nor yours will suffer prejudice; and according to the turn which things may take, measures may be taken for your return when expedient, and for whatever else there may be to arrange.

Was this dismissal? If it was, it was very delicately wrapped up in the convolutions of the royal prose. The Cardinal is to manifest a sudden desire to see his aged mother after an absence of fourteen years, and great care is to be taken to make the public record show that both Cardinal and Regent are asking the King to grant something he has already ordered. Furthermore, by a letter written to Orange, Horn and Egmont, drafted at the same time *but deliberately held back to be delivered after Granvelle had received his letter,* the King rebuked the nobles, ordered them to return to their seats on the Council of State, and pretended that no decision had yet been reached about the Cardinal. He would give more thought, he wrote, as to what was best to do.

So complex a plot to deceive the world certainly suggests that the King was putting up a smoke screen behind which he could maneuver in any direction and that he may have hoped to restore Granvelle when all the excitement had died down. There remains the distinct possibility that he was also deceiving Granvelle himself and that the removal of the unpopular minister was meant from the start to be as final as it proved to be in fact. With Philip one

never knows. He was a master of evasion: and in his secretary
Antonio Pérez, who may have drafted the letters, he had a past
master, as he was to find to his cost.

As for Granvelle, whatever he may have thought—and he was
after all a connoisseur of the royal methods—the path of duty was
plain; and after a momentary hesitation, to see which way the
cat would jump, he took to the road in March in the midst of a
brilliant cavalcade of horsemen, his coach drawn by a team of
mules supplied by the Regent who was in ecstasies to see him go;
and from Besançon in his native Franche Comté wrote dutifully to
the King of his filial desire to see his mother after so long an interval
and humbly soliciting the royal approval.

Philip's instructions were thus carried out to the letter. The
Regent wrote to the King, playing her small part in the comedy by
requesting leave of absence for the Cardinal, which she had taken
the liberty to grant, and the King solemnly replied that he could
not object to so pious and worthy a mission.

All this was for the file. But the people of the Netherlands were
perceptive. On the door of the Cardinal's palace in Brussels appeared a placard—FOR IMMEDIATE SALE.

Wild rejoicing broke out. Two of the disaffected nobles, Counts
Brederode and Hoogstraten, had no sooner seen their tormentor
pass through the gates of Brussels than they had galloped off
like a circus act astride the same horse to take their ironical farewell of him as he passed in his coach along the road to Namur
and the Franche Comté. Brederode and Hoogstraten were the
licensed clowns of the age. But even Orange himself, for all his
doubts about the royal intentions, expressed his formal gratitude to
Philip and returned with Egmont and Horn to the Council of State,
where they were all warmly welcomed by the Regent, now as
convinced an anti-Cardinalist as anyone in the Netherlands. Reconciliation was in the air and Orange's expressions of high and
grateful devotion to his sovereign had been met by a bland demand from Madrid for the services of his head cook. Months
later, the simpler-minded nobles were still celebrating the down-
fall of Granvelle in a series of ridiculous pageants and mimes in
which a horseman dressed up in cardinal's costume was scourged
by a pursuing devil with a whip of foxtails.

This buffoonery like the general rejoicing was misplaced. The Cardinal had gone. The policy remained. Four months before his departure, the great Papal council sitting at Trent in the Tyrol had set the seal on the Catholic riposte to Protestantism which we know today as the Counter-Reformation. Five months after his dismissal, while he still lingered hopefully in Besançon expecting his recall to power, his master sent instructions to the Regent to enforce the Trent decrees throughout the provinces, and in subsequent letters insisted that no alterations whatsoever could be made from the form in which they had been promulgated in Spain.

The decrees of the Council of Trent gave Catholicism back its soul, besides a sound doctrinal base from which the counter-attack on heresy was to be mounted. Many of the provisions which aimed at improving standards of discipline and piety among priests were admirable in every way and answered Luther, though forty years too late. But by their nature they involved an onslaught on the Protestant sects, which they outlawed, excommunicated, and on which they pronounced anathemas; their effect in the hands of bigots and Inquisitors amounted to nothing less than an attempt to burn out heresy at the stake.

To flaunt such a policy in the Netherlands in the circumstances of the time looks on the face of it an act of madness, particularly when one remembers that the statesman who might have been able to impose it, or could at least have been made the scapegoat in the event of failure, was cultivating his garden in Besançon. Without Granvelle there could be no Granvellism. The Regent, poor woman, was no bigot, for all that she had known Loyola in her youth. She would have liked to temporize, to follow the example of France, where the Trent decrees had been suppressed. Peremptorily from Spain came the demands for her to publish them. The city of Bruges, though staunchly Catholic, was already in ferment over the activities of the Inquisitor Peter Titelman, one of the choicest monsters of the period, of whom the Regent herself was supposed to be in awe. The Estates of the province of Flanders, inveighing against this same Titelman, besought the King to prevent the enormities being practiced by his servants. To take an instance, one Le Blas, for trampling on a consecrated wafer, had to suffer his right hand and foot to be wrenched off with red-hot irons, his tongue to be torn out, and to swing in chains over a slow fire till roasted.

Obviously it was an age inured to horrors. But already in
Granvelle's time the popular fury at such events had overflowed
and two heretic victims in Valenciennes had been forcibly rescued
from the stake on a day that was long remembered as that of the
"*Mals Brûlés,*" "the Unburnt," while the civil power had stood by
and done nothing.

The truth was that even the Catholics, who still formed the
large majority in every province, were increasingly sickened by
the sights they had to witness. The judges and magistrates—Catholics all—shared this distress. At the trial in Antwerp in October
1564 of Christopher de Smet (Fabritius in his better-known Lat-
inized name), a former Carmelite monk turned heretic and preacher,
the city sheriff was at pains to point out that not the court but
the King's decree was responsible for the death the victim was
about to meet. "Let us hope, then," replied Fabritius, "that this
decree will absolve and protect you at the great Day of Judgment."
Condemned he was—but observers noted the pallid faces of his
judges; and on the square, as he was strapped to the stake and
the fire was lit, the popular passions they had feared burst out
uncontrollably and the mob surged forward, scattering the officials
and guards around the pyre. The executioner, before fleeing from
the scene, stabbed the unfortunate victim to the heart and the
body was consumed in the flames, its remnants being later thrown
into the Scheldt; but Fabritius's death, like his life, was a sign of
the times. The fires were being lit for a greater conflagration.

On the Council of State both Regent and nobles were fully aware
of the dangers that were mounting every day. None of these
comfortable persons wanted rebellion—not even Orange at this time.
They were too well off and too well aware of the crushing power
that the King could wield against them. But they also had to live
with a people who were being driven mad by persecution and
bled white into the bargain by the flight of traders and capital
abroad. A solution of some kind had to be found, and it is typical
that they should have found it by sending another embassy to
Spain: this time in the person of the devoutly Catholic Count
Egmont, whose brief was not only to protest against the Trent
decrees, but to try to get the King to enlarge the aristocratic
State Council at the expense of the Finance and Privy Councils
staffed by the uppish jurists who had been worming their way into
power. No doubt Egmont was the perfect choice for such an

embassy, to which only Orange seems to have attached a serious purpose and which was regarded by the more highflying nobles in a light that was both frantic and farcical. At Cambrai, in the course of a series of Gargantuan banquets to speed the departing grandee, Counts Brederode and Hoogstraten, having contrived in their cups to insult an archbishop, signed a pledge in their own blood to revenge any harm that might befall the messenger by a personal assault on Cardinal Granvelle, still peacefully on his estates in Besançon! In the Netherlands, tragedy and buffoonery were inseparable companions.

In Spain, Egmont's reception was naturally more formal and in accord with protocol, though the King—who had tried hard to prevent the visit—is said to have rushed from his cabinet to embrace his guest, as Alva was later to embrace him on another memorable occasion. The hero of Gravelines and St. Quentin was received with every honor and distinction due to his rank and to the royal prospects of corrupting him. He was banqueted; feted; listened to with a flattering attention; asked for his advice; taken in the royal coach to the sierras beyond Madrid to see the progress of the Escurial, which commemorated the St. Quentin victory, and to the King's retreat at Segovia from which some of the most fateful of his orders were to go out. All the Count's pressing financial problems—of which he had a number—were settled to his advantage. Just one small urbane threat was issued. "Let us have no more of it, Count," the King remarked of past acts of rebelliousness as they were driving together in his coach. The Count was charmed by his visit. He had a quiverful of daughters approaching marriageable age and the King had expressed himself most encouragingly on the topic of husbands and dowries for them. In the matter of the main business of the visit Philip had also seemed affable and understanding, so that the impressionable envoy set off on his return journey declaring himself "the most satisfied man in the world."

By the end of April 1565 he was back in Brussels, still full of praise for the royal clemency. And a week later it was evident, even to him, that his mission had been as barren as Montigny's two and a half years earlier. In dispatches written only three days after the Count's departure from the Spanish court the King had made it plain that he would suppress heresy at whatever cost. He would, as he declared, prefer to die a thousand times rather

than allow a single change in matters of religion. Nor would
he enlarge the State Council to suit the grandees. The sole concession he would make to the popular cause was a project to call
a council of bishops and jurists to pronounce on the advisability
of publishing the Trent decrees and of substituting new methods
for executing heretics, whom it might be wiser to drown secretly in
prison rather than burn publicly.

In all conscience this sounds decisive enough, since the committee of bishops and jurists was practically certain to come down
in favor of the publication of the Trent decrees, as in fact it did.
Looked at with hindsight, the King's policy seems as unchangeable
as the laws of the Medes and the Persians.

But that was not how his counselors and servants saw it at
the time. His flattering attentions to Egmont, then his dispatches
which infuriated Egmont; his suggestion of committees; the enormous delays and gaps in his correspondence—all these created a
most painful impression among his secretaries and diplomats. All
were in despair over his indecisiveness, not least the Regent, who
was forever waiting for instructions which never seemed to come.
"Everything," wrote Chantonay, Granvelle's diplomat brother, in a
phrase which was later to be borrowed without apologies by Sir
Winston Churchill*—"Everything goes on from tomorrow to to-
morrow, and the main resolution in such matters is to remain
always irresolute." It was the opinion of such men that Philip
should certainly go to the Netherlands in person but they rightly
doubted whether he had any such intention. "The King would
be hard put to it to act like a man," wrote Chantonay, thinking
no doubt of the Emperor Charles, his father's friend and master,
who would hardly have lingered so far from the fray.

Times had changed however. The King's methods, based on
procrastination and a Jove-like brooding on the mountaintops, were
not necessarily wrong. If he was determined to impose an unpopular policy it was wise to do it by degrees, particularly with
a people as volatile as that of the Netherlands, where passions
rose and fell as quickly as in the nursery. It was a matter of
timing: and in the autumn of 1565 the King came down out of
the cloud and in his celebrated letter "from the wood of Segovia"
declared an end to all hopes of religious compromise.

* Of a prewar government when he was in the wilderness—"They are decided only
to be undecided, resolved to be irresolute, adamant for drift."

This *Diktat* had been signaled in advance for years, and it is proof of the Netherlanders' infinite capacity for self-deception that it should now be received by the Regent and the grandees on the Council of State with something approaching stupefaction. Heresy would be repressed, at the stake if necessary, and the Inquisition would continue to be administered by Inquisitors as ordained by the laws of God and man. It had been said often enough. The Emperor's edicts had laid down the policy fifteen years earlier. "Now we shall see the making of a fine tragedy," the Prince of Orange is said to have whispered to his neighbor as the King's letter was read.

When the details were published throughout the provinces that December the whole nation was stunned. Van der Vynckt in his monumental *Histoire des Troubles aux Pays Bas* says that a declaration of war could not have caused greater alarm. There was a large exodus of refugees. Broadsheets appeared on the streets of towns; prisoners of the Inquisition were forcibly freed; petitions were thrust at the Regent and nailed to the doors of Egmont's and Orange's palaces calling on them to rise for the national cause; there were even rumors that the King would come to the Netherlands with an army and that plans for a general massacre of Protestants throughout France and the seventeen provinces had been agreed on at a meeting at Bayonne between the French Queen Mother and her daughter, the Queen of Spain, supported by the Duke of Alva.

Through this outbreak of national hysteria—and it was nothing less—only the great nobles of the Council of State stayed calm. They could afford to. Perhaps they guessed correctly that the Bayonne conference had decided nothing and that the King was not one of the metal to come to Brussels, with an army or without one; in any case they made no move to seize the leadership that was being pressed on them. Egmont, as usual, was uncertain and wavering between loyalty to the King and to his own popular image as the defender of his country's liberties. But even the Prince of Orange seems to have been in a mood to wash his hands of the whole business. He had pressing economic matters to attend to that summer in his stadtholderates of Holland and Zeeland, and no doubt to a statesman of his skeptical turn of mind the zeal of the Protestant extremists who gathered round him on his return to Brussels (many of them in his own household) was almost as uncongenial as the Catholic bigotry of the King. What he felt is best seen in a letter he sent the Regent early in 1566 protesting against the evils of a policy so foreign to his own tolerant spirit, but written in a minor key, almost of abdication, to which the increasing unhappiness of his own married life may have contributed. "If his said Majesty will not reflect but insists on this inquisition and this policy," he wrote, "then I would prefer him to find someone else to take my place with more understanding of the national mood and more able than I am to keep peace and good order . . ."

Nature abhors a vacuum. Into the gap left by this failure of leadership at the top now stepped a group of men more resolute and grasping, with more to gain and less to lose: the minor nobility of the Netherlands, most of them Calvinist but numbering among them also a few Catholics and middle-of-the-road men who were prepared to work with anyone opposed to Spain. Count Brederode we have met already. More solid figures were Count Louis of Nassau (Orange's younger brother: a gay and debonair figure: "le Bon Chevalier" in the Prince's words); the two Marnixes (John of Tholouse and Philip of St. Aldegonde); Count Culemburg; Nicholas de Hammes (herald of the order of the Golden Fleece); and Count Charles Mansfeld, son of Count Peter Ernest Mansfeld, one of the Regent's staunchest and most Catholic councilors. A meeting of the minor nobility had taken place in the autumn of 1565 at Culemburg House in Brussels under cover of the festivities at the wedding of the Regent's son, Alexander Farnese (later Duke of Parma), who was to leave his own mark on the Netherlands in the years to come. After an attempt to draw in the high nobility had failed, the policy of these activists or "Leaguers" was set down in writing in a document of protest called a "Compromise," copies of which were sent out for signature in the provinces and attracted massive support.

Orange had not approved of these proceedings which seemed to him overhasty and backed by too little weight both inside and outside the Netherlands. He was regarded as the godfather of the movement, however, whether he wanted to be or not. Alarmed by the dangers he saw opening up around him, he tried first to associate Egmont with the scheme, and, when that failed, did his best to damp down the ardor of the signatories. That failed also. The ground swell of revolt was rising too fast to be contained.

News of what was afoot soon reached the Regent, along with still more disturbing rumors that the confederates had planned a massive descent on Brussels to present their Compromise in person. In her distress she turned, like everyone else, to Orange, forgetful of her recent attempts to humble him by favoring the Countess Egmont against the Princess Anna in the complicated game of precedence as played by the vice-regal court. And the Prince responded. At a meeting of the Golden Fleece called by the Regent in March 1566, and later on the State Council, his was one of the few friendly voices raised to comfort her, though his advice was clear and to the point—the King's decrees must be modified and any deputation of the Leaguers must be received as loyal subjects had the right to be received.

On April 3 the representatives of the minor nobility, to the number of about two hundred in the first wave, made a state entrance on horseback into Brussels, led by Brederode and Count Louis, who both settled themselves—to the Prince's considerable embarrassment—in his town house, the Palais Nassau. Next day the delegates met at Culemburg's mansion to swear a solemn reaffirmation of the League and to embody their program in a modified and more diplomatic version of the Compromise which had perhaps been suggested by Orange himself. On the fifth they marched in solemn procession to the vice-regal palace, where, in the same hall in which the Emperor Charles had abdicated amidst tears and lamentations nine years earlier, they now presented their bill of indictment against his successor.

The Regent, a woman of strong emotions, could barely contain herself as these terrible truths about her government were read aloud by Brederode in the presence of scores of her countrymen. The document's form might still suggest some lingering loyalty to the King, but she knew better. It was a program for rebellion. Retiring with her state councilors to an inner room, she wept. "*Quoi, Madame!*" exclaimed Councilor Berlaymont, enraged at what he had had to witness at the hands of impecunious nobles and mere gentry, "*Peur de ces gueux!*" ("What, Madam! Afraid of these beggars!")

At a banquet at Culemburg House attended by a horde of confederates, this gibe of Berlaymont's was repeated by Brederode, whose talent for burlesque had been fired by the words and who now produced a wallet and wooden bowl of the kind used by mendicants at street corners and along the roads of the Netherlands. As a piece of prepared theater this was sufficiently infantile, like most of Brederode's activities. But it was also a political stroke which took account of his audience's mood. The whole banqueting hall erupted with cries of *"Vivent lex Gueux!"* The Leaguers had been given a rallying cry which was soon to be heard on battlefields by land and sea and was to play its part in the making of a nation. Brederode was certainly an able buffoon. But further point was given to this adroit propaganda by the fact that the Prince of Orange with Egmont and Count Horn happened to be passing the Culemburg mansion at the time, and either by chance or design went in for a moment, where they too were caught up in the charade. The Compromise had compromised them also, and all of them were later to pay for it with their lives.

Meanwhile the Regent was debating what to do. As a defensive measure she had mobilized the Bands of Ordonnance, but loyalty to the King was at a discount and she could no longer be sure of being obeyed by the grandees, still less by the riotous and drunken gentlemen whom Brederode had brought to town. Obviously the time had come to make concessions. Another delegation would be sent to Spain to place the facts before the King—Count Montigny (for the second time) and the Marquis of Berghen being selected for this thankless and as it proved fatal task— while the Privy Councilors under their president, the Frisian jurist Viglius, assisted by co-opted magnates of the Golden Fleece, were charged with the task of working out a "Moderation" of the edicts against heresy, which they did to their own satisfaction if to no one else's.

What now [asks Motley in a trenchant passage] was the substance of those fifty-three articles, so painfully elaborated by Viglius, so handsomely drawn up into shape by Councillor d'Assonleville? Simply to substitute the halter for the faggot . . . It was most distinctly laid down that all forms of religion except the Roman Catholic were forbidden; that no public or secret conventicles were to be allowed; that all heretical writings were to be suppressed; that all curious enquiries into the scriptures were to be prohibited. People who infringed these regulations were divided into two classes—the misleaders and the misled . . . Every man or woman in the Netherlands might be placed in the list of the misleaders at the discretion of the officials . . . The superintendents, preachers, teachers, ministers, sermon makers, deacons, and other officers were to be executed with the halter, with confiscation of their whole property . . . *Other* heretics, however, who would abjure their heresy before the bishop, might be pardoned for the first offence, but if obstinate were to be banished. This seemed an indication of mercy, at least to the repentant criminals. But who were these "*other*" heretics? All persons who discussed religious matters were to be put to death. All persons, not having studied theology at a "renowned university," who searched and expounded the scriptures were to be put to death. All persons in whose houses *any act* of the perverse religion should be committed were to be put to death. All persons who harboured or protected ministers and teachers of any sect were to be put to death. All the criminals thus carefully enumerated were to be executed, whether repentant or not. If, however, they abjured their errors, they were to be beheaded instead of being strangled.

This passage, for all its caustic brilliance, does less than justice to the Regent, who seems genuinely to have had "Moderation" at heart. But the people dubbed it "Murderation." They were in no mood to accept the edicts in any shape whatsoever, for the new religious doctrines were spreading like wildfire in the provinces, both north and south of the great rivers. "Field preaching" and "hedge sermons" had become the rage. Preachers would appear outside a town. The word would go round and there would be a general exodus of the faithful to hear them. Those of the "Reformers" who had arms—an ever-increasing number—would provide guards to hold the ring against surprise from the Regent's officers, while from an improvised pulpit under the trees or the summer sky sermons in the popular tongue would be preached and presbyteries formed before the sun went down and the Catholic bells rang for the Angelus.

All that summer this field preaching spread through the land, working from the Walloon provinces northward. In Tournai in July a crowd of twenty thousand is said to have assembled to hear the Calvinist Ambrose Wille and to sing the Psalms in their French translation. At the end of the same month "tens of thousands," indeed "the whole population" (to quote Motley's words), poured out of Haarlem in the northern province of Holland to take part in similar services in Dutch. If these figures are given as evidence of Protestant numbers they should be accepted with reserve, for the new sects still formed only a leaven in the Catholic mass and thirty years later may still not have been in the majority in any province, even in the north, which by then had seceded from Spain. No doubt the crowds that attended these proceedings included a great number of the uncommitted who went there for the novelty of the thing—for something to do—and also a proportion of informers and vagrants, attracted by events which really resembled a gigantic fair or kermess of the kind for which the Netherlands had long been famous. Everything was provided, and provided free—religious fervor; mass singing; the excitement of forbidden things; even knockabout comedy, as at Antwerp, where a Catholic heckler of some learning so discomfited the preacher on the scriptural front that it became necessary to lambaste the victor for his triumph by beating him severely on the head.

All this was right and proper. Indeed about this field preaching there lingers an agreeably pastoral flavor of faith and the summer countryside: a sense of a fresher and more innocent world which John Wesley would have understood and for which his brother might have written the great hymns that saw the dawn of Methodism. But it was also a dangerous world. The edicts might seem to have lapsed, but by the letter of the law all these men and women were heretics: in Motley's fine words "an army of criminals doing deeds which could only be expiated at the stake; an entrenched rebellion, bearding the government with pick and matchlock, javelin and barricade, and all for no more deadly purpose than to listen to the precepts of the pacific Jesus."

The Regent was in despair about them. At Antwerp fourteen thousand on her own estimate had gathered outside the walls; thirty thousand were to greet the Prince of Orange when as hereditary Burgrave he rode in at the urgent request of the authorities to pacify the half-rebellious town. She had to confess to the King, "with sadness and anguish of spirit," her impotence to prevent what was going on. Even Orange, who seems loyally to have supported "Moderation" though without much optimism, could do no more for her in Antwerp than rebuke Brederode and his extremists and negotiate a compromise by which field preaching was to be permitted outside the city walls provided it took place in an orderly manner. The danger even threatened Brussels itself; but here the Regent showed the spirit of an emperor's daughter, declaring that she would attend any hedge sermons with her guards and would not neglect to hang the preachers on the spot.

It was growing late in the day, however, for such salutary

reminders that there was still a government in the Netherlands. Brederode's nobles, feeling that the tide was with them, were becoming daily more intransigent; and at a convention at St. Trond, attended by perhaps two thousand Leaguers, there was talk for the first time of enlisting armed help in Germany to force through a policy which no longer looked to "Moderation" but to the calling of the States General and even an end to the edicts. "I understand perfectly," replied the Regent to one of the delegates who brought her these insolent demands. "You want to take justice into your own hands and be King yourself." Truly, as she wrote to Philip about this time, everything was in such disorder that in most of the country there was no law, no faith, no king. Earnestly she besought him to come to Brussels or at least to authorize the calling of the States General as a safety valve for popular passions which might otherwise break over the Netherlands like a tidal wave, leaving sacked churches and cities in its wake.

Summer is a revolutionary season. Two hundred years later the Quatorze Juillet, the storming of the Tuileries, the September Massacres and the Day of Thermidor when Robespierre fell were all to underline this truth. In the Netherlands the ferment of field preaching had driven everyone a little mad. Suddenly-discovered freedoms have this effect. So have words repeated time and again with passion and the massed singing of great crowds. We have seen it in our own time at Nuremberg: Doctor Goebbels was no innovator. The field preachers were mostly Calvinist: men contemptuous of compromise: the chosen of the Lord in communion with the Lord's elect. And the Lord, amongst other prohibitions, had declared himself against idols and graven images. Against paintings, too, and gilding, and altars, and stained glass, and all the other abominations which were to be found in churches in every village and town in the Netherlands. A stern puritanism and hatred of superstition inspired many of these brave and often admirable men. They despised the old religion for the pride and ostentation of its ritual and the sloth and spiritual bankruptcy of its priests. It was a moral judgment.

But mixed up in all this there was also a great deal of rancorous envy of the haves by the have-nots. The preachers and their flocks were mostly poor men; the Church was fabulously rich. It was not hard for zealots to look on its priceless artistic treasures as loot acquired by the Whore of Babylon. That social protest was among the main causes of what followed is made clear by the fact that the first wave of destruction broke in the Walloon country near the French frontier where industrialization had created a kind of proletariat such as Marx himself might have chosen as the agent of revolution.

This was on the fourteenth of August. A sudden devastation swept over the churches in Poperinghe, Oudenaarde, St. Omer, and spread outward like the wind. On the eighteenth in Antwerp, on the eve of the feast of the Assumption, the famous black Madonna of the city was carried in solemn procession through streets crowded with pilgrims and sight-seers. Above the music and the beat of the drums cries were heard that "Marykin" was taking her last walk, and next morning a threatening crowd approached the sanctuary where the image had been placed behind grilles for greater safety (instead of being exhibited as usual at Assumption in the nave), with cries of *"Vivent les Gueux!"* and promises that her time had nearly come.

All this points to a deliberate plan. The cathedral clergy were obviously fearful of some outrage. The Prince of Orange, who was in the city, shared these fears, but by a singular mischance he was called to Brussels that very day for a meeting of the Golden Fleece, leaving behind him a magistracy on the verge of panic.

Next day, the twentieth, the blow fell. From early morning a crowd collected inside the cathedral, growing in numbers and boldness as the day wore on. The city fathers, making a timely and impressive entrance in procession, succeeded in persuading a large part of the mob to leave, and then retired themselves, feeling perhaps that enough had been done for honor. The great doors of the cathedral were closed behind them. But a side door was left open—so that those still inside could leave! The element of sheer farce, never absent for long from the Netherlands' affairs, played its part that day also.

Now grimmer things were at hand. Through the side door—as centuries later through the wicket that led into the palace of Versailles on the morning the women from Les Halles came to drag the Bourbons back to Paris—the agents of destruction re-entered Antwerp Cathedral. They had work to do. The shouts and insults and "Beggar" cries that had resounded all day under the great Gothic vaulting of the nave were now to be matched in action.

No longer men but a mob was at work: purposefully, as in an anthill. First the Madonna. It was dragged from behind its grille; its vestments were torn off; then it was hacked in pieces. This was only a beginning. But here one must pass once more to Motley.

A wild shout succeeded, and then the work which seemed delegated to a comparatively small number of the assembled crowd, went on with incredible celerity. Some were armed with axes, some with bludgeons, some with sledge hammers; others brought ladders, pulleys, ropes, and levers. Every statue was hurled from its niche, every picture torn from the wall, every painted window shivered to atoms . . . Indefatigably, audaciously—endowed, as it seemed, with preternatural strength and nimbleness—these furious iconoclasts clambered up the dizzy heights, shrieking and chattering like malignant apes, as they tore off in triumph the slowly-matured fruit of centuries. In a space of time wonderfully brief, they had accomplished their task.

A colossal and magnificent group of the Saviour crucified between two thieves adorned the principal altar. The statue of Christ was wrenched from its place with ropes and pulleys, while the malefactors, with bitter and blasphemous irony, were left on high . . . A very beautiful piece of architecture decorated the choir—the "repository" as it was called, in which the body of Christ was figuratively enshrined. This much admired work rested upon a single column, but rose, arch upon arch, pillar upon pillar, to the height of three hundred feet, till quite lost in the vault above. It was now shattered into a million pieces. The statues, images, pictures, ornaments, as they lay upon the ground, were broken with sledge hammers, hewn with axes, trampled, torn, and beaten into shreds. A troop of harlots, snatching wax tapers from the altars, stood around the destroyers and lighted them at their work. Nothing escaped their omnivorous rage. They descrated seventy chapels, forced open all the chests of treasure, covered their own squalid attire with the gorgeous robes of the ecclesiastics, broke the sacred bread, poured out the sacramental wine into golden chalices, quaffing huge draughts to the Beggars' health; burned all the splendid missals and manuscripts, and smeared their shoes with the sacred oil with which kings and prelates had been anointed. It seemed that each of these malicious creatures must have been endowed with the strength of a hundred giants. How else, in the few brief hours of a mid-summer night, could such a monstrous desecration have been accomplished by a troop, which, according to all accounts, was not more than one hundred in number? There was a multitude of spectators, as upon all such occasions, but the actual spoilers were very few.

Sufficient unto the day however. The cathedral was only one of thirty Antwerp churches. These were treated in the same way as the mob raged through the city without challenge spreading havoc in its wake, driving monks from their cells, nuns from their convents, burning the books and precious relics in one tremendous holocaust. Yet, if we are to believe the chroniclers, there was no killing, no rape, little if any robbery. The destruction swept over Antwerp like a whirlwind. In Flanders, Ghent had suffered a similar fate. In Valenciennes the Calvinists took over the town government. On the twenty-second it was Tournai's turn. That same day it reached Amsterdam. Hardly anywhere was it opposed by administrators in terror for themselves, their wives and daughters and possessions. On the twenty-fifth it was in Utrecht. Leyden and Delft soon succumbed to it—in Holland the authorities did not always wait for their churches to be attacked but were apt to be helpful and hand over their statuary in advance. All these towns were Catholic. Most if not all the magistrates were Catholic; so were the majority of the judges, stadtholders, governors and military commanders.

Nothing was done. The storm was allowed to sweep on northward till it reached Friesland and Groningen on the border with Germany. Within two weeks of its rising it had blown itself out, and score upon score of churches had been cleansed of their treasurers in the name of God.

The Brussels government had watched these events in much the same state of paralysis with which the Versailles of Louis XVI was to greet the fall of the Bastille and the Tsarist court the mutinies of 1917. There was dismay. There was a sense of outrage. But where Bourbon and Romanoff were pitifully unable to understand that the foundations of their world had shifted, the Regent was sure of it—so sure, that her first instinct was to escape from the convulsion to sanctuary in Mons, a staunchly Catholic town which had somehow managed to escape unscathed.

Foiled in this by the united opposition of the Brussels municipality, fearful of the fate of Antwerp if she left, and of the grandees who were reluctant to lose control of her, she gave way on every front, and on August 23 signed an "Accord" which authorized "Reformed" preaching in places where it was already established, provided that arms were laid down and there was no interference with Catholic worship.

On the face of it the Protestants had won a considerable victory. All the League's demands had been met. The government had been taught a humiliating lesson and had surrendered to the first show of force without the apparent will or power to fight. The Calvinists had not only been left in possession of their now legalized meeting places in the city suburbs, but by the intervention of Orange and like-minded governors in Antwerp and elsewhere were even permitted to keep some of the looted Catholic churches. Everywhere the radicals rejoiced. It seemed that their triumph could hardly go further or be more complete.

In fact it had already gone too far. In the Walloon south (except in Valenciennes and Tournai, both hotbeds of heresy) a strong Catholic reaction was springing up. Moderate opinion almost everywhere had been outraged by the excesses which had been committed. The leveling nature of the riots had not been lost on the prosperous burghers who had begun by supporting the League and the Beggars but now saw where all this might lead. Liberty of conscience was one thing. Liberty given to artisans to be as good as their masters was quite another, and they had no intention of permitting it.

A big swing back toward the Regent and public order was therefore built into the Calvinist triumph, and this feeling was not confined to Catholics but also embraced the Lutherans, who were as shocked as anyone by the success of their rampageous Calvinist rivals in snatching most of the benefits of the Accord. Orange himself was about to turn Lutheran, and, in his need to win support for his movement from his Lutheran relatives among the north German princes, looked on the Calvinists with some reserve as extremists who might ruin everything by their political incompetence and the provocations they were offering the King. As for the other grandees, the majority had been utterly alienated by recent events. Aerschot, Berlaymont, the elder Mansfeld, Aremberg and Megen were all openly committed to Spain. Egmont, always a loyalist at heart, was turning in the same direction, and was soon to be found persecuting heretics in his stadtholderates of Flanders and Artois with great severity. Nor were the minor nobles as a body any longer in the vanguard of rebellion. Their League had dissolved itself in compliance with the Accord, which had formally pardoned them for past disloyalties. A great number of them, disillusioned with their unwanted allies among the plebs, had gone over to the royalist side or into a disgruntled neutrality, leaving the rump of extremists under Brederode and Count Louis of Nassau in increasing isolation along with the Calvinist divines and the hard core of the faithful. Even the mobs had gone home.

It was a situation ripe for counterattack by a determined government, and the Regent had now found in old Count Peter Ernest Mansfeld just the adviser for the hour and the opportunity. Under his coaching she embraced it eagerly. She had never meant to keep the promises she had made in the Accord. They had been forced from her, as she explained to Philip in a revealing letter which displays both her duplicity and the real anguish with which she had suffered the affronts offered to her religion. The humiliations she had undergone had stiffened a nature that was not naturally cruel but was politic and cunning and now had a grievance to feed on.

For a while nothing dramatic happened. The first need was to preserve order; so the stadtholders departed to their various provinces to interpret the Accord in their individual ways—Egmont, by hanging heretics; Orange, by establishing a basis for a religious peace which might conceivably have lasted if others had been gifted with his own careful, dispassionate turn of mind.

Before long it became clear however that the Regent was interpreting her new religious settlement in the narrowest form. Her Accord had laid it down that Calvinist ministers might preach in the places where they had been in the habit of preaching and that their flocks might listen to them. Did this amount to freedom of worship? Did it mean that Calvinist services on the Genevan model could be held? The Regent expressed her horror at the very notion. Preaching had certainly been authorized. But not worship. That was something altogether different. That was reserved for Catholics. As her courage and confidence came back and she received from Germany reinforcements of mercenary troops paid for with money which the King had astonishingly been able to provide, her intransigence increased. To Orange she expressed her sharp disapproval of the license he had given to Calvinists in Antwerp to perform the full ceremonies of their religion. By February 1567, while rumors of some impending blow from Spain against the Netherlands were spreading throughout the country, she had reached the point of demanding that the grandees of her Council should take a new oath of loyalty to the government—proof indeed of how far things had moved since the days of her abject dependence on them during the image breaking of the previous August.

To this demand the royalists, Aerschot and Berlaymont, at once consented, and Egmont soon followed them. Orange and Hoogstraten declined. The lines of battle were being formed for a war which would outlast the lives of everyone then living and of their children too. Already the Calvinists, correctly gauging Philip's undying hostility, had called a synod at Antwerp and had declared the right of subjects to resist despotic kings. In the democratic pantheon these brave and stiff-necked men deserve an honored place along with Huss and Wyclif, but that was not how their enemies—or many of their friends—saw them at the time. Miscreants beyond the pale of mercy was how the Regent described them. Orange, more politic, merely declined to put himself openly at their head and lead them toward a disaster which he clearly foresaw. He was prepared to work for them, intrigue for them, favor them, to stretch the law for them, but not as yet to die for them.

Did he also "use" them as front-runners in his policy of resistance to Spain? It is hard not to see in his conduct about this time a certain ambivalence, not only toward the Regent, but also toward the Reformed hotheads who were raising armed forces under his very nose in Antwerp for an attempt on the isle of Walcheren and its port of Flushing where it was thought that Spanish sea-borne troops were about to land. We shall see how he treated these levies when their mission failed: but that he was unaware of their enrollment or objective passes belief.

Nothing can be proved, though it is noteworthy that Gachard, who translated and edited the Prince's correspondence in Motley's time and was an avowed admirer of the "immortal founder" of the Dutch nation, was certain of his rather humiliating involvement and connivance in the Walcheren attempt. Perhaps we should not be too harsh in our judgment of a man beset by so many problems and enemies. What is certain is that at this stage he gave no overt lead to the rebellion, which went off at half cock without any central direction beyond what Brederode was able to provide. The main struggle was to develop in the south, where the town of Valenciennes refused to admit a royalist garrison, and where groups of armed men were gathered in the countryside under leaders as untrained and unwarlike as themselves.

On these raw recruits, whom Sir John Falstaff might have been glad to muster on his celebrated visit to Gloucestershire, the Regent's professional levies now fell with brutal thoroughness in two engagements hardly deserving of the name of battles. A third rebel band under the young John Marnix of Tholouse—raised in Antwerp, with or without the Prince's connivance—fared little better in its attempt on Walcheren. Driven off from Flushing by the loyalist citizens, it came up the Scheldt to settle in the neighborhood of Antwerp, at Oosterweel, where it was surprised and destroyed by a royalist army under the lord of Beauvoir within sight and hearing of its co-religionists inside the walls. Marnix himself was hacked literally into pieces, in spite of the offered ransom which was traditionally paid for highborn captives—a foretaste of savageries to come.

Orange, Burgrave of Antwerp, was in the city at the time. On his orders the gates had been closed. This was represented as a measure to prevent the Regent's troops from entering in the flush of victory to massacre every heretic in sight, but to the Calvinists, including Marnix's distraught wife, it naturally seemed more likely that the aim had been to prevent their rushing to the rescue of their brothers whose bodies were now floating in the Scheldt.

As the enraged, half-demented crowds gathered on the battlements, the Prince was violently threatened and called a traitor to his face. Was the accusation unjust? The Prince was hardly a traitor to Antwerp, which he was in the act of saving from bloodshed and sack. Nor was he a traitor to the national cause which he was to uphold throughout his life. But his responsibility toward the extremists whom at the very least he had failed to discourage is not easily shrugged off. No doubt in these moments of pressing danger he had to choose between the few and the many, and the niceties of loyalty or betrayal had ceased to have much meaning.

It was no time for reason. The scene inside the city was apocalyptic, with armed men everywhere spoiling for blood: the Calvinists in one group, with cannon which they had seized from the arsenal; Lutherans and some Catholics in uneasy alliance in another; and the foreign communities in uproar. Never, said an

English observer, Sir Thomas Gresham, had he seen men so desperately eager to fight.

The crisis lasted for three days—from the twelfth of March, the day of the battle of Oosterweel, to the fifteenth—and at any moment a single spark might have set the city ablaze. Nothing happened. Those who have seen this as a near miracle achieved by the dominating genius of one man, the Prince of Orange, may have done less than justice to the stark effects of de Beauvoir's victory and of the massacre he carried out of his prisoners when a group of hotheads managed to scramble out of the city gates attempting rescue, only to retire with equal haste from the scene. In the Netherlands nothing was ever constant: heroism or cowardice, apathy or rage. Even hatred of the government was variable: and it is entirely fitting that these tremendous events, which had cost hundreds of lives and might have led to a small-scale Armageddon, should have ended in another compromise agreement hammered out by Orange and accepted by the Calvinist zealots to loyal cries of *"Vive le Roi!"*

So ignominious a movement deserved an ignominious end. Without Antwerp, the keystone of the Netherlands, the whole badly planned and premature revolt was doomed. Three weeks later Valenciennes surrendered and its Calvinist leaders were hanged. Like ninepins the other rebellious towns went down. Ghent, Ypres, Maastricht, Turnhout, Oudenaarde, all accepted the Regent's garrisons. In Holland, Amsterdam opened its gates, and throughout the north and northeast the royalists regained control. Brederode was soon to flee the country, to die in Germany; his party was disbanded or in flight. In Prescott's words, "The name of *Gueux* and the insignia of the bowl and the Beggars' scrip, which they had assumed in derision, was now theirs by right. It was too true a jest."

As for the Prince, a chapter was closing. The pacification of Antwerp was his last service to the Regent. But it was also his last service to an idea—to the creation of a new political order inside the framework of the old. The notion of some revolution by consent of the ruler was never entirely to leave him—indeed he was to carry out his most treasonable acts ostensibly in the King's name—but after Antwerp he had no real belief in it. Even in defeat the Calvinists had taught him a lesson: that there was no middle way of the kind he had tried to follow in his courtship of moderate opinion which in the end would always turn to Spain. Henceforth he was to be a Beggar, and Prescott's ironic words would be his epitaph also.

The rest is soon told.

On the tenth of April 1567 the Prince sent his resignation to the Regent and on the eleventh withdrew from Antwerp, where he had raised considerable loans. On the twenty-eighth at Willebroek, on his way to his estates at Breda, he had a last meeting with Egmont, whose capacity for self-delusion and loyalty to the hand that fed him had been almost as damaging to the national cause as the image breaking and extremism of the Calvinists.

At Willebroek Egmont was no more than the Regent's errand boy, primed with arguments for inaction, but the meeting of these old friends and onetime rivals was kind. According to de Strada, the Prince expressed the hope that the Count would escape the "furious tempest" soon to reach the Netherlands from Spain. He meant of course the Duke of Alva, who had left Cartagena for Italy that same month to conscript an army. It was a wasted warning, even if it was actually uttered—and indeed there is an apocryphal sound about many of the words supposed to have been uttered at this meeting: "Farewell, landless prince." "Farewell, headless count." More reasonable is the story that Orange, either at Willebroek or at the earlier Termonde meeting, told Egmont that his stubbornness would provide the bridge by which the Spaniards would cross into the Netherlands.

What is certain is that the Prince rode off alone to Breda. There he collected his entourage of children and resentful wife, closed up his house and went into exile in Germany. It was typical of his ambiguous nature and policies that he should have left behind him his sixteen-year-old heir, the Count of Buren, to continue his studies at the Catholic University of Louvain. Not even Motley has been able to excuse or explain it. Father and son were never to meet again.

7

THE GOVERNMENT AND ECONOMY OF SPAIN. COUNCILS, CHURCH AND INQUISITION.

Charles V had returned to Spain to die; his son returned to it to reign; but self-immolation was present in the one act as in the other and both were recognitions of Spain's special position in Europe as the crucible and defender of faith, the most Catholic of kingdoms ruled by the "Most Catholic" king.

At the end of an arduous life the Emperor had turned his back on imperial ambitions and dynastic dreams. Humiliated in Germany, defeated in North Africa and in his attempts to recover his old inheritance of Burgundy, thwarted by Mary Tudor's childlessness in his plans to unite England with the Netherlands in one satellite kingdom within the Spanish orbit, he had come to accept his limitations.

Philip was by nature far less European than his father. He was simply a Spaniard and had never had any desire to project himself as anything else, to live anywhere else, to enter into the thoughts of any other people. Even in Spain he was Castilian, not an Aragonese or a Catalan, and what he worked for was the welfare and glorification of Castile, but on a vast stage. This combination of extreme parochialism and world-wide ambitions was to be one of the hallmarks of his reign. The other was an intense hatred of dissent. It was entirely typical of him that one of his first public appearances in the peninsula as King should have been at an *auto-da-fé*, at one of the solemn ceremonies staged by the Inquisition to assert the need of absolute conformity in matters of faith. It was soon after his wedding to his third wife, the young Elizabeth of Valois, and Motley has a choice passage in which he sees the flames around the dying victims at the pyres lighting the King and his bride to their nuptial couch, in pardonable misunderstanding both of the mechanics of a *quemadero* and of the King's own passionate commitment, which was not to lust or to cruelty for its own sake but to an ideal.

And this ideal was shared by the overwhelming mass of his subjects. Like him they were conformist and Catholic. The distressing spectacle of religious wars in France showed that orthodoxy and one common faith had their advantages in this world as well as those to be expected in the next. Indeed it is very striking to note on how many fronts the King and his subjects were at one. Obviously the Protestant picture of the gloomy and bigoted tyrant needs a certain amount of correction in the light of the respect and devotion which were shown him during a life by no means free of defeats or troubles by a people who, if no better, were probably no worse morally than the inhabitants of other countries at the time. The truth is that even in the territories of the Crown of Aragon, with their fierce local loyalties, the majority of the population both liked and needed a king, even a Castilian one, and complained not of his tyranny but of his absence and of course his taxes. What troubled the Aragonese, the Catalans and the Valencians was not the institution of the monarchy they shared with Castile, or even the person of the monarch, but the difficulty they had in sharing in Castile's profits, in gaining admittance to the protectionist Castilian markets and the Castilian empire in the Indies. While seeking to preserve their jealously guarded rights against the Crown enshrined in their *fueros*, their provincial charters of liberties, they looked to the Crown to protect them from the tyrannies of local lords, along the pattern which Philip's great-grandfather Ferdinand had set in his famous Sentence of Guadalupe, a charter against serfdom.

In Castile, the dominant partner among the kingdoms which made up Spain, the relationship between monarch and subjects was infinitely closer and more direct. In the territories of the Crown of Aragon the King reigned; but in Castile he ruled. The embryo of what in England had grown into a parliament existed there also in the Cortes of Castile, but the limbs had long since begun to atrophy, and what had once been a lively three-chamber assembly of clergy, nobles and burgesses had shrunk into thirty-six representatives of eighteen towns, whose deliberations and complaints were as often as not ignored by the central government and whose only useful function was to vote supplies to the Crown without any corresponding check on expenditure.

In town and provincial government the King, through the agency of royal officials, was supreme—his problems were at the worst localized problems, and if we except the rebellion of part of the Morisco (Moorish) population in the Alpujarras south of Granada in 1568, and certain not very serious troubles in Aragon in the nineties, there was never the breath of an uprising against him such as had convulsed the first years of his father's reign during the *Comunero* troubles and the Valencian Germania. After the beating they had taken on the field of Villalar in 1521 the urban elements in Castile were in a chastened mood and sufficiently prosperous, in spite of inflation, to feel a sense of community with a king who lived among them and paid at least lip service to their cherished "liberties"; while in the countryside, a depressed peasantry was too deeply in debt and too securely held down in a still-semi-feudal structure to do more in the way of protest than to take to banditry or to flock in their thousands from the fields to the thriving towns of Andalusia and New Castile.

It might have been otherwise with the nobles. Secure on their vast estates, a warrior class, ambitious and immensely wealthy, they still had the power to rebel as their fathers had rebelled in the Emperor's time. They had cause enough, for their teeth were being drawn. The old feudal offices of state had lost importance; the sovereignty of the great orders of Santiago, Alcantara and Calatrava had become vested in the Crown; indeed for all their apparent power, the grandees who formed the top of the social pyramid had surprisingly little say in the actual administration of the country, which had fallen into the hands of lawyers and officials of the middle class. Yet in the course of the reign, though there was much grumbling about the pretensions of the *nouveaux riches,* no active opposition showed its head among these resplendent magnates. Immunity from taxation was no doubt one of the reasons for this docility. But the King also took care to appoint them, if not to power in Castile, at least to very glittering posts in the satellite and subject territories: to captain generalships in the Netherlands and viceroyalties in the Indies almost beyond the dreams of avarice. "Men," said Napoleon, "are ruled by toys." He meant by honors and decorations: and this dictum the Prudent King had certainly anticipated in his treatment of a class of men potentially dangerous to the state and to the monarchy itself. Shorn of power but showered with privileges, the grandees were tamed; and so

were the small nobility and gentry, the hidalgos, who found an outlet for their energies and ambitions in the King's armies and in the
Indies.

With the Spanish Church, Philip was to show himself even more
brilliantly successful. The Church, like the nobility, could have
been a disturbing factor inside the closed Iberian society, for in
theory it was international, a sprig of Rome, where policies were by
no means always Spanish ones. Yet, ironically enough, in its actual
government it had already been severed almost as effectively from
Rome as had the Church of England or the Lutheran and Calvinist synods in central Europe. The Spanish Inquisition, set up by
Papal bull in Ferdinand and Isabella's time, was a strictly Spanish
institution owing the Pope only a nominal allegiance. The appointment of Inquisitors, as of other Spanish clergy, was a matter for
the King alone. Only the Jesuits, a Spanish order by origin, showed
signs of looking to Rome; and in the course of time—though not
in this reign—they were duly expelled from the peninsula. It is
a remarkable paradox that the Church which most foreigners
thought of as the incarnation of inflexible Romanism and the
spearhead of the Counter-Reformation should have been in its
structure and spirit so national, so jealous of Roman interference,
and indeed in many of its attitudes so anti-Papal. Yet in spite of
this, Philip still managed to preserve the huge Papal subsidies of
the *cruzada,* officially for his services against the Turk and other
heretics. A masterly performance, though ultimately made possible
only because King and Pope needed one another.

Within Spain itself Philip nursed the Church and cared deeply
for its welfare. In his reign there were none of the lamentable
appointments to its hierarchy which had marked the early years
of Charles V, when the archbishopric of Toledo, the richest see in
Christendom after Rome, had been given to the sixteen-year-old
absentee nephew of his Burgundian favorite Chièvres. Philip's appointments were carefully made and went mostly to dedicated
and scholarly men whose failings were those of faith carried to
extremes. His interest and knowledge extended downward through
bishops and abbots to much humbler men in parishes and monasteries, large numbers of whom were known to him by name and
reputation. Nor did he neglect the claims of the unorthodox and
the mystics: souls like St. Teresa, whom he protected and whose
life and works were to be judged among the chief glories of his

reign. A fanatical enthusiast for the Church, nothing about it was too great or too small for his attention: the choice of an archbishop; the morals of a priest; the smell of heresy; the gift of a painting or a statue for a parish. Under his guidance it grew in influence and power and above all in wealth, in the vast extent of its possessions and revenues. But in this there was an element of worldly calculation, for though not assessed directly through the Cortes, as towns were assessed, it was expected to contribute to the royal exchequer, and the richer it was, naturally the more it could pay.

And pay it did. Through the *cruzada*, the *subsidio* (a tax on clerical rents), the *tercias reales* (a share of tithes), to which was later added the *excusado* to help finance the war in the Netherlands, the Spanish Church provided its king with an annual revenue little short of what he received from the Indies. Furthermore—and in this it was unique among taxpayers in that or any other age—the Church was *glad* to pay. The Archbishop of Toledo was one of the chief contributors toward the expenses of the Armada of 1588, in remarkable contrast to the Pope who managed to dodge *his* contribution to the crusade. When the great venture failed, the Archbishop sent another huge contribution to rebuild the shattered fleets. No other king in Christendom had such support. And the Church did not only support Philip with money; it gave steady backing to his policies at home and abroad and provided him in addition with an almost limitless supply of trained canon lawyers, propagandists and administrators.

To say that the Church was the most dynamic force in Spain would almost certainly be true, for the society of the time would have been unthinkable without it. Yet for all its virtues and vices, the Church no more governed Spain than did the grandees or burgesses. Spain was governed by its king. No ruler in history, not even Louis XIV or Bonaparte, attempted to shoulder so immense a task. And if it is objected that Spain was not governed very well, the fault lay less in Philip's deficiencies than in his virtues of superhuman industry and devotion to an ideal of kingship which had ceased to be practicable in an increasingly complex age.

It is here that one enters a kind of no man's land between fact and legend. The "Spider of the Escurial" ceaselessly plotting against men's liberties and their very souls is an easily recognizable image, and the small room they show to this day among the maze of corridors seems one more vindication of its reality.

In fact Philip was never the hermit of San Lorenzo that mythology would have us think. Only at certain times of the year did he go there; he was as often in Madrid, in his lodge in the "Wood of Segovia" or at his palace in Aranjuez, whose gardens, filled with the sound of nightingales, he remembered nostalgically in letters to his daughters during the Portuguese campaign. Yet it would be idle to deny that the Escurial was the place where he came to feel most at home. From a viewpoint on the hillside still known as the "King's Rock" or the "King's Chair" he had watched the progress of its building, and toward the end of his life his visits became longer and more frequent. It was there he died—in the bed facing the window through which he could see the high altar of the chapel and hear the chanting of the monks whom he had quartered there, not entirely with their enthusiastic consent, for the Escurial was—and remains—a cold and daunting place. Mountains of paper, still preserved in the archives at Simancas, witness to the work he did there in long hours of toil to the ruin of his health; to a marvelous industry and the misuse of the talents of an able man which invites pity. Yet perhaps it was not all done blindly out of stupidity and pride, as unfeeling critics have assumed. In the course of his life Philip suffered personal tragedy on a crushing scale, and it may be that his retreat to the more manageable and bearable world of state papers and memoranda was a kind of therapy which he needed in order to survive.

Much of what was accomplished in the famous night sessions either alone or with his secretaries was beneficent. We should not hold it against him that the Armada was planned in this small silent room, for at least in Spanish eyes it was the most justifiable of crusades. And almost without exception all the decisions that were born there, good or bad, were *meant* to be beneficent, as was recognized by his subjects and by many in a later time who came to look back on his reign as a golden age when there was still probity in Spain. That he was often wrong and in our terms tyrannical, with the moral responsibility for at least three murders squarely laid at his door, does not entirely detract from the fact that his aim was to provide justice for his subjects, both by the personal care he gave to their complaints and by the system of royal magistrates in the towns and superior courts in the provinces which provided a safeguard against arbitrary acts, at least for those who conformed in matters of religion.

All this was admirable. By sheer staying power and dedication the King managed, as no ruler managed before or since, to keep a personal eye on an infinity of problems. But of course a price had to be paid for it. Under this kind of direction the administration of an empire became reduced to its lowest common denominator, and pressing problems of state had to wait their turn while the King settled the details of a priest's vestments or a minute point of protocol. Nor were such blockages to be encountered only at the top. Bureaucrats of varying grades proliferated everywhere, from humble scribblers, through those who kept the records of the great councils, to the Principal Secretary of State, who above all men in Spain had the King's ear.

In Philip's early years this important office was held by one Gonzalo Pérez who had been trained in the school of the Emperor's great secretary Los Cobos, the prototype of the new breed of administrative man. After Pérez's death the office was split in two along territorial lines, one half going to Pérez's illegitimate son Antonio, of whom more hereafter. Toward the end of the reign this system was modified and the offices put into commission, but the immense power of influence and patronage remained undimmed. If not the driving force of the government, the secretaries provided the transmission to move the whole ponderous mass, and in their higher grades they were the essential links between the King and the viceroys who were the organs of rule on the periphery of the empire.

Inseparably connected with them were the royal councils, consisting of groups of magnates and jurists appointed by the Crown to sit in individual committees, each with its own secretariat and individual field of operation, part administrative, part judicial. It was a kind of solar system of planets revolving around the sun, the King himself.

Nearest to him, at least in theory, was the Council of State. But since the members of such a high-sounding body would have to be grandees, and since the King feared and disliked grandees, he used it sparingly, taking advantage of its tendency to divide into factions to disregard it at will. More useful, because less aristocratic, was the Council of Castile, a body supposedly devoted to Castilian problems but with a distinct inclination to poach. For Aragon there was a Council of Aragon, whose wings were soon clipped by the creation of a separate Council of Italy to administer the old Aragonese possessions in Naples and Sicily. There was a Council of War, in fairly constant session. There was a Council of the Indies. There was a Council of Finance: a very unenviable group of officials. There was a Council of the Inquisition.

Almost all these bodies were weighed down with an abundance of lawyers—economists had not yet been invented, though in the Spanish universities there were inquiring and farseeing minds already asking awkward questions about the real value of "money" and "wealth." It was natural that Philip should lean on such people. He was by nature a jurist himself; besides, they were of such low social standing that their ambitions could never become a problem, though their peculations sometimes did. Naturally the system as developed between a legalistically minded king and such advisers was a model of caution and ingenuity. Problems, wherever they arose, were directed to the appropriate council and with the help of the secretaries were answered in advisory memoranda (*consultas*) which were then submitted to the King. In the course of time—months were customary in even the simplest case—commands came back through the secretariat for action by the unfortunate viceroys in the territories concerned. "If death came from Spain," one experienced sufferer in Italy remarked, "we should all live a long time." Yet in the age of the mule train and the sailing ship the government of an empire which came to extend around the whole world would certainly have defeated any system. In terms of what had to be done, Spanish rule was the marvel of its age, and with the sole exception of the Netherlands kept its territories fairly well in hand, from Naples to the Philippines. The English were not even able to keep Ireland in order across the St. George's Channel.

Such in the very briefest outline was the government of Spain. In many respects no doubt it was a thinly disguised autocracy. Only in the Netherlands and in Aragon was the King faced with organs of popular opinion which still had life in them. In the Netherlands, driven by the factor of religious discord which did not arise elsewhere in his dominions outside the Morisco fringe, the King attempted to crush provincial liberties; and at the

end of his life he became embroiled with Aragon also, though
not on the religious front. His troubles with his Moslem subjects were a special case: the discord here was racial. Yet these were
aberrations. With so much power in his hands, so much *centralized*
power—for we must remember that the various councils were not
localized in their respective areas but attendant on the King—
the temptation must have been great to carry the system to its
logical conclusion and govern the Spanish empire as one unit.
Philip never succumbed to this temptation, but, faithful to his
separatist obligations, continued to think of himself and to act as
individual king of each of his individual kingdoms. No doubt
a natural timidity and his experiences in the Netherlands made
him shrink from the danger of pushing refractory subjects too far,
in particular the Catalans and the Aragonese, devoted as they were
to their precious *fueros*. But what may have counted just as much
was the fact that for taxable purposes they were as good as useless
and therefore as well left alone. Castile was what really counted:
and there he was the unchallenged and untrameled ruler, *Yo el
Rey,* "I the King," as he signed himself in state papers.

With its large preponderance in wealth and population over the
rest of the peninsula, Castile was the motive power behind Spanish
imperialism. It was a society on the move from its old northern
bases in Leon and Old Castile, with their commercial ties with
England and the Low Countries, toward Andalusia and the magnet
of the great town of Seville, a sixteenth-century California where
the streets were paved, if not with gold, at least with the silver of
the Amerindian mines.

Like all societies in a state of flux it was subject to gross in-
equalities in wealth, status and education. But opportunity beckoned to everyone who was not debarred by race or religion from
sharing in the national dream. These people, raised in a tradition
of conquest and cradled in religion, felt themselves capable of
anything. Sancho Panza, of a slightly later time, is not in the
least surprised to find himself made the governor of an "island."
As an Old Christian he feels himself well suited to the task, and
his poverty makes him particularly deserving. Nor is Don Quixote
disconcerted by the sight of giants and whole armies whom it is
his duty to overcome. Of course *Don Quixote* is the subtlest of
books; its message lies on a number of levels, many of them
ironic and critical of the past, yet whatever Cervantes' intention

may have been, the immense capacity of his characters both for deeds and for self-deception perfectly mirrors the men who in his youth drove back the Turk, built the Escurial, colonized the Indies and finally lost themselves in a dream of grandeur beyond their means.

Years later, after Cervantes himself was dead, an age in which defeat, not victory, had become the norm came to question whether the whole *Siglo de Oro*, the Golden Century, had not been as illusory as the Don's enchantments. This of an age which had seen the paintings of El Greco, Herrera's masterpiece at San Lorenzo, St. Teresa's *Life*, the poetry of St. John of the Cross, Louis de León and Garcilaso de la Vega, and the intellectual rebirth of the Counter-Reformation! The explosion of art and scholarship was real enough, and it carried within it the still greater seeds of Cervantes and Lope de Vega in their prime, the plays of Calderón and Tirso de Molina, the poetry of Góngora and Quevedo and the universal genius of Velázquez.

Even on the economic front the Spain of Philip's first decades had at least the appearance of a strong dynamic thrust. The revenues of a country are a fair indication of its power. By the 1560s, treasure receipts from the Indies had already reached an average of over three million ducats annually, of which the Crown's share was approximately a million, while Church and Papal dues provided the King with a similar amount. Subsidies from Aragon were negligible and the Italian and Netherlands revenues were swallowed up at source, but sums larger than those derived from the Indies and the Church combined came from Castile through the media of its notorious 10 per cent sales tax, the *alcabala* (which the towns compounded by a lump-sum payment known as the *encabezamiento*), customs dues, payments from the sheep breeders' guild of the *Mesta*, imposts on silk, and votes of supply made by the Cortes known as *servicios*, which were supposed to be grants for special purposes but came increasingly to be regarded as normal revenue.*

By the century's end all these figures had risen to a striking degree and the Castilian economy alone provided its king annually with six million ducats. But even at the start of the reign Crown

---

* These were supplemented later in the reign by an excise tax called the *milliones* at a level of eight million ducats over a six-year period. This was further stepped up in the nineties.

receipts were much larger and drawn from more sources than in any other European country. The economy of Spain was at least as buoyant as that of any competitor and she had a rising population to provide a surplus for emigration to the ranches and mines of the Americas, from which wealth flowed back to the homeland, not only in the treasure ships but in the consumer demand of a growing colonial society.

None of this is disputable. Yet those disillusioned critics of the next century who questioned the solid reality of Philip II's Spain were not simply being perverse, for they themselves were living among the detritus it had left behind, and as early as Philip's accession some of the pasteboard quality had been evident. Spain's economic growth was both synthetic and patchy. It was synthetic because it depended on a priming of specie from outside its borders, from an empire whose costs in administration and defense were always mounting and whose very existence embroiled the mother country with other acquisitive and jealous European states. In this context it would be interesting to strike a balance between Philip's receipts from the Indies and his expenses in protecting them, not neglecting the disastrous cost of the Armada of '88. Nor was Spain able to use her wealth creatively or for the benefit of the whole country. Except in Andalusia and the Biscayan ports her economy was already beginning to stagnate. Barcelona was only a shadow of her old self and the onetime centers of Castilian wealth in Burgos and Medina del Campo were in decline, their populations on the southward trek.

The King himself was from this region, from Valladolid in the repellent lunar landscape of the Castilian plain. In theory far wealthier than his fellow sovereigns, he had been born to the thin wind of penury and survived because, adopting his father's methods, he had licensed a national debt by a system of state bonds (*juros*) on which an ever-increasing percentage of his subjects lived. This in itself need not have been disastrous, since a *rentier* class can provide social ballast in a state, but in Spain it only accentuated an already existing trend to exalt the unproductive and, together with a fiscal system which exempted nobles and hidalgos from taxation, caused a rush toward the ranks of the illustrious unemployed. Anything was better than trade. The traders themselves thought so and hastened to marry themselves or their children into the gentry or to buy themselves titles from a king perpetually in need of ready money. The full effects of such a system which made the tax burden fall on those least capable of bearing it were surprisingly long delayed, not reaching their peak till the reign of Philip's grandson in the next century, but already in the 1560s the first danger signals could be seen in rural depopulation and in the crowds of beggars in the streets, monks in their cloisters, bureaucrats in their offices.

It was certainly a misfortune for Spain that though potentially the wealthiest of European countries, she was also the one where the true foundations of wealth were the least understood and therefore the least regarded. But the trouble went deeper than that. The leaders of her intellectual thought—nearly all of them churchmen—though prepared to accept what Mammon had provided in the way of worldly profits in their sees and universities, had for long been committed, as no other body in Europe outside the Calvinists was committed, to the promotion of purely spiritual values. What a man produced was of no importance: what he believed was everything. A society so oriented was almost bound to frame machinery to enforce conformity at whatever cost; and in Spain the need had been met by the creation of the most typical and basic of her institutions: the Spanish Inquisition.

The words themselves are as emotive as the Nazi camps of Belsen and Buchenwald. And by a strange chance both these tyrannies, which concerned themselves with racist theories and the imposition of a common dogma, owed their origin to a similiar cause and found the majority of their victims among the members of the same racial group.

Long before the Arab conquest of the eighth century there had been Jews in the peninsula; by the fourteenth they formed hard-working and prosperous communities in most Spanish towns; but their very success, the protection given them by the Crown and their employment in tax farming and other unpopular pursuits had already aroused jealousy against them, which only awaited the approval of the Church and of the envious in high places to take the form so sickeningly familiar in our own times. In the 1320s an outbreak of the Black Death in Navarre was laid at the Jews' door; passions mounted and toward the century's end exploded under the prompting of the Church into a holocaust; the ghetto (*judería*) was sacked; the flames spread throughout Castile; and in terror of massacre by the Christians, many of the survivors of the pogrom hastened to turn Christian and were baptized in droves.

By the mid-1400s therefore there were several distinct ethnic and religious groups within the peninsula: the Moors, soon to suffer their own conversion on the fall of their kingdom of Granada; the hard core of Jews who remained faithful to their religion; and the baptized Jews, now called *conversos* or "New Christians" to distinguish them from the dominant "Old" Christian population.

Dominant? So industrious and able were the *conversos* that before long they had not only recovered their economic ground but had begun to infiltrate into high offices of state, into marriage alliances with the best Old Christian families and even into the hierarchy of the Church itself. It was an astonishing performance, not confined only to the social and economic field, for one of the supreme masterpieces in the whole of Spanish literature was the work of a *converso*, Fernando de Rojas, in his novel in dramatic form popularly known as *La Celestina*.

This success however carried its own dangers. The *conversos* were now by definition Christians. But how Christian? It was not long before voices were raised among those whose ambitions in Church and state had been affected by this competition to suggest that these newcomers were only paying lip service to the faith and remained at heart—and indeed in secret practice—Jews who threw off their Christianity with their clothes. To a large extent this may have been true, for forced conversions of tens of thousands of people can hardly in every case have been sincere or lasting and left ample room for backsliding and secret "Judaizing" behind closed doors. But this was not the universal rule. Important numbers of *conversos* became either spiritually committed to their new faith or at least convinced that only by going along with it could they hope to live in peace and prosper, and this made them at least as hostile as any Old Christian to their wayward brothers who by remaining Jewish or by lapsing into secret Jewish practices were compromising everything which had been won by the conversion. They feared that the storm which had broken over the *juderías* in the massacres of the fourteenth century might easily break out again in still more terrible form to engulf them all.

This was precisely what happened: and not in the Castile of kings like Pedro the Cruel who had favored Jews, but of the sternly Catholic Isabella, whose chaplain was a Dominican friar by the name of Tomás de Torquemada.

It was a time when radical solutions were in the air. Christian Spain was soon to be on the march against the last Moslem stronghold in Granada, and the disciplining of Jews and *conversos* was a parallel task which had long been awaited by zealots at court and in the Church. When anti-Semitic rioting began to spread through southern Castile on a new wave of envious bigotry the "Catholic Kings" suppressed it, for they were the guardians of public order. But they took the opportunity at the same time of setting up a commission to inquire into heretical practices, and in 1478, satisfied on the evidence of their advisers that such heresies existed, they applied to the Pope for a bull to create an Inquisition on Castilian soil.

There was nothing new or revolutionary about such an idea, for the power to order an inquiry (*inquisitio*) into men's beliefs was part of Church doctrine and since the thirteenth century had found wider expression in a Papal Inquisition which had been exported to several European countries, including Aragon. For some time this body had slumbered everywhere for lack of heretics to torment, but it had organization and precedents behind it and on the face of things could have been transplanted to a Castile which had never enjoyed its benefits. The Catholic Kings thought otherwise however. They wanted an Inquisition of their own.

Such was their prestige that in November 1478 they managed to obtain it by Papal bull authorizing them to appoint three suitable persons "learned in theology" to form a special tribunal for Castile, and on September 17, 1480 this body was inaugurated in the persons of two Dominican friars, the forerunners of one of the most formidable organizations that have ever existed on this earth. Two years later seven other Inquisitors were added by Papal brief, among them Tomás de Torquemada, and further provincial tribunals were set up to reinforce the first, which had been planted in Seville, the hotbed of *converso* heresy. Under Ferdinand and Isabella's zealous protection the new organism spread rapidly to every corner of Spain. Aragon, which had its own Papal Inquisition and resented the intrusion of this Castilian changeling, was forced to toe the line and admit it, as did Valencia and Catalonia. Springing into the world fully armed, like Pallas Athene from the head of Zeus, it developed with astonishing speed a *persona* quite independent of Rome.

Let us glance at it for a moment as it existed in its prime within a decade or so of its foundation. In accordance with Spanish practice its organization was "conciliar," its governing body, working alongside the other royal councils, being the *Consejo de la Suprema y General Inquisición*, popularly known as the *Suprema*. Additionally it was graced with an Inquisitor General—Torquemada being the first incumbent—and this office and the presidency of the *Suprema* were often, though not always, held by the same person. One rung lower were the provincial tribunals established in the larger Spanish towns and ultimately throughout the Spanish empire, in Sicily, the Balearics, the Canaries, the Philippines, Mexico and Peru, indeed everywhere except in the Netherlands and Naples where the Papal variant managed to maintain itself—each with its own establishment of inquisitors, assessors, prosecutors (promoters fiscal), jailers and "familiars," who were laymen and provided its eyes and ears.

For all its formidable apparatus, the Inquisition's declared aim was not to punish but to reconcile souls to God. The confession of sins, above all the sin of heresy, was what it looked for and worked for with every resource of propaganda. It never ceased to protest its tenderness to all those who truly repented; and indeed at first sight there might seem some basis for this claim in the so-called "Edicts of Grace" which its tribunals promulgated at the time of their foundation and at set periods thereafter, by which all heretics and wrongdoers were allowed a period (usually of about a month) in which to come forward and obtain spiritual clearance for their sins.

In fact these Edicts of Grace were among the most dreaded of the Inquisition's activities. For confession had to be accompanied by denunciation of all heretical associates, real or imaginary; and by a second manifesto, known as an Edict of Faith, the faithful were also called upon to come forward with *their* denunciations of their neighbors, creating a snowball effect of charge and counter-charge. There is no need to dwell on the vices of such a system which paid a premium to the envious and malicious. It created a vested interest in heresy which was shared by the tribunal itself, its hangers-on and the mass of the population driven by fear and self-interest to collaborate, often by inventing quite fictitious crimes. Anything was better than suffering the fate of the denounced, who were forthwith carried off into the dungeons of the Inquisition, where they might linger for weeks, months, sometimes for years, without trial, without the least contact with the outside world which usually found it prudent to forget them.

For many of these unfortunates this was only the beginning of their sufferings. A supposedly neutral body of qualifiers (*calificadores*) had next to decide whether the crimes alleged against them came within the jurisdiction of the Holy Office, as in cases of heresy it always did. From that point onward there was a macabre travesty of ordinary legal action: a secret process in which a man, though allowed the illusion of a defense and even jurists to defend him, was deprived of all knowledge of the identity of his accusers and could be subjected to a variety of tortures, less refined than those used in our own more scientific age and perhaps no worse than those in use in other European countries at the time, but nevertheless bestial in the highest degree.

Of course acquittals were not entirely unknown, for some Inquisitors were humane and just and some victims emerged to resume their old occupations and even their old heresies, though the familiars were usually quick to catch up with them and the system was never twice cheated of its prey. Similarly it would be wrong to think that death was the invariable or even the usual end, for the Inquisition concerned itself also with minor matters, such as bigamy and usury, and even serious errors of faith were more often than not expiated by spiritual penances, scourgings, public "shamings," imprisonment or service in the galleys, accompanied by a public abjuration of sins which could be of the light variety (abjuration *de levi*) or *de vehementi*, which was a graver matter and from which any relapse led inevitably to the stake. Yet even these comparatively minor sentences could be ruinous to the victim. The Inquisition had a long memory as well as a long arm and had by no means finished with a man when it had sent him to the galleys, or had "relaxed" him to the civil power to be burned, or had seized all his goods by confiscation and transferred them to its own pocket. The garments of shame which had to be worn by a convicted heretic at his abjuration were often hung as trophies in the parish church like the bodies on gamekeepers' gibbets, and the crime was remembered not only against the wrongdoer himself but also against his descendants, who found themselves debarred from entry into the professions and from public office under the Crown. The whole aim was to fix in the public mind a detestation of heresy and a dread of its consequences. Thus the culmination of a process which had taken place in the dark, often indeed literally by night behind the walls of the Inquisition's prisons, was played out in full sunlight in the central squares of Spanish towns at the great public cere- mony of an "act of faith," the notorious *auto-da-fé* so often pic- tured in the art of the times.

An *auto* was not a public burning, for that took place later at a *quemadero* or *brasero* usually outside the city walls; it was a religious ceremony carried out with great pomp and with a spiritual aim in view; yet in all conscience its by-products were horrifying enough—the huge crowds in gala mood, drawn by morbid curiosity and the promise of spiritual benefits; officialdom enthroned in its tiered seats as in boxes at a theater; the mass declarations of faith; the sermon preached by some eloquent friar; the procession of penitents, many of them bizarrely dressed in miters and yellow gowns with a St. Andrew's cross emblazoned on them, the *sam- benito* or "sacred sack"; the corpses of dead heretics disinterred and carried with the rest; the sentences proclaimed from the pul- pit; the posses of friars urging repentance on those condemned to be relaxed; and for those supremely unfortunate ones the last jour- ney under military escort to the *quemadero*, where the lighting of the first brand might be allotted to some distinguished guest, much as the wife of the chairman of the line is invited to launch a ship today.

Critics of the Inquisition have spoilt much of their case against these horrors by overplaying them and letting it be thought that to be burned alive was a commonplace. In fact this fate was ex- ceptional and was reserved for the "contumacious" who persisted in their beliefs to the end, the relapsed who fell back into error after abjuring *de vehementi*, the "dogmatizers" who preached heresy and those who refused to make confessions or shielded their friends —for the rest a recantation, even at the last moment, was enough to earn a more merciful garroting before the dead body was thrown into the flames. It would be possible to make out a case for the Holy Office as being less cruel than other tribunals of its time, more sparing in its use of torture, more just and more enlightened at least in its treatment of witchcraft than the good people of Salem

two centuries later; just as it certainly killed far fewer people than
its enemies chose to believe and killed most of them far less
odiously.

But in the end every defense breaks down before the facts. Here
was a system which even at its mildest was the enemy of light. The
censorship it exercised over books was one aspect of its sterility.
Another was the vast and lucrative trade it did in the issuing
of certificates of unblemished ancestry, of pure blood, to candidates
in search of public office. All else pales before the proofs of its
inhumanity still preserved among the archives—here a *procès verbal*
of a forced confession; there an accusation or one of the *listas*
of proceedings at an *auto,* with its macabre resemblance to a race
card or the program for a graduation. Pilar Rodriguez must do
penance for licentiousness and present herself weekly for instruction by her parish priest. Sancho de Rojas will abjure *de vehementi*
and his property is confiscated. Carlos Morero must serve a life
sentence in the galleys. Juan d'Aguila will be relaxed.

Such was the system which in its cruelty and blind bigotry in a
rapidly changing world was to be one of the main causes of Spain's
decline. But for a while at least it was an agent of her greatness.
Divided racially and politically into a number of competing groups,
she needed unity above all things, and only through religion could
she hope for it. This the Inquisition went some way toward achieving for her by its vigilant attention to the backsliding *conversos* and
later to the few Protestant cells which dared to raise their heads in
Valladolid and Seville. The Inquisition was less fortunate in its
treatment of the Moorish population (Moriscos) whom it had inherited as nominal Christians as a result of the capture of Granada
and the edicts of Charles V. These it first neglected and then by
ill-timed severities drove into actual rebellion against the Crown.
The Moriscos apart, however, by the 1560s all traces of heresy in
the nation had been ruthlessly burned out. If Waterloo was won
on the playing fields of Eton, the victories of Lepanto against the
Turk and of the royalist armies in the Netherlands came out of the
smoke of a hundred *autos* throughout the length and breadth of
Spain.

8

THE NETHERLANDS. REGIME OF THE DUKE OF ALVA. 1567-73

All ages have their mystiques. The sixteenth century is even more enigmatic than most, for this was an age of discovery and re-assessment by land and sea and in the human soul where the greatest mysteries are hidden. Even now that the archives are open and most of the secrets are known, the policies, motives and even the natures of Elizabeth Tudor, of Catherine de Medici, of Philip and the Prince of Orange remain shrouded in uncertainty. Calvin and Loyola are hardly explicable in modern terms, and the Inquisition at which we have been glancing seems more an Orwellian nightmare than anything else. Only in the Duke of Alva, Philip's choice to succeed the Duchess of Parma in the Netherlands, do we encounter a major figure who needs no interpreting but is instantly recognizable to this as to every other age: the man of blood and iron.

No man had studied more deeply or practiced more constantly the military science. In the most important of all arts at that epoch he was the most consummate artist. In the only honourable profession of the age, he was the most thorough and the most pedantic professor . . . As a disciplinarian he was foremost in Spain, perhaps in Europe . . . Such were his qualities as a military commander. As a statesman he had neither experience nor talent. As a man, his character was simple. He did not combine a great variety of vices, but those which he had were colossal, and he possessed no virtues. He was neither lustful nor intemperate, but his professed eulogists admitted his enormous avarice, while the world has agreed that such an amount of stealth and ferocity, of patient vindictiveness and universal bloodthirstiness, were never found in savage beast of the forest, and but rarely in a human bosom.

This is vintage Motley—he needed a full parade of villains to balance his heroes in his enormous canvases. Instantly the man springs to life, as formidably as to the gaze of his victims on the scaffold and battlefield: the very prototype of the tyrant: persevering, ruthless, cold, implacable. A brilliant likeness—truer than many of Motley's judgments.

In 1567 Fernando Alvarez de Toledo, Duke of Alva, was fifty-nine: a not unbenevolent-looking gentleman with a small head, yellowing complexion, dark eyes, and a forked beard falling patriarchally over his chest.

Eight years younger than his master, Charles V, the Duke had been trained in his school of warfare and had been at his side through the triumphs of Tunis and Muhlberg and the disaster of the siege of Metz. The Emperor, an excellent judge of men, had recommended his abilities to Philip along with certain warnings about his ambition and bent for intrigue. These Philip had heeded. He was never to trust Alva; only to use him. But if the chastisement of rebellion and heresy in the Netherlands had become the royal aim, no more logical choice could have been made than this soldier of high ability and inflexible purpose who for years had been advising a policy of cutting off heads.

After a final briefing from the King at Aranjuez, Alva had sailed from Cartagena on May 10, 1567, in a fleet commanded by Spain's invaluable Genoese ally, Prince Andrea Doria, and by early June he had assembled from the Spanish dependencies in Italy a force of approximately nine thousand foot and twelve hundred horse for the passage of the Alps by the Mont Cenis pass. On this miniature army —*gentille et gaillarde,* as Brantôme calls it—the commentators of the time were to lavish rhapsodies of praise. Everything was of the best: from the engraved armor of the musketeers, to the brilliant cavalry under command of the Duke's natural son, the Grand Prior of the Knights of St. John, and the agreeable reinforcement of a cadre of whores, marching with the best of them. "Such was the moral physiognomy of this army which came to enforce the high religious purposes of Philip!" exclaims Motley, his Puritan soul revolted by these arrangements. "In such infamous shape was the will of God supposed to manifest itself before the eyes of the heretics in the Netherlands." The Duke, always a realist and an innovator in military affairs, would no doubt have replied that he was merely making sensible provision for human appetites, and the proof of his wisdom shows in the fact that his army marched the five hundred miles from

Lombardy to Brussels with hardly a rape or robbery of the civilian population on the way—a record unprecedented in sixteenth-century warfare.

As this paragon of an army wound its way through the long summer days, marching in three divisions which bivouacked each night on the campsite of the corps immediately ahead, all Europe held its breath. On the west, a sizable French force shadowed it; to the east, six thousand Swiss were on the watch. The line of march passed almost through the outskirts of Calvin's stronghold of Geneva, which the Pope had hoped would be treated like the Cities of the Plain, but no violence was offered it. The Duke had his objectives; he was never a man to engage more enemies than he had to. Early in August he crossed into Netherlands territory in the outlying province of Luxemburg, where he was waited on by the Regent's ambassadors, Noircarmes and Berlaymont, anxious to know the terms of his commission, and by Egmont, drawn to the destroyer like a moth to a flame. "Here comes the archheretic," Alva is said to have remarked in his hearing; and it was some time before he could bring himself to mask his contempt for this pitiful dupe.

On August 22 the Duke entered Brussels and presented himself at the vice-regal palace, where he was received with a very comical mixture of formality and offhandedness in the Regent's bedchamber, her somewhat bizarre choice of venue for affairs of state. What the Duke thought of these arrangements may be imagined—he was the soul of punctilio and certainly no longer the impressionable cavalier who in his youth had galloped the length of Europe, from Hungary to Spain, for a few brief hours with his young bride. His tone at the interview was mock deferential: he held the winning cards. As for the Regent, she had been almost beside herself with rage ever since learning that she was to be replaced. "By the extraordinary restrictions which your Majesty has set to my authority," she had complained to Philip that April, "you have taken away all powers from me and prevented me from settling the country's affairs. Though at present everything is quiet here, you want to give the credit for it to someone else, though I alone had all the trouble and danger." The choice of Alva of all people exasperated her beyond measure: he was a man, she wrote in July with passionate resentment, whose reputation was so odious in the Netherlands that he would make the whole Spanish race detested.

The Duke's intention was simply that it should be feared. He had no belief in the virtue of terror, only in its results, which he had found effective, and he had a series of lessons to teach to the too squeamish Regent, the backsliding grandees, the rebellious mobs. That the lesson had been learned and that the situation in the Netherlands was now more settled in Spain's favor than at any time since the King's accession, and that his mission was therefore both unnecessary and potentially destructive of the hard-won peace, would not have concerned him. He was a believer in rigorous measures and the therapeutic values of punishment. He had no understanding of the forces at work in the world or of the Netherlanders, "men of butter" as he called them, whom he had come to "tame."

No time was wasted. On the day after the bedchamber interview he showed his commission as Captain General to the Council of State. By this appointment—which fell short of the regency but gave him effective power in the sphere where it mattered—the King and Alva had shown that if they did not understand the Netherlands, they certainly understood the character of the Duchess of Parma, whose resignation and retirement from the country could now confidently be looked for without the actual need of dismissing her. Within a matter of days the Duchess was asking the King's gracious permission to lay down her now odious task of responsibility without power. And in this she was not merely being selfish and huffed—she was after all Netherlands-born and a woman with some compassion in her soul. The first lesson, that of taming the Regent, had thus begun. The Duke turned immediately to the second.

In spite of every warning and the flight of most of his old associates, Egmont had remained at court. This irresolution has been greatly blamed, but in fact he was being true to his inmost nature and to self-interest too, for all his wealth lay in the Netherlands and unlike Orange he had nowhere else to go. Alva, knowing his man, had taken great care to play on these susceptibilities once he had overcome his first instinctive feeling of contempt; and his efforts to lull the victim into a sense of security had been ably seconded by the King in letters full of cordial regard and praise for Egmont's high services to the state. These blandishments were unnecessary: Egmont would have remained anyway. But the skill and subtlety of the treatment may be seen in the remarkable fact that Count Horn, the third of the old triumvirate, should also have allowed himself to be lured back to Brussels from the safety of his estates.

Early in September the trap was sprung in true Netherlandish fashion at the tail end of a banquet attended by most of the high-ranking Spanish officers, including the Duke's natural son, the Grand Prior, and by the Duke's own military band specially loaned for the occasion. At the height of these festivities, so reminiscent of Brederode and the Beggars' dinner, the Grand Prior in a whispered aside seems to have warned Egmont that he should leave Brussels at once. It is a credible tale, the more so from the chronicler's version of Egmont's response, which was to leave the table, as though to escape, and then in one final act of irresolution to return, on Berlaymont's advice, to finish the last of the many banquets he had graced. Later that night, after a conference arranged by the Duke at his lodgings to discuss the plans for a new citadel at Antwerp, both Egmont and Horn were arrested and the Captain General sat down to announce this *coup de main* to the King, with apologies for the fortnight's delay which circumstances had forced on him since his arrival in Brussels.

In this the Duke showed himself a severe self-critic. No one else, at the time or since, ever complained that he was slow to punish. That same night of the arrests, he outlined to Philip proposals for a new court to deal with the recent unrest, and by the end of the month this body was actually in operation under the title of the Council of Troubles or of Tumults, soon to be known to the world under the more acceptable title of the Council of Blood.

Not for two centuries, till the Revolutionary Tribunal of 1793, was such a court to be seen again, though our own age has become sadly familiar with its successors. It was the purest tyranny: a private instrument of terror without a shred of legality to its name, based quite unashamedly on the principle that the security of the state demanded procedures very different from those existing in the Netherlands, where crimes had actually to be proved. In order to overcome such time-wasting formalities, it was now provided that of the judges, including a quota of Netherlanders who thought it wise to accept appointment, only the Duke and two Spanish advisers had the right to vote. Decisions were apt to be unanimous and the verdict was often death. The crimes hardly mattered, for they had been so widely defined as to include almost any act of commission or omission during the recent troubles to which the Duke felt in the mood to take exception or which appealed to the macabre humor of his principal deputy, Juan de Vargas, of whom Motley has preserved an immortal portrait:

To shed blood was, in his opinion, the only important business and the only exhilarating pastime of life . . . He executed Alva's bloody work with an industry which was almost superhuman, and with a merriment which would have shamed a demon. His execrable jests ring through the blood and smoke and death cries of those days of perpetual sacrifice. He was proud to be the double of the iron-hearted Duke, and acted so uniformly in accordance with his views, that the right of revision remained but nominal. There could be no possibility of collision when the subaltern was only anxious to surpass an incomparable superior.

For the details of this extraordinary court—say for a glimpse of Councilor Hessels waking from a nap on a hot summer's afternoon to bawl out sentences of death, or of Vargas in happy mood at the discovery that a victim had been executed somewhat ahead of sentence—we must indeed go to Motley, remembering always that he has a genial way with stories, many of which were palpably invented, and a tendency to accept atrocity figures greatly in excess of those now credited by more sober commentators, who allow just over eleven hundred killed or banished and twelve thousand condemned to smaller penalties in the six years of the Council's life. Yet the very smell and feel of persecution is in his pages— the cloud of fear over town and countryside; the secret accusation; the tramp of soldiers in the night; the parody of justice; the "hideous fruit of human bodies hanging from the trees"—and can one doubt that this was truly the Duke of Alva's "vineyard" which, in his own phrase, he had promised not to "uproot" but to "prune"?

The first effects of the terror were to paralyze the country. Not a breath of resistance stirred in the most turbulent of cities—Ghent— as Egmont, stadtholder of its province of Flanders, was brought with Horn under strong guard to imprisonment in the grim citadel which still watches over the town. Those who could not escape across the frontiers or who thought their past acts of rebellion too small to have been noticed bowed their heads and waited for the storm to pass. Wiser men took no chances. Hoogstraten, on his way to Brussels, heard at the eleventh hour of Egmont's arrest and returned to Germany. Count Peter Ernest Mansfeld, most fervent of loyalists, sent his son Charles out of the country—the young man had signed the Compromise, and though he had later turned his coat, this was no guarantee of safety in the age of Councilor Hessels and Juan de Vargas. Nor was the terror confined to the Low Countries, for on September 19 one of the grandees' envoys to the Spanish court, Montigny, Horn's brother, was arrested in Madrid*; the other, Count Berghen, had been fortunate enough to die.

By early October the Duke was reporting to Philip that God be praised! the provinces were perfectly quiet and pacified. He was in excellent humor as he saw his garrisons installed in the provincial capitals and the progress of his new citadel in Antwerp, built to overawe that center of heresy and disaffection. In December he had the ironic pleasure of ushering the Duchess of Parma as far as the borders of the Netherlands into retirement, having already succeeded to her place through his new commission as Lieutenant Governor, with more power in his hands than any ruler of the Low Countries had ever held. Not even the Emperor in his heyday had possessed a Blood Council, nineteen bishops and three *tercios* of Spanish regulars to obey his slightest whim.

With the new year of 1568 the tempo of persecution quickened as the new system got down to its work, now free of such small restraints as the Duchess had been able to impose by her presence in the country. On January 4 eighty-four notables died on the scaffold; in February ninety-five more were charged and thirty-seven condemned; in March there were fifteen hundred more arrests, five hundred in a single day. Meanwhile the Prince of Orange had been summoned by proclamation to appear before the Council to answer for his acts; his estates had been sequestrated *in absentia;* and his heir, the Count of Buren, kidnapped from his studies at Louvain and removed to Madrid, where in the course of time he was to grow up into a proper Spaniard. When the university authorities protested against this breach of the decencies, they

---

* Montigny was later condemned to death and secretly strangled in prison in Simancas by the King's express order. Philip's very detailed instructions for this crime make chilling reading. The aim was to suggest death from natural causes.

were silenced by Vargas in execrable Latin and informed that the Blood Council cared nothing for their privileges.

This was the keynote of the new regime, which did not stop at religious persecution but aimed to sweep away all the old customary rights and local autonomies of the seventeen provinces and to replace them with one centralized bureaucratic Catholic government, ruled from Brussels and subject only to the will of the King. Prejudice should not blind us to the fact that in many ways this was a sensible and modernizing aim, long overdue. The provinces needed some of the policies of the Duke of Alva—unfortunately they had to swallow the medicine whole, in one bottle, which proved peculiarly lethal to a great number of the patients for whom it was prescribed.

For some months under these hammer blows the provinces remained stunned and almost unprotesting, but then resistance began to stir, first of all in Friesland, where groups of refugees had returned from England and had taken to the woods, earning for themselves by robberies and outrages against country monasteries and priests the name of the "Wild Beggars," the *Gueux des Bois*. This brigandage was soon put down; but in Germany, where the remnants of the Beggar party had gathered around Orange and his brother Louis of Nassau, a more serious threat to Alva's regime was gradually being mounted.

As the legal base for it—for this was rebellion against one's sovereign in a still semi-feudal and very legalistic age—the Prince now produced his personal "Justification," which was published and secretly distributed throughout the Netherlands, calling on the King to turn from evil counselors toward his loyal subjects who still wished him well, with reservations. Having said so much, the Prince proceeded with the raising of an army for operations against the King's Lieutenant Governor on three fronts—in Friesland, which was to be invaded by Count Louis; between the Rhine and the Meuse, where Hoogstraten was to command; and in Artois, where French Huguenot forces had been enlisted to draw off the Duke southward, while Orange himself waited with reinforcements to exploit the situation as it developed.

Once again we encounter the Prince at his most devious. Poised on the brink of action, he remained obsessed with the finer shades of meaning which might be read into his manifesto and with its effects on public opinion in Germany. On April 17 we find him wondering aloud to the Landgrave of Hesse:

I am not quite sure of that little word *"kriegsrustung"* [preparation for war]. Is that perhaps too hard and sharp and likely to be understood as though we meant to undertake hostilities from wanton pleasure rather than for simple defence?

As Ruth Putnam somberly remarks of this in her fine biography of the Prince, "The terms of the formula by which the demon of war was summoned made little difference. The proclamation was the signal to let him loose, and he ravaged the Netherlands for nearly eighty years."

The Prince was not of course to guess that the struggle for liberty would last so long. Cassandra herself could not have foreseen such an effusion of blood. No doubt his casuistry has its unattractive side, but like any other man faced with a perilous decision he was trying to make the most of his material and weighing up the chances and prospects as they stood. These seemed good: and that spring the offensive was launched across the borders of the Netherlands. Both the southern prongs met with disaster, but in Friesland Count Louis was warmly welcomed and on May 23 near Heiligerlee, the monastery of the Holy Lion, won the first patriot victory of the war, the royalist commander, Count Aremberg, paying for his rashness and bad dispositions with his life and the wholesale destruction of his army.

Never was there a more Pyrrhic triumph. The Duke's rage at hearing of this disgrace to his arms may be imagined, and the steps he took to restore the situation were marked by a brilliant display of his qualities as a leader, in which ruthlessness and caution were exquisitely blended.

To march toward the sound of the guns was the natural reaction of the soldier, and he had had three *tercios* of the best troops in Europe at his disposal. But first he had to secure his base in Brussels and the south. On May 28, five days after Heiligerlee, the Prince of Orange and Count Louis of Nassau were pronounced guilty of levying war against the King and sentenced to perpetual banishment. On the first of June, nineteen of the old Beggar party were publicly executed in Brussels, and during the two following days the executioners were kept busy. This was the small change of terror. On June 3, at the center of a crushing display of military power, Egmont and Horn were brought back from Ghent to Brussels to be lodged in the Broodhuis, the guild house of the crossbowmen on the Gran' Place. Accusations of high treason, rebellion and conspiracy against both men on numerous counts had long since been laid before the Blood Council, and on the fourth of June the Duke formally passed sentence of death upon them.

It was not quite judicial murder. Egmont and Horn in their flirtation with the League and Beggar policies had committed acts and uttered words with a treasonable flavor about them, and they were more fortunate than many humbler victims in having defenders in high places, including the Emperor Maximilian himself, to plead their immunity as knights of the Fleece, and in Horn's case as a Count of the Holy Roman Empire, from the jurisdiction of Alva's courts. But of the real substance of the charges, which alleged a plot to destroy Spanish sovereignty in the Netherlands and subvert the Catholic religion, both men were of course quite innocent. At the worst they had maneuvered to reduce the King's powers a little; and Egmont in particular had acted since the image breaking with a zeal for the Roman Church and the hanging of heretics which should have satisfied Vargas himself. The condemnations in fact were simply acts of terror carried out in haste in answer to the defeat at Heiligerlee, with the twin aims of discouraging wobblers and of freeing the very substantial forces which had been needed to guard the prisoners for use in the coming campaign in the north. As such they were successful; and those who claim that they were blunders, depriving Spain of two biddable supporters, have conveniently forgotten both the military problem facing the Duke and the chance that both victims might easily have turned their coats again in the dangerous times ahead.

The executions themselves, passing into legend with the years, ensured that only the injustice should be remembered. It was an age when those condemned to die were expected to enter very actively into the spirit of the occasion, and this was one of the most imposing scenes ever staged on the Gran' Place, most theatrical of settings, which the Duke had filled with phalanxes of troops in battle order and all the solemn panoply of death—a scaffold draped in black, two velvet cushions, two iron spikes for exhibition of the victims' heads, a table with a crucifix. In this drama which he had

staged, both victims played their roles and submitted to the executioner's sword with the Spartan rigor of an age of heroes, and that
is what the world saw and remembered. Few present that day
can have guessed the poignant fact that almost to the last moment
Egmont remained unreconciled to his fate; that on the scaffold
itself he was still asking the Spanish general Romero whether a
pardon might not be granted. These emotions of Egmont's, the
prayers he had uttered for the King's welfare on his way to die,
and his anguished remorse for the part he had played in leading
Horn into the net by his too sanguine example, give another dimen-
sion to this ritual killing of two men of moderate talents who were
to figure among the patron saints of a rebellion which one of
them certainly had tried to prevent. Observers reported seeing
tears even on Alva's cheeks. Both the Counts, he assured Philip,
had died "very Catholically and modestly," which was high praise,
a producer's tribute and probably sincere. He hoped the example
would be "fruitful."

Once they were dead and in their temporary resting place in
St. Gudule, the troop movements which had been among the reasons for their prompt dispatch from the world went forward without delay. The small loyalist force in the north under Count
Meghem was ordered to stand on the defensive, avoiding combat,
while five columns of regulars moved up across the great rivers of
the Waal, Rhine and Meuse and concentrated on the tenth of
July at Deventer, where on the next day the Duke himself arrived
to take command.

Among the rebels the fruits of Heiligerlee had already been
wasted by their failure to get possession of the important town of
Groningen, which would have given them a secure base in the north
and perhaps the means of paying their semi-mutinous German
levies. Once this failure had become clear, the Prince of Orange
had urged his brother to rejoin him in Germany and above all
things not to allow himself to be cornered in open country by the
vastly superior Spanish forces; but these warnings went unheeded,
and in mid-July Count Louis was forced out of his entrenched
camp near Groningen by Alva's advance guard and driven back
on the small town of Jemmingen in a loop of the Ems, where he
found himself in a trap of his own making, between an unfordable
river and fifteen thousand veterans under the Duke's personal command.

What followed was a massacre—the rebel army was not so much defeated as butchered at the unhurried tempo of the slaughterhouse and with about as much resistance from the victims, whose losses were in the region of seven thousand killed for a maximum of eighty Spaniards, or seven on the Duke's estimate, which may have been a piece of black humor on his part. The Spaniard Mendoza records the macabre detail that the people of nearby Emden learned the results of the battle from the multitude of hats floating past their city on the ebb tide; and for weeks afterward peasants working in the fields near Jemmingen and on the banks of the Ems would come upon a litter of corpses, armor, weapons and all the wreckage of an army which had entirely ceased to exist.

This tremendous proof of the Duke's talents was not wasted on Europe, where the fainthearted and the compromised who had secretly supported Orange or allowed him to recruit troops in their territory were hurrying to excuse themselves. The Emperor Maximilian, reputedly a crypto-Protestant or at least a sympathizer, had seen the danger signals very early and had protested against Orange's dangerous proceedings, which the results of Jemmingen had now underlined. Count Louis had survived the battle, escaping across the Ems in the last moments as the beaters closed in, but the cause he had fought for was obviously in ruins and the provinces which had lent him some small if timorous help now lay completely prostrate under Alva's hand, without the power or even the will to resist.

Into this vacuum of defeat and apathy the Prince of Orange now advanced in September with an army which in July might have turned the fortunes of war. A politician of brilliant gifts, he was a very inadequate soldier, and he was faced with almost exactly the same situation which had defeated the genius of Hannibal at the height of his powers after Cannae—a subdued and hostile countryside; a lack of supplies; a wasting army; a general whose policy was to avoid battle.

Alva in fact, like Fabius the Cunctator, had no need of victories. He was not a showy commander or one who cared for the world's opinion, still less for the applause of his soldiers who were simply there to obey him. Faced with Orange's army of thirty thousand, which was slightly larger than his own and richer in cavalry, the master arm in the wide fields of Brabant, his aim from the start was defensive. As the Prince advanced, he watched him from entrenchments near Maastricht. The Prince took Tongres and advanced on Loos. The Duke quickly slipped round his flank, re-took Tongres, then marched back across his path, as impalpable as a shadow. This was scientific soldiering of a kind very repulsive to Orange's French and German mercenaries who had enlisted for loot. They were to get none. There was no bringing the Duke to battle except on his own terms. Once, catching a unit of the Prince's army at a disadvantage at a river crossing, he destroyed it with one quick rapier thrust, which Motley, on the authority of de Strada, has preserved as a vignette of sixteenth-century war:

. . . In the meantime the whole rearguard of the patriots had been slaughtered. A hundred or two, the last who remained, had made their escape from the field, and had taken refuge in a house in the neighbor-hood. The Spaniards set the buildings on fire, and standing around with lifted lances, offered the fugitives the choice of being consumed in the flames or of springing out upon their spears. Thus entrapped, some chose the one course, some the other. A few, to escape the fury of the fire and the brutality of the Spaniards, stabbed themselves with their own swords. Others embraced, and then killed each other, the enemies from below looking on, as at a theatrical exhibition; now hissing and now applauding, as the death struggles were more or less to their taste. In a few minutes all the fugitives were dead.

This fight near the river was the only real engagement of the campaign, costing Orange about two thousand dead, including Hoogstraten, who was mortally wounded in the course of it. All the rest was chessboard maneuver. But it was a game between a master and a tyro. The Prince advanced his pieces almost to within gunshot of Brussels, but not a town or a village stirred to help him. Baffled, he drew back, with Alva always close at his heels, recrossed the Meuse and made for the French border, where civil war was raging. Many of his soldiers wanted to take part in it, no doubt preferring any other opponent to the Duke of Alva; the rest were openly mutinous and in a mood to kill their unfortunate commander.

By November it was all over and Orange's army, like its pred-ecessors, had melted away. It was a worse disaster than Jem-mingen, where at least there had been a battle. "We may consider the Prince of Orange as a dead man," the Duke reported complacently to his King.

This was the low ebb of patriot fortunes and for Orange himself a time of deep humiliation. Barely escaping with his life from the troops whom he had no means of paying, he found employment for himself and his brother with the Huguenot forces under Coligny which were now engaged in the third of France's interminable religious wars. Perhaps fortunately, he was not present at the bloody Huguenot defeats of Jarnac and Moncontour; he had little heart for the campaign, and in the spring of 1569 he made his forlorn way back to Germany and to the wife whose amours and eccentricities had become the talk of Europe. A brief reconciliation took place between them at Mannheim, but the wayward Anna was not to be controlled and was soon taken in adultery with a refugee Antwerp lawyer by the name of John Rubens, not yet the father of Peter Paul, whose marvelous canvases were in some danger of being un-events, since at this social level adultery could be a capital crime.

The Prince chose to be merciful; he was probably glad to be free of a burdensome and hateful union; but the divorce that followed was still a blow to his pride and played its part along with the fiasco of the Netherlands campaign in the gradual darkening and sobering of mood that marked the change of the grandee on the make into the selfless and patient statesman of the later years. At about this time he began to worship as a Calvinist. Motley sees this approvingly as an act of deep conviction. It was much more probably political, for the Prince was always more statesman than saint. Born a Lutheran, brought up a Catholic, he had gone back to Lutheranism in his duel with Philip because the Lutheran German princes had seemed his natural allies, but when they failed him, there was simply nowhere else to turn for support in the desperate game he was playing but to Calvinism and the Huguenot forces which were miraculously working their way back to favor at the French court after their defeats of 1569. In the words of the "Wilhelmus von Nassawe" ballad, soon to be sung in his praise throughout the Netherlands, he had been "constant in adversity," perhaps because he had the wit to see, where others could not, that the game could still be won.

For the truth was that the enemy's condition was little better than his own. 1568, in which Philip lost both his much-cherished third wife, Elizabeth of Valois, and his heir Don Carlos, was also a year of acute danger for Spain, faced by a rising at home of the Moriscos, the descendants of the Moors who had held the kingdom of Granada before its conquest in Ferdinand and Isabella's time. Gross mismanagement and the cynical betrayal of promises made by the Catholic Kings to respect the culture of the defeated were chiefly to blame for this outburst of Moslem feeling which for two years set the villages of the Alpujarras in the mountains south of Granada ablaze and invited intervention by the Turks or the Moslem pirates of the North African coast.

Faced with the choice between rebellion and the suppression of their cherished language and customs, which they had managed to preserve by judicious bribery in spite of the fierce edicts of the Emperor's day but which the new fanaticism of Philip's government seemed determined to destroy, the Moriscos had sprung to arms under "kings" of the old royal line, the last successors of the emirs who had ruled in Córdoba when Spain beyond *El Andaluz* had been a patchwork of semi-barbarous kingdoms beyond the light of the Arab sun. Another Motley—Stirling Maxwell in his biography of Don John of Austria—records the desperate bitterness of this war and the atrocities against the Christian minorities caught unawares in the first frenzy of the revolt:

But whether the fortresses were surrendered or stormed, the garrison was, with scarcely an exception, massacred with the most revolting cruelty. The Christian *Alguazil* was repaid with usury for his exactions and his severities; and the wretched curate became the victim of tortures like those which his cloth inflicted in the dungeons of the Inquisition. Their feet and legs were roasted over fires of charcoal; tied by the wrists to the tops of towers, they were let fall time after time on the pavement below until their lower limbs were beaten to a jelly; their eyes and tongues were torn out; their ears and noses were cut off; their joints were hacked asunder from their extremities upwards; their mouths were filled with gunpowder, which was then ignited; their heads were beaten to pieces with hatchets; and their mangled corpses were sometimes sewed up in the carcases of swine and burned, sometimes exposed on the hillside to feed the fox and the wolf. More than one Morisco, fiercer than his fellows, tore out and devoured the heart of his enemy.

Such horrors—repaid in the end with interest by the victorious Christians—were probably as inevitable as the outbreak itself in a land divided into deeply irreconcilable social and religious sects. The rebellion in the Alpujarras is an event which it is hard to consign to a footnote. Too much blood was shed, and it is impossible to forget that with the final collapse of the rising and the dispersal inland of the defeated Moriscos to the towns and villages of the Meseta, we are witnessing the last stage but one° in the extinction of the great flowering of Moslem culture in the peninsula which went back seven centuries.

What is more to our purpose is the fact that it took Philip's government two years to put down the rebellion of part of a minority racial group. Here was the first sign of chronic weakness at the center of an empire extending around the world and engaged in a double crusade against Moslem and heretic. If the whole Morisco population and not just a small percentage of it had risen, and if Spain's most formidable rivals—the Ottoman Turks—had listened to the pleas of their co-religionists and had struck against the coasts of Valencia or Andalusia, either alone or in alliance with the Barbary pirates, the verdict of the *reconquista* might well have been reversed and the Crescent carried to the gates of Toledo as well as Vienna.

Instead, the Turks chose to attack Cyprus, a Venetian possession: the first of a series of misjudgments which were to lead to a drawing together of the *Signoria*, the Papacy and Spain, and in the autumn of 1571 to a great Christian victory over the Ottoman fleets in the gulf of Lepanto.

For almost every Spaniard and for most Catholics Lepanto was the great, the fabulous day, a new Salamis. Titian painted an allegorical picture. Years later Cervantes, who was wounded in the battle, remembered it in *Don Quixote*, and one can feel in his words the sense of deliverance and the exultation of it still. And though Lepanto was in many ways a wasted victory and within two years of it Ottoman fleets were once more at sea as rampant as ever, popular opinion in Spain was right to regard it as a turning point in her history. Never again were the Turks to pose a major threat to Spain or her dependencies. The danger which had loomed between 1568 and 1571 had been dispelled at last and

° In the next reign the whole Morisco population was finally expelled from the peninsula.

there was no longer the chance that she might be caught and broken up in war on more fronts than even her enormous resources could have sustained. If the Mediterranean did not become a Spanish lake, at least it was no longer a springboard for her enemies, and the real focus of her problems had shifted with the victory westward to the Atlantic and northward to the Netherlands where most of the military, naval and diplomatic lines now crossed.

Here was the cockpit for future struggles which would engage Spain for the rest of the reign and another half century beyond.

In the provinces these crisis years which had begun with the Morisco rising and ended with Lepanto had been marked by Alva's highly efficient disposal of rebel threats to his regime.

Apart however from the ever-present danger of French intervention in Netherlands affairs, the Duke was not entirely without his anxieties, since England, once the traditional ally, had been showing herself increasingly prone to challenge and thwart him.

Such a clash of interests and antipathies had been bound to come. Catholic Spain and heretic England impinged on one another at too many points in Europe and the Indies. The first slaving voyage of John Hawkins to the Caribbean had been followed in 1564 by the Spanish seizure of English shipping in the peninsula; his third and most impertinent foray had been punished by armed attack and the execution and imprisonment of many captured seamen. In 1568, as English indignation mounted at the brutal regime in the Low Countries, the Queen and her Council seized a number of Alva's pay ships which happened to have put in at Plymouth, ironically enough to escape from pirates!

The rights and wrongs of this matter were endlessly and acrimoniously debated. Since the specie aboard was on loan from foreign bankers and not yet in Alva's possession the English had perhaps a technical right to "protect" it, even to use it for themselves. In clumsier hands the incident could easily have led to war, for the King about this time and for a year or two thereafter was at his most hawkish where England was concerned, full of plans for a descent on the island in support of Norfolk and the northern earls in '69 and the more imaginative attempt to remove Elizabeth altogether through the ramifications of the Ridolfi assassination plot in 1571, which the Pope regarded as "of the highest importance for God's service and the welfare of His Church."

Alva had disapproved of the whole policy. A breach with the Queen, he told his master, was undesirable, if only because of the danger of driving England and France into one another's arms in joint hostility to Spain. For all his militancy against Orangists, he was a moderate where England and the wider fields of diplomacy were concerned. For that matter he did not in the least approve of Philip's other aggressive leanings at this time against the Turks in the Mediterranean in pursuance of the Papacy's Holy League. "It is less the Turks who menace Christianity than the heretics who are in its entrails," he was to write to his master in 1573, and even before Lepanto and the renewal of rebellion in the Netherlands his absolute concentration on the problems and opportunities which he saw before his eyes in Brussels had made him indifferent to everything but his provincial plans. There he was full of resource. "Everyone must be made to live in constant fear of the roof falling on his head," he had written to the King, arguing against the issue of a general pardon for those who had offended in the troubles of the Duchess's time. "In this way the towns will accept what is being arranged for them; private persons will offer high ransoms and the States will not dare refuse what is proposed for them in your Majesty's name."

As usual the Duke's mind was running on money. It was one of the main preoccupations of his life. He had promised Philip a golden stream of cash to irrigate the treasury out of confiscated rebel estates, and up to a point had succeeded. There was a limit however to what could be won in this way once the properties of Orange and his lieutenants had been seized. What was obviously needed was some more radical measure of fiscal reform to make his government independent of provincial whims by substituting a series of centrally imposed taxes for the time-wasting votes of supply which had to be wheedled out of the country down to the last recalcitrant village; so now in the spring of 1569 he summoned the States General to Brussels and laid before it proposals for three new taxes: the Hundredth Penny, a 1 per cent capital levy; the Twentieth Penny, a 5 per cent charge on all transfers of land; and the Tenth Penny, a 10 per cent purchase tax on all sales, on the model of the notorious *alcabala*, the time-dishonored stand-by of the Spanish treasury.

It often seems easier to tax a man's soul than his pocket. From end to end of the Netherlands a tremendous outcry went up against these proposals to force the provinces into the fiscal strait jacket which for decades had been ruining Spain. The States General were prepared under extreme pressure—and with Alva the pressure was bound to be extreme—to concede the Hundredth Penny, but the Twentieth and the Tenth were judged quite simply to be ruinous and unworkable.

So no doubt they were; though less sensitive economies have since learned to live with much the same kind of thing. The Duke however had not come to argue the merits of financial theses. When the Estates of Utrecht refused point-blank to accommodate him, he first quartered a unit of Spanish troops on them, and when this failed to produce the desired results, had them formally indicted before the Blood Council, and of course convicted, for failures of duty during the image breaking of '66. Motley has enormous fun with Vargas's part in these proceedings, which were marked by more than his usual zest for justice:

It was six months, however, before the case was closed. As there was no blood to be shed, a summary process was not considered necessary. At last, on the 14th July, the voluminous pile of documents was placed before Vargas. It was the first time he had laid eyes upon them, and they were, moreover, written in a language of which he did not understand a word. Such, however, was his capacity for affairs, that a glance only at the outside of the case enabled him to form his decision. Within half an hour afterwards, booted and spurred, he was saying mass in the church of St. Gudule, on his way to pronounce sentence at Antwerp. That judgment was rendered the same day and confirmed the preceding act of condemnation. Vargas went to his work as cheerfully as if it had been a murder.

Here was indeed an invaluable assistant. And for just so long as the Duke continued to employ such strong-arm methods his affairs prospered and the provinces meekly obeyed him. As de Tocqueville has observed, however, despotic governments are never in such danger as at the moment when they begin to reform; and a desire for reform, or at least for some moderation of Alva's rule, had for some time been agitating the King's advisers at the Spanish court and even the King himself.

As early as the summer of 1569 Philip had reached the conclusion that some kind of general pardon was desirable in the Netherlands. By the year's end, constantly prodded by pacific advice from his cousin the Emperor, he had sent off four possible drafts for Alva to choose from. An activist where England was concerned, in this being the exact antithesis of the Duke, he had much more accurately assessed the dangers of driving a trading society away from its profits. The Tenth Penny, he was to write to Alva in 1572, on the eve of the holocaust, would no doubt be an admirable contribution to the funds, always supposing that it could be collected without trouble. Yet in all countries, in his experience, the introduction of new taxes was dangerous and displeased people more than anything else. Earnestly he begged the Duke to weigh the affair very carefully and consider the possibility of some compromise.

In days to come, under other governors, the King's lightest wish had the force of law. The Duke of Alva did not scruple to shelve even the royal pardon, which he contrived to sit on for six months before proclamation in a grand state ceremony at Antwerp in a form which in fact exempted from amnesty all those even remotely guilty of taking part in disturbances. "By its provisions," complains the indignant Motley, "not a man or woman was pardoned who had ever committed a fault. The innocent alone were forgiven. Even they were not sure of mercy until they should obtain full absolution from the Pope."

Perhaps it was not the most liberal of documents, though the town of Antwerp was at least sufficiently impressed or wary to thank its governor for the honor he had done it. But by its publication the damage was done and the government had deprived itself of its most potent weapon, the aura of implacability and frightfulness of the Duke himself. Hope began to stir again; people took heart—they were not quite sure why. But whereas in 1569 the Tenth Penny could have been enforced at the cost of a few processes before the Blood Council which would hardly have taxed Vargas's energies to the full, by 1571, when the final decision was reached to collect the quotas in a slightly toned-down version, opinion throughout the provinces had hardened to such a degree that even the pro-Spanish stalwarts like Berlaymont and Aerschot— even Viglius the Frisian jurist, most servile and timorous of men— found the courage to protest against the hated scheme which in Noircarmes' view would cause two thousand emigrations. When the Duke looked like insisting, the Antwerp exchange closed and the economic life of the country came nearly to a halt.

But even then the resistance was passive. It is untrue to say, as unkind critics have said, that the Netherlanders accepted religious butchery, only to rebel when their pockets were about to be picked. The facts are even more dismal. They would have suffered this indignity also if a quite fortuitous happening had not intervened: the work not of merchants or martyrs, but of pirates.

When the remnants of the Beggar party had broken up, the more desperate, the *Gueux des Bois*, had taken to the forests, while the sailors among them had found themselves ships and become the *Gueux de Mer*, the "Sea Beggars," raiding along the exposed and vulnerable coasts from a base in Emden beyond the borders of the Netherlands. This was simple piracy. It happened however that by virtue of his sovereign powers in his small French principality, Orange had the right to issue letters of marque to ships which he permitted to fly his flag, and at Coligny's suggestion these sea captains and their crews suddenly found themselves legalized and rendered respectable, at least in Calvinist eyes.

Having taken them under his protection, the Prince did his best to lay down standards of decorum. Hostile acts were only authorized against the Duke of Alva's regime, with whom Orange had declared himself at war. Christian piety was to be preserved among the crews by ministers shipped for the purpose, and only seamen of good character were to be enlisted or received on board.

There admirable precepts did not entirely change the character of the Beggar fleet. Exhorted to godliness, it remained a band of cutthroats. Many of its members would have been surprised to be considered as anything else. Its admiral, Lumey de la Marck, was a noble-born ruffian. It had no real base. When not raiding, it took shelter where it could, relying on the tolerance of rulers who had no love for Philip. The early spring of 1572 found a squadron of its ships in English waters recovering from a mauling at Spanish hands. Those who supped with Queen Elizabeth however were wise to use a long spoon, also to bring their own provisions. A sudden shift in her policy, which was now turning toward an accommodation with Alva, made the Beggars unwelcome in her ports, and their supplies were forthwith cut off.

This squadron, under de la Marck and his deputy Bois de Tres-long, numbered twenty-five ships and perhaps seven hundred men. It set sail for Holland, making for the Texel channel and Enkhuizen in the Zuider Zee, where Beggar sympathies had been reported. But wind and tide were against it; and sailing back rather aimlessly down the coast, it anchored on the first of April off the port of Brill which commanded the entry to the lower Rhine. Brill normally had a Spanish garrison—it was a recognized strong point. But this garrison had been temporarily moved to Utrecht. The Beggars, much to their own astonishment, found themselves off an unde-fended town, which they took, not promptly—for no one acted promptly in this extraordinary affair except the magistrates who had fled at the first alarm—but at least with the thoroughness of buccaneers.

Few decisive events have been accomplished as quaintly or with as large an element of burlesque. Within a matter of hours the churches had been looted and Adam van Haren, one of the Beggar captains, was parading his decks in helmet and chasuble. In similar fancy dress—for so they evidently conceived it—Treslong and a Beggar contingent from Brill went down the coast a few days later to Flushing, where rebellion had also raised its head. Motley de-scribes the journey:

The expedition seemed a fierce but whimsical masquerade. Every man in the little fleet was attired in the gorgeous vestments of the plundered churches, in gold embroidered cassocks, glittering mass-garments, or the more sombre cowls and robes of Capuchin friars . . . So swept that resolute but fantastic band along the placid estuaries of Zeeland, waking the stagnant waters with their wild beggar-songs and cries of vengeance.

The capture of Brill had been a haphazard and piratical act in which the townspeople had played no part; from which indeed the large majority had fled. But at Flushing the fishermen under the prompting of Orange's agent, Jan van Cuyck, had led a popular uprising against the town magistrates, defying the introduction of a Spanish garrison, and had sent to Brill for help. We have seen how that call was answered. And this was to be the general pattern as the tide of rebellion rose and spread across the islands and the provinces north of the great rivers: first through Walcheren, then to Holland, then eastward into Gelderland and Friesland. Veere on Walcheren was the next Beggar capture, thanks again to van Cuyck and his fishermen. By the end of May Enkhuizen, the principal port on the Zuider Zee, had placed its magistrates under arrest and sent for Beggar aid. Medemblik and Hoorn followed suit early in June: the northern quarter of Holland was collapsing into rebel hands. On June 18 Oudewater fell; a short while later, Gouda. On June 23 the important town of Leyden opened its gates to a Beggar garrison, and Dordt followed. At the end of June the Beggars took Gorcum at the meeting of the waters of the Waal and Meuse. On July 23 Haarlem came to terms with them. The revolt was becoming general, and by the end of that month, with the exception of its greatest town, Amsterdam, almost the whole of Holland was in rebel hands, including Rotterdam and Delft from which Alva had withdrawn his garrisons. "With one fierce bound of enthusiasm," writes Motley, "that nation shook off its chains." He means of course the north, the nucleus of the seven provinces of the future Dutch Republic which were finally to make good their breach with Spain. And even here his enthusiasm must be qualified. Professor Geyl in his *Revolt of the Netherlands* puts the matter in perspective:

One thing appears at once from this outline—namely that in the extension of the revolt the Beggars fulfilled a function of the greatest importance. Everywhere the magistrates had to be compelled to recognise the Prince, and it was not often that the party of the revolution, which most easily found support among the lower classes, was able to apply sufficient pressure from within the walls. It was the Beggars, under their aristocratic chiefs, who spread the revolt from town to town; and if occasionally a town did come over to the Prince spontaneously, their assistance was immediately required to confirm it in its choice. Nor should it be thought that all these Beggar bands did was to reveal the towns to themselves. The two were by no means animated by the same spirit. The Beggars were the men of '66, the iconoclasts; men who had suffered on account of their faith and who bore a grudge not merely against the Spaniards but against the Church; men whose Calvinist faith found vent most readily against priests and papists. But the bulk of those who called in the Beggars most certainly had no thought of breaking with the country's Catholic tradition. To the town populations on whom Orange called in the summer of 1572 his cause meant detestation of the Spanish garrisons and the Tenth Penny

. . . When the burgomasters of Gouda, in their anxiety at the approach of the Lord of Swieten, cautiously sounded part of the citizen guards as to whether they were ready to defend the town, all the reply was: "No; for the Tenth Penny we won't lift a finger."

So the rebellion was on two levels: the social-religious and the economic. The Prince of Orange seems to have been one of the few to appreciate this fact which has bedeviled judgments about the rising ever since, but he saw also that for the time being the two parties formed one united front which might be used for a truly national purpose.

As yet he had no thought of a complete break with the past. Traditions of feudal loyalty died hard. He did not send agents into Holland to call a conference of its Estates as rebels against Philip but rather in the royal name to fight Alva's allegedly illegal and usurping government. If this was a fiction, it was a necessary one in the climate of the times, when rebellion against an anointed ruler was a crime in the eyes of God and man. And this was not altogether a sham. As late as 1573 the Prince was almost certainly prepared to recognize Philip and Spanish sovereignty in the Netherlands in return for freedom of worship, the restoration of the old provincial charters, the suppression of the Blood Council and the recall of the Spanish troops.

No doubt these were large aims; but then much water had flowed under Dutch bridges since Alva had first come to Brussels. Throughout the north in the summer of 1572 rebellion was organizing itself and acquiring a legal basis. The first rebel congress was called that July at Dordt, and there the Prince's delegate, Philip Marnix of St. Aldegonde, sketched out a program of reform. All illegal taxes were remitted. The Prince was recognized as the King's stadtholder of Holland, Zeeland and Utrecht and commander of their provincial armies, with a vote of 100,000 crowns in cash—truly a superfiction, since a royalist stadtholder, Count Bossu, had been appointed to succeed him in '66. More idealistically, liberty of conscience was decreed: the right of every man to worship as he pleased. Needless to say, this vision of the future, the far-distant future, in which perhaps the Prince alone believed, was a dead letter from the start, and the cries of persecuted Catholics soon rose loud and anguished on the liberated air. But few heeded them.

These events had spread themselves from the capture of Brill on

April Fools' Day till well past midsummer with hardly a reaction from the hard-pressed government forces under Bossu, Alva's deputy north of the rivers. It may be wondered why so experienced a commander as the Duke had allowed such a situation to develop without some lightning counterstroke of the kind that had crushed the rebels at Jemmingen. A blow in the south, near the heart of his defenses, had prevented any such move—Count Louis of Nassau with Huguenot help had seized Mons in the Walloon province of Hainaut, near the border with France, not forty miles from Brussels.

To this threat the Duke had reacted with all the fierce promptness of his nature. His son Don Frederick (Fadrique: not to be confused with his natural son Don Ferdinand, the Grand Prior) was sent at once to besiege the town. It was a moment of the gravest peril in which the whole Spanish position in the Netherlands hung on a thread, for the French king, Charles IX, seemed to be in almost open alliance with the Protestants, and the Prince of Orange was poised to strike from Germany with a fresh army numbering perhaps twenty-four thousand men.

On July 8 the Prince crossed the Rhine; on the twenty-third he took Roermond on the Meuse. Here he was delayed by his usual financial difficulties—his army was not unreasonably demanding to be paid before it consented to cross the river onto the Duke's midden. Also there was a diplomatic battle to be waged, since the normally well-disposed Emperor Maximilian had been showing himself much more Spanish-minded since the marriage of his daughter the Archduchess Anne of Austria to Philip in 1570, and was now threatening to launch the imperial "ban" against the disturber of European peace.

In August the Prince replied in suitably stately but submissive terms to this threat. He had done what he could to come to some accord with a regime which Maximilian himself had dubbed "highly pernicious," yet all his efforts had been in vain, and short of abandonng the Netherlands to an "insupportable yoke" he had seen no other choice than to take to arms.

I profess before God and your sacred Imperial Majesty [he wrote] that since they refuse me justice, it is no fault of mine that I am forced to begin a war in which I seek only what is my due and every man's natural rights. . . . That is why the Christian charity I owe to the maltreated peoples of the Low Countries, my emotion at their sufferings and their just demands, the obligations I have had to undertake in their name for the defence and well-being of the hereditary provinces on behalf of His Majesty the King of Spain (my most honoured and clement sovereign) have forced me to oppose this cruel and insupportable tyranny of the Duke of Alva with all the strength lent me by nature, by right, and by the laws of the Empire.

He ended:

I humbly beg your Majesty to take me and mine under your protection, praying that Almighty God will grant you long and perfect health, that He will make your reign fortunate and leave you to enjoy a lasting peace.

Humbug perhaps, but necessary humbug. The Prince had to keep everyone sweet and use every argument and every weapon to hand. Bad news had been coming in of the rout of a Huguenot force which had attempted to relieve Count Louis in Mons, but he had the Frenchman Coligny's pledge of massive support for his invasion, and on August 27, the day of his letter to the Emperor which should at least ensure neutrality in that quarter, he crossed the Meuse from Roermond, threatening the heart of Alva's citadel across the plain of Brabant.

Unknown to him, three days earlier, the massacre of St. Bartholomew had taken place in Paris and Coligny and nearly all the Huguenot leaders were dead.

The massacre itself is one of the most extraordinary events that ever occurred: a brew of politics, blood lust, fear and neurosis on a scale fortunately rare. One of its most poignant figures is the young French king himself, coaxed into the betrayal of a man whom he had rightly honored and loved, for Coligny was truly his friend. The details belong to French history—the wedding celebrations of Henry of Navarre and Marguerite de Valois which brought the Huguenots to Paris; the first attempt on Coligny's life; the reassurances; the plottings of the Queen Mother and the Catholic nobles; the mass killings; the royal marksman with his arquebus at the window in the Louvre.

Just as the much smaller affair at Glencoe a century later will always be remembered as the epitome of treachery, so St. Bartholomew's has a special place in the anthology of crimes. Even in its own day it was hailed with the extremes of revulsion and joy. In Rome Te Deums were sung—officially in gratitude for Charles's escape from an imaginary Huguenot plot, and not, as Motley implies, as a thanksgiving for thousands of Protestant dead. The Papacy was seldom crude. In Spain Philip was seen to smile, even to laugh, as well he might, for his brother of France had been converted overnight from a dangerous foe into a virtual prisoner of the Catholic faction of the Guises, and therefore of Spain. In England the Queen went into mourning and berated the French ambassador. But for Orange the news, in his own words, was a "sledge-hammer blow." He had run out of allies. The Huguenot party at the French court had ceased to exist; its supporters in the country were being butchered as the waves of terror spread outward from the Louvre to the south and west where the movement had its base; and there remained to him only the liberated territories of the northern Netherlands and Count Louis in Mons, closely pressed by the besieging forces of Don Frederick.

Toward Mons the Prince now turned in a long wheeling march past Louvain and Mechlin which took him north and west of Brussels, then sharply back southeast in the direction of Nivelles. Rebellion had been brewing in many Flemish and Brabantine towns, but for fear of royalist reprisals few of them would have any truck with him, and there can be no doubt that he would have done better to march north toward the real center of the revolt in the cities of Holland which alone could have supplied his expensive and insubordinate army. On the eleventh of September he lay with his headquarters close to Mons and the Spanish covering force. And that night a band of raiders under Julian Romero, one of the most enterprising of Alva's generals, fell upon him in an *encamisada,* wearing nightshirts over their armor for mutual recognition in the darkness, and nearly finished off the rebellion at a blow.

The guards were sleeping. The prince was awakened by his pug dog Kuntze whining and clawing at his face. Motley, who for some reason omits the little creature's name, assures us that from that day the Prince always kept a "spaniel of the same breed" in his bedchamber, and indeed in statues of Orange he is sometimes shown with just such a companion.

In the event, the Prince escaped from the burning camp and the raiders were beaten off. But there was no more to be attempted for the relief of Mons, where Count Louis was advised to make what terms he could. The main rebel army, as mutinous as its forerunner of '68, recrossed the Meuse and the Rhine to be disbanded at Orsoy, and its unfortunate and bankrupt commander was once more lucky to escape from it with his life. But this time he did not choose to go into exile: instead he returned by a roundabout route to Holland, intent, as he wrote to his brother John, on finding his grave there.

Already in these tentative actions the shape of the future of the Low Countries had been sketched out. North of the rivers and on the islands at the mouth of the Scheldt, where Alva's garrisons were few and the Sea Beggars active, the Calvinists were elbowing their way into power and carrying the Catholic majority along with them into total war with Spain, while in the northeast, in Gelderland and Overyssel, Orange's brother-in-law, Count van den Bergh, was covering a similar take-over of the market towns with an army he had brought from Cleves. But in the south the Calvinist cells, which might have made a revolution there also, had been held in check by the presence of large Spanish forces and by the overmastering fear of the Duke which had prevented all but a handful of places from throwing in their lot with Orange.

Mons had been one of the exceptions: a prime one, for it had raised a threat to the Duke's whole position. Count Louis and his garrison, much reduced by sickness and mutiny, were allowed to march out with the honors of war—such civilities cost the Duke nothing, and he needed Don Frederick's siege force for work elsewhere. Once the garrison was gone, the hangings began. Noircarmes, an industrious butcher, took charge of operations there, while Don Frederick moved on to Mechlin, which had not withstood any siege but had been unwise enough to welcome Orange on his inward march from the Meuse. This ancient town, the ecclesiastical capital of the Netherlands and once the see of Cardinal Granvelle, was now handed over to the *tercios* as a warning to the rebellious-minded. The Duke was a believer in the merits of example; his men simply followed their instincts; and the results no doubt satisfied them both.

From Mechlin Don Frederick's army marched north into Gelderland and Overyssel, from which Count van den Bergh had hastened to evacuate himself, though not the unfortunate townsfolk who had accepted his protection. Here another example was deemed expedient for the general good, and Zutphen was chosen, or rather chose itself by a crass attempt to fire upon the *tercios*. As in Mechlin, so in Zutphen. Its epitaph is written in a contemporary report that a "frightful outcry and sound of slaughter" had been heard by those outside the walls, though no one quite knew what had happened. All the garrison and "some burghers" had been put to the sword, the Duke reported. In Naarden the details are firmer. In a frenzy of unwisdom, this small town on the Zuider Zee close to Amsterdam—a hotbed of Anabaptism, according to the Duke—first rejected a summons to admit Don Frederick's troops, and then decided to fete them as its guests. Let Motley tell the sequel as some indication of the horrors of the times:

The great bell had been meantime ringing, and the citizens had been summoned to assemble in the Gast Huis Church, then used as a town hall. . . . Suddenly a priest, who had been pacing to and fro before the church door, entered the building, and bade them all prepare for death; but the announcement, the preparation, and the death were simultaneous. The door was flung open, and a band of armed Spaniards rushed across the sacred threshold. They fired a single volley upon the defenceless herd, and then sprang in upon them with sword and dagger. A yell of despair arose as the miserable victims saw how hopelessly they were encaged, and beheld the ferocious faces of their butchers. The carnage within that narrow space was compact and rapid. Within a few minutes all were despatched, and among them Senator Gerrit, from whose table the Spanish commander had but just risen. The church was then set on fire, and the dead and dying were consumed to ashes together.

Inflamed but not satiated, the Spaniards then rushed into the streets, thirsty for fresh horrors. The houses were all rifled of their contents, and men forced to carry booty to the camp, who were then struck dead as their reward. The town was then fired in every direction, that the skulking citizens might be forced from their hiding places. As fast as they came forth they were put to death by their impatient foes. Some were pierced with rapiers, some were chopped to pieces with axes, some were surrounded in the blazing streets by troops of laughing soldiers, intoxicated, not with wine but with blood, who tossed them to and fro with their lances, and derived a wild amusement from their dying agonies. Those who attempted resistance were crimped alive like fishes, and left to gasp themselves to death in lingering torture. The soldiers, becoming more and more insane as the foul work went on, opened the veins of some of their victims, and drank their blood as if it were wine. Some of the burghers were for a time spared, that they might witness the violation of their wives and daughters, and were then butchered in company with those still more unfortunate victims. Miracles of brutality were accomplished. . . . Men were slain, women outraged at the altars, in the streets, in their blazing homes. The life of Lambert Hortensius was spared, out of regard to his learning and genius, but he could hardly thank his foes for the boon, for they struck his only son dead, and tore out his heart before his father's eyes. Hardly any man or woman survived except by accident. . . . Shortly afterwards came an order to dismantle the fortifications . . . and to raze what was left of the city from the surface of the earth. The work was faithfully accomplished and for a long time Naarden ceased to exist.

At this point in the autumn of 1572 it would have seemed to a detached observer that the whole rebel cause must follow Naarden into oblivion. Of the territories which had acknowledged Orange in the spring, the Duke had reduced all but Holland and Zeeland to obedience, and even there he held the largest city—Amsterdam —and the fortress of Middelburg on the isle of Walcheren together with its supply base of Goes, recently saved for him by a feat which he rightly acclaimed as among the greatest ever performed by soldiers.

In this half-drowned country of islands off the mouth of the Scheldt, Goes had been besieged by a rebel army and Beggar flotillas had cut its communications with the mainland of Brabant. But there had still been one way in which a relieving force could reach it—a ten-mile march, waist-deep even at low tide, across the sandbanks of the eastern Scheldt, broken in places by channels of much deeper water. This almost incredible journey was accomplished in five hours of an autumn night by three thousand men, Spanish, German and Walloon, under their veteran commander, Mondragon. If they had lost their way or been delayed an hour the rising tide would have accounted for them all; but only nine men were drowned and Goes was duly relieved.

Freed from the immediate threat to his foothold on Walcheren, the Duke could turn his attention to the rebels' land base in Holland, where Orange had been busily establishing himself. The rebellion had geography on its side. Zeeland was a congeries of islands easily dominated by the Sea Beggars from Brill and Flushing. And though on modern maps Holland has a substantially earthy look, in the sixteenth century it too was a land of waters: protected on the south by rivers, on the west by the ocean, and on the east by the Zuider Zee and the meres around the town of Haarlem. Whoever held Amsterdam held the key to its back door, however, and this advantage the Duke enjoyed. If Don Frederick's army could take Haarlem, a dozen miles off in the narrow neck of the peninsula, the rebel province would be cut in half and could be reduced at leisure, by northward thrusts on Alkmaar and the Beggar-held ports on the Zuider Zee, or southward on Delft and Leyden.

And Haarlem nearly submitted without a blow; its magistrates and many of its citizens had no desire to share the fate of Naarden or resist a besieging force of fifteen thousand veterans. A revolution from below at Beggar prompting defied the fears of the fainthearted and took the town to war.

From that moment, the mood of defiance was absolute. The fortifications were weak; the Orangist garrison amounted to perhaps four thousand men and a corps of three hundred Amazons, "all females of respectable character" as Motley solemnly assures us. Don Frederick had confidentially expected to reduce the place in a week.

Yet Haarlem held out for nine months. This is one of the great stories of human endurance which it is impossible to recall without emotion. Even the case-hardened Spaniards showed a grudging admiration for the endurance of the town under months of almost constant bombardment, and we may share their point of view as we read of the assaults; the subterranean battles in the saps and mines below the walls; the desperate, and to the Spanish, novel, skating forays on the ice; the slow grind of starvation as the spring thaw cut off the relief route from Orange's camp at Sassenheim across the meres. It was a war, Alva informed his king, such as had never been seen before. His sense of puzzlement is obvious, for these were rebels and burghers and their heroism a freak of nature. But what can be sensed also is his growing alarm. The reduction of Haarlem was proving immensely costly. Three new regiments had to be called up from Italy, and even these could barely guarantee the communications of the besieging army or of Amsterdam itself from Beggar sea-borne assaults from Enkhuizen on the Zuider Zee.

The Duke in fact was wearying of the struggle. His health was suffering from the prevailing cold and dampness of the climate and for some time his petulant complaints and requests to be relieved of his burdens had been reaching the Spanish court: the first storm signals to be hoisted by the regime.

Some of these requests had actually been answered: a successor as Lieutenant Governor and Captain General had been sent him in the person of another magnifico, the Duke of Medina Celi, whose commission was however then deferred by royal command pending the settlement of the unrest caused by the Tenth Penny legislation and finally lapsed altogether, though not before the newcomer had provoked his rival by displays of pique and insult that made their own chaotic contribution to Netherlands affairs. "There is not on earth a more irascible man," Alva lamented. "There is nothing I can do to please him. Since I have been here I have suffered all the pains and persecutions that there are; only this last contrarity was missing."

Half silly with rage and disappointed ambition, Medina Celi had even accused the Duke of a slothful and craven refusal to bestir himself or march against the enemy. Alva resignedly replied in measured letters to his king that he would go swimming in the canals of Holland if that would serve the royal cause. Nevertheless he remained in a kind of purdah, first at Nymegen, then at Utrecht, far from the battlefield, lamenting his ailments, his "chair-borne" life, the slights put upon him by Medina Celi and his master, and the lack of recompense for his vast services in terms of "honor, life and fortune." He was as usual desperate for money. Even the fall of Haarlem—after titanic exertions which had involved Don Frederick in the transportation of a whole fleet overland from the Zuider Zee to the Haarlem lake—brought only new problems: first a mutiny of the army of occupation in the conquered town; then another siege—of Alkmaar—on the far perimeter of the Netherlands, in the narrow "horn" of Holland, where the all-conquering *tercios* were turned back by a Beggar cutting of the dykes and the encroaching waters of the North Sea.

When all was over, it became a popular saying in the Netherlands that victory had begun at Alkmaar. It was certainly a victory, but so had Heiligerlee been a victory, and the snap seizure of Mons, and further back the "Compromise" and the forcing of the Duchess's "Accord." The taking of Brill and Flushing had far more right

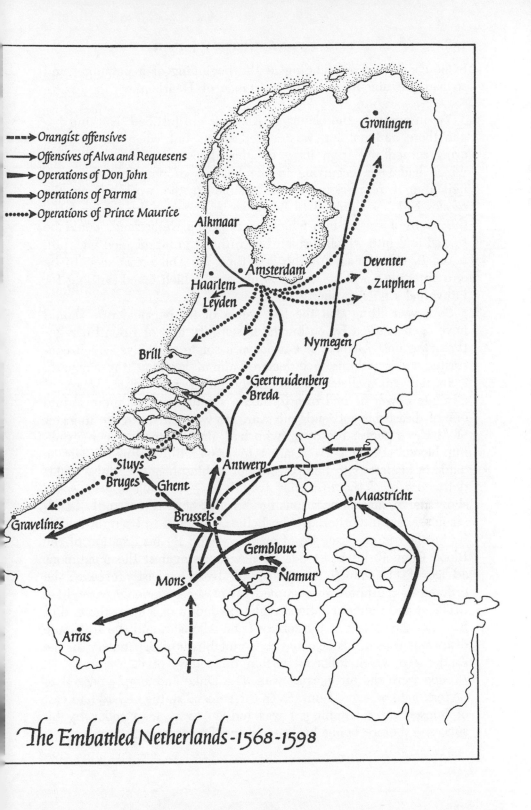

Legend:

- ---→ Orangist offensives
- → Offensives of Alva and Requesens
- ➤ Operations of Don John
- ➤ Operations of Parma
- ••••→ Operations of Prince Maurice

Groningen

Alkmaar

Deventer

Amsterdam

Zutphen

Haarlem

Leyden

Nymegen

Brill

Geertruidenberg

Breda

Sluys

Antwerp

Maastricht

Bruges

Ghent

Gravelines

Brussels

Gembloux

Mons

Namur

Arras

The Embattled Netherlands · 1568-1598

to be considered as standing at the beginning of a new age; and so had the nine-month-long resistance of Haarlem.

Yet in one way the claims of Alkmaar are justified. Nothing began there and nothing was settled there, but when the Spanish army turned tail from its gates the almost imperceptible swing which had been occurring in the balance of power between rebellion and repression became visible to the world. Even the *tercios* had been proved to be powerless against the *genius loci*—the waste of waters into which parts of the Netherlands could be turned and into which a small but ruthless group of men was prepared to turn them. For the first time the Duke was seen to be encountering a will as strong as his own, which cared nothing for individual rights, property or lives.

So it was fitting that the last weeks of his personal rule should have been marked by outbursts of self-pity and of resentful rage: threats against Alkmaar not to leave a single soul alive which contrasted oddly with his once declared aim of "pruning" the vineyard.

In fact his policies had entirely failed, and in six years of absolute power he had transformed a situation full of promise into one of disastrous and endemic war. He was not quite the monster of Motley's pages: the man "who had almost literally been drinking blood." Perhaps the claims to a merciful nature which he made in his letters to Philip were not as blasphemously false as his detractors over the centuries would have us believe. He *could* show mercy, and on occasions he did. But he was that sadly familiar figure, an authoritarian who believed himself to be right and to be justified in any exercise of arbitrary will. By his creation of the Blood Council, his insistence on new taxes against the unanimous advice of his council and above all by the ghastly excesses he ordered or permitted in occupied towns, he had richly earned retirement and the humiliations that crowded in on him at the end of his rule—the retreat of the *tercios* from Alkmaar, and the still more disastrous rout of his fleet under Count Bossu off Enkhuizen in the Zuider Zee which followed within three days of it.

Such were the fortunes of war. The Duke had simply ceased to be fortunate on every front. Even the colossal statue he had had cast of himself after Jemmingen was hidden away in a cellar by his successor before being broken up by the insurgents.

9

PHILIP IN MIDDLE AGE. DON CARLOS. 1568.
THE GRAND COMMANDER. SIEGE OF LEYDEN.
TURNING OF THE TIDE. 1573–74.

Philip was now in his forties and had been more than a decade on the throne. He had never really been young, and the aloofness which had so affronted the pleasure-loving Netherlanders and Italians was hardening into the image of the "Prudent King" whose self-control and freedom from all human passions was to become a byword.

This was how he chose to be seen, for he had a theory of kingship which set him apart. And naturally the court painters of the time obliged. Indeed they obliged too well. Where Titian had impressed his own vision of a man's soul on his state portraits of the Emperor, the artists who served Philip produced only the likeness of a taciturn gentleman in black velvet: a lethargic, somnolent man of whom we may well believe with Professor Merriman that his "only recreation was repose."

This was certainly one side of the King's nature. "God did not send your Majesty and all kings, His viceroys on earth, to waste their time reading or writing, nor yet in meditation or prayer," one contemporary complained, with memories of the Emperor's more active regime. But Charles himself had ended by renouncing the world. The same strain of melancholia which had taken him to Yuste and his unfortunate mother Queen Joanna into outright madness showed itself in his son in a lack of physical resilience and a morbid concern with privacy, in a preference for the written over the spoken word and in secret actions, not all of which have been unraveled to this day.

What none of the portraits show and none of the state papers reveal is that this closed-up, fanatical side of Philip's nature, which brought great cruelties and injustices in its train, was only half the man. "He is an adept at concealing his affections," wrote one perceptive critic. The King had learned the art in a hard school. His first two marriages were dynastic and arranged for him by his father. He himself negotiated the third, also for dynastic reasons, when it became desirable to set the seal on his *détente* with France. This marriage to a young girl who had originally been intended for his own son turned out to be an extremely happy one, bringing him two daughters who were to provide the chief solace of his life. But Elizabeth of Valois, whom the Spaniards long remembered with affection as the "Queen of the Peace," died young, as did the fourth wife, Anne of Austria, his own niece.

These bereavements, and the loss of the children whose coffins lie in the obscenely prissy vaults of the Escurial, should help us to understand the King. The impassivity which so impressed his subjects was partly a disguise. For a moment now and then, in the famous letters to his daughters,* another man shows through: fussy, banal, affectionate:

The peaches have arrived in such a state that I wouldn't have known what they were if you hadn't written to tell me. I haven't been able to eat them, and that I regret very much, because coming as they do from the little garden beneath your window, they would have given me so much pleasure.

It's a fine thing that you've already got lemons at Aranjuez, as you my eldest write. I don't think I need answer your other letters, as they're already some days old now and I burnt them so as not to over-load myself with paper. I don't suppose they contained anything that required an answer, but if they did you can write about it again. Yesterday we received news of the arrival in a port forty leagues from Lisbon of one of the ships from India. . . . I don't know what the fleet is bringing us; I only know that on this ship is an elephant, a gift to your brother from the viceroy whom I've just appointed. . . . Tell your brother about the elephant; tell him also that I'm sending him a Portuguese book so that he can learn the language, which I wish he could speak already.

* These letters were written in 1581–82, a decade after the point we have now reached, during the King's visit to newly conquered Portugal. The recipients were the children of the third marriage to Elizabeth of Valois: Isabella Clara Eugenia, aged fifteen, and Catalina, thirteen. The boys referred to are the Infante Don Diego, who died in 1582, and Philip, later Philip III, the King's sons by his last wife, Anne of Austria, for whom he was in mourning at the time.

This desire to instruct and edify is a constant theme:

Your letters and news from Aranjuez have given me much pleasure. The thing I miss most is the song of the nightingales, which I haven't heard this year, since this palace is so far from the country. . . . Coming back to Aranjuez, you must both be great marksmen now, judging by your success with the deer and such a lot of rabbits. You, my eldest, tell me that your brother distinguished himself; you probably meant that your sister did, to judge by what you write further on. You have put an o for an a and have also missed out a word. You were probably writing in a hurry.

It's excellent that you understand Portuguese as well as you say. Try and see to it that your brother understands it as you do. . . . Make him read in Portuguese and explain it to him, since you understand it so well. I think he'll now be able to fill in the coloured letters; that is why I'm sending you some more which will keep him occupied for some time; and I still have some left. See that he fills them in, but little by little, so as not to tire him, and sometimes set him to copy them. He will learn that way and, I hope, acquire a good hand. . . .

There is also an unexpected strain of humor:

It's excellent news that you're all well. It strikes me that your little sister's canine teeth have come very soon: they must be to replace the ones I'm about to lose—I'm sure they'll have gone by the time I return. I've just been reading the letter in which you tell me that I've already mentioned my sister's windows at the chapel, and I've written about them again in my last letter, so that in fact I've told you about it three times. So you'll see what a state my poor head is in with so many things to occupy me. . . .

So as to prevent embarrassments on the journey I gave the order of the Fleece to-day to the Duke of Braganza; he helped me at mass and we both wore the Collar—mine made a sad effect against my mourning clothes. The Duke was more elegant. . . . For the first time he had bootees on, which almost everyone here except myself is wearing.

One of the Infanta's maids, Madalena Ruiz, was with Philip in Portugal. As we see from her portrait in the Prado she was an elderly dwarf; she was also apparently a problem:

I don't think Madalena is quite as cross with me as she was; but she's been ill for some time; she's been purged and she's still in a bad temper.

She came here yesterday in a poor state: weak, old, deaf and semi-infirm. I think all this comes from what she drinks. . . .

I told you the other day how bad the bull-fight was. There's nothing more to add, but I must tell you about Madalena, who has had a fever ever since and has had to be bled twice and purged. . . . To-day she came to see me, still very feeble and with a bad colour. She told me that she'd lost all taste for wine—a bad sign with her.

The King's love for his children and interest in every detail of their lives appears time and again:

Everyone gives me a good account of you and says you've grown a lot, certainly you, my second daughter. If you've taken measurements, let me know how much you've grown while I've been away, and send them to me, measured exactly in silk ribbon or thread. Add those of your brother. I'd love to have them with me until I can see you all for myself. I pray God it may be soon. . . .

It comes therefore as something of a shock to find the following written in the same tender terms:

Yesterday my nephew and I attended an *auto;* we watched it from a window and heard everything very well. Everyone was given a paper with the names of the participants on it. I'll send you mine so that you can see who they were. First of all there was a sermon, as is customary. We stayed for the pronouncements of the sentences. Then we withdrew, because they needed the house we were in for the civil power to condemn to the fire all those whom the inquisitors had handed over. It was eight o'clock when we arrived and we didn't dine till one. May God keep you as I pray He will,

Your good father.

We see here the dichotomy between paternal feeling and the implacable will that had men burned at the stake and secretly strangled in prison, and we meet it again in almost clinical form in the fate of the King's eldest son, Don Carlos, long since in his grave when these charming letters came to be written to his half sisters.

Carlos, the child of Philip's first marriage, was a product of the

interbreeding which was to prove the ruin of the Spanish Hapsburgs. From the Prado portrait there emerges a young man, certainly thin and unprepossessing, but no worse than Charles V at a
similar age. The famous deformity of the Hapsburg jaw is there,
but the mishapen body, the hump on the back and the uneven
height of the shoulders which figure in contemporary reports are
not insisted on. Outspoken critics were soon declaring however that
the boy was also sadly unhinged in his mind, and a head-first fall
down a flight of steps, followed by a trepanning of the skull and a
"cure" by the introduction into his sickbed of the miracle-work-
ing remains of a dead Franciscan cook, can hardly have improved his wits.

As Carlos neared manhood these tales multiplied, and the picture was built up of a half-crazed buffon with a pathological lust for
blood which showed itself in a desire to see animals tormented,
young women whipped, and in physical attacks on the most sacro-
sanct grandees at court. Though highly colored, these accounts are
believable of a descendant of *Joanna la Loca,* and they are partly
borne out by the antipathy to his grandson which the Emperor
showed during his last years at Yuste. Indeed we may go further
and say that if Philip himself did not believe them, then he was
truly the monster of Protestant legend, a Saturn who devoured his
own children.

What are the facts? The unbalanced nature of the boy can
hardly be doubted on the evidence surviving. We can accept the
perversions, the insulting adolescent behavior, the hatred for his
father on which almost all reports agree. But equally we must
allow that at least the hatred was rational. There is no need to
suppose with Schiller that Don Carlos and Elizabeth of Valois felt
an illicit love for one another before agreeing that to find one's
prospective bride transformed into a stepmother gives some cause
for complaint. Nor is this all. A young man is rightly impatient of
his elders. Heirs to thrones are probably no less impatient than
others, and they are apt to have more impatient supporters. Here
we approach the great political and religious issues of the time; for
there were elements in Spain and in the Netherlands which may
well have looked to the heir to the throne to provide active opposition to Philip's policies. That Don Carlos can have been a heretic
is an amusing notion which we can dismiss, while remembering that
his Austrian kinsman, the Emperor Maximilian, was almost certainly

a Protestant sympathizer. But that the boy may have intended to fish in Protestant waters and even to flee abroad where he could have formed a focus for discontent is by no means impossible; and even the more sensational reports that Carlos had confessed to a priest an intention to kill his own father are not more irrational than other details of the extraordinary and tragic story. Certainly what followed is only explicable on the assumption that in *some* way—either politically or because of his mental state—Don Carlos had become so dangerous and unstable an element in Spain that it had become vitally necessary to destroy him.

The final scenes have a starkness unsurpassed by anything in Shakespeare or Greek tragedy. On a January night in 1568 the King, with a small group of intimates, forced his way into his son's room in the royal palace in Madrid. The bolts of the door had been tampered with: clearly some resistance was expected from the Prince, who was supposed to sleep with loaded pistols at his side. Awakened by the sudden ghostly appearance of a father armed and helmeted like some visitant on the battlements of Elsinore, the unfortunate boy seems to have asked if they had come to kill him. Hardly any other words were spoken. The windows of the Infante's room were boarded up, and the heir to Spain, the Netherlands, Naples, Sicily and the Indies was handed over to the custody of a jailer, never to be seen again by his father or the outside world.

Six months later he was dead—probably of natural causes, for the poor young man had a bad ancestry, his health was poor and his practice of sleeping through the heat of a Madrid summer in a bed packed with ice was hardly conducive to a long life. Most historians now believe that the King, fearing for the fate of the monarchy and of Spain itself in the hands of a madman or moral degenerate, shut up his son under conditions in which he could not be expected to live long: and this, if tragic, and indeed worthy of Aeschylus, is not dishonorable to the King. His letter to the Pope announcing the Infante's death certainly suggests some such explanation in the guarded and wary phrasing which seems to conceal and yet reveal between the lines the writer's anguished certainty that Don Carlos was insane, an innocent victim of God's providence. Few reading these words would doubt the intensity of grief behind them: they come clearly from the heart. Yet there were rumors of a more sinister truth behind the story—natural in a

Europe which by and large feared and hated Philip and rejoiced in his discomfiture. Some years later the King's principal secretary of state at the time, Antonio Pérez, claimed to reveal that Don Carlos had been poisoned on the King's orders: a most specific and detailed accusation. Was it true?

When Pérez wrote this he was a disgraced exile, full of hatred for his master. Charges by so unreliable a witness may well be disbelieved. Yet one thing gives us pause. Two and a half centuries after Don Carlos's death, during the brief reign of Joseph Bonaparte in Madrid, the Infante's remains were exhumed, when, so the story goes, the head was found severed from the body. A tall tale? Or proof of an execution? And for what offense? The marble tomb still lies at the far end of the second vault of the Escurial. So coolly desolate a place which conceals in its rows upon rows of tombs an infinity of tragedy and suffering may also conceal a crime, however well intentioned. It would have been in keeping with Philip's character, fond father though he was, to act as Abraham would have done with Isaac if there had been no voice from the heavens and no ram caught in the thicket.

That same year, 1568, perhaps the saddest of the reign, saw also the death of Elizabeth of Valois. The widower, left with two small daughters but no heir, soon married again, but of the five children of this union with his Austrian niece, all but one were to die in infancy.

Gradually as he grew older the King retreated from the world. He was never the recluse of legend—indeed in Tordesillas there is a charming painting of him in an arbor at a *fête champêtre* apparently playing a mandolin—but his bent had always been solitary, and ill-health, combined with the immense burdens of a working life in which he set himself to know everything and decide everything, drove him increasingly into the society of secretaries and confessors and the few advisers whom his proud, reserved character could admit into his confidence.

He had no friends. Perhaps the nearest to one was Ruy Gómez de Silva, Prince of Eboli, with whom he had been brought up, though Eboli was five years the elder and was divided from his master by an immense gulf which even the most experienced and professional courtier could never cross. Eboli, as we have seen, was not Spanish by birth but Portuguese, and when he died his successor in the King's affections, Don Cristóbal de Moura, was of the same race. This is significant, for the most Castilian of kings never trusted the Castilian grandees who surrounded his throne, but preferred the society of those who owed their fortunes to him and to him alone.

There were some sound reasons for this, for little more than a century earlier, in the time of Henry the Impotent, Castile had all but been torn to pieces in the hands of grasping and powerful nobles, yet a price had to be paid for this insistence on the second-rate and for the jealous distrust which Philip showed throughout his reign for the able and the independent-minded among the men who served him. He had great talents at his disposal—Alva and Parma in the field; Santa Cruz at sea; men of the caliber of Garcia de Toledo as his viceroys; and diplomats like Bernardino de Mendoza to dazzle Europe with their expertise—but he gave his trust to none of them. A patron of the arts, he was displeased by El Greco's altarpiece for the Escurial. Only in the protection he gave to religious reformers like St. Teresa did he show any appreciation of genius, which otherwise he distrusted as a potential threat to his authority. Thus, as the reign went on, the quality of those about him declined—certainly in the field of action, though by his encouragement of artists he deserves some share of credit for the brilliant outburst of talent that followed during the reigns of his son and grandson. In a sense he had prepared the way for its lushness by the sterility of his own regime, whose perfect monument is the Escurial, a vast mausoleum where even the books in the splendidly proportioned library are turned the wrong way round with their faces to the wall. Not even Versailles provides so grandiose and frigid an impression. But it will undoubtedly be there when the Last Trump blows, fashioned as it is in its creator's image out of the rock of the sierra which surrounds it: the basic element of Spain.

For twenty-one years—from the spring of 1563 to the autumn of 1584—it rose stone by stone among the foothills, near Madrid in the almost exact center of the peninsula. It was the King's one hobby. He watched its building; it was his favorite place of refuge; and there eventually he died, in the small room through which the guides hustle their hordes of victims on the way to the chapel and the royal tombs.

The symbolic importance of this building for any proper appreciation of its creator has often been pointed out. But it goes further: it mirrors Spain itself. The combination of bare, massive exterior and the brilliant decor of the chapel which is its heart is very revealing of a country where the battlements of apparently ruined castles in the depths of the countryside and the unwelcoming walls of *paradors* conceal marble floors, exquisite furniture, and the most modern and luxurious lavatories, the property of marquises or the State Tourist Board. On one level it is just another legacy of the Moors who once ruled this land and kept the charm of their patios and their women carefully veiled from prying eyes behind the blank walls that still line the streets of Andalusian towns. And on another it typifies something schizophrenic in the national soul: the velvet in the iron glove; the longing for display and for disengagement which from the seventies onward began to color the austerity of Spanish attitudes, even with regard to the interminable problem of the Netherlands.

Throughout his years in Brussels Alva's policy had been forward and extremist. It came naturally to him—he was a Castilian in the tradition of those who had led the centuries-long struggle of the *reconquista* against the Moors and won vast empires in the Americas with a handful of penniless adventurers.

But there were other Spains and other policies. The history of Philip's reign is not only one of aggression and bloodshed, but also of the Jesuit missionaries; of Las Casas fighting for the rights of landless Indians against their oppressors; of St. Teresa, St. John of the Cross and the jurists who drew up enlightened colonial laws. At court the Duke's attitudes were not unchallenged. A Netherlands peace party—doves against hawks—had existed from the earliest days of the reign, led by the Portuguese Ruy Gómez de Silva, Prince of Eboli, the statesman who, in the words of the Venetian Soriano, formed with Alva the "two pillars" which upheld the vast machine of Spanish rule and on whom depended "the government of half the world."*

Eboli died in 1573, the same year as the Duke's retirement from Brussels. But his protests against Alva's barbarities, which had been echoed by such unlikely seconds as the Pope and Cardinal

* On other fronts, particularly with regard to England, Eboli and his friends were hawklike, Alva dove-ish.

Granvelle, had already led to a change of heart at court, where the influence of the Emperor's ambassadors had also been very actively exerted in the quest for peace. The ill-starred amnesty of 1569 had been one proof of this; another had been the attempt in 1572 to replace the tyrant with the ineffable Medina Celi, the Governor who never was.

This milder policy had not been decided on only in answer to these pressures or to the voice of conscience. Fantastic though it may seem, the brush fire war in the Netherlands was already eating up far more than half the royal revenue from the Indian mines. The *tercios* were the best troops in Europe but they were abominably expensive. Furthermore they expected to be paid, as the mutiny which followed the capture of Haarlem had shown with brutal clarity, besides causing their famed commander more pain than he remembered in forty years of soldiering. A policy of retrenchment, of ending the ruinous struggle on any reasonable terms, had thus become a need; and in 1573 the Spanish government acknowledged this by performing an abrupt *volte-face* from the crudities of the Duke's regime toward the more accommodating spirit of the Duchess Margaret which had made excellent sense six years earlier.

The new Lieutenant Governor and Captain General of the Netherlands charged with these new policies—Don Luis de Requesens y Zúñiga, Grand Commander of Castile and lately Governor of Milan—was a man of very different stamp from Alva. He had fought at Lepanto and in the campaign of the Alpujarras, but by training he was more diplomat than soldier and had certainly shown a very diplomatic reluctance to shoulder an appointment in a land which was fast becoming the grave of reputations.

Motley, always hostile to Spanish measures of any kind, sees in all this no more than a plot to snare the patriots where attempts to bludgeon them had failed, and some observers at the time were equally suspicious. "His [Alva's] successor is pretending the greatest moderation," wrote Hubert Languet to Philip Sidney that December. "The threads of his net are too coarse and he will not catch many birds. He promises immunity to all who give themselves up to be tortured." This was the orthodox Protestant view, but the Grand Commander's first and enormously detailed letters to his master on his arrival in Brussels in no way bear it out. On the contrary, it is perfectly clear from them that he genuinely regarded a pardon in the widest terms as absolutely indispensable for the provinces, and the suppression of the Blood Council and of the Tenth Penny likewise.*

Poor Requesens! It is hard not to feel for him: a simple gentleman of "cape and sword" in the shoes of Spain's most renowned grandee, struggling to turn the clock back to an age of reason. Alas, it was far too late. He could not even obtain a balance sheet of the finances—the Duke judged such an exercise "impossible." Nor could the Grand Commander hope to find a "middle way" with opponents more intransigent than himself and more unwilling to negotiate on any meaningful terms. The time for that had passed too. In fact with good will but singular ineptitude the King had removed Alva from Brussels at precisely the moment when his fiercely anachronistic policies had begun to make sense.

The proofs of this were not long in coming. Rebellion in the northwest had escalated into full-scale war; and that winter the lines were drawn around Leyden in central Holland, which the Spaniards were besieging, and Middelburg on the island of Walcheren, still held by the veteran Colonel Mondragon for the King.

Middelburg fell. The Spanish relief fleet was driven off under the eyes of the new Governor, watching from a dyke-top like Xerxes on the day of Salamis. With Middelburg went Zeeland and control of the coast as far south as the mouths of the Scheldt above Antwerp—a formidable strategic and indeed diplomatic gain for the patriots, for in the articles of surrender Mondragon had recognized Orange as legal stadtholder of the province. And now the tide of war seemed decisively on the turn in the Protestants' favor, not only in the north but in the far east of the country, where a fresh army of German mercenaries under Count Louis of Nassau was advancing on Maastricht, the fortress commanding the crossing of the Meuse on the direct route between Cologne and Brussels.

This was to prove the last foray of the gay and chivalrous adventurer whose activities since Heiligerlee had been so unfortunate. On this occasion in the spring of 1574 he had every advantage of surprise and more importantly of numbers, at a ratio of nearly two

* This tax was already effectively in abeyance—commuted for down payments of two million florins.

to one over the scratch levies which Requesens and his lieutenant Sancho d'Avila had been hastily drumming up from the Spanish garrisons throughout the country. Yet from the start of the campaign the initiative was firmly in Spanish hands, and when in April Count Louis was finally brought to battle on the heaths near the village of Mook on the border between the Netherlands and Cleves, his numerically superior cavalry of mounted pistoleers was swept away in disgraceful rout by a resolute charge of horsemen trained to drive home with lances through the peppering of shot. It was a disaster comparable to Jemmingen, and somewhere in the carnage Count Louis died, along with a younger brother and a cousin— their bodies were never recovered, and it seems probable that they were thrown unrecognized with a multitude of others into a common grave.

"If they are dead, as I can no longer doubt," wrote the Prince of Orange to his one surviving brother John, "we must submit to the will of God and trust in His divine providence that He who gave the blood of His only Son to maintain His Church will do nothing but what will redound to the advancement of His glory and the preservation of His Church—however improbable it may appear. And though we were all to die, and all this poor people were massacred and driven out, we must still trust that God will not abandon His own."

These are moving words. The Prince felt the bereavement perhaps more keenly than any other event in his life, for he had always loved and trusted Louis, and since his other co-adjutor, Marnix of St. Aldegonde, had been for some weeks a captive in Spanish hands, he believed himself completely alone with his burdens—"without one man at my side to help me." Yet in this same letter to John we glimpse something of the spirit that sustained him:

If no prince or power will give us help, and for want of it we were all to perish, so be it in God's name. Yet we shall have the honour of having done what no nation ever yet did, of having defended and maintained ourselves, in so small a land, against the mighty and dreadful efforts of such powerful enemies, without any aid from others. And if the poor people of these parts, abandoned by all the world, still resolve to hold out as they have done till now, and as I trust they will

continue to do, and if it do not please God to chastise us and utterly destroy us, it will still cost the Spaniards the half of Spain, in wealth as
well as in men, before they will have made an end of us.

At the time these words were written, the faith behind them was
already being justified by events—d'Avila's victorious army had
mutinied and marched, not against the fugitives from Mook or
Orange's own small army in the marshes of Bommel between the
Meuse and the Rhine, but on the town of Antwerp in search of pay.

As the wits had it, the Spanish Army mutinied after a battle, the
Orangist mercenaries before one, and this was almost literally true,
for the *tercios* never flinched from an enemy in the field. These
indisciplined acts, repeated time and again in the years ahead, were
however to cost Spain half her empire in the Netherlands and are
therefore of great significance, both in their own right and as
symptoms of the economic cancer which was to be among the
causes of that empire's decline.

Only a minority of perhaps an eighth of Philip's army in the
Low Countries was actually Spanish—7900 in December 1573 as
against 16,200 High Germans, 9600 Low Germans, 20,800 Walloons
and 4780 cavalry of various nationalities. But throughout it, Spanish
methods prevailed; and its *esprit de corps* was almost wholly
Spanish. Like all armies of occupation in all ages it felt both its
superiority as a fighting body and its spiritual isolation, far from
home among the prosperous foreign burghers who distrusted and
feared it. What marked it out, and what it had come to depend on,
was its sense of corporate discipline, never more necessary than
when it had defied its own officers and was operating on its own,
like a chicken running around without its head.

Spanish mutinies were therefore always marked by a rigorous
sense of order and followed a rigid and invariable pattern in
pursuit of a communal aim: which was simply to be paid. First,
elections would be held to choose a council from among the senior
soldiers, under a chief deputy or *Eletto*, much on the lines of the
early commissars in the Soviet armies of the civil wars. Then the
body of mutineers would march off in strict military formation to
seize a town—any town which was thought large enough and
wealthy enough to be held to ransom and to provide creature
comforts until the ransom was paid.

On this occasion the sufferer was Antwerp: a choice destined to be very fatefully repeated. Probably it had to be Antwerp, for no other city was rich enough to afford the three-year arrears of pay due to even this small section of the sixty-thousand-strong army in the Netherlands. Requesens, in a letter to Philip, had estimated the total arrears at over six million ducats, which was more than the King's total annual revenue from all sources at the time, and though in Antwerp the mutineers from Mook were no more than three thousand, the unfortunate Grand Commander had not even the resources to pay *them. "Dineros y non palabras,"* "Cash, not speeches," they shouted at him as he appeared before them on horseback to make a personal appeal.

Providentially, Antwerp had the means to rid itself of this gross incubus which had settled down upon it like a cloud of locusts. In typically Netherlands fashion the whole affair was settled with cash promises and part payment in goods—whereupon the mutiny ended with a grand drinking party, in the course of which the Spaniards, dressed like the Beggars of Brill in a wonderful array of silks and satins, were recalled to the colors to beat off a sudden sea-borne assault by Orangist forces on the Scheldt. Brederode would have appreciated so Rabelaisian an ending. And, equally typically, this buffoonery was the curtain raiser to a supremely great and decisive event: the siege of Leyden.

To be exact, it was the renewal of a siege. For nearly five months, from the end of October 1573 to March 21 of the following year, a Spanish force under Francisco de Valdez had lain before the city, until drawn off by the threat of Count Louis' invasion which had ended at Mookheyde. On the twenty-sixth of May it returned and began to set up its strong points and redoubts in depth in a wide circle through the surrounding countryside, for this was to be no campaign of direct assault of the kind which had cost heavy Spanish casualties at Haarlem and Alkmaar, but a blockade to starve the city into surrender.

This new policy, the fruits of hard experience, had been Alva's legacy to his successor and is lucidly expressed in a letter to Philip just before his departure from the Netherlands. "I am now engaged," he wrote, "in distributing the troops in carefully chosen quarters, from which they will be able to prevent the Beggars from drawing any further support from the country districts. I expect great success from this measure. By these means the rebels will be imprisoned in their towns and will perish by starvation. Some wintry night, when the canals and ditches are frozen hard, I may succeed in surprising and overwhelming them."

Almost certainly Leyden had been foremost in his mind when these words were written in the immediate aftermath of his failure against Alkmaar. On the principle of the fox and the grapes, if for no other reason, it was a tempting prize—the key to central Holland and the Orangist strongholds along the Meuse which now lay in a wedge between the Spanish-held Amsterdam-Haarlem line and the bulk of the Spanish territory south of the rivers. To attack these mainland strongholds rather than the islands of Zeeland was sound strategic sense. But for a proper understanding of what happened it is at first sight puzzling that the assault, when it came under the Duke's successor, should have been launched not against the southern flank of Orangist territory and from the south, where the main Spanish strength lay, but on Leyden and from the northeast. The explanation lies simply in the geography of Holland, which was well protected by its water defenses except against an enemy who held the entrance to its back door—Amsterdam—and the roads and canals radiating down from it through the low-lying country of Rhynland, of which Leyden was the capital.

The Prince of Orange, whose strategic instinct was much superior to his ability as a field commander, had seen the danger of such a thrust and had done his best to guard against it. But Leyden, after triumphantly enduring its first five-month siege, had been in no mood to listen to his warnings. When Valdez had moved off in March the last thought in anyone's mind had been that they would see him back in May. The town had not been reprovisioned; its small Orangist garrison, which cost the citizens money, had actually been sent packing. And even when the Spaniards did return and with sinister precision seized and fortified their blockading points across every road and canal on the perimeter, the mood in the town remained astonishingly calm. Not till July, when the siege had lasted well over a month, was a register made of grain stocks available to feed the fourteen thousand inhabitants of the place. The tally came to less than nine thousand bushels; but even then no central collecting points or rationing system were set up; the brewers were allowed to brew; the rich to supply themselves with vegetables from their market gardens outside the walls.

Small wonder that as the summer wore on signs of famine began to appear; and with them the plague, which was raging throughout the provinces, and the first symptoms of discontent, for it must be remembered—*pace* Motley—that Leyden was no more a wholly Calvinist town than any other in the Netherlands and contained its fair share of the fainthearted and the disloyal, even when its actively pro-Spanish citizens (known as Glippers) had left it and gone over to the enemy.

For Orange, the siege had set a problem of the gravest kind. He could not abandon the town, for rebel morale could afford no more disasters like Haarlem. But he had no field army worthy of the name, and just as certainly there seemed no point in using up the last resources of his towns along the Meuse to pay for a new batch of German mercenaries to be treated as Sancho d'Avila had treated Count Louis on the heaths of Mook. Since the rebels could not face the Spaniards in the field, only one possible plan remained—to cut the dykes and open the sluices on the Meuse and Ysel* and allow their waters to flood north over the low-lying land, as the sea dykes had been used to save Alkmaar. But even here there were difficulties. Alkmaar lay close to the shore; Leyden was fifteen miles from the Ysel, and expert opinion was divided as to whether the river waters could be made to flow to a sufficient depth to allow a fleet of barges to breach the dykes guarding the polders of Delfland in a series of concentric rings, or flood to any depth at all in the slightly higher ground in Rhynland immediately south of the town.

Since there was no other way, however, the plan had to be tried, and on July 30 the States of Holland decided to attempt a relief "by boats or barges" and decreed that all costs and damages arising from the inundations should be borne jointly by the country and towns of Holland. The unfortunate peasants on the land now to be drowned were not consulted; no one had consulted them at Alkmaar either; they were simply ordered on the first of August to remove their goods and stock within eight days to an Orangist town or fort on pain of confiscation. On August 3 the Prince in person watched the first cutting of the Ysel dykes at Kapelle, soon followed by the opening of the sluices of the Meuse near Rotterdam, and the water began to flow over the polders of Delfland toward the raised dyke called the *Landscheiding* which ran in a

* The Ysel near Leyden is to be distinguished from the much larger Yssel draining into the Zuider Zee.

wide arc round the south and east perimeter of Rhynland. It was a slow business, slower even than the least hopeful of Orange's engineers had expected. But by the end of August, as the fleet of flat-bottomed barges assembled under the Prince's admiral, Louis de Boisot, and his Zeeland crews, the villages of the middle land between Delft and Leyden had become islands in a vast and spreading lagoon.

Inside the town the fatuous optimism of the first weeks had given way to anxiety and bitter debate. The main organs of power, including the civic guard, were in the hands of the Orangists, but they had many enemies, and the propaganda of Valdez and the Glippers which continued to reach the town became increasingly persuasive as hunger began to lay its grip on the fainthearted and the not inconsiderable body of the well to do, who wanted to accept the pardon which Requesens was now offering to all those who would acknowledge the King and the Catholic religion.

For more than a week, between the twelfth and twentieth of August, no messages came in from the Orangist camp. The beleaguered city felt itself abandoned. On the twenty-seventh a mutiny broke out among the freebooters who formed part of its defense force: though soon quelled, it was a portent. On this same day new food regulations were announced; hoarding was prohibited, somewhat late in the day; surplus stocks were commandeered; all animals, including horses, were registered for slaughter. Four days later the grain supplies of the town ran out, and on the second of September the first distribution from the abattoirs of half a pound of meat and bone a day per person was made in the choir of St. Peter's Church.

The writing was on the wall and there were plenty to read it. Resistance among the discontented rose to a new height, fortified by a letter from Valdez offering terms "for the last time" to all the "stiff necked" who cared to listen. Bronkhorst, the Prince's governor, was on his deathbed with the plague, and in his absence the Chief Burgomaster, van der Werf, though himself an Orangist, felt the need to call an assembly of the magistrates, aldermen, nobles and officers of the civic guard to debate the answer which the town should give.

It was an almost fatal decision. Of the corporation of the "Forty," as they were called, only seven were resolute for resistance, in spite of the lead given them by the elderly Jacob van der Does, member of the States of Holland, and a few supporters from the nobility and guard captains. This was not the heroic Leyden of legend but something more humdrum, more human and infinitely more credible. And from the great debate the most perfect of compromises emerged. Delegates would be sent to ask Orange and the States to release the town in its extremity from its solemn oath to resist the Spaniards—a prescription in fact for surrender which satisfied all those who desired it. But these delegates were sent through the Spanish lines under a flag of truce with the quite unacceptable request for a week's consultation with the Orangists in Delft. Of course Valdez cut short the whole abortive mission. On the sixth and the tenth of September other assemblies were held and despairing letters were sent out by the grapevine to the Prince. The Orangists still controlled the city, but by a constantly narrowing margin. And then on the eleventh, soon after dawn, the sound of heavy firing was heard from the south.

Early that day Boisot's fleet of barges, manned by a Beggar force and two companies of French arquebusiers, had surprised the enemy on the *Landscheiding* and had cut it to allow the Delfland floods to flow northward into Rhynland. Beyond the *Landscheiding*, another road, the *Groeneweg*, raised itself on its dyke the few vital feet above the polders, now filling with water, on which the barges were advancing. For some reason the existence of this road had not been known to Boisot or his engineers, but no Spanish forces had established themselves along it, and that same day—the eleventh of September—the relief force sailed through the breaches they had made in it and found themselves within two miles of open water of the Zoetermeer lake, more than halfway to Leyden from their start line in Rotterdam. Again unknown to them—one wonders why—another road, the *Voorweg*, stretched in an arc across their path, lined with peasants' huts and outbuildings which Valdez had taken care to fortify and garrison with three thousand men. So shallow was the water flowing from the rivers through the breaches in the *Landscheiding* and *Groeneweg* that navigation up to the line of this unexpected barrier was only possible for Boisot's barges along the courses of the drainage ditches, which grew shallower as they approached the *Voorweg*, or up the line of a canal which was commanded at its crossing point on the road bridge by the well-sited Spanish artillery.

On the seventeenth of September Boisot assaulted this immensely strong position. The delay of nearly a week since the cutting of the *Groeneweg* had been due to the need for calling up not only reinforcements of the troop-carrying barges but also a flotilla of cannonfiring vessels which it was hoped would neutralize the Spanish cannon at the bridge. The result was a rebel disaster. Not for the first time in the history of warfare it was proved that land-based guns had the mastery of the guns of a fleet—and this was a fleet of mudlarkers adrift on a few ditches in fields perhaps one to one and a half feet deep in water. Clearly the direct route to Leyden was impregnable to this kind of assault; but while the disconsolate Orangist leaders were debating what to do, a member of the Prince's council arrived at their headquarters with the suggestion that a fresh attempt should be made to breach the ring of dykes much further to the east, from Schieland, where the floods were reported to be higher and still rising in the gale now blowing off the sea.

The plan was immediately adopted and a scouting force of eight galleys, with a picked body of arquebusiers and pioneers aboard, set out on a wide sweep into Schieland, passing without difficulty over the submerged eastern extension of the *Landscheiding* and breaching their old bugbear of the *Voorweg* on a day of teeming rain without interference from the stormbound Spaniards in the nearby villages. The main fleet of barges was now brought up, and on September 21 Boisot and an advance guard of galleys broke right through the enemy defenses to the small Noordla lake beyond the Zoetermeer, only a few miles from Leyden, whose steeples could be clearly seen next morning when the Beggar flotillas were drawn up on the Weeport Vliet canal to fire a triumphant salute of guns toward the town.

That same day in Leyden the first of the horses were slaughtered to make up a ration of a quarter pound of horseflesh and a quarter pound of beef, including bone and fat. "It is the truth," reads one journal of the siege, "that some go to bed seemingly in good health, but are found dead in the morning, killed by famine, three or four together in one house." By famine alone? The plague was raging in the city, whose sufferings, set out in the stark narratives of the times, make no light reading.

But from the eleventh of September, when the gunfire of Boisot's fleet had first been heard from the *Landscheiding*, the Orangist authorities had the town well in hand, in spite of occasional defeatist outbreaks and the despair of the sick and starving. "I cannot break my oath," the Chief Burgomaster, van der Werf, had told them, "but if my body can serve you, cut it in pieces and distribute it among yourselves"—heroics which may ring false today but were not without point in the context of an hour that demanded fine gestures on the model of Haarlem, where the last loaves of bread in the starving city had been tossed in defiance into the Spanish camp. So in Leyden, on the twenty-second of September, with famine stalking the streets, negotiations with the enemy were finally broken off. That was the day when the salute of Boisot's guns had been heard from the Noordla lake, but only silence followed—no letters reached the town; there was nothing to be seen of the relieving fleet or indeed of the floods beyond a trickle of water in the polders.

For since the storm which had launched the Beggars on their offensive from Schieland the wind had changed into the east and the flood levels had dropped. The lightest of Boisot's craft drew one and a half feet of water, while only an average of one foot lay over the meadows north of the anchorage on the lake, except in the two canals leading toward Leyden which were blocked by Spanish strong points at Leyderdorp and Zoeterwoude. There was no choice but to wait for a change of weather to float the barges across the fields and the barrier of the *Kirklaan* road which lay like another *Voorweg* across their path.

Nearly another week of almost unbearable frustration went by for the Orangist leaders and their crews cooped up in open barges on the lake. For well over a month the Prince of Orange had lain dangerously ill at Rotterdam, but on September 28, a day of brilliant sunshine, he was rowed out to review his fleet and bring what comfort he could. The very next day the weather changed and a gale blew from the northwest, driving the high September tides of the North Sea into the estuary of the Meuse, whose waters piled up and burst through the sluices and breaches in the dykes, flooding into Rhynland to a depth of three feet or more.

No time was wasted. At midnight on the first/second of October the whole rebel armada got under way, driving the Spaniards off the *Kirklaan* in the storm and darkness lit by the flash of cannon, and forcing their barges through the cuts into the waterlogged country beyond, among the "quiet orchards" Motley describes, with the "chimney stacks of half-submerged farmhouses" rising above the floods. The great Dutch historian Robert Fruin, in a book written to commemorate the three hundredth anniversary of the siege, has a passage in which he describes these midnight capers, surely among the oddest in the history of war:

Meanwhile the water was rushing in the direction of Leyden through the wide openings that had been cut. It was barely given time to rise sufficiently. Hardly was it deep enough to carry the galleys, when they all pushed through and over the Kirklaan, and the early morning of October 2nd found the whole flotilla struggling in the shallows beyond. It could hardly be called sailing: the galleys went sliding and scraping over the ground. Rather than wait for the water to fill the vast polder, the crews jumped overboard and shoved and hauled the ships along by main force over the shallows, until at last they reached the wide and deep canal of the Meerburg.

Ahead of them lay two Spanish-held redoubts. One—Zoeterwoude —had already been outflanked and its garrison was in flight westward through the floodwaters toward safety in The Hague. But the second, at Lannen, within three hundred yards of Leyden and little more than a mile from Valdez's headquarters at Leyderdorp, was a more formidable proposition altogether, since it stood on higher ground impervious to floods and commanded the canal which was the one entry point for shipping coming from the south.

On the afternoon of October 2 Boisot carefully reconnoitered this new obstacle, all too reminiscent of the Spanish positions on the *Voorweg* which had given him a bloody nose. He had graver cause for concern, for before making his assault across the *Kirklaan* he had sent off a carrier pigeon with a request for a diversionary attack on Lannen by the Leyden civic guard, and not a sign of movement on the walls had even acknowledged it. To taut nerves, this inactivity suggested either the extremes of famine or the actual fall of the town.

In fact there was a simpler explanation. The pigeon—perhaps the most provoking bird in history—had lost its way. Not till late on October 2, well after the piercing of the *Kirklaan*, did it eventually turn up inside the walls with its message. But early on the morning of the third the civic guard set out to remedy their failure with a last desperate assault on the blockading fort. Right to the end the fates played their game with Leyden: even to the provision of a thick morning mist which lay over the polders, masking the approach of Boisot's fleet from the spearheads of the town militia—both advancing on a fort no longer occupied.

For in the night the Spaniards had decamped. Brave to a fault in battle, the *tercios* of Valdez had not stood to face the advance of a few feet of river water. And who shall blame them? A great number—perhaps a thousand—had died further back toward the *Kirklaan* in the inferno of the night battle as Boisot's fleet had swept through the defenses. The fall of their last and perhaps impregnable post in Lannen was announced through the morning mists by a boy from Leyden who had seen their torches moving in the night on the path to Leyderdorp and waved his cap from the battlements of the now deserted fort.

On such a note, Leyden was relieved. A few hours later, when the obstacles in the canal had been cleared, Boisot's ships were anchored at its quays. That same day the news reached Delft, where the Prince of Orange was at worship. No one interrupted the sermon for an announcement.

10

THE PRINCE OF ORANGE. MUTINIES.
THE SPANISH FURY. 1574–76.

For Orange the relief of Leyden was a watershed. Before it his aim
had been simply survival in face of overwhelming Spanish power.
But after Leyden had been saved and the whole of southern
Holland cleared of the mutinous defeated troops, the future
beckoned to much wider liberties and his main preoccupations
were less military than diplomatic, in a search for allies to help
him free the "entire fatherland" of seventeen provinces, not all
of which seemed aware of their common heritage.

These new problems were to prove just as intractable as the old
ones, for even in the liberated lands of Holland and Zeeland the
Prince was by no means free to act as he pleased. His anomalous
position as "governor" on behalf of a King with whom he was at
war was certainly the least of his troubles, for this was a fiction
which everyone understood. But his powers were derived not
from one unified state but from two provinces very diverse in
character and jealous of their independent rights. Not for nearly
two more years were they to federate. As a humanist, a man who
would have been at home in the more liberal climate of Erasmus,
he desired freedom of conscience for everyone—Lutheran, Calvinist,
Catholic. Yet the highly organized Reformed Church, of which he
was now himself a member and which provided the indispensable
dynamic of revolt, had no intention of tolerating anyone who was
not of God's elect. This made for trouble and indeed for massacres
on Protestant soil appallingly reminiscent of Alva and the Blood
Council but which the Prince had no power to check. And even the
more aristocratic and tolerant "Regents" of the towns and the
delegates of the provincial "Estates," though they professed their
boundless devotion and pressed honors upon him of "absolute
might, authority and sovereign control," were not always as generous with gifts of cash and political understanding. Small wonder

that in his loneliness his thoughts should have turned to a third marriage, no matter what the cost. And diplomatically it was enormous, since his chosen bride, Charlotte de Bourbon, a French princess of the house of Montpensier, was an ex-nun, indeed an ex-abbess, and by taking her he offended not only the Catholics of the southern provinces but also the Lutheran relatives of Anna of Saxony, who was still living in confinement in Germany. What the world felt was well expressed by the old Landgrave of Hesse:

I cannot understand what the Prince is thinking of. . . . *Nam si pietam respicias.* If you consider piety, you must remember that she is French, and a nun, a runaway nun at that, about whom all kinds of stories are told of the way she kept her cloister vows before the Prince wanted to jump from the frying pan into the fire.
Si formam. If it is beauty he is after, you can hardly believe that he was charmed by that, since undoubtedly no one can look at her without being more frightened than pleased.
Si spem prolis. The Prince has indeed already too many children for his needs, and if he were in his senses would wish himself without wife or child.
Si amicitiam. If he wants friendship, we do not believe he will get it. Her own father is so incensed against her that the Prince cannot expect much gratitude from him and her relatives.
So we cannot imagine what has led him into this business, which will estrange many of his friends. . . .

All of which was forceful and true. Yet the marriage was a domestic success and brought the Prince much happiness along with a fresh brood of children. *Si spem prolis!*

In Spain there was a *need* for heirs, not for continence as advocated by the Landgrave. The Infante Don Carlos had been dead nearly seven years. But about the time of the Prince's marriage, a son, Don Diego, was born to Philip by his third wife and niece, Anne of Austria. The King's problems were usually the converse of his rival's, their natures curiously similar in the tenacity and stoicism that marked them as they grew old in enmity together. Where they chiefly differed was in the King's almost pathological inability to make up his mind about the provinces. He desired peace but not the means by which it could be won. He was prepared to make concessions, but only irrelevant ones, like a general pardon and the abolition of the Tenth Penny which had been buried in the rubble of Alva's regime and the waters outside Leyden. Beyond that he would not go. Had he not said that he would rather lose the Netherlands than reign as a king of heretics? Yet no one—not even his unfortunate representative in Brussels—knew more certainly that he had not the means or the sinews for waging war. In the autumn of 1575 he was declaring the second suspension of payments of his reign. The brush-fire affair against two small rebellious provinces had bankrupted the Spanish exchequer.

Along with Spain and its empire, Philip had inherited from his father twenty million ducats worth of debts, which was more than twice his income, plus a liability for *juros* (annuities chargeable to revenue) to the tune of perhaps another fifty million.

This appalling situation had resulted in the first suspension of payments in 1557, in the form of the creation of a floating debt at interest of 5 per cent. The manipulation had not impressed the moneylenders of Augsburg, Antwerp or Genoa, where the royal bonds became negotiable only at a heavy discount, and interest rates for future borrowings were raised proportionately.

As a result, by 1575, the Crown's debts to its bankers had gone up to nearly forty million ducats. Yet even in the affluent 1580s, annual revenue did not exceed ten million ducats from all sources; in 1575 it was perhaps eight million, made up roughly in a ratio of two and a half/to one and a half/to one/from the Castilian taxes, ecclesiastical dues including Papal contributions, and the royal share of silver from the Indian mines. None of the other Spanish dependencies contributed anything; and even Aragon, Valencia and Catalonia, though integral parts of the peninsula, were for taxable purposes worthless.

As against this, the war in the Netherlands was already costing two million ducats annually, nearly twice the Crown's receipts from the Indies at the time—the provinces which had helped to pay for the Emperor's wars were now no more than an encumbrance.

As we can see now, with the benefit of hindsight, there were three possible ways out of an intolerable situation. The King could have made over the Netherlands to some third party allied to

him by interest or blood. This was the solution which the Emperor
had had in mind when he had married Philip to Mary Tudor
in the hopes of an heir who would unite England and the Netherlands under one crown, and Philip was himself to resurrect another
version of it at the end of his life, when he handed over what
remained of his seventeen provinces to his daughter and her
Austrian husband as joint rulers. A similar result could have been
obtained much earlier and at far less cost by coming to terms
with the Orangists and partitioning the provinces along the lines
of military occupation after the relief of Leyden, which would
have saved the bulk of them for Spain. Best of all might have
been to cut all political connection with the Netherlands and
treat them not as a possession which cost money but as a trading
partner in the great capitalist expansion of Europe which lay
ahead. But that is to enter the world of the ideal. Trade could
not be confined to Europe. The Dutch seamen and merchants of
the northern provinces would certainly have wanted their share
of the Indies trade, Castile's most jealously guarded preserve.

In any case the King did not think of his problem in such
terms. He was concerned as a Catholic to guard the faith in all
its purity throughout the seventeen provinces; and as a Spaniard
and his father's political heir he was determined to keep his pat-
rimony of Burgundy from the embrace of France, the ancestral
enemy, whose aim over centuries had been to absorb it.

These beliefs and these policies were not unreasonable in themselves; they were merely unenforceable, except at the price of
national bankruptcy which could be disguised but not evaded. The
greatest care was taken by the King and his councils to explain
that the suspension of payments of 1575 was merely a move against
profiteers and that in good time the deserving would be paid
in full, if at a lower rate of interest. Estimable provision!—destined
indeed to enjoy a considerable success and to stave off the next
bankruptcy for twenty-one years. No one seems to have thought
of the short-range effects of a lowering of interest rates which
amounted to a cancellation of half the royal debts. In Seville,
two of the largest banks defaulted. The Indies fleet could not sail.
The great fair at Medina del Campo, the barometer of Castilian
prosperity, was forced to close. Suddenly, throughout Europe,
among the financiers who had sustained the Emperor and his
son in their adventures, Spanish credit went sour. No one would

lend money, even on the old *asiento* system by which the royal revenues were mortgaged in advance at the most appealing rates of interest. There was simply no more money to be had. And certainly no one seemed to have pondered very deeply on the reaction among the Spanish garrisons in the Netherlands once they became acquainted with this fact. It was a fateful omission.

The Spanish retreat from Leyden had been followed by a winter and spring of diplomatic maneuvering, during which Requesens had first tried to extract money from the fifteen nominally loyal provinces and had then entered into direct negotiations with the Orangists in a conference at Breda in the presence of an imperial ambassador. Both these initiatives had failed, and in the summer and autumn of 1575 the Grand Commander had launched a three-pronged offensive against the rebel provinces, culminating in an attack on their sea bases in Zeeland under his own personal direction.

Seldom had the Spanish Army performed such prodigies; even Mondragon's fantastic march over the mud flats of the Scheldt was emulated as the assaulting columns waded through sea channels commanded by a Beggar fleet to pen their enemies into the port of Zeirickzee, whose capture would open up the coastline of Walcheren to Spain. Motley describes the scene, which can stand for countless other deeds of Spanish valor in these campaigns:

On the night selected for the enterprise, that of 27th September, the moon was a day old in its fourth quarter, and rose a little before twelve. It was low water at between four and five in the morning. The Grand Commander, at the appointed hour of midnight, crossed to Philipsland, and stood on the shore to watch the setting forth of the little army. . . . Don Osorio d'Ulloa then stripped and plunged into the sea immediately after the guides. He was followed by the Spaniards, after whom came the Germans, and then the Walloons. The two hundred sappers and miners came next, and Don Gabriel Peralta, with his Spanish company, brought up the rear. It was a wild night. Incessant lightning alternately obscured and revealed the progress of the midnight march through the black waters, as the anxious Commander watched the expedition from the shore, but the soldiers were quickly swallowed up in the gloom. As they advanced cautiously, two by two, the daring adventurers found themselves soon nearly up to their necks in the waves, while so narrow was the submerged bank along which they were marching, that a mis-step to the right or left was fatal. Luckless individuals repeatedly sank to rise no more. Meantime, as the sickly light of the waning moon came forth at intervals through the stormy clouds, the soldiers could plainly perceive the files of Zeeland vessels through which they were to march, and which were anchored as close to the flat as the water would allow. Some had recklessly stranded themselves, in their eager-ness to interrupt the passage of the troops, and the artillery played unceasingly from the larger vessels. Discharges of musketry came con-tinually from all, but the fitful lightning rendered the aim difficult and the fire comparatively harmless, while the Spaniards were, moreover, protected, as to a large part of their bodies, by the water in which they were immersed.

At times, they halted for breath, or to engage in fierce skirmishes with their nearest assailants. Standing breast high in the waves, and sur-rounded at intervals by total darkness, they were yet able to pour an oc-casional well directed volley into the hostile ranks. The Zeelanders, how-ever, did not assail them with firearms alone. They transfixed some with their fatal harpoons; they dragged others from the path with boat-hooks; they beat out the brains of others with heavy flails. Many were the mortal duels thus fought in the darkness, and, as it were, in the bottom of the sea; many were the deeds of audacity which no eye was to mark save those by whom they were achieved. Still, in spite of all impediments and losses, the Spaniards steadily advanced.

These were the preliminaries to the nine-month-long siege of Zeirickzee, which duly fell in the summer of 1576. It was a great triumph for Spanish arms and for Requesens' strategic insight. Un-fortunately he was not there to see it, for he had died of fever that March. And still more unfortunately for Spain—indeed fate-fully as things turned out—the besieging army had barely seen the rebel garrison march out from the fortress with the honors of war than it broke into mutiny and marched off to the mainland, where it was joined by other mutinous units in search of pay or at least a town to sack.

With the Grand Commander's death the government of the Netherlands had devolved on the Council of State, a high-sounding body which in fact comprised one Spaniard of force, by the name of de Roda, and a group of timeserving Catholic grandees under the leadership—if such a word can be used of him—of the Duke of Aerschot, the supertrimmer of the age. This was of course a profoundly unrepresentative body without power of authority, and its efforts to halt the tide of anarchy, rising fast as the *tercios* seized the town of Alost, near the threatened capital, were so obviously doomed to failure that the province of Brabant took fright and began to enlist troops for self-defense. Everything was in flux. The Prince of Orange, sensing the opportunity, was busy pulling strings from an advanced base at Middelburg. The hub of the Netherlands, which still lay in Flanders and Brabant, was in uproar, and for the first time since the "Compromise of the Nobles" in 65–66 the prospect had opened up of a large-scale rising which could possibly be fanned to embrace all seventeen provinces.

That September a young enthusiast in touch with Orange, Baron Hèze, in command of the defense force recently raised in Brabant, took the first illegal step by invading the Council of State and arresting its members, though not de Roda, who had fled to the army and was proclaiming himself the King's sole representative pending the arrival of a new Governor General from Spain. Through the general chaos the forms of long-submerged organs of power began once more to show themselves. The "States" of Brabant met and summoned the fifteen nominally loyal provinces to send representatives to a new States General, this revolutionary move being buttressed and given a show of legality by the release of some of the state councilors, including Aerschot, who reconstituted themselves and gave their official blessing to the scheme.

The response was disappointing, for only Brabant, Flanders and Hainaut attended the first meetings. Interprovincial fears and jealousies ran high, and among the Catholic grandees who were now embarked on this halfhearted revolution against the King there was a natural reluctance to burn boats or to throw themselves into the arms of Orange and the Calvinist-dominated states of Holland and Zeeland with whom they were still officially at war.

In this crisis the Prince was at his most persuasive: his fraternal letters to the southern delegates were masterpieces of logic and good sense:

Understand your own position. Steer yourselves away from this dire confusion, which is the true base of tyranny and has been the source of ruin to republics from time immemorial. To do this, union among yourselves is important above all. . . . My advice, subject to your correction, is, write to the King that you resolutely refuse to endure any

longer the incubus of his foreign troops or to submit to the an-
nihilation of all your rights. Express yourselves clearly, without am-
biguity. Let this letter be signed by all the provincial estates . . . by
all individuals of dignity in the land. . . . This action would act like a
spur to your deliberations. Your position would be defined. . . . You
will then be in a position to act together and to feel mutual obligation
to defend your action. Weighty deeds must bear the stamp of their own
importance. . . . Let him [the King] see that it is the general voice of
the people speaking, that the Estates are supported in their protest
by great and small.

Nevertheless he was distrusted by a wide section of opinion in
Brabant. There was an element of preaching, and worse, a strain
of demagogy and republicanism in these outpourings highly repugnant to men like Aerschot who wanted the Spanish troops
out of the country but certainly no break with the age-old loyalties
of the provinces to their ruler. Reminders set out in this same
letter to "See what Holland and Zeeland have done in five years"
were scarcely tactful when addressed to magnates who had contrived to sit on the fence throughout that time. Indeed, so deep
was this distrust, and so wide the gulf in religion and social
theory between the Catholic nobles of the States General and the
Orangists of the northwest, that even when the two sides were
brought together that October in conference at Ghent, progress
toward union was slow and might never have been achieved at
all if a startling event had not occurred to force everyone's hand.

Throughout that autumn the Spanish garrisons had lain in their
fortresses like so many time bombs primed and ready to explode.
Such sacking and pillaging as had come their way had been on a
comparatively modest scale and insufficient to meet their now
enormous arrears of pay. Yet, "If ever labourers were worthy of
their hire," wrote Motley, "certainly it was the Spanish soldiery.
Had they not done the work of demons for nine years long?" Resentment, anger, a hatred of heresy, a bitter sense of betrayal and
injustice had been building up pressures whose outward signs were
clearly visible. Observers were astonished at the ferocious self-
discipline and religious fervor of these mutineers, whose devotions
were marked by ceremonial oaths and scourgings and displays
of banners and sacred images reminiscent of some *auto-da-fé* staged
by the Inquisition in Toledo or Seville. Few could doubt however

that the dominant emotion was greed for gold. The Spanish Army, abandoned by its paymasters and shut up in its citadels throughout Flanders and Brabant, had become a vast freebooting enterprise, a joint stock company only seeking a suitable object to exploit.

Pat to its purpose lay Antwerp, in the Italian Bentivoglio's words an "Indies of a city," perhaps the richest in the Western world, the home of every bourgeois comfort, yet lying temptingly at the mercy of a fortress of enormous strength. By the end of October it had become obvious that some attempt on this treasure house was imminent. On the twentieth the town of Maastricht on the Meuse had been sacked with the utmost savagery; by the twenty-ninth, Sancho d'Avila, commanding Antwerp citadel, was busily at work subverting the German contingents guarding the town itself. The danger was so evident that for once the authorities in Brussels were moved to act with energy and dispatched a mixed force of six thousand Walloon infantry and cavalry, which took up positions inside the walls on the third of November.

It is impossible not to feel a certain impatience with Antwerp. Here was a city of perhaps a hundred thousand souls, well garrisoned once the reinforcements from Brussels were in place, under a resolute governor, yet no defense works of any kind had been attempted or *were* attempted until the very last hours before the assault, and even then they were skimped and grossly inadequate. Only the governor, Champagney, Cardinal Granvelle's youngest brother but no lover of Spaniards, seems to have shown any energy or understanding of what was required of a city in a virtual state of siege and liable to instant bombardment and sack of a kind sickeningly familiar from the recent fates of Naarden and Maastricht.

In the citadel, where d'Avila's veterans were under arms, there was only impatience for the work to begin. Reinforced at dawn on November 4 by a large body of fellow mutineers from Alost eager to "dine in Paradise or sup in Antwerp," the garrison marched out to the attack, perhaps five thousand strong, supported by the guns of the fortress and the comforts of religion. Motley describes the scene with indignant scorn:

In the counterscarp they fell upon their knees, to invoke, according to custom, the blessing of God on the devil's work which they were about to commit. The *Eletto* bore a standard, one side of which was emblazoned with the crucified Saviour, and the other with the Virgin Mary. The image of Him who said, "Love your enemies," and the gentle face of the Madonna, were to smile from heaven upon deeds which might cause a shudder in the depths of hell. Their brief orisons concluded, they swept forward to the city.

Within minutes the battle was decided. The Walloons broke at the first onslaught and the disciplined columns of mutineers burst through the pitifully weak defenses and fanned out into the heart of Antwerp which they grasped in a ring of steel and fire. Motley describes the fury of the assault:

Meanwhile, the Spanish cavalry had cleft its way through the city. On the side farthest removed from the castle, along the Horse-market . . . the States dragoons and the light horse of Beveren had been posted, and the flying mass of pursuers and pursued swept at last through this outer circle. Champagney was already there. He essayed, as his last hope, to rally the cavalry for a final stand, but the effort was fruitless. Already seized by panic, they had attempted to rush from the city through the gate of Eeker. It was locked; they then turned and fled towards the Red gate, where they were met face to face by Don Pedro Tassis, who charged upon them with his dragoons. Retreat seemed hopeless. A horseman in complete armour, with lance in rest, was seen to leap from the parapet of the outer wall into the moat below, whence, still on horseback, he escaped with his life. Few were so fortunate. The confused mob of fugitives and conquerors, Spaniards, Walloons, Germans, burghers, struggling, shouting, striking, cursing, dying, swayed hither and thither like a stormy sea. Along the spacious Horse-market the fugitives fled onwards towards the quays. Many fell beneath the swords of the Spaniards, numbers were trodden to death by the hooves of horses, still greater multitudes were hunted into the Scheldt.

There remained the mopping up.

Meantime, while the short November day was fast declining, the combat still raged in the interior of the city. Various currents of conflict, forcing their separate ways through many streets, had at last mingled in the *Grande Place*. Around this irregular, not very spacious square, stood the gorgeous *Hotel de Ville*, and the many-storied, fantastically-gabled, richly-decorated palaces of the guilds. Here a long struggle took place. It was terminated for a time by the cavalry of

Vargas, who arriving through the streets of Saint Joris, accompanied by the traitor Van Ende, charged decisively into the mêlée. The masses were broken, but multitudes of armed men found refuge in the buildings, and every house became a fortress. From every window and balcony a hot fire was poured into the square, as, pent in a corner, the burghers stood at last at bay. It was difficult to carry the houses by storm, but they were soon set on fire. . . . The conflagration spread with rapidity, house after house, street after street, taking fire. Nearly a thousand buildings, in the most splendid and wealthy quarter of the city, were soon in a blaze, and multitudes of human beings were burned with them. In the City-hall, many were consumed, while others leaped from the windows to renew the combat below. The many tortuous streets which led down a slight descent from the rear of the Town-house to the quays were all one vast conflagration. On the other side, the magnificent cathedral, separated from the *Grande Place* by a single row of buildings, was lighted up but not attacked by the flames. The tall spire cast its gigantic shadow across the last desperate conflict. . . . Women, children, old men, were killed in countless numbers, and still, through all this havoc, directly over the heads of the struggling throng, suspended in mid-air above the din and smoke of the conflict, there sounded, every quarter of every hour, as if in gentle mockery from the belfry of the cathedral the tender and melodious chimes.

After the battle, the massacre, then the search for treasure; rape was the last in time of Antwerp's sufferings. In a letter to the King, de Roda estimated the dead at over eight thousand, a figure which has been questioned but may not be far from the truth.

De Roda counted this a victory for the King over his enemies. He was mistaken. The events of November 4, 1576, destroyed Antwerp's pre-eminence, for never again was the troublesome city to dominate so completely the trade of northern Europe. But the "Spanish Fury," as it was long remembered, was a still greater calamity for Spain. The shock of it united, if only for the moment, forces, by no means all of which had been inimical to Philip. Within a week of the massacre the Catholic States General and the Orangists of Holland and Zeeland overcame their differences and signed the Pacification of Ghent, a treaty of peace between the provinces and of alliance against tyrannical rule. What diplomacy had been unable to do in ten years the Spanish Army had accomplished in a day.

11

PACIFICATION OF GHENT. SUMMIT OF
PATRIOT FORTUNES. ORANGE AT BRUSSELS. 1576–77.

The Pacification of Ghent was a landmark in Netherlands history: the first truly independent act of provinces feeling their way toward self-government and liberty of person if not of conscience. In prints of the time we see charming idealizations of what the Pacification meant or was intended to mean to contemporaries. Inside a low, circular wickerwork cage, whose open gate is guarded by a heraldic lion, seventeen maidens representing the seventeen provinces sit demurely with shields in their laps emblazoned with their respective coats of arms, oblivious of the threatening gestures of a besieging ring of Spanish soldiers in full armor who aim everything at them from lances to sizable cannon.

This has a distinct flavor of Orangist propaganda, not to say wishful thinking, for the seventeen provinces were not all that cozily unanimous or anything like as secure from danger as the artist would have us believe. Only a minority actually signed it. But the Pacification was at least a beginning. By this treaty the Catholic center and south made peace with their Orangist sisters and all jointly agreed to expel the Spanish garrisons. On the religious front, where some accord was urgently needed, Holland and Zeeland were to profess the new religion, the Catholic provinces the old, without interference from one another, and everywhere the savage edicts of Charles and Philip were suspended pending a final settlement which the States General were to work out.

Such were the main terms. Though it had an Orangist bent and contained many provisions personally beneficial to the Prince, the Pacification was a popular act and met needs and aspirations that were widely felt at the time. Some months later, in January 1577, it was enlarged into a broader consensus in the Union of Brussels, signed not only be representatives of every province (except Luxemburg), but also by almost all their important dignitaries, in solemn reaffirmation of unity in face of a new danger. For on November 3, 1576, the day before the Spanish Fury in Antwerp, Requesens' successor as Governor General had arrived in Luxemburg from Spain—the King's half brother, Don John of Austria, the victor of Lepanto.

On the face of it this seemed an excellent choice, for as the son of Charles V Don John could appeal to the memory of his father's popularity in the Netherlands and to the tradition by which the provinces were always held to have prospered under the rule of royal siblings, whether legitimate or not. Admittedly his mother, Barbara Blomberg,* a lady of Ratisbon, had in a moment of pique cast some doubt upon his parentage and provided Motley with one of his best comments, straight out of Gibbon—"Baseborn at best, he was not sure whether to look for the author of his being in the halls of Caesar or in the booths of Ratisbon mechanics." But this was just Motley's fun, since this "last crusader whom the annals of chivalry were to know" was clearly a chip off the Emperor's block, a fine fellow, handsome, charming, gifted, and wearing the laurels of the most celebrated victory of the age.

Why then have historians been so unkindly critical of the appointment and the man?

The obvious answer must be that Don John failed in the Netherlands; but then others with greater qualities have failed when given impossible assignments. The King wanted peace, wanted it sincerely—even Motley concedes this. Desiring peace, it was perhaps unwise to confide the getting of it to a man whose reputation had been made in war and whose interests were not in the Netherlands at all but were concerned with romantic dreams of a throne to be won and a damsel in distress to be rescued—in fact the throne of England and the hand of the imprisoned Mary Queen of Scots! These were not insuperable drawbacks, however, since Don John was never to pursue his chimeras very far. More to the point were the King's instructions, which were to ensure by "good, just and reasonable means . . . a true, stable and durable pacification," by adhering "in love, gentleness and benevolence" to the

---

* She was now the widow Kegell. Even Alva had been unable to control her scandalous activities. She was finally shipped off to Spain where she died.

laws of Charles V and giving "just and reasonable contentment to all."

How these surpassingly contradictory things were to be attained was not set out in the royal rescript. The placards of Charles V would have entailed burning at the stake a vast number of Calvinists, even without the assistance of the Blood Council which was officially suppressed. Yet in the same breath a general pardon was ordered to be proclaimed, excepting only the Prince of Orange, the author of all known evils. All means of pacification were to be employed, but subject to the proviso that the rights of the Catholic faith and of the Crown were to be maintained intact— by implication in Holland and Zeeland as well as in the still-Catholic south and east.

These were absurd provisions which could only have come from the King's cabinet, isolated as it was by hundreds of miles from the cockpit where they were supposed to be carried out; and to blame Don John for his failure to implement them is to show even greater ignorance and insensibility than Philip himself. No doubt the King should not have appointed a figure from the chivalry books to carry out a program which demanded the wisdom of a serpent and the duplicity of a born man of affairs. Appointed the unfortunate was, however. And within his limitations Don John did surprisingly well. Even his mistakes redounded to the credit of his successor.

The new Governor General had arrived in Luxemburg (rumor had it in the disguise of a Moorish slave) in the autumn of 1576 at precisely the moment when hatred of Spain was at its zenith and there existed an almost frantic desire to get the Spanish garrisons out of the provinces at almost any cost. This was not unpleasing to Don John, whose hopes for the moment were to embark the *tercios* on a squadron of Spanish ships still in Netherlands waters and descend with them on England to the rescue of the imprisoned Scottish queen. He was faced with harsh realities, however. From Luxemburg, the Cinderella of the seventeen provinces, he had first to get to Brussels to take up his inheritance in accordance with the ancient forms.

The States General, not to mention the Orangists, were in no wise prepared to allow this except on the most stringent terms.

The new Governor must be put in leading strings before being permitted to advance a yard further: he must subscribe to the Ghent Pacification as enlarged by the Union of Brussels.

Here was a bitter dose to swallow. To make it more palatable, the States General had procured a document signed by no less than eleven doctors and professors of theology at the University of Louvain to vouch for the fact that the Pacification did not contravene the Catholic religion, as it patently did, since it authorized heresy in at least two provinces and possibly in all seventeen. Faced with an ultimatum—and a very short-termed one at that—Don John behaved predictably: he fumed and nearly assaulted a delegate of the States with a weighty metal object. Reconsidering the matter with the assistance of the Duke of Aerschot, whose changing loyalties over the years defy analysis, he agreed to sign.

It was a surrender; but surrenders can be shrewdly timed. In fact Don John had little choice, since he had been enjoined to pacify and use no force. And by his agreement to abide by the Pacification, which was enshrined in a document called the Perpetual Edict, Don John, an innocent in diplomacy, managed to outflank the acknowledged master of the craft. The Prince of Orange had recommended a "flat and total breach" of any negotiations with the enemy. The States General, deeply suspicious of Orange anyway, jumped at the chance of self-assertion against the extremists on their flanks. In their eagerness to rid themselves of the Spanish garrisons, whose dismissal Don John was ready to concede, they even side-stepped the Pacification by agreeing with him that the Catholic religion should be maintained everywhere, just as the King was insisting.

Only Holland and Zeeland protested against the Perpetual Edict, which was signed on February 12 at Marche-en-Famine and published on the seventeenth in Brussels. The Prince's nose had been effectively put out of joint and Holland and Zeeland had been diplomatically isolated—no mean feat for a newcomer to Netherlands affairs, though neither Don John nor his mentor Aerschot have received many tributes from historians for their expertise. Orange's position in the matter was understandable. He distrusted everything that came out of Spain. Yet it is now accepted that Don John was loyally prepared to stand by his word. At the end of March the Spanish troops began to evacuate their citadels, soured by what they regarded as unmerited defeat but at least in receipt of their long-awaited pay: by the end of April these deadly succubi were on their way out of the provinces, going southward along the "Spanish Road" and not by sea, since the Queen of England had intervened forcibly to ensure she did not have to suffer their company.

By this time Don John had reached Louvain, close to Brussels, where he was well received, and in May he made his "Joyous Entry" into the capital which gave itself over to junketings on a scale not seen since the early years of the Duchess Margaret, with triumphal arches, parades, odes, banners, minstrelry and a pageant depicting the battle of Lepanto.

Motley suggests that nothing could have exceeded the hatred Don John felt for the provinces and the inhabitants who were providing him with so choice a display. This is unlikely. The Joyous Entry into Brussels was very much Don John's kind of ceremony, and as his father's son, and a bastard at that, he no doubt relished every allegorical moment.

Only for the moment, however. For some time his mind, and that of his faithful shadow and secretary Escovedo, had been somber in the extreme. The forced departure of the Spanish troops with whom they had hoped to descend on England had thoroughly embittered them, as their letters to Antonio Pérez abundantly show. "You are aware," Escovedo had written to the man who in a year's time was to have him murdered, "that a throne—a chair with a canopy—is our intention and our appetite, and all the rest is good for nothing. Having failed in our scheme, we are desperate and like madmen. All is weariness and death." Nor was Don John himself far behind in his own letters to Pérez—"Ah, Señor Antonio, how certain is my disgrace and my misfortune. Our enterprise is ruined, after so much labour and skilful enterprise."

This is ripe comedy, and one can imagine the astonishment of Philip when these extraordinary confidences found their way to him, as they assuredly did, for Pérez was playing a double game. But in his more responsible letters to the royal cabinet, even when not suffering from the enchantments of lost thrones, Don John had not proved much more reassuring. He was too artless and honest a correspondent. Before his entry into Brussels he had gone out of his way to assure the King that the royal name was execrated in the Netherlands and that only Orange's was respected. Hotfoot on this highly tactless truth, he had attempted to negotiate with the Prince, infinitely too wily a bird to be caught in the embrace of the first of Philip's governors, whom he felt sure he could outwit. The negotiations naturally failed. Now in Brussels, in Alva's chair but without the *tercios* whom Alva had commanded, the disconsolate Don John chose to reopen the dialogue with the antagonist whom he correctly saw as the pilot of the disaffected and the sole stumbling block to Spanish rule.

Thus opened the second diplomatic battle of the campaign, fought over ground where the Spaniards sought to show that the Perpetual Edict had replaced the Pacification of Ghent as the basic settlement, and Orange's delegates set out to prove that the Edict was no more than an illegal gloss on an agreement which the whole nation now adhered to.

In such maneuvers Don John was bound to fail: he was facing opponents who were utterly intransigent and who felt—correctly —that time was working on their side. He himself had undoubtedly done his best to curb his own impatient and choleric nature where heretics were concerned and to carry out the very uncongenial brief laid down for him in Madrid. His good faith at this time is indisputable and has the best documentary proof. "I negotiate with the Prince of Orange," he wrote to Philip, "so as to give him every surety, because I see that the establishment of peace, the maintenance of the Catholic religion and of the obedience due to Your Majesty now depend on him, and that the time has come when we must make a virtue of necessity. If he will only listen he will find my proposals are very advantageous to him. . . ." No doubt they were. Perhaps they were *too* advantageous for it became evident very soon that even the Governor's natural allies among the moderates of the States General were beginning to fall away as they sensed his impotence in face of the Orangist challenge and the halfhearted support he seemed to be receiving from the King.

Don John's inherent melancholia began rapidly to increase with these undeserved reverses. He felt himself to be unwanted, friendless and forlorn among "winebibbers" and "scoundrels" who increasingly despised and rejected him; for the enthusiasm of the people of Brussels had not long survived once the tinsel decorations of the Joyous Entry had been put back into storage, and he had begun to fear that plots were afoot to take his life.

In many ways Don John is a tragic and sympathetic figure. The extraordinary events of a life in which the fates had dealt him almost equal measures of triumph and frustration had created deep inroads in an ego never basically strong and had made him a prey to almost pathological despondency and self-doubt. In mid-June 1577, either feeling himself stifled in the political atmosphere of Brussels, or, according to one story, being warned at dead of night of plots to capture or assassinate him, he left the capital for Mechlin, ostensibly to arrange for the pay of certain German units which had remained behind after the departure of the *tercios*. From there he withdrew still further south to Namur on the more agreeable pretext of entertaining Marguerite de Valois,* the French king's sister, on her way to take the waters at Spa, and having sped her on her journey in her gilded barge along the Meuse, he suddenly arrived with a picked body of troops at the citadel on the heights above the town and seized it in a well-planned and ingenious coup. "This is the first day of my government," he is supposed to have exclaimed to the astonished castellan who had been peacefully breakfasting with him when the assault party rushed in.

As Regent and Captain General of the Netherlands, Don John had of course a perfect right to any fortress within its borders, and if he had acted more like a brigand than a ruler on this occasion, no one, not even the States General, had any legal right to complain.

Complain they did, however, with considerable acrimony, for the capture of this fortress at the confluence of the rivers Sambre and Meuse, where it could easily become a springboard for invasion if the *tercios* were ever to return up the "Spanish Road," had originally been planned to coincide with an attempt by the Governor's agents on Antwerp citadel, garrisoned by troops supposedly loyal to the States General.

Such an enterprise could not afford to fail, for "Antwerp citadel" were emotive words, the symbol of Alva's tyrannical rule and the place from which the Spanish Fury had been launched only months

---

* Marguerite was the wife of Henry of Navarre, later King Henry IV of France. Her wedding celebrations had been graced by the massacre of St. Bartholomew. She was really in the Netherlands to spy out the land for her favorite brother Anjou, who was about to make his own disastrous contribution to provincial affairs.

before. It was not a bad plot in its conception. Don John had a
fervent supporter in actual command of the fortress and colonels
of units stationed in the city who were prepared to act in the
King's name to restore the royal writ.

Yet in the event the plan collapsed in the most ignominious way
before it was even properly attempted, in face of an Orangist coup
which not only forestalled Don John by seizing the castle for the
Beggars but captured the very compromising letters he had addressed to the castellan and the colonels.

This time the outcry was enormous and was soon to result in the
partial dismantling of the great fortress, from whose cellars Alva's
vainglorious statue, cast from the cannon taken at Jemmingen,
was dragged into the light of day and hacked to pieces, while
throughout the country there was a huge revulsion in favor of
Orange, the one man who had consistently warned against Spanish
intentions and treachery. The unfortunate Governor was almost
overwhelmed by the disgrace of his failure and the appalling results which day by day became more evident. Humiliation after
humiliation was being heaped upon him, for several other dispatches which he and Escovedo had written to Spain had recently
fallen into the hands of Orange's Huguenot allies in Gascony and
had been forwarded to the States General, who were thus privileged
to learn what their erstwhile ally and ruler really thought of them.

At first the culprit tried to carry things with a high hand, with
peremptory demands that all armed forces should be placed under
his control, all rebels and heretics chastised and Antwerp citadel
returned to him. This was whistling in the dark, for his real
feelings, as revealed in a letter to his half sister the Dowager
Empress, had a much more despairing ring:

In truth they [the people] are willing to recognise neither God nor
king . . . they love and obey in all things the most perverse and heretical tyrant and rebel in the world, this damned Prince of Orange. . . .
I know not what to do with such rebelliously obstinate men.

These words were from the heart and their poignancy speaks
for itself. Yet even in the midst of his tribulations Don John
still had one remaining asset—the sheer inability of the conservative forces in the country to visualize any other government

than the one they had always been accustomed to, which derived from Spain under the wing of a Spanish governor.

The States General were deeply imbued with these traditionalist feelings. In a country rapidly moving toward revolution they remained half believers in an old establishment. Left to themselves they would no doubt have found some means of accommodation with the Governor (who for his part was prepared to accommodate himself to *them*), and some formula whereby the old loyalties to King and Pope could be continued, in a suitably modified form.

Events however had already made such policies meaningless, since the whole country was aflame with libertarian dreams and passionate resentment of the tyrannies of the past. This wave of hope, of protest, of faith, swept Orange into Antwerp in triumph on the eighteenth of September. Five days later, summoned by the distrustful but impotent States General, he made a grand progress by barge into the capital itself—an event preserved for us in contemporary prints imbued with the sense of a pompous but deeply meaningful ceremonial. Motley too preserves this to perfection:

On the 23rd of September he was attended by a vast concourse of citizens to the new canal which led to Brussels, where three barges were in waiting for himself and suite. In one a banquet was spread; in the second, adorned with emblematic devices and draped with the banners of the seventeen provinces, he was to perform the brief journey; while the third had been filled by the inevitable rhetoric societies, with all the wonders of their dramatic and plastic ingenuity. Rarely had such a combination of vices and virtues, of crushed dragons, victorious archangels, broken fetters, and resurgent nationalities, been seen before, within the limits of a single canal boat.

This was Don John's Joyous Entry all over again, with variations, less than six months after the event, but this time there was a steadier and more deliberate purpose behind the pageantry. Far off in Namur, Don John, who had all but agreed to a compromise with the States General which would have preserved Spanish rule in the Netherlands, if not his own governorship, was now presented with fresh terms wholly Orangist in character and raised to a level which no Spaniard could possibly accept—in effect an invitation, indeed a command, for him and his royal master to turn republican.

The wheel had come full circle. The Prince of Orange was no longer an exile, no longer the forlorn leader of two small provinces; he was no longer one element in a movement or conspiracy, but *de facto* ruler of the Netherlands.

12

ARCHDUKE MATTHIAS. GOVERNMENT AND DEATH OF DON JOHN. 1577-78.

The Prince had been brought to this position on a wave of national-ist fervor and detestation of Spanish rule which was common to almost all classes in the Flemish-speaking states, from the magnates of the States General to the burghers and artisans of the towns and the peasants of the countryside.

One must beware however of equating this nationalist feeling with a widespread sympathy for Calvinism, as Motley is apt to do. In fact two dynamics existed side by side: nationalism and Calvin-ism. Sometimes they overlapped. The Calvinists were all national-ists, but the converse was not true: only a small percentage of nationalists were sympathetic to the Reformed faith. Even in Hol-land and Zeeland the majority were probably still Catholic, though now completely under the domination of a Calvinist government which held every organ of power. In the Walloon provinces, where Calvinism had made its first appearance in the Netherlands, it had completely ceased to count in face of a strong Catholic reaction only waiting to become counterrevolutionary and pro-Spanish once given a lead. This applied also in the northeast, particularly around the Catholic stronghold of Groningen. At the heart of the Nether-lands, in Flanders and Brabant, the magnates and most of the countryside were also firmly Catholic. In the towns however Calvinism had been making headway; but whereas in Holland and Zeeland this Calvinism had become with success almost as conserv-ative and socially respectable as Catholicism itself, in Brabant and Flanders it was a revolutionary creed with strong demagogic under-tones.

The Prince's problem was how to use and at the same time bridle this Jacobin ardor which he needed in his struggle to free the provinces from Spanish rule but which compromised him in the eyes of the Catholic moderates and in particular with the jealous, self-seeking grandees of the States General: men like Aerschot who had a personal grudge against him going back for years.

These "moderates" were in one sense tied to him, because without his prestige and resources they would have been unable to resist the Spaniards, but they had been deeply affronted by the semi-royal entry into Brussels and by what they took to be his dangerous ambitions. A three-way tug of war therefore developed between Don John, the States General, who wanted only a limited revolution which would retain the King's title under a new governor, and the Prince, who found himself directing a national struggle with only one reliable ally, the Calvinists, and that ally filled with demagogic notions of its own. This is the key to the perplexing political maneuvers of the next two years.

Ten days after Orange's entry into Brussels the young Austrian Archduke Matthias left his brother's palace in Vienna in his night clothes and took the road to the north; by the end of October he had reached Maastricht and one of the most bizarre interludes in Netherlands history had begun.

The Archduke, a political innocent if there ever was one, had come by invitation of a caucus of grandees (among whom no one should be surprised to find the Duke of Aerschot) to offer him-self as Regent and Governor in the place of Don John, whom the States General no longer recognized.

The move to install this royal nonentity in Brussels was of course anti-Orangist—Aerschot's name among its sponsors was sufficient guarantee of that—and was intended as a counterpoise to the Prince, now Ruward of Brabant, an office similar to that of Roman *dictator* which public opinion had pressed on him and which gave him vastly increased powers. Aerschot's part in the intrigue had actually been checked before his nominee's arrival by his own arrest in Ghent in the heart of his stadtholderate of Flanders by a group of Calvinist radicals in touch with Orange. The puppet master was thus removed, if only for a limited season. There remained the puppet waiting for someone to manipulate him.

This task the Prince now decided to undertake himself, for if the young man's arrival had complicated an already chaotic situa-tion, there might still be advantages to be gained from the proper use of him as a "front" against Don John and as a wedge between the Spanish and Austrian branches of the Hapsburg family. There was even a chance that he might prove a rallying point for the Catholic moderates, whom it was necessary to attach and hold; whereas to send him back home would needlessly antagonize Vienna, where a new emperor had just succeeded the crypto-Protestant Maximilian whose sympathy for the Reformed religion had played a restraining part on Spanish policies. These were factors which had to be carefully weighed.

In December therefore, under Orange's prompting, the States General were induced to declare Don John a public enemy and to invite Matthias to assume the governor generalship on the basis of the Union of Brussels, with a new (Orangist) Council of State to assist him and Orange himself as Lieutenant General in the real position of power. The Prince had effectively stolen the Duke of Aerschot's clothes. On December 10 a new act of union was signed at Brussels—noteworthy as being the last confederation of the United Netherlands—and early in the following year the Prince escorted his puppet archduke into the capital for the third Joyous Entry which the indomitable town had chosen to celebrate within ten months.

Retribution this time was swift, for Don John in his remote provincial exile had not been idle and the *tercios* were already on the march back to rejoin the Governor in Luxemburg. By the year's end he has twenty thousand of the famous "black-beards" under his hand, including the most welcome reinforcement of all, his nephew and comrade in arms at Lepanto, almost exactly of an age with him, Alexander Farnese, future Duke of Parma,* the Duchess Margaret's son, whose wedding celebrations had provided the cover for the first meetings of the Leaguers and embryo Beggars in '65.

Parma (to give him the name by which history knows him) found the Governor sadly reduced in health and spirits, a mere shadow of the man who had led the Christian fleets in the greatest of all victories over the Turk. Successive disappointments and humiliations had turned Don John from an eager searcher after thrones into a figure quite strikingly reminiscent of Don Quixote in the hour when he recovers his sanity and loses his will to live. The Governor had just learned from Parma's mother, the Duchess

* Farnese only succeeded to the dukedom on his father's death in 1586.

Margaret, then in Italy, that the King had chosen her to replace him in the Netherlands, this without a word of warning or of gratitude from the King to his unfortunate and long-suffering servant. It was a bitter blow, but Don John was too chivalrous a man to visit these unmerited slights on his half sister, who was certainly innocent of any intrigue against him, or on her son, his oldest and most valued friend. Awoken at dawn with the news that Parma had reached his camp, he hastened to embrace him and press money and honors upon him, which Parma tactfully declined—the whole scene of the meeting between these paladins is imbued with the spirit of the chivalry books, full of high-flown but genuine emotion on both sides. And the result was a great feat of arms which Amadis himself might have envied.

On January 25, 1578, Don John issued a proclamation to the provinces, in effect a declaration of war. The army of the States General, which included English and Scottish units, was in the neighborhood of Namur, about twenty thousand strong. Most of its commanders were absent in Brussels at a wedding—another typically Netherlands touch. Near Gembloux the royalists came up with this force which had prudently turned tail from an attempt on Namur citadel and was retreating in wooded country through a defile above a marshy stream. Over Don John's head waved a banner with a cross and a Latin inscription—"By this Sign I conquered the Turks. By this Sign will I conquer the heretics."

Seldom have promises been so quickly justified by events.

Riding forward with the advance guard to reconnoiter the enemy's line of retreat, Parma was struck by their lack of balance, the bunching of units on the narrow track between the river and the hills. By nature he was the most calculating and scientific of commanders, the first great master of the chessboard maneuver which was to be the pattern of warfare for more than two centuries till Valmy and the French Revolutionary armies destroyed the mold, but at Gembloux he was still a young man with his mark to make in the world, faced with an opportunity which might not recur. "Tell Don John of Austria," he is said to have cried to an aide-de-camp as he spurred his horse into the marsh, "that Alexander of Parma has plunged into the abyss to perish there or to come forth again victorious."*

It is hard after four centuries to accept the heroics of an age in

* There is another version of the words, but the sense is much the same.

the spirit which was then expected and commonplace. Cervantes in his immortal book was soon to puncture them forever. Indeed Parma himself in a letter to his mother after the event was at pains to deny that he had had any intention to settle matters at a blow. However that may be, a small body of his cavalry, almost certainly less than a thousand and probably half that number, rode through the stream, at imminent risk of foundering, and fell with devastating force on the center of the retreating army at its weakest link.

No resistance whatever seems to have been offered by the panic-stricken nationalist force which simply disintegrated under the blow. The tally of the dead and captured as recorded by contemporary chroniclers makes almost incredible reading, but the States General's army of twenty thousand men was certainly routed and to a large measure destroyed at a cost of a handful of Spaniards.

The shock to the provinces of this event was immense, setting off a chain reaction of revolutionary feeling against the grandees, who had chosen to attend a wedding rather than a battle. In Ghent, always a radical town, the mob burst into a frenzy of protest and insurrection; the whole province of Flanders seemed to be veering to Calvinism. This in turn caused a revulsion among the nobles and well-to-do Catholics whose hatred of Spain was secondary to their regard for their own privileges: a sentiment still more widespread in the French-speaking provinces, where the reoccupation of towns by the royalists in the wake of their victory was producing a climate ripe for counterrevolution against the Flemish-speaking and heretically inclined north.

If the King at this point had chosen to reinforce his Governor General with troops and a siege train, Don John might well have been able to restore Spanish rule up to the line of the great rivers and pen the Orangists into the territories they had occupied at the death of Requesens. But the King had totally withdrawn his confidence from his half brother. For motives that still remain obscure, Secretary Pérez had for long been poisoning the royal mind with talk of Don John's dangerous ambitions, and though nothing in the Governor's or Escovedo's confidential letters shown by Pérez to the King disclosed even an inkling of any treasonable plot, there was certainly sufficient evidence of Don John's intemperate and bellicose state of mind to convince Philip that the appointment had been a calamitous mistake.

For Spanish policy now required quite another sort of person to represent it in the Low Countries. The King was very clear about it. On September 1, not long after the seizure of Namur (which he deplored), we find him declaring to his half brother that his aim is to win back the provinces to obedience and Catholicism by negotiation, not by war, in which victory would only bring suffering to his people. On the same day he began to explore the possibility of replacing his now too martial Governor by his old consortium of the Duchess Margaret and Granvelle. His search for a compromise was heartfelt, for even after he had reluctantly allowed the *tercios* to be recalled to the provinces in face of rebel provocations, he was continuing to insist that a peaceful settlement must be found. A recourse to arms, he wrote on September 11, would entail the ruin of the country and the loss of "many good vassals." Again in October he was repeating this. And all the while, far off in Namur Don John was assuring him that the only remedy left was war; that clemency should follow victory, not precede it; that the fire of heresy then raging was worse than the one Luther had lit.

The gulf between King and Governor was unbridgeable. Despairing of prodding the Duchess Margaret and Granvelle into immediate arrival on the scene, Philip decided to take the matter to its source and to negotiate with the States General behind his half brother's back, even offering to replace him with another governor of Hapsburg blood if only the supremacy of the Catholic religion and the royal sovereignty were accepted as in the time of Charles V.

References back to this alleged golden age mark the correspondence of almost all parties except the Orangists at this time, though precisely what was meant by the prescription varied widely. Even Don John himself used the phrase, though he found this royal intervention "very pernicious" and encouraging to the rebels, as indeed it was, for these were the days after Gembloux when rebellion might have been crushed by resolute action.

But from his point of view, something far more "pernicious" than this hole-in-the-corner diplomacy was soon in the air. Far off in Vienna the new emperor, Rudolf of Hapsburg, had become concerned with the dangers of the Netherlands revolt and the increasing chance of French intervention.

Gembloux had been won in January 1578. Throughout the spring and summer the Emperor was bombarding Madrid with suggestions of imperial mediation. Was this desirable? In Spain the King and his Council of State earnestly debated the matter. This new diplomatic intervention seemed to match their own pacific mood which stemmed from their lack of men and money to wage full-scale war. Perhaps a deal could be made with the Emperor's help whereby the King would withdraw Don John and the States General would withdraw Matthias, leaving the way open for the appointment of a new Governor General in the person of the Dowager Empress, Philip's sister, or the Archduke Ferdinand.

In order to smooth the way for this eventuality, Philip now canceled his invitation to the Duchess Margaret and also to Cardinal Granvelle, who had already tactfully declined it. Instead, a conference under imperial management would be held at Cologne; and to his ambassador to that conference, the Duke of Terra Nova, the King declared his intention to recall Don John. He did not think to tell Don John of this himself. In fact he now hardly bothered to write to him at all, since all the royal eggs were now in the diplomatic basket being carried to market elsewhere.

It was not a bad policy in itself. Peace *was* desirable—for Spain as much as for the Netherlands—but the King had come to desire it on terms entailing a return to Catholicism and obedience to his sovereignty which were unacceptable to the Orangists, who now controlled the States General, and unacceptable also to the proposed mediator, the Emperor, who wanted a settlement along the lines of the Pacification of Ghent.

Perhaps in the light of his many perplexities we should excuse Philip. He had not wanted the seizure of Namur. He had not really wanted the victory of Gembloux. He was a man of peace. But by his distrust of his half brother, his duplicity, his ingratitude and his sad misjudgment of realities, he had gone far to deserve the ridiculous yet menacing complications which now beset him.

The first of these, the ambitions of the Archduke Matthias, we have already noted.

But Matthias was only one of the restless intriguers who were now hurrying to fish in the muddy waters of the Netherlands. A more formidable figure was John Casimir, brother of the Elector Palatine, who offered his services to the States General at the end of May 1578.

In the aftermath of Gembloux the Prince of Orange had hustled the States General and his puppet archduke out of Brussels to the greater security of Antwerp, where he set himself to hammer out the basis of a religious peace which alone could give unity to the provinces in the face of the enemy. But if this was the soul of his policy he was also in urgent need of a sword, and John Casimir with twelve thousand men at his back (to be paid for by the Queen of England) was an asset which could not lightly be set aside. The Prince was not to know that this stiff-necked Protestant would choose to intrigue against him and become the ally of the Calvinist divines and the mobs which were setting up a reign of terror in Ghent and other Flemish towns, burning monasteries and desecrating Catholic churches on the model of the image breakers of '66. In the chaotic conditions of the times one could not always choose one's friends. Often, as in the case of Matthias, they were chosen for one; and this pattern was repeated when in July, at the invitation of Lalaing, Catholic stadtholder of the Walloon province of Hainaut, yet another contender entered the lists—Francis of Alençon, now Duke of Anjou, the brother of the French king and most odious of the progeny of Catherine de Medici.

Here was certainly the figure with the greatest capacity for good or evil who had yet intervened in the affairs of the provinces. Anjou was not only a man with time on his hands, one of a gallery of aspiring adventurers in search of a "throne with a canopy" like Don John, but a person of major political importance, standing very close to the seat of power in Paris and commanding a large military following in his own right.

There lay the rub from the Netherlands point of view, for if Anjou was in many respects a most desirable and potent ally, it was not possible to forget that he was also the heir to Gallic ambitions in the Low Countries which dated back for hundreds of years, and was likely one day to succeed a brother in Paris whose sexual tastes seemed to rule out children. If Anjou, in the name of the States General, were invited to capture Spanish-held fortresses in Hainaut and Artois, would he later show a disposition to keep them in the name of France?—this was the problem, and it was not only a Netherlands problem but one which also concerned England, where the Queen's diplomacy had always aimed at weakening the Spaniards' hold on the provinces but never to the point of letting the French replace them, since France in her eyes was the more menacing power. So strongly did she hold this view, that she showed her displeasure at Anjou's arrival on the scene by freezing her subsidies to the Orangists, who were thus placed in the delicate situation of having to offend either their new French ally or their English paymaster.

Here was a shrewdly judged blow, for the Prince, who had spent the last decade in a frantic search for money, was peculiarly susceptible to such arguments. But the Queen, thinking only of English interests, had been too parsimonious in the past, too full of double-dealing where the provinces were concerned, and what Anjou had to offer in the way of immediate troop reinforcements was of a nature which was bound to override all other considerations in the military situation of the time. The Prince succumbed to necessity—with typical reservations—and on his prompting the States General made haste to accept Anjou's offer of aid in return for the high-sounding title of Defender of the Liberties of the Netherlands, which it was hoped would mean everything to the French and nothing to Elizabeth.

By midsummer of 1578 a triple threat to Don John's position had therefore developed—John Casimir, temporarily immobilized with his Protestants at Zutphen for lack of money; the army of the States General in Brabant, now commanded by the old royalist general Bossu who had turned his coat; and Anjou, Defender of Liberties, at Mons in the Walloon country, issuing declarations of war against the Spanish king.

The Governor General meanwhile had been enjoying mixed fortunes in the field. In eastern Brabant and Hainaut his troops had reduced a number of small towns, including Sichem where Parma massacred the garrison after its surrender and hanged its commander from the battlements quite in the style of Don Frederick at Naarden. This act of terrorism which was greatly out of character had its effect, and other surrenders followed more expeditiously. On the debit side of the balance sheet, and far outweighing it, was the loss of Amsterdam which now passed irrevocably into the rebel camp, taking with it the last royalist pocket in Holland.

The loss of this once devotedly Catholic town which rivaled Antwerp in importance was one of the most decisive events of the decade. There was no siege, no battle, the Papist magistrates were simply chased out. Yet from Don John's point of view the major problem lay not in the north but in the Walloon states, in the shadow of Anjou, and in Brabant, the rebel base for an offensive against Namur. To meet these threats, he planned to fall upon Bossu's force near Mechlin before a general concentration could be made against him, and in theory at least this made excellent sense. But the need to provide garrisons for captured fortresses and a corps of observation to keep watch on Anjou had reduced the royal army to twelve thousand infantry and five thousand horse, numerically inferior—though it was stronger in cavalry—to Bossu's twenty thousand strongly posted in an entrenched camp near the village of Rijnemants; and in the ensuing engagement (which Parma had opposed at a council of war) the Spanish forces were outmaneuvered and were fortunate to escape with a drawn battle. It was the first check to their arms since the affair at Heiligerlee in the early days of Alva's governorship and it put an end to any hopes of further royalist penetration into Brabant.

That August near Don John's camp, under the shade of an oak tree irresistibly recalling the court of justice of his spiritual ancestor St. Louis in the forest of Vincennes, another abortive conference took place between the Governor General and his opponents in the person of Queen Elizabeth's staunchly Protestant secretary, Francis Walsingham, and another English envoy, Cobham, who had been deputed to find some means of accommodation with Don John which would also satisfy the rebellious provinces and cut out the danger of French intervention.

There were many forces working for peace. The Queen desired it. So did the Emperor. The States General might have been expected to be in the mood for compromise in the light of recent Calvinist excesses, the activities of John Casimir, and the "Religious Peace" which Orange had forced on them and which licensed Calvinism in the Catholic provinces as an "equal" religion without much hope of any corresponding concession from Holland and Zeeland where the old faith was firmly suppressed. Yet the terms presented to the Governor through the English envoys could hardly have been stiffer. The truth was that for the moment the States General was completely under Orangist control, a mere mouthpiece for the Prince, who had judged that the time was now ripe to make an end of all Spanish pretensions of dominance or even of influence in the Netherlands. So harsh were the terms that even Walsingham, who secretly hoped for the failure of the negotiations, found himself unable to defend them when pressed for his opinion by the Governor.

This time Don John did not argue, did not threaten. If before in his endless round of charges and countercharges against his enemies he had shown petulance or arrogance, all this had gone. He said little beyond telling Walsingham, "Such terms will not do for me." There was nothing to say. Walsingham himself was impressed, or so at least he claimed in a letter to the Lord Treasurer, Burghley, a more pacific and moderate person who was by no means as anti-Spanish as the envoy. "Surely I never saw a gentleman for personage, wit and entertainment comparable to him," wrote Walsingham, saving the sting for the tail. "If pride do not overthrow him, he is like to become a great personage."

But it was not pride that was to be the enemy. The Governor was already a sick man, worn down by disappointment and the rigors of campaigning in the summer heat. In Namur typhoid had broken out among the troops in their grossly insanitary and overcrowded quarters—two thousand had died, according to dispatches which fell into Orangist hands. Partly as a defense measure to guard the crossings of the Sambre and Meuse, and partly for the sake of hygiene, an entrenched camp was built for the army on the heights of Bouges about a mile from Namur citadel, and there in September Don John himself was carried in a camp bed to be housed—for he had no wish to displace any of his officers— in a disused pigeon loft which was hastily furnished for the occasion with a few curtains and damask hangings and a wooden staircase in place of the ladder which had provided the only means of entry.

From this lodging the victor of Lepanto wrote his last despairing letters to his friends. "His Majesty is resolved upon nothing; at least I am kept in ignorance of his intentions," he lamented to Don Pedro de Mendoza, the Spanish agent at Genoa. "Our life is doled out to us here by moments." In another letter of the same day to Giovanni Andrea Doria, admiral of the Genoese fleets at Lepanto, he expressed himself in the same terms of resignation. "Again and again have I besought His Majesty to send me orders, which shall be executed if they do not come too late. They have cut off our hands; nothing now remains but to stretch out our heads also to the axe. I grieve to trouble you with my sorrows. . . ."

To the King, who had come to regard him as an encumbrance,

an obstacle to peace, he wrote simply for orders—this was on September 20 and was to be his last letter to Philip. "I assure your Majesty that the work here is enough to destroy any constitution and any life." Two days earlier, at the first serious onset of fever, he had already despaired of his life. Probably he did not wish to recover, not even to retire as he had once dreamed to the sierras like the contemplatives and wronged shepherds of pastoral literature. But always he returned to his complaint, his justification before the King and the world—"Thus I remain perplexed and confused, desiring more than life some decision on your Majesty's part, for which I have begged so many times." and he asked again for "orders for the conduct of affairs."

"To the underlined I will not respond,"* noted the King in the margin of this letter when it was placed before him—it was the keynote of his whole treatment of his servant, and though his wider aims were just and merciful the Fates did not forgive him.

With this outpouring of his emotions of loyalty and despair Don John laid down a burden which had always been uncongenial. On September 28 mass was said by his confessor at his bedside. That same day Don John formally transferred to Parma his insignia and titles as Governor General and military commander in the Netherlands, subject to the approval of the King, for it was important that there should be no breakdown in the chain of command such as had followed the death of Requesens. In his last moments the dying man, whose life had been spent in the pursuit of glory and self-assertion in a hostile and jostling world, found a humility which was heartfelt and yet at the same time a reflection of his knight-errantry, his vision of the way the son of a Christian emperor should die. Having dictated his will to his confessor, leaving such possessions as he had to the King together with a plea for the support of his dependents, "And now, father, is it not just," he said, "that I who have not a hand's breadth of earth to call my own in this world should desire to be at large in heaven?"

On the first of October, the eve of the anniversary of his great victory, he died: the most forlorn of all the governors of the Low Countries in two centuries of Spanish rule. But the romantic nature of his life, something of that same spirit that had brought him

* *Lo rayado no yo le diré.*

galloping across France in disguise to his government in Luxemburg, has survived the almost complete oblivion which has swallowed the memories of Spanish rule. In the most popular of tourist guidebooks to Belgium to this day Don John is solemnly declared to have died not of typhoid (as he probably did), or conceivably of the plague, but of poison administered to him in a pair of gloves by a wronged lady of Namur. The King had certainly bidden him in his instructions on his appointment to the Netherlands to be particularly careful of his amours.

13

SPAIN AND THE INDIES. NEW TRENDS IN SPANISH POLICY. 1579. THE CONQUEST OF PORTUGAL. 1580.

With 1578, the year of Don John's death, we reach the watershed of the reign. The arrival on the Netherlands scene of a successor in the Prince of Parma was to mark the beginning of a policy toward the rebel provinces much subtler and more diplomatic than the late Governor's blundering moves but at the same time more purposeful. Where Don John had blustered, Parma cajoled. But he did it sword in hand and increasingly with royal support. Conciliation with rebels and heretics was no longer the royal aim: it was conquest.

This was soon to be true on a much wider front than the Netherlands, for 1578 was the last year of the old regime of moderation which by and large the King had followed, apart from the aberration of Alva's time. Before the next year was out his principal secretary Antonio Pérez, who had succeeded the dead Ruy Gómez, Prince of Eboli, as leader of the moderate faction at court, had been arrested and replaced in the King's confidence by the far more activist Granvelle. New attitudes and ambitions were in the making. In '78 there was a new king of Portugal: an elderly celibate, the last of his line. Here was opportunity, for through his Portuguese mother Philip could claim to be his heir. And the year had seen also the first appearance of English raiders on the unguarded Pacific coasts of Peru—a very different kind of event but conducive to the same line of thought. Its focal point was the trade route to the Spanish empire in the Indies.

Already for well over half a century this had been the life line of metropolitan Spain and her dependencies. Without the silver of Peru the Spanish fleets which had held off the Turk

Zacatecas
Pachuca
Mexico · S. Juan de Ulúa
Vera Cruz

Havana

CUBA

HISPANIOLA

Santo Domingo

MEXICO (NEW SPAIN)

Nombre de Dios

Cartagena

SPANISH MAIN

Panama

R. ORINOCO

R. AMAZON

PERU

Callao · Lima
Cuzco

BRAZIL

Potosí

CHILE

Santiago

RÍO DE LA PLATA

MISSISSIPPI

	Spanish Possessions
	Portuguese Possessions
Potosí	Major Mines

The Spanish Empire   in the Indies

from Europe could not have sailed and the armies which had trounced the Orangists at Gembloux could not have kept even a small royalist toe hold in Luxemburg and along the Meuse.

No more bountiful gift had ever befallen a deserving nation. If the English of a later time were said to have picked up an empire in a fit of absence of mind, the Castilians had got theirs in a place which no one had even dreamed existed. Their agent Columbus had stumbled on it thinking he was in an archipelago off the coasts of Asia. Nor at first were they particularly pleased with being presented with what soon gave every appearance of being a continent most inconveniently placed across the sea route westward to "Cathay" and "Cipangu" which had really been their goal. For some years they went on looking for a way around it or a strait through it, somewhere on the arc between Mexico and Venezuela—it was this quest, in the days when Charles V was still a boy, which had taken Vasco Núñez de Balboa into his treetop in Darien to glimpse the waters of the Pacific gleaming in the tropic sun.

Such as they were, these discoveries were solely Spanish. The Pope had decided the matter in his famous bull *Inter Caetera* of 1473, which in effect purported to carve up the still-undiscovered oceanic worlds between the rival Christian kingdoms of Castile and Portugal, giving to the former all lands and islands west of a line drawn a "hundred leagues" to seaward of the Azores—a demarcation which was later moved substantially westward by mutual agreement between the parties in the Treaty of Tordesillas.

The new Caribbean lands were therefore a monopoly: but what were they worth? The islands first settled—Hispaniola (modern Haiti) and Cuba—were suitable for farming and the raising of cattle, sheep and pigs, and even better adapted for sugar cane, but few of those who had adventured into the unknown across an uncharted ocean had done so to engage in the modest pursuits of husbandry, even with the help of an unpaid labor force of docile, naked savages. No one in Spain would work with his hands if he could possibly avoid it, and the future *Conquistadores* were more reluctant than most. As the islands settled down and the bureaucrats moved in from Spain to demarcate boundaries and promulgate laws, and as the supplies of alluvial gold which could be washed (by native labor) from the rivers and streams began to dwindle, the more adventurous moved out, drawn by a dream of treasure in great and distant kingdoms somewhere to the south and west—of El Dorado, the gilded man—but drawn also by a sheer desire to perform great deeds which has no parallel outside the chivalry books on which many of these desperadoes had been weaned.

As it happened, many of these dreams were true. Cut off for millennia from his African, Asian and European brothers, man in the Americas had been developing the last and most sophisticated of the Stone Age cultures of which history has any record. Its best artistic achievements, which have given Mayan art a unique prestige, were already over and its great ceremonial cities lay deserted and half buried in the jungles of Guatemala and Yucatán: but in the north, in Mexico, a new barbaric power had arisen in the armed theocracy of the Aztecs of Tenochtitlán, and southward, beyond the Isthmus, the Incas of Peru had created a full-fledged empire for themselves which extended from what is now Ecuador to the southern borders of Bolivia.

This Inca realm must have numbered some millions of people, and it was highly organized, with tracks and bridges and a courier system not unworthy of imperial Rome. In Mexico, the capital of Montezuma, war chief of Tenochtitlán—the future Mexico City— was of a size to astonish the Spaniards who first set eyes on it: a city larger than Seville and built dramatically in the midst of a lake. Yet both these powers, which were so much more formidable than the primitive tribal societies of the islands, went down before a handful of attackers who would certainly have failed to take the smallest fortress in the Netherlands. Cortés brought five hundred men and a few horses to the conquest of Mexico: Francisco Pizarro one hundred and eighty men and twenty-seven horses to the conquest of Peru.

The results startled the conquerors themselves: even their faith in God and gold had scarcely promised so much. Indeed what happened is hardly explicable in terms of reason, for though in Mexico Cortés was helped by a native tradition which looked to the return of the white god Quetzalcoatl out of the east, and though there and in Peru the Spaniards were able to use jealous tributary states against their overlords to profit by a policy of "divide and rule," the physical odds alone of many thousands to one and the appalling terrain of Mexican jungle and the high cordilleras of Peru should have made the whole thing impossible.

The invaders, mostly ignorant, uncomplicated men, gave no more rational thought to what they were doing than Don Quixote faced with some "adventure" on the plains of La Mancha. With the certainty of sleepwalkers they went their way across deserts and mountains, into strange and populous cities, tormented by thirst, hunger and disease and in constant danger of death in a variety of hideous forms. Numbers of them fell in battle; many were left to perish in the jungles and the high passes of the Andes or came to a sacrificial end on the altars of savage gods. Very few lived to enjoy the gold that had brought them or even the more modest profits of the estates they had carved out for themselves. Their conquests were soon cut down and regulated by a bureaucracy and a Church which found their crudities embarrassing. Even Cortés, the most diplomatic and successful of their leaders, died, a rich man it is true and a marquis, but powerless and neglected in a Spain which had no use for his talents, thousands of miles from his estates in the valley of Oaxaca: Balboa was beheaded: of the five Pizarros who with Almagro had led the conquest of Peru, only one was alive ten years later, and he was a prisoner in a Spanish jail.

Yet their work was done, as none could have done it but the extraordinary galaxy of impoverished gentry, younger sons, soldiers of fortune and the sweepings of Castilian prisons and bordellos whom we call the *Conquistadores*. By the middle of the century, fifty years after Columbus's first voyage, when Philip succeeded the Emperor on the throne, the huge territory of Spanish America had been brought under control of the Crown. Of course there were vast areas where this control was nominal. Peru, outside of the coastal strip dominated by its new capital of Lima, was still largely "Indian" and unabsorbed; and elsewhere the Spanish writ did not run far beyond the settled country of the towns and great estates. Still, from what is now Florida, through Mexico, Central America and the islands, to Venezuela and Colombia on the Atlantic coast (the Spanish "Main") and the Pacific territories as far south as Chile, Spanish laws and administration had been established.

It was a prodigious achievement, in which the jurists, bureaucrats and friars who had followed hard on the heels of the

Conquistadores had played their full part. Though Spanish rule was to degenerate into one of the most torpid and repressive colonial systems ever devised, this should not blind us to the dynamism which drove it in the early years, when the enlightened self-interest of the King in Spain and of a devoted band of radical missionaries, lawyers and great viceroys all combined to build a new civilization on the wreckage of conquest and the ruin of powerful states. Nowhere else in Europe or indeed in the sixteenth-century world could the machinery have been found to reduce so vast an empire to obedience in so short a time.

Of course in terms of human suffering the cost of it all was appallingly high. Discouragement, famine due to agrarian changes, and the white man's diseases to which they had no immunity carried off the natives in Cuba and Hispaniola in such numbers that slave labor from Africa had to be brought in to replace them; and the same ghastly tragedy was soon to be repeated on the mainland on a much vaster scale. No pleas of well-intentioned paternalism or spiritual care for the subject peoples can atone for the fact that in little more than half a century the population of Mexico fell from twenty-five millions to less than two.

Even genocide as practiced by the Nazis pales before such figures, which sound incredible but which modern scholarship has established.* Nor were the survivors much more fortunate. The *Conquistadores*, practical men, not greatly concerned with social effects or human rights, had buttressed their victories by building or rebuilding cities, whose municipalities they of course controlled, and by dividing up the best agricultural land into estates worked for them by tribal labor on a basis of serfdom not far removed from slavery. This system of *encomiendas* as they were called was almost certainly necessary if the conquest was to be perpetuated and the land and its mineral wealth worked economically, but it was one which if left unchecked would have developed into petty satrapies and the purest tyranny.

That this never quite happened, and that the Spanish empire in the Americas became at least in theory one where the subject peoples had legal and spiritual rights, was due to the natural jealousy of the Crown toward overmighty subjects and to the missionary fervor of a Church which, in spite of the Holy Office,

* Notably the researches of S. F. Cook, W. Borah and L. B. Simpson.

was still very radical in its thinking and took literally the Christian doctrine that all believers were equal in the eyes of God.

It was not the policy of either Charles or Philip to encourage men like Cortés and the Pizarros to become independent rulers of states prolific in precious metals. Steps were speedily taken to curb their ambitions and to replace them with more trustworthy and biddable officials who also by a fortunate chance were men of probity and high administrative skill. And it was certainly not the policy of the Church—as represented by its activist wing of friars and other regular clergy—to let slip an opportunity of converting souls on a scale unknown since the time of the Apostles. Everywhere throughout the subject territories the royal agents moved in: bringing law and order and new taxes and cutting the "old conquerors" down to size, even in their strongholds of the city councils. And alongside and often ahead of them went the missionaries: preaching, baptizing, building churches and schools, even dreaming in their innocence of a native priesthood which one day would carry on their work.

Toward the social system set up by the conquerors, and particularly toward the serfdom of the *encomiendas,* the parceling-out of human souls, the good friars felt a deep antipathy. They had spokesmen with expert knowledge of the problems—men of fanatical enthusiasm like Las Casas—and a powerful lobby at the Spanish court, where the Emperor's conscience had been deeply troubled by reports of depopulation and ill-treatment of Indian labor. In 1543 the so-called "New Laws" attempted to dismantle the whole *encomienda* system—perhaps the most strikingly benevolent legislation ever passed by a despotic government. And though the New Laws were doomed to failure, and were never put into practice in a continent whose social structure was too frail to stand such idealistic tamperings with hard economic facts, they were symptoms of a regard for justice which at least sought to curb the worst excesses of exploitation and might have succeeded if the Indies had been less rich in lands and minerals to excite the extreme cupidity of man.

For of course at heart exploitation had been the aim which had brought the Spaniards from the islands to the mainland, and such it remained to the end. All the impressive trappings of the Spanish empire in the Indies with its two great viceroyalties of Mexico and Peru, the apparatus of laws and courts of justice, of town councils, parishes and bishoprics—all this was the framework for the efficient extraction of money. The actual gold and silver which the *Conquistadores* had managed to squeeze out of their victims had not amounted to very much, since the Indians themselves were ignorant of their true wealth, but Spanish prospectors soon revealed it—silver in profusion: the mines of Zacatecas in northern Mexico and the huge mountain of silver at Potosí in the viceroyalty of Peru, in present-day Bolivia, the find of the century.

From 1505 onward this stream of treasure began to flow from the New World to irrigate the Old. By 1510, annual consignments were already averaging two hundred thousand ducats; by 1545 they had topped the million mark; by the time of Philip's accession, two millions. In the early days much of the total value had been made up of gold from the Antilles, but with the discovery of Potosí in 1545 and the introduction in the sixties of new methods of refining silver with an amalgam of mercury, silver shipments began to predominate heavily over gold, both in bulk and value. By 1580 the annual receipts had reached four million ducats; by 1585, seven million (the equivalent of three million dollars in modern money); and after a slight recession during the next five years, reached their all-time peak in the last decade of the reign at a level of eight million ducats, some three million of which went to the Crown in the form of the royal fifth and the proceeds of taxes levied in the Indies.

These enormous shipments of treasure accounted for most of the eastbound trade, though there were also consignments of cochineal, hides, sugar, pearls from the short-lived pearl fisheries at Cubagua, and more exotic Americana in the shape of native jewelry and featherwork for the amusement of the court. In return the settlers received the necessities of life—seeds, wine, oil, textiles, books, arms, horses, cattle—and the luxury goods of the Old World which they craved. This trade was jealously protected by the home authorities, who kept it a strict monopoly in the hands of the Seville merchants organized in their guild of the *Consulado* and the bureaucratic machine of the *Casa de la Contratación*, the Seville-based "House of Trade" which regulated every detail of the *Carrera de Indias*, from export licenses to the inspection of ships and the training of pilots.

At first the ships engaged in the *Carrera* had been small, and

easy prey for the pirates and privateers who swarmed among
the Caribbean islands; but a convoy system soon grew up and by
the sixties had taken definite shape with the organization of two
annual fleets under protection of the royal galleons of the Indian
Guard.

The first of these, the *Flota*, would clear from Seville and her
satellite ports on the Guadalquivir in the spring, and once in
Caribbean waters would divide, some of its ships making for the
islands, while the rest sailed on the Vera Cruz and its twin port,
San Juan de Ulúa, the terminus for Mexico (New Spain), where
they wintered and took aboard the treasure which had come down
from the hinterland through Mexico City and the fever-ridden
jungles of the *tierra caliente* which lay along the shores of the
Gulf.

The second, known as the *Galeones*, left the Guadalquivir in
August for Nombre de Dios on the Isthmus, where the Peruvian
silver was loaded after its thousand-mile journey by mule train
and Pacific coaster from the wilds of Potosí. Then in March the
Galeones, after wintering with their cargo in Cartagena, the safest
harbor on the Main, would join the *Flota* out of Vera Cruz at
Havana for the long haul homeward.

As an organizational feat this would have been respectable in
the early days of steam, and when one remembers that it was
repeated year in, year out, throughout Philip's reign, with only
minor breaks in the routine, in seas plagued by hurricanes and
privateers, the virtues of the system and of those who ran it emerge
in a remarkable light. Now and then land convoys were ambushed
and the odd straggler was snapped up in the Florida channel,
but when disaster finally befell a whole fleet it was not at sea
but in harbor in Cádiz, where the *Flotas* of 1587 and 1596 were
destroyed by English action, on the second occasion, incidentally,
causing the third and last of Philip's bankruptcies. The system
was good: perhaps the best that could have been devised. But
the pressure upon it was enormous. The sheer value of the treasure
carried made it the most tempting target in the world. And
though once aboard ship it was safe enough, there were weaknesses
further back along the tenuous lines of communication between
the mines and the ports and in the weak land defenses of an
empire covering half a continent but with a population of fewer
than two hundred thousand settlers. By the 1560s the Indies and

their treasure had become a necessity for Spain and an open invitation to her enemies. It was a situation fraught with danger for everyone.

Into this pickle the French had been the first to put their hand. Under Francis I they had had a great potential for making mischief, and even under his less competent successors there were times when colonies of Frenchmen had managed to get a toe hold at sensitive points on the perimeter of the Indies, notably at the southern tip of Florida, before the Spaniards blasted them out.

By contrast the English, with their traditional friendship for Spain, had started with high hopes of getting into the field not as poachers but as gamekeepers. When this illusion died and it became clear that the Spaniards would police the Caribbean for themselves, there were still optimistic souls among them who thought they could trade there peaceably with the tacit consent of Spain and no questions asked. It was on this basis that John Hawkins made his first voyage in those waters, as a trader with goods to sell—slaves from Africa in fact, for this was three hundred years before the "Peculiar Institution" became one of the causes of the greatest of civil wars.

The Spanish colonists in the remote townships along the Main were only too happy to trade with Hawkins at his price, which undercut the official rates charged by Spanish slavers. When this compliance drew down upon them the displeasure of the Spanish government an agreeable comedy was mounted, in which the English would put on a grand display of force, with much banging off of cannon into the bush, and the local townspeople would graciously declare themselves defeated: after which business could begin to everyone's satisfaction except the slaves. However, on his third voyage the comedy came to an untimely end. Forced off his course by hurricanes, Hawkins was unwise enough to put into San Juan de Ulúa, the terminus of the silver route from the Mexican mines, and there, trapped by the incoming *Flota* and its guard galleons with the newly appointed Viceroy of Mexico aboard, he was first treated to civilities (until the *Flota* had got inside the harbor) and then set upon in overwhelming strength.

The treachery of this attack and the grim fate of the captured seamen—of whom four were burned by the Inquisition and many

were to languish for years in Spanish jails—was never forgiven by
Hawkins or Drake (who was present in a minor role) or by
Protestant opinion in England, which was deeply shocked when
the remnants of the expedition limped home. In this sense San Juan
de Ulúa was a turning point which marked the end of English
good will toward Spain and of hopes of peaceful penetration into
the Indies.

But too much should not be made of this. The real significance of
the event is not that a few sea captains were driven to feel themselves personally at war with the King of Spain, but that events
nearer home about this time—the Papal excommunication of Elizabeth in 1570 and the Ridolfi plot against her life—brought important
elements in the English government to share their view and made
possible a policy of aggression toward Spain which would have
been unthinkable five years earlier. The fate of the prisoners of
San Juan merely added an edge of Protestant religious fervor to
what would otherwise have looked like piracy, and gave English
captains in the Caribbean much the same attitude of mind which
had inspired Moses and his followers when they came down out of
the wilderness armed with the sword and the Word to smite the
ungodly Canaanites. The combination of profit motive and crusade
was irresistible. Even the pacifically minded Queen was affected
by it. Hostilities in the Indies in the shape of raids on Spanish
treasure routes appealed to her, not only because they sometimes
paid handsome dividends, but also because they were arguably
not acts of war against Spain itself and could in any case be dis-
avowed as the work of hotheads who had exceeded their instructions. Her aim in the Caribbean, as everywhere else, was a limited
one: to pester and harass her royal brother-in-law into an accommodating frame of mind, but never to defeat him outright.
Yet for a while she could easily have achieved it if only she had put
her mind to it.

The affair at San Juan de Ulúa had been on Drake's second
trading visit to the Indies. The third in 1571 was an armed reconnaissance, in the course of which he spent some time in Darien, on
the Atlantic coast of the Isthmus, striking up a working partnership with groups of escaped African slaves known as the Cimaroons
and learning from them a number of details about the treasure

route from Peru which ran through Cimaroon country to its terminus at Nombre de Dios.

Next year, after returning to Plymouth to refit, he was back to launch his first attack on this coast. With a handful of men he stormed the town of Nombre de Dios, and, finding no gold there, succeeded after further hair-raising adventures in ambushing one of the mule trains on the road from Panama, returning home with enough specie to have gladdened the Queen's heart if in the meantime she had not changed her policy to one of *détente* with Spain, which necessitated the captain's hasty withdrawal from the stage till the outcry in Spanish circles had died down and her own policy had begun to veer again.

Hazards of this kind were normal in the Queen's service: no one ever allowed himself to become too discouraged by them. In any event in the course of his wanderings Drake had stumbled on certain strategic truths far more important than any capture of a treasure convoy, however large. The vast empire which looked so impressive on the maps had shown itself on closer acquaintance to be very ill-protected: its harbors were poor, their defenses weak, and though there were a few armed fighting ships on patrol, there was not a guard squadron permanently stationed in the Caribbean which could dispute a resolute attack in force.

Nor did the matter stop there: for of the two main treasure routes the more important, that of the Peruvian silver, ran through the territory of tribes bitterly hostile to Spain and depended for its security on three weak garrisons in Panama, Venta Cruces and Vera Cruz, in what was otherwise a wilderness. Whoever held the Isthmus controlled the treasure route and had his hand on the jugular vein of the Peru viceroyalty which depended for its life on Panama; for like Balboa before him, Drake too had climbed a tree in Darien and dreamed of sailing those sunlit waters of the Pacific on the empire's unguarded flank. With half a dozen ships and as few as a thousand men the whole ramshackle edifice of Spanish power might be shaken to its foundations and its financial credit ruined.

This was near the sober truth and no dream. A decade later he was to try it in the most ambitious of his raids, capturing not only Cartagena, the winter base of the *Galeones*, but also Santo Domingo, capital of Hispaniola, which for years had been the seat of Spanish administration in the Caribbean, a town of massive proconsular dignity whose origins went back to the second voyage of Columbus. But in 1576, a decade before this sensational event, a similar plan was attempted by a force of fifty seamen under John Oxenham, who had been with Drake on his raid of '72, had seen the Pacific from his treetop and was the first Englishman to sail its waters—in a few makeshift pinnaces which for weeks on end terrorized shipping off Panama and came close to cutting the life line of the Isthmus.

Oxenham's venture just failed, and he himself was caught and duly hanged in Lima. But in the year he died Drake was on his circumnavigation of the globe, which took him through Magellan's Strait and then northward in the Pacific along those same coasts: past Callao, the port of Peru, and out among the undefended shipping which carried perhaps a quarter of the annual revenues of Spain.

It was one more proof if proof were needed of the vulnerability of the Spanish position in the Indies, and it had been given by the one man whose almost magical reputation magnified every threat and pointed the need for new allies and new methods. Drake's circumnavigation was not of course the cause of the shift in Spanish policy from caution to aggression which suddenly became evident at this time. But it was in the atmosphere that grew out of his legend and the very real pressure of Protestant sea power in the Indies that the Enterprise of Portugal was born.

Its conception dated back nearly five centuries to the day when the small territory around Oporto emerged as a county independent of Castile, to graduate over the years, first into the kingdom of Portugal, and then, by a combination of commercial expertise and feats of daring as wildly improbable as anything performed by the *Conquistadores*, into a world empire holding the monopoly of the Eastern spice trade, with interests from the Persian Gulf to the Moluccas and Macao on the mainland of China.

Castile next door had of course done even better—from the start she had seemed the candidate most likely to succeed. But the affront to her honor was never forgiven. In Castile's eyes Portugal remained the cherished but faithless bride who had deserted her in their adolescence as nations and must at all costs be recovered, "for richer for poorer, in sickness and in health"—it was not the least of Portugal's attractions that she seemed immensely well endowed.

To this aim, which was both emotional and plain acquisitive, Philip's ancestors had devoted a great deal of blood and treasure. In the fourteenth century they had tried straightforward rape, and on the field of Aljubarrota had been soundly thrashed for their pains. In the fifteenth and sixteenth, now allied to the more civilized Hapsburgs, they had adopted Hapsburg methods, and by a series of wholesale marriages of Castilian princes to Portuguese princesses and Castilian princesses to Portuguese kings had set out on a sustained attempt to marry the lost territories back into the fold. Thus two of Charles V's aunts and a sister had been wedded in turn to one particular Portuguese monarch, Manoel the Fortunate (who did not get his soubriquet for nothing); Charles himself had married Manoel's eldest daughter; Philip, his granddaughter. Still the Portuguese royal house, blessed with virility and excellent luck, continued to absorb every Spanish match and to provide legitimate Portuguese heirs.

Then at last the luck ran out. The great-grandson of Manoel, King Sebastian I, was a crusader four hundred years out of date, filled with an obsessive urge to conquer and convert Moslems in Morocco in emulation of St. Louis, who had also come to grief along the infidel coast. Lured inland from its base to the plain of Alcazar-el-Kebir, the Christian army which included in its ranks all that was best in Portugal in leadership and courage was utterly destroyed. The King's body was never found. He had not thought to marry and his successor was an aged cardinal, vowed to celibacy, with whom the house of Avis which had presided over Portugal's glories from the days of Henry the Navigator would come to an end.

Actually there was no lack of heirs—there seldom is to a going concern; and though Portugal was nearly bankrupt through finding ransom money for the captives of Alcazar and the overstrain of running a world empire with a home population of only a million, she still had an affluent look in the eyes of Europe. The French Queen Mother, Catherine de Medici, had a claim of sorts, notable if only for its nuisance value. But Manoel the Fortunate had not neglected to provide a suitable posterity. The Duchess of Braganza was the daughter of his youngest child Edward. Her sister Maria had married Alexander of Parma and had produced a son, Prince

Ranuccio. The old dynast's second son, Louis, had fathered one Antonio, prior of the commandery of Crato: young, personable and beloved by the Portuguese masses, but unfortunately illegitimate. The best, indeed in Spanish eyes the only, claim of course belonged to Philip in right of his mother the Empress Isabella, eldest daughter of King Manoel, through whom, after decades of frustration, the Hapsburg policy of marrying the right people seemed about to pay its usual dividend.

Immediately the news of Alcazar-el-Kebir reached the Escurial the proper steps were taken to exploit the opportunity which fate had so undeservedly delayed for five hundred years. But it was still a diplomatic game. There was still a king in Portugal. To his credit, Philip had tried to warn his nephew Sebastian against the Moroccan adventure, and his activities after the presumed death of the battlefield were marked by the same careful desire to keep on the right side of the Portuguese by stressing his strict legitimate claim. To help future subjects come to the right conclusion, Don Cristóbal de Moura, a trusty Portuguese nobleman long resident at the Spanish court, was sent to Lisbon with pockets stuffed with bribes for the deserving. Attempts by the King-Cardinal to get Papal dispensation to try a belated hand at matrimony were deftly frustrated by the Spanish representative in Rome.

It was a good beginning. But the master hand was still lacking to co-ordinate all these widespread activities, and in the spring of 1579 Philip summoned Cardinal Granvelle to Madrid.

Since leaving the Netherlands Granvelle had been employed in Italy in posts of high-sounding importance but hardly worthy of the most gifted administrator in Spanish service. Philip's method was always to cut down and isolate superior talents and to replace them as soon as they had served their turn. He had done it with Alva; he was to do it with Parma; he was to do it with Granvelle himself; but for the moment there was a pressing need for statesmanship at the center of power. As soon as word came of the newcomer's landing in Spain the remnants of the old Eboli faction in the disreputable persons of Eboli's widow and her lover, Secretary Pérez, were hustled off into arrest, and the way was clear for a man of much wider-ranging mind and deep commitment to the imperial idea.

In the Netherlands under the Duchess Margaret Granvelle had seen the results of timidity and half measures, which had among other things cost him his office and fifteen years out of power. A polished diplomat and certainly no lover of force for its own sake, he hoped that the strength of Spain's legal claim, supported (however reluctantly) by the King-Cardinal Henry and important sections of Portuguese opinion among the nobles and merchants, would take Philip to Lisbon without bloodshed when the old man died, as must soon happen. Don Cristóbal's bribes were also expected to be helpful. But Granvelle was also aware that among the urban masses and lower clergy there were many who were implacably opposed to Spain. Don Cristóbal's gold had not reached *them.* And as a student of the European scene he was uneasily aware of the dangers of French or Papal intervention to prevent any further increase in Spanish power. Clearly when the time came it would be wise to have an army already mobilized under a commander whose name would carry its own message across the Tagus and indeed to the whole of Europe—naturally the Duke of Alva, whom a benign providence had preserved in retirement on his estates for just such an occasion.

In January 1580, after a troubled reign of fifteen months, the expected happened and the old King-Cardinal died, leaving behind him a regency council, the majority of whose members supported the Spanish claim. Granvelle's advice was for immediate invasion to forestall trouble. Yet Philip hung back. His ingrained legalistic turn of mind made him too trustful of the value of appeals and proclamations where a prompt show of force would probably have settled everything without fighting. Not till five months had passed since the old king's death did he bow to the inevitable and order his army across the border against the usurping Don Antonio, who in the meantime had established himself in Lisbon and had been proclaimed by the people as successor.

It was a major blunder which might also have resulted in Papal recognition of the pretender's claims—a legate with full powers was on the way from Rome and might have proved a most disturbing factor if he had not been delayed en route to Portugal from Barcelona by receptions thoughtfully staged for him in every town along the road. Fortunately for Philip, Alva's army, which was over thirty thousand strong, supported by levies almost as numerous raised privately by Castilian grandees and by a Spanish fleet from

Cádiz, was able to retrieve the situation without further waste of time. In a smooth joint operation the royal army was brought by sea to Cascais, outflanking the Tagus barrier, to crush Don Antonio's ill-trained rabble of defenders in one sharp engagement at the bridge of Alcántara almost in the suburbs of Lisbon, which fell the same day without further resistance.

It was not quite the end of the fighting. A number of unfortunates were to die at the hands of Alva's hangmen—and Don Antonio's—before the usurper fled abroad and Portugal submitted to an embrace which was to last for sixty years. The rest of the vast empire made no trouble in accepting a change of masters, except that at Terceira in the Azores French squadrons and forces loyal to the pretender put up a stern fight before being subdued by the Spanish fleet.

In a campaign which otherwise had stayed within the borders of a small corner of the peninsula Philip had won himself a trading empire which extended from the Persian Gulf to the Moluccas, the important Atlantic staging posts of the Azores and the Cape Verde Islands, and the huge and splendid territory of Brazil which had lain till then on the wrong side of the boundary line settled at Tordesillas. He had also acquired the two fine Atlantic harbors of Lisbon and Oporto, and, in the Portuguese royal squadron, a round dozen of the finest galleons afloat. On paper at least it was by far the largest concentration of force that had ever existed under one man's hand. Castile and Portugal were once more united—no longer two jealous provinces, but one empire girdling the whole earth. And there were further triumphs to come.

14

ALEXANDER OF PARMA. UNIONS OF ARRAS AND UTRECHT. THE PROVINCES DIVIDE. ANJOU. DEATH OF ORANGE. 1578–84.

A new broom was now to sweep the Spanish Netherlands. Alexander of Parma was thirty-three, the great-grandson of a pope and the grandson of an emperor, whose qualities were reflected in the very complex nature of their descendant.* "His personal appearance," says Motley, "corresponded with his character. He had the head of a gladiator, round, compact, combative, with something alert and snakelike in his movements," and indeed there is a print of him as he may have looked about this time which perfectly bears out this description—the small head with the hair cut *en brosse* raised at the end of the elongated neck like the hood of a cobra about to strike. The formal portraits, of which there are a number, show us a variant on this theme: the man born to command, arrogant and self-assured, with the upward curl of the moustaches, the full beard above the ruff and the somber splendor of the clothes adorned with the collar of the Golden Fleece. Yet this may be partly an illusion. Cover that self-assertive, almost swashbuckling beard with one's hand and there emerges quite another image, of a wary, watchful person full of guile but also of sensibility, certainly no desperado or seeker after impossible ideals.

This duality appears in every aspect of Parma's character. He was immensely brave, almost suicidally so at times, because only in this way could a commander become a legend to the troops he led. Yet as a general he seldom took a risk; he was the meticulous architect of victory. He could show himself as cruel as Alva. But this also was deliberate. Significantly, he showed cruelty only in the early days of his command when a lesson had to be taught which

* He was the younger of twin sons. The elder was named Charles after the Emperor: he was named Alexander for the Pope. Charles died in infancy.

people would remember. As a rule he was compassionate. But his compassion like his cruelty came from the head, not the heart: the response to a situation where it paid to be clement, to charm and bribe rather than destroy. This politic character of his did not escape the notice of the Netherlanders, who observed that though brought up in Spain with Spanish tutors and companions, he was by nature (as of course by birth) far more an Italian with an Italian's devious, subtle mind, a Machiavelli in gold inlaid armor.

Blessed with an intelligence far greater and more adaptable than Don John's, Parma was also faced with a more favorable situation, or at the very least a situation on the turn which could be exploited by an agile and opportunist mind. Calvinism had overreached itself in the central and eastern provinces and particularly in the Walloon states where it had become a discredited and alien creed. Even Motley acknowledges this, though he seems to have felt that there existed some special affinity between the hardy Germanic races and Protestantism on the one side, and between Rome and the more excitable Latins or "Gauls" on the other, which in some mystical way made it inevitable that the Reformed faith should triumph in the north and Catholics in the south.

Here Motley is guilty of uttering great nonsense, as a moment's thought would have reminded him, since in the French religious wars which he himself recorded in his book it was precisely in the south, in Provence and Gascony, that the Huguenot heresy had thrived.

Indeed the whole notion is misconceived, like every other racist theory. There was no natural affinity between any particular territory and any particular faith. Poland and Ireland, both northern states, are Catholic to this day, as England might have remained but for the matrimonial difficulties of Henry VIII. In the Netherlands the Walloons were turning against Calvinism not because they were by race or nature attuned to Rome, but because the quickening effect of a reformed Catholicism which we know as the Counter-Reformation was already beginning to be felt there and because the dominant Catholic nobility and town governments were affronted by the leveling tendencies they saw in John Casimir and the mobs under Calvinist divines. This feeling was soon to affect the central states of Brabant and Flanders also, for much the same reasons, and because, unlike the submerged Catholics of Holland

and Zeeland who had no hope of rescue, they had a champion conveniently close at hand in the royalist army under a new and alert commander with patronage and cash at his disposal. For it was not to be the least of Parma's blessings that his governorship coincided with the first period of solvency in Philip's reign and that a leap in the treasure receipts from the Indian mines was soon to provide a decade of affluence, of *largueza*, when there were ample funds available for judiciously placed bribes.

This royalist reaction did not happen all at once; it had to be worked for. Even in the south there was no immediate rush to Parma's standard, and indeed one of the first results of the forward probing of his agents was to stir up a further wave of demagogic fervor in Ghent, where even Orange was denounced from the pulpit for his trifling with the idolaters.

But all the material for the Catholic riposte was already to hand. A party known as the "Malcontents," formed by some of the leaders and troops which had received such a drubbing at Gembloux, was already taking a line independent of the Orange-dominated States General and even of Anjou, who might have been expected to form their natural rallying point. Rumors were rife in the south that the northern provinces were considering some form of Protestant union of their own. These rumors were well founded; but in any event the community of interest between Calvinist north and Romish south had all but ceased to exist, and throughout the Walloon provinces there was an increasing disposition to believe that some accommodation with Spain was possible on the basis of the Pacification of Ghent and the Perpetual Edict, which Don John was held to have broken by his aggressive acts but which nevertheless provided a possible *modus vivendi* now that Don John himself was dead.

Within a fortnight of that event and before the King had even recognized his rights as successor, Parma had already taken the first step to exploit this diplomatic opportunity by letters to the Walloon "estates" of Hainaut, Artois, Lille, Douai, Orchies and Tournai, offering on behalf of the new administration the withdrawal of foreign troops, a general amnesty and a guarantee of local privileges in return for obedience to the Catholic religion and the King.

Parma did not neglect the chance that *all* the provinces might listen to such promptings and took an early opportunity of offering reconciliation to the States General on Philip's "two terms" of obedience to Church and King. But the reply was negative, and it was on the Walloons that he naturally concentrated the full resources of his propaganda. The Walloons were Catholic anyway. Very little was being asked of them except that they should turn their backs on Anjou and French policies. The dual aim was to shut the door on France and by playing the religious card to divide these power-ful provinces from their Calvinist-infiltrated neighbors to the north.

Small wonder that the Walloons responded. The Prince of Parma was far more to their taste than John Casimir and the image-breaking radicals of Ghent: besides, he had perhaps more to offer than Anjou. In January 1579, led by Artois and Hainaut, the more influential sections among them banded themselves together by a declaration of mutual interest—the Union of Arras—which took them the first step along the road of reconciliation with the King. Yet the signatories at Arras still regarded themselves as a regional grouping within the Ghent Pacification and would have disclaimed any desire to destroy the general union of seventeen provinces which had been enshrined at Brussels.

Two weeks later the northern tier of Protestant states drew up a document which was claimed, if not believed, to be within the meaning and spirit of the Pacification—the Union of Utrecht, signed by Holland, Zeeland, Friesland, Utrecht and Gelderland, the last-named Catholic-minded province having been dragged in against its will by Orange's sternly Protestant brother, John of Nassau, who had managed to impose himself as its stadtholder.

To outward appearances the signatories of this treaty had no more abandoned hope of a workable union of seventeen than had their opposite numbers at Arras. They did not break with the King or as yet deny his title. Their representatives continued to sit in the States General, protesting that nothing significant had hap-pened; and indeed, if one took the clauses of the agreement at their face value, there was some justification for the view that this was nothing more than a strengthening of a section of states within the Brussels union to meet the threat of an impending royalist offensive against Gelderland.

Yet protest as they might, something far more decisive had hap-pened at Utrecht, as at Arras—a hiving-off of power blocs which had at last begun to face up to the realities of their basic dis-harmony. Perhaps these differences could have been overcome.

But certainly the divorce between them had opened the door to great dangers. Orange in particular was aware of this, and though a Calvinist and accepted by Motley as the hidden hand behind the Union of Utrecht, he was in reality deeply opposed to this narrowing down of his dream of the "entire fatherland." "This one is no good," he remarked when the treaty was submitted for his signature. Nevertheless after a delay of some weeks he signed— it was the first proof that his influence had waned in the face of his extremists.

The trends in the Walloon provinces naturally struck the States General as far more menacing than any regrouping in the north. Everyone on the Flemish side of the language line could see quite well what Parma was up to and how vulnerable the French-speaking sisters might be to Catholic pressure and a diplomatic hand played with finesse—"*la politique de douceur*," as Parma's biographer calls it.

As they quite rightly feared, the Governor General was abundantly blessed with such talents; yet it was a game of almost lunatic complexity that he was called upon to join. He was not dealing even yet with one common body of opinion which wanted to make peace with him but with a whole spectrum of divergent interests, Artois demanding one thing, Hainaut another, the nobles a third, though *they* at least were united in pursuit of titles and money. The Governor General was not even supported by his king, who continued to respond to requests for instructions either with silence or an even more unhelpful insistence on the need for a return to the state of affairs existing in the reign of Charles V. Would the King agree to ratify the Pacification of Ghent (as everyone at Arras was demanding) or would he not? Parma had set himself to avoid the tactless and time-wasting complaints with which Don John in his agony of soul had bombarded Madrid, but there were limits even to his own exemplary patience. "For the love of God," he wrote, "will your Majesty consent to give me an answer without delay to these most pressing questions?"

What then of Philip? Throughout 1579 his hopes had been high of some final settlement of his problems through imperial mediation at the conference in Cologne. Not till November was he to write resignedly to Parma that all prospects of a general pacification had collapsed, but already by the summer it had become clear from

the reports of his ambassador that the influence of Orange—
"that monster," in Terra Nova's words—had made any compromise
impossible.

This was a very real turning point in the reign. The search for
peaceful solutions with the Netherlands, with France, with England,
was about to be abandoned. Hopes of a general settlement with the
rebel provinces were replaced by attempts at a step-by-step reconquest, using a mixture of diplomacy and force for which the
King's new (and as yet "temporary") Governor General was ideally
suited.

So instead of the resistance which Don John had met with in
his dealings with his master, Parma found compliance—hesitant at
first but warming into life as time went on and his activities began
to prosper. Negotiations with the Walloons and not reliance on the
Emperor became the King's watchword; and Parma's ambassadors,
who had been received at Arras with some reserve, were at last instructed to give assurances that the King would ratify any accord
which they could negotiate within the spirit of the Pacification of
Ghent.

This was soon qualified, both by the King and by Parma himself, but at least it prevented the States General's Orangist delegates, also present in force at Arras, from arguing that Parma was
an unauthorized negotiator, a mere cuckoo in the nest. Increasingly
the Orangists were thrown on the defensive, unable seriously to
pretend that the Pacification, on which the Walloons set such store,
had been hallowed by the Calvinist mobs which had terrorized
Catholic cities and interfered with the freedom of worship in
Antwerp itself. All that was left to them in the way of bargaining
was an appeal to the Walloons not to make a separate peace but to
await the outcome of the conference at Cologne—in whose success
no one, least of all the States General themselves, believed for a
moment.

The result was probably inevitable. The Walloon provinces went
over to Parma, but they went over inch by inch, with endless pre-
varications and squabbling between the King, the acting Governor,
and the discordant voices within the Arras union, and even between
Parma and his own ambassadors, who grossly exceeded their instructions in their anxiety to make peace. Nevertheless by April
1579 the Malcontents had been brought over to the royalist side;

in May the preliminary accord between Parma's delegates and the Walloons was signed at the abbey of St. Vaast; and by the autumn the King had actually ratified the treaty and its text had been published—to no one's satisfaction, for it was a most reluctant meeting of minds.

To judge from its terms, the Treaty of Arras (not to be confused with the earlier Union) was hardly the diplomatic triumph claimed for it by Parma's admirers, who find it none too easy to explain his failure on no less than two occasions to control his own ambassadors and prevent them from bargaining away his Spanish and other foreign veterans in exchange for the promise of a national army of Walloons! Had no one remembered Gembloux? Motley, writing of course from the Orangist viewpoint, calls the terms "not bad," but in fact they were very unfavorable to Spain. All foreign troops were to leave within six weeks. The Ghent Pacification, imposed on Don John, was ratified. The King promised to provide within six months a governor general of legitimate royal blood—so that Parma had apparently signed away even his own job.

So tame a surrender of vital interests calls aloud for an explanation, which some historians have found in charges that Parma was insincere and had no intention of carrying out clauses which would deprive him of the elite troops on whom all his plans depended. It is certainly true that he accepted the hard necessity of their going in anguish of spirit and that he straightway set about persuading the Walloons to let him have them back. Go they did, however—if only for a time. It seems more likely that Parma was prepared to concede even this—and here may lie his real claim to genius—because his own knowledge of the Walloons and of the desperate conditions in the provinces had convinced him that the Treaty of Arras, for all its apparent disadvantages, would provide a Spanish foot in the door of the Orangist house, and that once "reconciliation" had been agreed on it would speedily be followed by a return to obedience and active help in the reconquest of the whole Netherlands. It was a small price to pay. Diplomacy was only one of his weapons.

Equally important was war: indeed it was a principle of his to proceed "with a pardon in one hand and a sword in the other." Even before the Arras treaty took away his Spaniards, the forces at his disposal were small by the standard Alva had enjoyed, but this had not prevented him from carrying out a raid as far afield as Antwerp and then fastening on the States General's stronghold of Maastricht on the Meuse, around which he threw up a complex of walls and redoubts more formidable than any yet seen in Europe.

As at Haarlem, this siege was a desperate affair of mine and countermine deep underground. Motley preserves one unforgettable picture which also puts the whole epic struggle in the Netherlands into perspective:

At the same instant the new mine, which was to have been sprung between the ravelin and the gate, but which had been secretly countermined by the townspeople, exploded with a horrible concussion, at the moment least expected by the besiegers. Five hundred royalists were blown into the air. Ortiz, a Spanish captain of engineers, who had been inspecting the excavations, was thrown up bodily from the subterranean depth. He fell back instantly into the same cavern, and was buried by the returning shower of earth which had spouted from the mine. Forty five years afterwards, in digging for the foundations of a new wall, his skeleton was found. Clad in complete armour, the helmet and cuirass still sound, with his gold chain around his neck, and his mattock and pickaxe at his feet, the soldier lay unmutilated, seeming almost capable of resuming his part in the same war which, even after his half century's sleep, was still ravaging the land.

Maastricht fell in the summer of 1579 to a surprise assault, and the victorious commander, who had been seriously ill with fever, was carried in state on the shoulders of his veterans to a thanksgiving mass inside the walls. A print of the times shows us an idealization of this extraordinary scene—Maastricht aflame, the mines exploding, the soldiers in their finery and Parma himself borne aloft under a surprisingly modern sun umbrella through a throng of courtiers and yokels who wave their hats. Motley has a more savage way with him:

The pavement ran red with blood. Headless corpses, an obscene mass of wretchedness and corruption were spread on every side and tainted the summer air. Through the thriving city which in the course of four months Alexander had converted into a slaughter-house and a solitude the pompous procession took its course to the church of St. Servais. Here humble thanks were offered to the God of love, and to Jesus of Nazareth, for this new victory. Especially was gratitude expressed to the Apostles Paul and Peter, upon whose festival, and by whose sword and key, the crowning mercy had been accomplished and by whose special agency eight thousand heretics now lay unburied in the streets.

Whatever one may think of the means, the capture of Maastricht was a resounding event whose echoes were heard throughout the provinces. Yet by the Treaty of Arras, ratified within a few weeks of his triumph, Parma had bound himself to send away the troops who had achieved it.

Seldom in history has a victorious commander allowed himself to be disarmed in so striking a way, and when we remember that this was his first real taste of power and that by the treaty he had also cut himself down to a six-month term as Governor General we can only marvel at his self-possession. Did he already guess that neither the King nor the Walloons could do without him or the *tercios?* There are hints of it in his correspondence both with Philip and with his own father in Italy. Sometimes despair seemed to overcome him and he begged to be allowed to march away from the ungrateful provinces at the head of his veterans, yet these were only momentary expressions of pique which may have had another motive in reminding the King of his indispensability, and in his letters we find him more often turning to thoughts of the great part he might still have to play in Netherlands affairs. After all, what other candidates for his office were available beyond the young Infantas, the Austrian archdukes, or his own mother, whom the King seemed to have in mind, though it was perhaps stretching things a little to regard *her* as a legitimate princess of the blood?

This matter of the succession was to prove troublesome: a saga in itself. Once the Austrian branch had ruled itself out for the time being by the failure of imperial mediation at Cologne the Duchess Margaret had become the only candidate, but would she take up the governor generalship once her son's six-month probation had expired, or would she not?

For more than two years the tussle lasted; the King cajoled, nagged and commanded his half sister into the breach; while she for her part timidly obliged him by advancing as far as Namur.

And there she stuck—halfway between Philip's urgent goadings and proddings and the equally daunting refusal of her son and the Walloon notables to accept her as their Vicereine.

In the end the King accepted the inevitable and gave way before an inertia greater than his own. The Duchess left the Netherlands, never to return. Her son remained for another thirteen years in an office which he had agreed to lay down in six months. The question of the succession, though long deferred, solved itself in the happiest way. But the problem of the troops was more intractable, and at a great parade outside Arlon Parma sent off the Spanish units which had provided the core of his army. They went off like lambs, even accepting half pay for their services, unlike their German brothers-in-arms who were as usual in open mutiny and ravaging the countryside. All that Parma had left under his command were the "reconciled" Malcontents from Gembloux, a ghost force of the "national" army promised under the Arras treaty, and a personal bodyguard of Italian and Albanian light horse, for whom the Walloon "estates" were soon clamoring to help them hold off the ravening Protestants of Ghent.

On paper it looked a desperate situation, and so it would have been in fact if the States General had not been in even worse shape —deserted by Anjou and by John Casimir's Germans, who had retired from the provinces, still unpaid, with safe-conduct passes which Parma had thoughtfully provided.

For these disasters, and particularly for the fall of Maastricht, everyone had combined to blame the Prince of Orange, whose anguished call for troops to save the doomed city had been met by an offer of the Antwerp town guard, excellent hands at a pageant! The Prince's stream of letters to the States General about this time disclose a profound concern if not despair at the way the life-and-death struggle was being regarded in the circles around Matthias. "But the real cause of the ills which befall us is our irresolution," he wrote in a solemn remonstrance early in the new year of 1580, "for we meet often enough, consult often enough, and are as lax in doing things as we are busy in talking about them."

No one could have expressed more clearly the shortcomings of a system of running a war by parliamentary committee, and the Prince went on to list the necessary changes that would have to be made if Maastricht were not to become the pattern for new defeats and ultimately for the loss of the entire free Netherlands. There must be a communal war chest on the model set up at Utrecht; a standing army as opposed to local levies hastily recruited to meet crises as they arose; and above all there must be a central direction of the war in order to impose the national will on the enemy and not merely to react to his moves.

What gave special urgency to these plans was Orange's appreciation that in Parma the Netherlands had found by far their most dangerous antagonist. And this of course in reverse was exactly the view that the King and all Spanish governors in the Low Countries, including Parma, had formed of *him*. As early as Alva's time plans had been afoot to remove the Prince by assassination since he seemed to be unbribable, and this idea, which was by no means repugnant to the ethics of an age which was to witness the murder of at least five royal or semi-royal persons, not counting judicial murders like that of Mary Queen of Scots, had made its reappearance under Don John* and Requesens as a neat solution to an intolerable problem. It was now to reappear again at the suggestion of Orange's old enemy Cardinal Granvelle in the form of a thundering royal denunciation called a "Ban," which was conceived in November 1579, hotfoot on the final breakdown of the peace talks at Cologne, declaring the Prince of Orange a public enemy of mankind for whose head large rewards would be paid in cash and patents of nobility. "We declare him traitor and miscreant," the solemn document declared. ". . . we banish him in perpetuity from all our realms. . . . We allow all to injure him in property or in life. . . ."

The Jackdaw of Rheims was no more soundly cursed. Yet for the time being at least the King and the Cardinal hurt only themselves. This ill-advised exercise in propaganda rebounded, as Parma had prophesied it would. When eventually published in the Netherlands, in the summer of 1580, it was the prime cause of three important events, all highly damaging to Spain—the return of Anjou to the Netherlands stage; the publication of the Prince's counterblast in his famous "Apology"; and the solemn renunciation by the free provinces of their king.

All these happenings were closely interrelated. Orange's Apology was not only a personal vindication of his own part in events but provided the groundwork for a renunciation of Philip by a recital of all the villainies, real and imagined, which made him unfit to rule.

* Don John had indignantly rejected the notion. The assassin whom it was proposed to send to him for briefing had previously considered assassinating Don John himself!

Such a move had been on the cards ever since the Beggar seizure of Brill gave the revolt a base; the arguments in its favor had grown much stronger now that a majority of the provinces were openly at war with a man whom many thought of as anti-Christ and whom all regarded as a tyrant. And since so lawless a king had to be replaced, he had to be replaced by someone. A strong faction, particularly in the north, wanted the radical solution—Orange in the King's stead as Count of Flanders, Duke of Brabant and so on. Orange would have no part in this—not because he was without his share of ambition, but because he was a realist who understood that personal and provincial jealousies ruled him out and the state of the country made it necessary to find a foreign protector of royal blood.

For this role Anjou had for some time been the only possible candidate, since the Queen of England and the King of France were both reluctant to offend Philip in so direct a way as usurpation and Matthias had proved a broken reed without influence or even the ability to command respect. It was true that as Defender of Netherlands Liberties Anjou had shown himself almost as impotent as Matthias, deserting at the first check. But since then he had been coming up in the world: a suitor whom the English Queen seemed to be taking seriously and whom the Netherlands would have to take seriously also if powerful friends in France and England were not to be antagonized. The title of Defender of Liberties would obviously no longer do: nothing less than the succession to Philip's titles would attract so powerful a prince or meet the vacuum to be caused by Philip's deposition. Yet so objectionable was this Catholic Valois to Calvinist interests that there would have been small chance of getting his sovereignty accepted if just at this vital moment the King's Ban had not united all the Flemish-speaking provinces behind Orange and Orangist policies.

On this favorable tide the Prince carried his brain child of a new Anjou alliance with few dissentient voices, except perversely enough in his own strongholds of Holland and Zeeland where sovereignty would be offered to him and to him alone—no nominee would do, and certainly no Papist. And once agreement with Anjou had been reached in September 1580 at Plessis-les-Tours, Orange went on to the next step—his reply to the King's Ban in his own Apology, which was shown to the Estates at Delft in December and published at Leyden in the next year.

This remarkable document, which Motley treats with the reverence due to a declaration of the rights of man, was in fact propaganda, much of it probably ghosted for the Prince by his chaplain and spiced with scurrilous attacks on the King, whom it accused among other things of bigamy and of the murders of his wife and his heir Don Carlos. These are the details which have naturally been remembered; indeed the extreme Protestant view of Philip as tyrant and monster owes a great deal to the Apology, as does Verdi for some aspects of his celebrated opera. Yet these were only the by-blows of a manifesto whose wider aim was to pave the way for Philip's deposition by providing proof, or a specious appearance of it, that the title of King was unknown to Netherlands law and that even the dukedoms and the countships of the various provinces were mere contractual rights, subject to local privileges and dependent on the ruler's good behavior.

To say as Motley does of this tirade that in the course of it the Prince towered morally over his opponent is grotesque. It was a clever thesis dressed up in self-righteous dogma to provide the justification for a unilateral act of power. This soon followed. In May 1581 the States General assembled at Amsterdam to draft a Declaration of Independence, which was put into its final form of an "Abjuration" and ratified at The Hague on July 26 by delegates of the States of Holland, Zeeland, Utrecht, Friesland, Groningen, Overyssel, Mechlin, Flanders and Brabant, renouncing their allegiance to a ruler "appointed by God to cherish his subjects, even as a shepherd to guard his sheep," who had nevertheless oppressed and conspired against them.

Thus the watershed was reached. For years, in some cases for a decade, the signatories of this act of state had resisted their sovereign, had libeled him, deposed his representatives, appointed new ones, fought against him in arms, and had done all these things ostensibly in his name as his loyal subjects. Thus humbug had now come to an unlamented end. The Abjuration had sent him packing in theory as well as in fact. Incidentally it had also neatly disposed of the puppet governor, Matthias, who had resigned in despair earlier that summer but was now by inference dismissed, since he could hardly be the representative of a monarch whose writ no longer ran. All this had cleared the air: overdue steps had at last been taken.

But the sentiment of the age made the notion of a republic unacceptable, and by an unfortunate chance the candidate for sovereignty whom it was now proposed to put in the King's place—Anjou —was no longer a free-lance adventurer at odds with his royal brother, as at the time of his first foray into the Netherlands, but a man working in close accord with powerful interests at the French court and a serious suitor for the hand of the Queen of England. It was of course for these very reasons that the provinces had turned to him for a "sovereign and seigneur," yet in Philip's eyes the affront to his own dignity and to his deeply held conviction of his divine right to rule, which was implicit in the Abjuration, had been sharpened beyond measure by the political undertones of what appeared in Madrid to be an Anglo-French conspiracy to replace him in his father's own homeland, and by a Valois, the hereditary enemy!

The time was ill-chosen for any act that could disturb the delicate balance of power which had been maintained since Câteau-Cambrésis by cautious and politic rulers who had kept the temperature low and avoided any direct confrontation with one another. By invading Portugal Philip had broken this principle himself, since command of Portugal gave him Atlantic ports and a fleet which could be a direct threat to England and to her dreams of overseas expansion in the New World. His new chief adviser, Granvelle, was an advocate of a forward foreign policy, and this attitude was matched by the growing intransigence of the Protestant zealots on Elizabeth's Council, men like Leicester and Walsingham who welcomed the thought of a breach with Spain.

Thus everywhere moderation was in retreat before new fears and new ambitions. Policies were hardening. And inevitably they began to center round the political vacuum created by the Netherlands revolt which the Abjuration had widened and which the personality of the new "sovereign" had turned into a threat to the general peace.

Francis Hercules of Alençon, Duke of Anjou, was a squat, pockmarked man of twenty-eight who suffered from the occupational disease of younger sons: ambition. His three elder brothers had become kings of France; one sister, Marguerite, whose favorite he was, had become a queen if only of Navarre; another had married Philip.

These accidents of birth had increased a natural aptitude for intrigue which was coupled with a complete lack of principle.

It was this aspect of the man which particularly enraged the moralist in Motley and made him almost as hostile to Anjou as to Philip himself, even to the point of descending to sneers at the ducal nose, which was allegedly so swollen and distorted as to appear to be double:

This prominent feature did not escape the sarcasm of his countrymen, who, among other gibes, were wont to observe that the man who always wore two faces might be expected to have two noses also.

Much of this was unfair, for Anjou was not the only intriguer of the age and had amiable qualities. At least Queen Elizabeth thought so, and she was an excellent judge of a man. The extraordinary saga of their courtship has never been completely explained. In encouraging him, was the Queen acting with the aim of defusing French ambitions in the Netherlands? Was she after an alliance with France? Was it an economical way of asserting her influence in that quarter and checking the Protestant extremists abroad and on her own Council? Or was she simply acting as a woman, as with Leicester many years before?

If she was playing a game, then almost all those closest to her were deceived—none more so than Anjou himself, who after a preliminary foray at Cambrai with his army in the summer after the treaty of Plessis-les-Tours had taken himself off to England with all the optimism of a lover. Probably the Queen was angling for a French alliance, to be signed and ratified before she committed herself. But that she liked Anjou is evident. He amused her. He was her "Italian," her "frog," and for all his faults more real, more satisfying than the court poets who made love only in pastoral verse. Perhaps the man who saw furthest into her dilemma was Sir Ralph Sadler in a few blunt words when asked for his opinion on the Council—"in years the Queen might be his mother. Doubtfulness of issue more than before. Few old maids escape."

It was a tragic problem if one remembers the Queen's past life and her nature, which was not without its passionate side, as to be expected of the daughter of Henry VIII and Anne Boleyn. Her Council were either lukewarm about the match, like Burghley, or deeply opposed to it, as were Walsingham and Leicester. Even the courtly Sir Philip Sidney had expressed his misgivings of how English hearts would be "galled" by her marriage to a Frenchman and a Papist "in whom the very common people know this, that he is the son of the Jezebel of our age"; and an obscure bencher of Lincoln's Inn by the name of Stubbs had voiced the same sentiments in a pamphlet splendidly entitled "The Discovery of a Gaping Gulf, wherein England is like to be swallowed by another French Marriage, if the Lord forbid not the Banns by letting her see the Sin and the Punishment thereof."

For this impertinence the too impetuous Stubbs and his printer had to suffer the public chopping off of their offending right hands. The Queen was not to be trifled with. Her vengeance on this occasion and her behavior throughout the Anjou courtship do seem to show a deeper personal involvement than at any time since she had had to give up Leicester. But now she was a much better actress, and the tragicomedy of her *pas de deux* with Anjou was played to its end with baffling skill, with gifts of rings and public embraces which convinced many foreign observers that the engagement was an accomplished fact.

In February 1582 Anjou landed back on Netherlands soil at Flushing accompanied by Leicester himself: a very flattering attention which hinted to the world that if the comedy was over—as in fact it was—the new lord of the free Netherlands at least enjoyed that highest favor reserved for ex-lovers of the Queen. Did he also enjoy the hidden support of France? This possibility, as his correspondence shows, had haunted Parma ever since Anjou's reappearance on the scene, for French intervention on anything like the scale of Henry II's war in 1557, before St. Quentin, would have faced him with an impossible situation. Yet the threat of it also provided him with an opportunity—with an argument for the return of the Spanish troops whom he had sent away under the terms of the Treaty of Arras.

Whilst Anjou was still lingering in England Parma had begun to work on the fear of the French which was strongly held by the town oligarchies throughout the Walloon states, though only to a lesser degree by the nobles, who preferred two paymasters to one. By February 1582 he had carried his point and the Walloons were begging the King to show his clemency and "consent" to bring back the troops whom they had insisted on packing off only two years earlier! "Blessed be to God," Parma wrote triumphantly, "that at last by His grace there has now been accomplished the thing I have most desired in this world and on which depends the preservation of the Holy Catholic Faith and of the Low Countries. It is a miracle. . . ." In June the King announced that everything had been arranged for the dispatch to the provinces of two *tercios* of Spaniards, that four thousand Italians were ready in Milan, and that permission was given for the enlistment of two thousand infantry and sixteen hundred horse in the Franche Comté, plus a corps of two thousand Swiss to guard against any French interference with the concentration; and two months later the advance guard of the *tercios* was back in the southern provinces, magnificently equipped: every man with the look of a captain, as admiring observers reported.

Meanwhile the Duke of Anjou, armed with letters to the States General from Queen Elizabeth commending him to their favor as her "other self," had been ceremonially installed as Duke of Brabant in Antwerp on February 17 with the usual flummery which had greeted Don John and the Archduke Matthias in the past. The rejoicing on this occasion was even less heartfelt. Holland and Zeeland wanted no part of him; had indeed already pressed their provincial sovereignties on Orange for the duration of the war. And though the Protestant majority on the States General—for Protestant this body had become—were prepared to give Anjou the appearance of power in the remaining provinces, they were in fact determined to hedge him around with restrictions and muzzle him as they had Matthias.

To the Calvinist preachers and city mobs he was simply an object of aversion and intense distrust as a Papist who had shed Huguenot blood and the son of "that Jezebel" who had inspired the massacre of St. Bartholomew. Indeed Anjou was not a very trustworthy person—his own sister gave it as her opinion that if all double-dealing were to vanish from the earth he would easily make up the deficiency himself. But it was to say the least unfortunate that when on his birthday, only a month after his arrival, an attempt was made on the life of his protector, the Prince of Orange, everyone should immediately have jumped to the conclusion that he was to blame for it.

"It's a pity that he [Orange] and others of his kidney didn't die eighteen or twenty years ago," Cardinal Granvelle remarked with tart satisfaction when the false news reached him that the Prince was dead. It was of course a Spanish plot, engineered by a Portuguese merchant and executed by his servant with Parma's knowledge and approval, and was fortunately recognized as such just in time to prevent a general massacre of every Frenchman in Antwerp.

Though no work of his, the crime hardened opinion against Anjou, if only for the reason that people felt him fully capable of such treachery. And these attitudes naturally deepened his own resentment and jealousy of the public eulogies of Orange which accompanied the hero's convalescence from an almost mortal wound. Detested by his subjects, closely watched by the States General and a new (Protestant) Council of State specially appointed to curb him, with the overmastering shadow of Orange always at his shoulder—it was no marvel that the newcomer felt tempted to justify the popular opinion. There were always voices to tell him that his role as a *roi fainéant* was ignoble and unworthy of a son of France. Indeed in many ways the Duke is to be pitied: he was as misused as Matthias, another victim of the Netherlanders' almost pathological distrust of their rulers.

By the new year he had reached a state of unbearable frustration —Lord of Brabant, Friesland and Gelderland, newly inducted as Count of Flanders, but consigned to a draughty abbey in Antwerp, where, as he said, he was "The Abbot of St. Michel by grace of the Prince of Orange." This role was one which he was not prepared to play once he had accumulated a sizable French army of his own. Secret plans were drawn up with his captains for simultaneous attacks on a number of important fortresses held for the States General in southwestern Flanders, and in mid-January 1583 a body of his troops to the number of perhaps three thousand under his personal command seized one of the main gates into Antwerp and attempted to rush the town to cries of "Long live the mass! Long live the Duke of Anjou! Kill, kill, kill!"

This so-called "French Fury," to distinguish it from the "Spanish Fury" after the death of Requesens, was a thoroughly botched and incompetent job. Motley asserts that the French made straight for the jewelers' shops, and though this may be an amusing libel it does illustrate the frivolity of the attempt when compared with the savage rape of the city by the *tercios* and accounts for the much more spirited response of the Antwerpers on this occasion. Let Motley bear witness:

Gentlemen came with lance and cuirass, burghers with musket and bandoleer, artisans with axe, mallet, and other implements of their trade. A bold baker, standing by his oven—stark naked, according to the custom of bakers at that day—rushed to the streets as the sound of the tumult reached his ear. With his heavy bread shovel, which he still held in his hand, he dealt a French cavalry officer, just riding and screaming by, such a hearty blow that he fell dead from his horse. The baker seized the officer's sword, sprang, all unattired as he was, upon his steed, and careered furiously through the streets, encouraging his countrymen everywhere to the attack, and dealing dismay through the ranks of the enemy.

With such protagonists was Antwerp saved from its own lawful ruler, who eleven months earlier had entered it in state! By nightfall a large part of the invading force of French were either dead or prisoners and Anjou himself was a fugitive from a city he was never again to enter. Soon they were singing in the streets:

> 't Is better met den ouden vader,
> Dan met den verrader.

> (Better the old father [Philip]
> Than the traitor.)

Nor were these only Catholic voices. What was sung in Antwerp was preached from Calvinist pulpits everywhere, but with this gloss on it—"Better an open enemy than a treacherous friend." The revulsion against Anjou was passionate and widespread throughout the liberated provinces.

Yet to whom else could the Netherlanders turn? In ruling circles no one had yet seriously thought of rebuilding bridges to Spain. The crying need for an ally in the face of Parma's army, now sixty thousand strong, had not been lessened by what had happened but had actually increased, since Anjou had not failed elsewhere as dismally as at Antwerp but had seized fortresses—Dunkirk among them—which he might keep for himself or even trade with Parma if pressed too hard. How else but by a reconciliation with Anjou could these fortresses be recovered and an army found capable of facing Parma in the field? If Anjou chose to feel affronted, how could a small rebel confederacy defend itself against him and the world power of Spain combined?

In what was to be the last of his great state papers Orange now pointed out these unpalatable facts. His own credit was badly damaged by Anjou's disgrace, since the man had been his candidate, but the force of that orderly, dispassionate mind could still command the respect of all but the most purblind and bigoted of his followers. There were, as he explained, only three possible courses open—to treat with Spain, which was unthinkable; to fight on alone, which was impossible; or to return to an ally who had at least brought benefits:

Remember how deeply we pondered before accepting Anjou as our sovereign and how every one of us, without exception, was convinced that there was no one else to defend us. . . . I don't deny that the Duke has broken faith and his contract with us. But if you reflect well, can you deny the advantages he brought us? For three years he has enabled us to defend ourselves, while two powerful armies which Spain brought against us melted like snow in the sun.

The logic was inescapable, since even Elizabeth was pressing for a compromise; and bowing to necessity the States General reopened discussions with their treacherous protector. It seemed as though the clock were to be put back three years—to an Anjou alliance for the third time of asking: a coalition between a Calvinist government and a Catholic sovereign: a deep mutual distrust.

In June 1583 the Duke of Anjou left Dunkirk and retired to France. In July his governor surrendered the town to Parma, who was busily engaged in snatching fortresses in Flanders as bases for a general offensive to the north. Anjou however was by no means unhopeful of returning to the provinces which had swallowed the bitter pill of his treason; and preparations to this end were already well advanced when in the summer of the following year he died— of typhoid? of consumption? of poison? There were the usual rumors.

Throughout his short life this able and unscrupulous man had done little but make trouble, first in France, then in the Netherlands, and always for his own selfish ends. But by his death he did the world an even worse service, for he was the last of the male Valois, except a king, who was never likely to have children, and the heir to the French throne was now Henry of Navarre, a Huguenot who was anathema to the Catholic majority of the country and its ambitious leaders of the house of Guise. This one fact changed the whole political balance of Europe by converting the French Catholics from rivals of Spain into allies and fellow conspirators against the heretics and the weak, temporizing Valois king.

If this was a result which might have amused Anjou, a witty and irreligious man, he would certainly have relished beyond measure the other by-product of his own death.

The news of it had to be taken to the Netherlands, to the Prince of Orange, who had left Antwerp the previous summer for Holland. In the south, in Brabant and Flanders, the Prince had failed, and this move had been a tacit admission of it. His connections with Anjou had ended by destroying his credit with the Calvinist zealots who now ruled the roost in Ghent and Antwerp. His wife Charlotte de Bourbon had died during his convalescence from his wound, and his remarriage to another Frenchwoman, Louise de Coligny, had seemed to underline a growing dependence on a nation whose activities in Antwerp during the Fury had by no means been forgiven or forgotten. Only in his northern base from which the revolt had sprung was his influence still undiminished, his policies accepted, if not always understood. There in Delft he had set up house in a disused convent, the Prinsenhof, which still stands by the placid, leaf-strewn canal in the shadow of the leaning tower of the Oude Kirk; and to this quiet place there came in July the courier from France, apparently a sternly Calvinist young man already known to the Prince by the name of Guion.

In fact he was a bigoted Catholic, Balthazar Gérard, who had pressed his services on Parma as a man appointed by God to cleanse the world of anti-Christ.

But the executioner had brought no pistols with him. Parma had not thought him even worth the price of one. Nor had Gérard himself expected to be admitted to his victim's bedchamber with the dispatches from Paris, as in fact he was. Only next day was this deficiency remedied—paid for with a gift of money from the Prince himself! Was this *hubris*? If Orange suffered from the sin of pride, it lay in too great a reliance on his own inviolability—the Prinsenhof was badly guarded, and the persons in it hardly at all.

On the day after his purchase—Tuesday the tenth of July 1584—Gérard once more gained admission to the house. Orange's wife saw him and remarked on his desperate appearance, but nothing was done. *Hubris* again? As the Prince came from midday dinner and turned to go up the flight of stairs to his private rooms above, Gérard stepped from a dark alcove near the door into the court- yard and shot him through the body at point-blank range. Accord- ing to tradition the Prince cried out: "My God, have mercy on my soul. My God, have mercy on this poor people." A few minutes later he was dead.

The assassin was captured, put to the torture, and later executed in the square facing the New Church, where today in summer the cars are parked in serried ranks. They tore off his right hand, lacerated his body with red-hot pincers, ripped out his heart and flung it in his face. Then they dismembered him and struck off his head.

There are few memories in Delft of this savage and bestial scene. But they still show you in the Prinsenhof under a glass sheet the marks on the stone where the shots struck.

15

ADVANCE OF PARMA. FALL OF ANTWERP.
1584–85.

With the events in Delft and a grand apotheosis of Orange as father of a nation Motley ends his *Rise of the Dutch Republic*. Dramatically it was fitting to close his book on the death of a hero; and it is also true that the seeds of the future state known to seventeenth-century Europe as the United Provinces and to us today as Holland had been sown in the Union of Utrecht before the Prince's guiding hand was removed forever. But "Rise" is a misnomer. "Birth" might have been better—a rickety, uncertain birth which it seemed all too likely the infant would not survive. If 1584 saw anything, it was the near extinction of the rebellion. And this was not because Orange's death left it without a heart or a head. Ten years, even five years, earlier it would have been true, but it was true no longer. The threat to the nationalist cause did not lie in the loss of a man who for all his genius was no longer irreplaceable, but rather in the developing thrust of Parma's offensive from his Walloon base into the heartlands of Flanders and Brabant.

To start with, this had been a hand-to-mouth affair, hampered by a lack of money which at one stage had reduced the *tercios* to beggary and had driven the German units to a mutiny which Parma put down singlehanded by an expedient which would have delighted the elder Dumas: by swooping down on the mutineers and carrying their ringleader off bodily across the crupper of his horse. In the aftermath of Anjou's disgrace Parma had managed to pick up the fortresses of Eindhoven, Diest, Dunkirk, Nieuport, Zutphen and Ypres; and in the months immediately preceding the death of Orange, "that pernicious man," as he called him in an exultant letter to the King, he had begun to move against the four key cities of Brussels, Bruges, Ghent and Antwerp, whose capture would ensure the reconquest of Flanders and Brabant.

By then the worst days of penury were over and Parma had

money—large consignments from Spain, much greater than anything previously enjoyed by the royal government. And he had a
considered policy. The victorious advance had been marked by a
display of moderation which first astonished and then captivated
his opponents. He explained his motives in a letter to Cardinal
Granvelle *à propos* of the terms he had given Ypres:

Although many wanted me to kill the Burghers and their leaders who
had surrendered at my discretion, I felt I should not do this, both
because of my present aims and because of the discredit which might
have resulted and have affected the negotiations. For I know by experience that clemency is the one remedy to use on these people and
that past severities only exasperated them. The right course now is to
reassure them and win them over step by step.

If cunning and coldhearted, these principles were strictly observed and there were no executions or atrocities of the kind he
had allowed at Sichem and Maastricht. When he entered a town
the mass entered with him and everywhere the practice of the
Reformed religion was suppressed, but the Calvinists were allowed
a generous period of grace to leave in peace, taking their goods
with them, and could in fact stay forever if reconciled with the
Church. It was a far cry from Alva. The new Governor General
knew how to limit his objectives: he looked to no sudden large-scale
triumph but to a gradual eating-away of the rebellion, literally
town by town. "To treat each individual case apart; that's what
is necessary and what we ought to aim at," he informed Granvelle.

Here was good political doctrine, since the strength of Calvinism
varied widely from town to town. But on the military front it certainly did not apply, and he was now to alarm the more conservative officers on his staff by moving against all four rebel towns
at once. Of course he had neither the troops nor the siege trains
to do this in the formal sense of sitting down before their walls as
Don Frederick had done at Haarlem. Moving across a wide arc
of rebel territory, he simply cut off the towns from one another
and from their sources of supply by building forts at strategic
points on road and canal links, and then relied on economic strangu-
lation and on his own reputation for reasonableness to do the rest.

Bruges was the first victim of this method: in May 1584, two
months before Orange's death, it passed into the royalist camp.

Ghent was more troublesome. The turbulent and ungovernable city which had become the forcing ground of Calvinism in the south now responded to Parma's overtures with the reminder, through the mouth of its ruling demagogue, that it could tear up more letters in any given day than the royalist secretariat could write.

This was a typical piece of bombast. Even when the city was near to desperation, with its food supplies cut off and no hope of rescue from Brussels or Antwerp, its representatives were still trying to write their own terms of surrender—no Spanish troops to be garrisoned in the citadel, and Calvinist worship to be permitted in certain wards at least for a limited time. "The King, my master and yours," Parma replied with cold politeness, "is Catholic and is honored with the title of 'Catholic King.' As for myself, I belong to a family of Christian princes. I risk my life for the Catholic faith and I do not mean to sully my name by authorizing people to worship in an un-Catholic way. It was for these principles that the war between us began, and it is on these principles that it will end."

He was in a position to enforce such prophecies, and in September the besieged themselves recognized the fact and signed the instruments of surrender in his camp at Beveren. "Such was the end," writes Van Essen, Parma's biographer, "of this celebrated Calvinist republic of Ghent . . . which defied the States General, opposed the policies of the Taciturn [Orange] and bore the main responsibility for the separation of the Walloon provinces. For years its Catholics had been oppressed by a minority of violent sectarians, while priests and regular clergy were made the chief victims of its crimes."

Yet the terms given it at Beveren were so mild that even Parma felt obliged to justify them to the King by pointing out the excellent results which his methods had already achieved at Bruges. An equally powerful motive had no doubt been his hope—soon to be abundantly justified—that once purged of its Calvinists it would become the base and arsenal for his war machine against Antwerp, the huge emporium on the estuary of the Scheldt which was the pivot of rebel resistance in the central provinces and the main target of his campaign. This was a still more formidable nut to crack. When told they were to besiege it, Parma's council of war, with only two dissentient voices, expressed something close to disbelief, for Antwerp's fortifications had been built by Charles V, its citadel by the Duke of Alva, and it was hallowed by military opinion as impregnable to any force not holding command of the sea.

These objections Parma swept aside with unusual curtness. He had no intention of attacking the walls of Charles V or Alva's star-shaped citadel. He would starve the town out by cutting off its access to the sea by the building of a fortified bridge across the narrows of the Scheldt.

In the last months of his life the Prince of Orange had foreseen just such a plan and had urged the Antwerpers and their burgo-master, St. Aldegonde, to breach the dykes and flood the country on the right or Brabant bank well down-river from the town, thus facing Parma with the impossible task of bridging a lake several miles wide.

But the Antwerpers—and particularly the guild of butchers, whose cattle would have lost their grazing—had refused this re-quest point-blank, threatening to resist by force if anything so ob-jectionable to their profits were attempted. As a concession they had let St. Aldegonde cut the left-bank dykes and flood the country on the Flemish side, thus actually helping the Spaniards to bring up their bridging material by boat, as Orange had also foreseen and warned against. It was Parma's luck in this siege to be uniquely blessed by the shortsightedness of his enemies—even some of the blockships and much of the timber for the piers and causeway had lain under the noses of the Calvinists in Zeeland ports for over a month without anyone suspecting their destination.

So enormous and audacious a project of bridging half a mile of tidal water in the front yard of a city of a hundred thousand people and in the face of vastly superior fleets was rightly judged one of the marvels of the age. An army of carpenters and smiths had to be recruited. An entirely new canal was needed to float up the heavier material from Ghent. Enormous quantities of timber and flotillas of boats had to be assembled, batteries of cannon placed in the ravelins on the bridge and in the forts guarding the narrows; the force of sappers and covering troops had to be fed—all this in a countryside flooded to a depth of several feet, with few roads across it, in a wilderness where, as Parma himself said, there was nothing but dykes and salt water.

Through the depths of a cheerless winter the work went on; the piles were driven into the silt to carry a causeway from either bank; the central span, a quarter of a mile long, formed of a bridge of boats anchored and chained together, was towed into position; and on the twenty-fifth of February—St. Matthew's Day, which the Emperor Charles had always regarded as specially fortunate—the whole vast project was complete and Antwerp cut off from the Beggar bases in Zeeland. Very handsome it looks in engravings of the time, with its flags and cannon and galloping horsemen on its causeway against the distant prospect of spires and shipping on the river. The artist has even shown us Parma himself, standing hatless in doublet and hose in the fort of Ste. Marie on the Brabant bank, gazing out on the animated scene so wonderfully evocative of the power and genius of the Spanish empire at its height. Never was his urbanity more evident or turned to a neater purpose. A spy, sent out from Antwerp to examine the bridge, was captured in the act and taken into the presence. The poor man, hourly expecting to be hanged, was courteously conducted round the works, shown everything, besought to count the forts and the one hundred and fifty cannon, was entertained in the royalist camp at Beveren and sent back into the city, a living argument for a settlement of the kind Parma was offering and the peace party in Antwerp, the so-called "Peiswillers," was anxious to accept.

But for the ruling Calvinists—a minority well entrenched in power—no terms were acceptable that did not include guarantees for a religious toleration they had certainly not shown their Catholic fellow citizens. Their negotiations with Parma had been marked by a mutual polish and courtesy which would greatly have astonished the Duke of Alva, but on this point they were adamant, and even the fall of Brussels, which surrendered on very generous terms in mid-March, did not alter things one jot. They remained buoyed up by hopes that the king of France, to whom they had offered the sovereignty of the Netherlands, or the Beggar fleet, or both, would come to the rescue before starvation set in.

By early spring the first of these hopes had been dashed—the king of France was too much the prisoner of his own extreme Catholic wing to look for new heretic subjects. Even the Zeeland fleets were inexplicably delayed—not till the beginning of April did two hundred sail under Orange's bastard son, Justin of Nassau, appear in the Scheldt and begin operations against the Spanish forts guarding the estuary approaches to the bridge.

Obviously something had to be attempted from Antwerp itself. There an Italian engineer by the name of Giambelli had prepared his own solution to the problem in the form of two stupendous floating bombs: ships whose hulls were lined with brick and stuffed full of explosives to deck level. On the night of April 4/5 these vessels, the famous "hellburners" whose reputation lingered long after them, were launched on the ebb tide against Parma's bridge —the most monstrous and showy piece of pyrotechnics since the siege of Constantinople. One drifted wide to explode harmlessly on the Flemish bank; the second got through the outer line of stake boats and struck the northern ravelin which Parma himself had just quitted under the urgent promptings of his staff. Van Essen has a fine descriptive passage:

Scarcely had he got clear, when the mine hidden in the bowels of the *"Espérance"* exploded with terrifying force. Huge pillars of flame spouted into the air, lighting up the countryside for miles around. Forts, bridge, shipping, the banks of the Scheldt and the fantastic shapes of flooded villages seemed to leap out of the darkness in a flash of eerie light. The earth shook with a rumbling sound which spread like thunder under the feet of the terrified troops. Huge waterspouts were formed and a kind of tidal wave broke over the forts on either bank, sweeping everything away and swamping the Spanish posts. Witnesses of the scene thought that for an instant they had glimpsed the river bed itself. They claimed to have seen the waters, mixed with a film of brilliant fire like molten lead, invade the bank, destroying everything in its path. Tombstones, marble blocks, scraps of iron, bricks and beams which Giambelli had packed into his bomb were flying in all directions and spread destruction among the garrison of the bridge and its forts. Cannon balls, chains, lumps of iron and piers from the river bed were scattered over the fields for a distance of more than half a mile from the centre of the explosion. The worst destruction was on the bridge itself. The northern ravelin where the Prince of Parma had been standing only a few moments before was completely smashed; nails and chains, wrenched violently out of place, became air-borne; the causeway was broken up. Four large pieces of artillery were hurled skywards and disappeared; four ships moored close to the bridge caught fire and sank; two others were destroyed. Several officers were flung violently through the air by the blast and landed on the banks or in the waters of the Scheldt. Some, like the Vicomte de Bruxelles, Jacques de Bossu, had miraculous escapes from death. Not so fortunate were the Marquis of Richebourg and de Roble de Billy, who lost their lives in the catastrophe. Richebourg's body was found some days later, rolled round an iron chain hanging from one of the guard boats in the middle of the river; the re-

mains of Roble de Billy were only identified after the surrender of
Antwerp, literally stuck to the causeway planks. He was only identified
because of the gold chain he always wore. Between one o'clock and half
past one that morning nothing was heard but the cries and groans of the
injured, crushed by the fall of masonry, wounded in the explosion, or
drowning in the river.

Giambelli's bomb in other words was a decided success. It
created an ineffaceable impression, which three years later was to
play its part in the defeat of the Armada, attacked by fire ships
—though not in fact by hellburners—in Calais Roads. The savage
force and intensity of the explosion, far surpassing anything
dreamed of in military thinking in the West, was vividly preserved by artists who were either present themselves or were told
about it by horrified eyewitnesses; and there in the engravings
is the inferno of the blast, the huge mushrooming cloud of fire
and smoke like some ancestor of the atom bomb, and—carefully
labeled—the Vicomte de Bruxelles flying through the air above
the ruined ravelin like some virtuoso of the high wire, halfway
between the sky and the Scheldt. It looks apocalyptic. And no
doubt that was how it felt.

Yet, incredibly enough, nothing was done to exploit the opportunity thus presented. Perhaps the wind was in the wrong
quarter or, more probably, nobody had really believed in Giambelli
and his bombs; at all events the Beggar ships in the estuary made
no move, and within little more than twenty-four hours Parma's
engineers had repaired the worst of the damage and sealed off the
breach. This failure did not spell the end of rebel resistance, for
a most determined two-pronged assault was launched some weeks
later to cut the Kouwenstein dyke to open traffic to the city over
flooded country on the Brabank bank of the river; but the psychological pressure of the siege by that time was running deep,
and the peace party in Antwerp had begun to embrace even its
Calvinist burgomaster and Orange's old disciple, Philip Marnix of
St. Aldegonde.

There was no sudden panic surrender; nor on the royalist side
was there any intemperate demand for one. Feelings were respected. Proper regard was paid to Antwerp's special position as

the commercial capital likely to house large colonies of foreign heretics. But in August all resistance came to an end and the capitulation was signed at Beveren on terms even more magnanimous than had been granted Ghent and Brussels—a four-year amnesty for Calvinists, provided they created no "scandal" by public worship; a fine to cover the expenses of the siege; the imposition of a garrison; though even here the susceptibilities of the inhabitants were consulted and none of the hated Spanish or Italian troops were to form it, only Germans and Walloons. No one was hanged. No one was proscribed.

"I give infinite thanks to God," the victor wrote to Philip, "for His great and singular grace in guiding me with His divine hand and allowing me to bring this wearisome and dangerous task to so happy an end." The note of joyous reconciliation, of safe return to legality, was the one he meant to strike, and he took care to stress it in his own entry into the town, surrounded not by his victorious generals but by the high Netherlands nobility: the Duke of Aerschot, the Prince of Chimay, Count Charles of Mansfeld, Count Egmont, the son of Alva's victim. This was to be no triumphal parade in a captured town. The King's representative was entering into his own—by the same gate through which his grandfather Charles V had passed on another "Joyous" occasion, surrounded by much the same crowds of cheering and rejoicing people. Van Essen does justice to the delicious irony of the scene:

At every cross-roads he was brought to a halt by entertainments created in his honour by poets, comedians, and others, declaimed in Latin, French and Flemish. There were also tributes delivered in Spanish and Italian, probably commissioned by the equally enthusiastic foreign merchants at a cost of several thousand florins. Everywhere triumphal arches, set pieces and columns decorated with flowers and inscriptions recalled his victories, comparing them to Alexander the Great, Caesar and Scipio Africanus.

But then Antwerp had perhaps always been at heart a Catholic town. Hundreds of its Calvinists had already gone into exile and were spared the sight of this Babylonish captivity. On the Scheldt bridge the Italian and Spanish troops, denied their triumphal entry into the city, held their own celebrations which were spread over three days of pageants, banquets and a ball graced by almost everyone of note in the reconciled provinces, including a corps of eight hundred ladies of gentle birth. Conducted tours of the bridge and its outworks were arranged for the good citizens, who could thus see for themselves Giambelli's handiwork and the rotting corpses on the Kouwenstein dyke where the last attempt to raise the siege had failed.

Soon the news had reached Spain; and according to Strada's story the King, roused for once from impassivity by the arrival of couriers in the night, was hammering at his elder daughter's door with the ecstatic words, "Antwerp is ours."

He might well rejoice. The rebels, who at Don John's death had held all the provinces but Luxemburg and a small strip of land along the Meuse, had been driven back behind their water defenses. Not since Lepanto had there been such a victory for Spanish arms. The end of the rebellion itself seemed to be in sight.

16

INTERVENTION OF ELIZABETH. 1585.

In fact at this precise point the balance of the struggle began to change. Victory resembles defeat if only in this, that both have to be paid for, and the very completeness of Parma's triumph had brought into action forces which had always been present in the European situation but had lain dormant in the limbo of Elizabethan policy.

Traditionally France was England's national enemy. The Empire and Spain had seemed her natural allies: this had been doctrine for both Henry VIII and his elder daughter, and Elizabeth herself had at least paid lip service to it for most of her reign. Even at the height of the Spanish maltreatment of the Netherlands under Alva she had been reluctant to intervene on the rebel side, and Alva for his part, though perfectly willing that Spanish or Papal agents should assassinate her if they could, had been careful to play down any talk of crusades against her or invasions of her territory; he had been as moderate in his English policy as he had been ruthless in his suppression of the Netherlands, and the Queen had recognized the fact.

That is not to say that she ever spared Spanish susceptibilities when they conflicted with what she judged to be English interests. She had had as little compunction in turning down Philip's offer of marriage at the outset of her reign as she had in seizing Alva's treasure ships in '68 or in supporting by proxy the slaving ventures of John Hawkins in the Caribbean or the still more piratical exploits of Drake along the Spanish Main. As we have seen, in 1572 the famous corsair had launched an unprovoked assault on Nombre de Dios and had attacked the narrow life line of the treasure convoys —in a sense the life line of Spain itself—on the Isthmus of Panama; in his circumnavigation of the globe he had raided all along the unprotected Peruvian coast. For these exploits the Queen had had

him knighted, and by the French ambassador in her presence—
a highly provocative act.

These were the pinpricks of a cold war. In a sense they were
unavoidable. No popular ruler such as Elizabeth aspired to be could
have resisted the forces of expansion which permeated English
society at every level and nowhere more so than in the ports
dominated by an aggressive class of Protestant merchants and
seamen. Drake was a national hero, and the policies he stood for
were supported in the Privy Council by a group of able and
determined men led by Walsingham and the reigning favorite,
Leicester. Nor was the Queen reluctant to countenance Drake and
like-minded adventurers. They brought her money. She was a share-
holder in several of their enterprises. Nevertheless she kept a tight
hold on them. When cornered by Spanish ambassadors, a suffering breed of men, she was always ready to deny any personal
responsibility for what was done by her servants in her ships. She
had no desire to enter into any duel to the death with Spain.
Whenever possible she negotiated—with the King, with Alva, with
Don John, with Parma—often behind the backs of her own advisers,
who were constantly pressing her to intervene more directly against
Spain, particularly in the crucible of the Netherlands where the
greatest danger lay.

For this policy of strictly limited confrontation the Queen had
many excellent reasons. As a woman she disliked war; it was all too
apt to get into men's hands and give them ideas above their
station. The expenses of it appalled her parsimonious soul—cold
war in all conscience was ruinous enough. Also as a ruler she had
a natural distaste for rebels, and as a person of cool and skeptical
mind she had an aversion for religious bigotry of any kind, especially the Calvinist kind which she saw disturbingly reflected
among her own Puritan extremists. Rather than support rebellion
à outrance in the Netherlands she would prefer a *détente* with Spain
—on her own terms of course.

And in these attitudes she was almost exactly matched by her
onetime suitor. Philip too had a hatred of war. As early as 1557
a Venetian ambassador had commented on it. And he too was a
temporizing person. Another Venetian ambassador, Contarini, expressed it excellently: ". . . the King is very slow to make up his
mind on important matters, and puts off decisions more often than
he ought, imagining that time will come to the rescue. . . ."

For years, acting on these principles, the King had put off any final solution of the English problem, concerning himself more with the hereditary rivalry with France which was in fact by far the less pressing danger. On several occasions he had thought of having the heretical queen assassinated or even of invading her territories in association with plots devised in Rome and supported by Catholic groups in Scotland and England itself, but always at the last moment he had drawn back. Several promising opportunities had been lost in this way, notably in 1567, in the winter of 1571 at the time of the Ridolfi plot and in 1576, when his governor in the Low Countries—Don John—had been an enthusiast for an invasion across the Channel: a project which both Alva and later Parma distrusted. What had stuck in the King's throat was the thought that if Elizabeth were killed or deposed, her legal successor was Mary Queen of Scots, a woman whose religious orthodoxy might be all that could be desired but who was half French by blood and wholly French in sympathies.

Thus for two decades the peace of a great part of western Europe had been kept by the mutual fears, idiosyncrasies and wisdom of two cautious rulers who distrusted one another but thought rather worse of their respective allies. It had been a triumph of common sense in the face of provocation and religious bigotry. But then throughout that time, London, Madrid and the Spanish government in Brussels had all been aware of another factor, the balancing force of a strong French monarchy which could intervene decisively against either side.

All this was now changed. The King of France in 1585 was little more than a cipher in his own country, which under the auspices of the ambitious Guise princes and the ultra-Catholic League had become almost a client state of Spain.

In such a context Parma's successes were much more menacing to English interests than Alva's had ever been. There were other factors too. Spain had swallowed Portugal with its fleets and Atlantic harbors. The sudden change which had come over Spanish policy since the death of Eboli and the arrival in Madrid of Cardinal Granvelle was too obvious to be missed by the Queen's advisers, well briefed as they were through the brilliant intelligence network which Walsingham had created. After the subjugation of the Netherlands it might well be England's turn. Few doubted it. Even Elizabeth was a reluctant convert to the notion, though she had constant second thoughts, to the despair of her servants. She always did the right thing in the end, however. So in the days when Antwerp was falling she made a defensive alliance with her uncongenial suitors of the Netherlands States General and engaged to send an army to defend their liberties, even appointing Leicester to command it, a special mark of her favor.

By so doing she was able to save the balance of Europe in her time. And by the same token she made certain the dispatch of the great Armada of '88.

17

THE ARMADA. 1585–88.

In 1585 the notion of invading England from the continent could not have seemed the harebrained scheme it appears to us. The island had fallen many times to invading waves of Celts, Romans, Angles, Saxons, Danes and Normans up to the day, exactly a century before, when Elizabeth's own grandfather had landed at Milford Haven on his way to find the crown on Bosworth Field.

Almost without exception over a millennium these ventures had succeeded, partly because of the inviting physical shape of the country, whose low-lying eastern shore was indented with bays and estuaries and whose capital lay on a tidal river only sixty miles from the sea.

To Philip the invasion of the heretic island had therefore a long and encouraging ancestry, even if times had changed since the perhaps legendary Hengist and Horsa had been invited ashore and the Viking long ships had stolen up the Trent and Humber. England had a fleet, reputedly the strongest in western Europe outside of the Mediterranean where the oared galley still ruled.

On the oceans Spain was a comparative newcomer. The great sea-going fleets of the Atlantic had been Portuguese. But Portugal was now subject to the King of Spain, whose own galleons of the Indies' treasure convoys had become a formidable force in their own right. And in the course of the recent war against the pretender to the Portuguese throne a royalist squadron under Philip's famous admiral Don Alvaro de Bazán, Marquis of Santa Cruz, had won two resounding victories off the Azores against French and (it was believed) English warships.

In the flush of this imagined success—imagined, since none of the Queen's men-of-war had actually been present—Santa Cruz had suggested an invasion of England by a sea-borne armada from Philip's Atlantic ports.

The King's reaction was cautious: he had firsthand knowledge of England and realized, if Santa Cruz did not, that the enter-

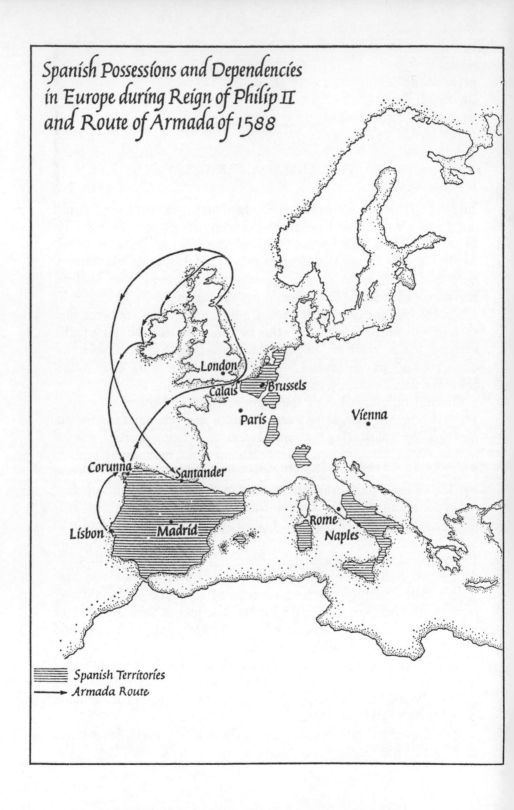

Spanish Possessions and Dependencies
in Europe during Reign of Philip II
and Route of Armada of 1588

London
Calais •Brussels
Paris
Vienna
Corunna Santander
Lisbon Madrid
Rome
Naples

Spanish Territories
Armada Route

prise would devour men and money. However, the idea lodged in his mind. By 1585 the times were propitious, with the Turks fully engaged elsewhere along their frontiers and France firmly held in check by his treaty of Joinville with the Guises, and on the seventeenth of August, the day of the capture of Antwerp, he recognized the force of what Santa Cruz was urging by charging Parma to prepare a plan for the invasion of England and to advise what contribution could be made from Brussels.

Thus from the outset the King had recognized the vital part the Netherlands would have to play and had modified the notion of an assault by armada from Spain. He can only have been confirmed in the soundness of his judgment by the details with which Santa Cruz soon provided him: demands for a fleet of 150 galleons and large armed merchantmen, 40 storeships, 320 auxiliary cruisers and picket boats, 6 galleasses and 40 galleys, with crews and an invasion force together numbering little short of a hundred thousand men at a cost in the region of four million ducats. Such resources were not to be had in Spain or its empire or anywhere in Europe. The Ottoman Turks had not been able to match them at Malta or Lepanto: indeed it is hard to credit that Santa Cruz can really have believed in what he proposed or could have been doing more than make a staff appreciation of what was desirable in the ideal world of the military planner.

Yet if most of this was visionary, the central idea behind it had gained in force, since circumstances were rapidly driving Philip to accept that some kind of invasion of England would have to be attempted. The arrival in the Netherlands late in 1585 of the Earl of Leicester with seven thousand English troops had been an intolerable provocation, and Drake also was at sea again on a raid which had taken him to Vigo and was to unroll through the Caribbean among the half-defended harbors of the islands and the Main. The need for chastisement of heretics, revenge for insults and the security of Spain all cried aloud for action, and in the spring of 1586 the King received through Parma's agent Piatti a detailed scheme which seemed to promise retribution at conveniently cut rates. "The enterprise," Parma had written from his Netherlands headquarters, "could well be carried out from here." What he was envisaging was a sneak landing in Kent or Essex to be undertaken by a force of thirty thousand infantry and five hundred cavalry (who were to find their mounts in England), carried from Flemish ports in flat-bottomed barges under the escort of twenty-five warships.

On the face of it this was an appealing scheme which took good account of one of the principles of war—economy of means— for the Netherlands army was already in being and separated from its objective only by the narrows of the Straits of Dover which its commander hoped to cross "in ten or twelve hours," eight if weather conditions were fair. A huge armada at ruinous cost was therefore ruled out: no armada at all would be required from Spain unless the secret of the enterprise were to leak.

There however lay the rub, and Parma himself was underlining it by insisting that only if complete secrecy were kept could the operation be mounted with any hope of success. How then was a force of twenty-five warships and flat-bottomed boats for thirty thousand men to be assembled in the canals and harbors between Antwerp and Dunkirk without word of it reaching England or at least without its destination being guessed, however good a cover story were put up for a proposed assault on Zeeland? The King himself was to note and comment acidly on the value of any such assumption. Looked at in this light, Parma's plan was every bit as impracticable as Santa Cruz's and is open to parallel interpretation —that it was not a serious plan at all but a piece of window dress- ing, perhaps with the aim of attracting large Spanish reinforce- ments into the Netherlands, to be used, not for the King's "great enterprise," but to attack the rest of the heretic provinces, a pos- sibility which we find reflected in certain significant utterances of Piatti, and in Parma's own oddly supine and devious conduct throughout the Armada affair from first to last.

Philip's own conduct at about this time shows a surprising lack of resolution and decisiveness for one so apparently committed to a great objective. Plans were debated but nothing was decided beyond the need for postponing action till the spring, eight months off. Preparations for an armada went forward in the dockyards and arsenals but disjointedly, without urgency or central direction. Probably in his heart of hearts the King still shrank from the vast expenditure of blood and treasure that the enterprise must cost him and hoped that God would provide a less expensive solution to his problem in the shape of a rising of English and Scots Catholics, stiffened by a nucleus of Parma's troops put across the Channel for the purpose.

Through the autumn of 1586 the long-suffering Governor General found himself bombarded by increasingly shrill royal demands for action on these lines which he knew to be ridiculous. He had no belief in the chances of any Catholic conspiracy succeeding in England without armed aid on a scale which he had no means or hope of providing for many months to come, and it must have been with relief that he learned that the projected rising, which we know as the Babington plot, had been penetrated by Walsingham's agents and had ignominiously collapsed, involving in its ruin the woman in whose interests it had been made.

Babington's was only the latest of a number of plots which over the years had been mounted with Spanish or Papal money against Elizabeth's life and the Protestant succession. But when for her complicity in it Mary Stuart went to the block in Fotheringay Castle on a February morning in 1587 everyone knew that something irrevocable had been done beyond the taking of a life. Elizabeth's frantic show of grief and anger at a deed she had ordered by her own signature on the warrant was just one proof of this. It was her practice to disown all unpopular or compromising acts of her own servants, even though carried out on her behalf and with her approval, and never had the need to lay the blame elsewhere been more evident than on this occasion, when royal blood had been shed and she had kicked away the last prop of the shaky edifice of peace which she and Philip had erected and kept in some sort of repair for over twenty years.

For in spite of all that had happened she still wanted peace: her ministers were to remark that summer that never had her passion for it been stronger or more willfully obtuse. For their part, the radicals on her Council had long since accepted that war must come, and even the moderates like Burghley had become resigned to it. For them the execution of Mary Stuart had become a necessary act, inviting the chance of immediate attack, perhaps from France and Spain together, but cutting the risk of a rising at home by removing the figurehead and patroness for whom alone the Catholic gentry of England would "come out" against a well-entrenched and vigilant government—what they would do for Mary, whom they thought of as their lawful queen, they would never do for Philip.

In Spain and its dependencies the execution was greeted with horror and outrage. Even Parma, who may well have been at one with Elizabeth in his desire for peace—if for different reasons, for he wanted it to make war better in the Netherlands—wrote to the King in the most solemn terms of the "punishment" which the English queen deserved; while in the Atlantic ports of the peninsula the build-up of ships and stores was hurried on under urgent orders from the small workroom in the depths of the Escurial where the King toiled till all hours with his secretaries.

There was still no agreed plan—in a sense there never was to be one. The Armada was one of the most debated, most cared-for, most regimented and worst-directed events in history. Well over a hundred sail were being collected with stores and crews ticketed down to the minutest detail. Immense care was to be taken that every soul aboard should be shriven and warned against blasphemy and incontinence. Yet the ports and roadsteads where these huge forces were assembling had only rudimentary defenses and lay temptingly open to raiders from the sea, as was dramatically shown that spring when Sir Francis Drake with a powerful squadron sailed out of Plymouth (pursued at a decent interval by the Queen's urgent, but not too urgent, summons of recall) and swept down on the crowded harbor of Cádiz for two days and nights of impudent pillage—the famous singeing of the King of Spain's beard which has joined the game of bowls on Plymouth Hoe in the pantheon of "all the glories of England." Accurate advance warnings of Drake's intentions had been sent out by Spanish agents in London, but they arrived too late to save Cádiz. Neither the galleys on duty in the narrows nor the antiquated cannon of the town's defenses could prevent the leisurely destruction of some thirty sail of varying tonnage, not all earmarked for the Armada but including one newly built galleon, the property of Santa Cruz himself, and a number of indispensable storeships. "This service, which by God's sufference we have done, will breed some alterations," Drake wrote triumphantly of the vast disruption he had caused.

It was a striking display of English power, and of English daring, on which Philip particularly remarked,* and there was more to come. Lisbon itself, the main concentration point, was for a while in danger of suffering a similar fate; and from a temporary base which Drake seized ashore at the castle of Sagres vast damage was done to coastal shipping and stores, including the destruction

* He wrote to Mendoza, his ambassador in Paris: "The damage it [the English fleet] committed there was not great, but the daring of the attempt was so."

of large quantities of barrel staves needed for the fleet's storage casks—most essential of commodities.

All of this was to have the effects which Drake had foreseen. Philip's plans were thrown seriously awry. For weeks no shipping could move in the waters between Lisbon and Cape St. Vincent, and it became clear that no Armada would sail that year. But the King did not allow himself to be cast down or too deeply impressed by what had happened. God would repay the injuries he had had to suffer in His name. June—the month after the insolent descent on Portuguese soil at Sagres—saw the development of the King's thinking on the form the enterprise should take. Two plans, two irreconcilable attitudes, of Parma and Santa Cruz, were forcibly united—it was to be a shotgun wedding. Parma would invade from Flanders as he had wished—or had appeared to—with his barges and escort fleet from Antwerp, having first provided the Scots Catholic nobles with enough men and cash to raise diversionary troubles on the English border. Meanwhile the Marquis of Santa Cruz's Armada (in a suitably cut-down form) would seize the Isle of Wight as a base for operations in the Channel and intervene as opportunity offered.

Philip might have claimed with justice that here was an advance on the strictly individual plans which the admiral and the Governor General had each in turn put up. But if marriage there was to be, it was still one without much chance of issue. Though two forces were now to be used, they were placed well over a hundred miles apart, where neither could help or influence the other, and the more vulnerable—Parma's army in its flat-bottomed craft—was apparently seen as the spearhead, crossing in advance of the Armada which might have been expected to protect it. The plan in fact was amateur and ill-balanced: there was no concentration of force, no common objective, no interrelation between the two fronts, unless one accepted Parma's thirty thousand innocents-at-sea as bait to attract the English men-of-war up-Channel from their other prey.

Yet the Governor General, who had proposed to invade England without any supporting fleet from Spain *at all*, as Philip was soon inconveniently reminding him, was hardly in a position to object to these arrangements, and for a while things proceeded in perfect conformity with a plan in which no one (except the King) could possibly have believed. New ships were fitted out in the

Tagus and the Biscayan ports. The ravages of Drake's raid were
slowly made good. Parma dutifully supplied advice as to whether
Santa Cruz's Armada could maneuver in The Solent and Spithead.
And he sat down to besiege the Flemish town of Sluys, whose
capture would give him another harbor, though much silted up in
the two and a half centuries since the Plantagenet Edward III had
lambasted the French there at the start of the Hundred Years War.
Perhaps the fact that in recent months he had received massive
reinforcements of men and money had helped to sweeten his
mood.

Then abruptly in July 1587, while still before Sluys, the mood
changed, and in a letter to the King he referred for the first
time to the need for warships which must escort the barges and
effect the crossing of the troops. He himself had not a war fleet
big enough; yet, without one, his transports might well be sunk.

It says much for the atmosphere of sheer fantasy in which the
"great enterprise" was conceived that no one had thought of this
before. Years had passed since Santa Cruz had first put forward
the notion of an armada and Drake's open act of war in Cádiz Bay
was nearly three months old, yet the invasion planners had not even
agreed on the elementary risks of what they were proposing. Some
of them were *never* to understand it. To his credit the King did
not long resist this glimpse of the obvious but set to work on
modifications, which were ready by the beginning of September.
Parma was now told that Santa Cruz would not halt at the Isle
of Wight but would take his fleet to the mouth of the Thames off
Margate Point (the North Foreland); would anchor there, sending news of his arrival to Flanders; and by his presence would
cover Parma's crossing. Once Parma was ashore the Armada
would disembark six thousand Spanish reinforcements for the advance on London and would then remain on guard to keep communications open with the Netherlands and Spain.

These instructions are among the most crucial in the whole
disastrous story that was to end in the stormy waters off Kerry and
Donegal. The King had abandoned the notion of halting his
Armada at the Isle of Wight, where it would have been hopelessly
out of touch with its Netherlands partner. But though he was proposing to bring it a good deal nearer, he was still assuming that
Parma could join it off the North Foreland with his barges. He
said so specifically. "You in the meantime will be quite ready, and

when you see the passage assured by the arrival of the fleet at Margate or at the mouth of the Thames, you will, if the weather permits, *immediately come out with the whole army* in the boats which you will have ready."

Any hope for the Enterprise therefore depended (even in the absence of an English fleet) on a period of calm weather in the straits. Without it the Armada itself would be in danger, for it had no harbor to go to, only an anchorage, and that off the enemy coast. Dunkirk and Nieuport were too small to hold it. Its nearest haven was Santander. As for Parma, his share in the operation depended entirely on good weather and a coast clear of the enemy—two most unlikely contingencies.

Yet no one seems to have raised any immediate objections. The macabre quality in the Armada story lies in this, that though almost all those concerned in it felt the gravest doubts about it, amounting almost to an acceptance of disaster, no one except Medina Sidonia at the eleventh hour could ever bring himself to tell the King the truth. The infinite distance which divided a Prince (now Duke) of Parma or a Captain General of the Ocean Sea like Santa Cruz from his royal master made impossible any real sharing of opinions or doubts, which had to be expressed obliquely, by polite evasion, by degrees. The King's servants often managed to thwart and obstruct, even sometimes to advise, but they were seldom candid. Thus Parma, faced with a plan which his acute intelligence must have told him was founded on illusions, made no outright protest but fell back on lamenting the state of his military affairs in the provinces and his lack of resources in men and money.

In fact they had seldom been better. The army he commanded in the autumn of 1587 was in every way superior to anything seen in the Netherlands since Alva's time, and seemed poised for similar victories. Sluys, to Philip's great joy, had fallen in August. The Earl of Leicester's Englishmen, so greatly feared on arrival, had done no more than slow down the pace of the Spanish advance, and Leicester's own intrigues with the more radical and leveling of the Calvinists had caused so strong a resentment among the conservative-minded oligarchs of Holland and Zeeland, on whom the real burden of the war fell, that both he and his royal mistress had come to be regarded as opportunists who would sell the free provinces either to the demagogues or to the Spaniards.

It must be confessed that there were some grounds for this belief.

The town of Deventer and an important fortress outside Zutphen had both been betrayed to Parma by captains in whom Leicester had shown a most ill-advised trust. As for the Queen, her own anxiety to make peace with Spain and desert her uncongenial Netherlands allies, unless they too came to the conference table with Parma in a suitably flexible mood, was an open secret and was soon announced by the actual presence of her negotiators on Flemish soil. This had already bred between the rebels and the English an atmosphere of distrust which had bedeviled their joint operations to save Sluys and made any close co-operation impossible, at least for the time being.

Knowing this, and the extent of the reinforcements he had poured in from Italy, the King could be forgiven for thinking that the hour had struck. His Netherlands army was at its peak. The enemy were weak and divided. The impatience of a normally patient man in the grip of an obsession burst out through the usual meanderings of the royal prose into urgent commands for action. On hearing reports that the English fleet had left the Thames to concentrate at Plymouth—"If as a result of these movements," he wrote to Parma, "you judge that the Channel is unguarded, you may, if you are ready, start the venture without waiting for the Armada." A month later Philip's urgings had become more strident—"If you can cross the Channel before the arrival of my fleet, do it boldly. The Armada will come to join you afterward."

That same November Parma reported that the convoy squadron was ready at Antwerp and Dunkirk, and so were the barges. He must have meant that he hoped they were, for nine months later their number and condition were to horrify the liaison officers from Spain. More realistic was the doubt he now expressed as to how these canal craft would fare in the winter waters of the Channel. God willing, and if there were no English fleet in the straits, he hoped to be ready within a fortnight: but it was a very fatalistic letter. Man being so inadequate, there was much need for heavenly assistance—this was to be the philosophy of all those engaged in the Armada.

Still in this mood of resignation, prepared to "sacrifice" himself, as he had long since written to the King, the Governor General left Brussels on November 17 for Bruges and the discovery that the Zeelanders under their admiral Justin of Nassau had blockaded the

Scheldt and Antwerp where most of his escort ships lay. That something of the kind would happen had been one of the major certainties of a war in which sea power lay overwhelmingly on the rebel side, and this alone, without any regard to interference from English squadrons in the straits, would have made Parma's plan for a solo crossing an impossibility. But however unwise he had been to feed such fictions to his master, at least he now had the good sense to correct them and write with the utmost urgency to insist that the two wings of the plan must act as one. Santa Cruz would have to be on the spot and must detach part of his fleet to escort the barges out of Nieuport and Dunkirk—otherwise the plan could not be worked. He was quite clear about it. "We cannot attempt to cross with the expeditionary force," he wrote, "without being sustained and supported by the Marquis of Santa Cruz's armada."

Unfortunately he had not said this from the beginning, but it was now the fundamental point on which he stood and on which he was to insist with a growing desperation in letter after letter to Spain. The Netherlands army was no self-contained expeditionary force of all arms, for its naval complement was blockaded in Antwerp. Even on land it was a wasting asset in the bitter cold of a Netherlands winter which was rapidly cutting down its strength from its autumn peak to perhaps eighteen thousand effectives, where fifty thousand would barely be enough to hold the ring in Flanders and provide the cross-Channel force. But in the calm of the Escurial things were seen differently. "If on receipt of this letter," wrote Philip that December, "you are on the coast of Flanders and no enemy force is there to dispute your passage, then cross immediately in God's name. . . . I have ordered the fastest vessels in the Armada to leave at once, and on the assumption that you will be on enemy soil I have ordered them to bring you six thousand Spaniards as a reinforcement. These same ships will bring you large sums in specie."

Orders of this kind in the Spanish service were seldom translated into action. But the notion that in the depths of that melancholy midwinter he was supposedly ashore in England was to draw from Parma the most anguished cry he uttered in a lifetime of thankless service—"You have accepted that I cannot make the crossing without the Armada's support. If I cross now we must all perish, for it is evident that I must blindly obey your Majesty. You are aware that the Marquis of Santa Cruz has not arrived and you know the reasons for this delay. Yet in spite of this your Majesty seems to imagine that I can be at this moment in London. I am profoundly distressed. What am I to do?" He did not want to make difficulties but was prepared to set out across the Channel "in a pinnace" if that would satisfy the King. In the same letter he set out the true condition of his barges: small craft unfit for fighting and unlikely to survive "a freshet," much less a tempest.

That even Philip had now begun to grasp some of the truth of this and to appreciate that the Armada must shepherd Parma's barges across the straits is clear from a letter which he wrote in January 1588. It was a knowledge however which appeared at times to desert him, and in his instructions to Parma and to his admirals we encounter frequent proof of an ambivalence of attitude in the King's own mind. This was to cause much trouble in the months to come.

Meanwhile the main planning went ahead. Santa Cruz was hounded on by a stream of messages to get an armada of sorts out of the Tagus by the second week in February at the latest. Of the great fleet of which the Marquis had dreamed, a motley array of thirteen galleons, four galleasses and some sixty lesser craft had actually been drummed up, most of them short of stores, guns and even crews. If the sailing date had been kept, this ill-found flotilla would have had to brave the winter weather in Biscay and the Channel on its way to a phantom rendezvous off the enemy coast with a force which all too probably would never have got to sea.

But infinite are the "ifs" of history, and can one be sure that the proposed February armada would necessarily have failed? Whatever the state of mind of those in London like Walsingham who had correctly gauged Spanish intentions, the Queen was in her most pacific mood, busily issuing instructions for the departure of her peace mission to Flanders, and hers was the voice which counted and set the tone of the English preparedness. The fleet was not in the strength or state of alertness it was to reach by midsummer and there was hardly an army worthy of the name. If an armada, even in embryo, had stolen up the Channel that February it might have achieved complete tactical surprise. And though we have no reliable records to guide us, the weather could hardly have been worse than the cycle of storms which were to scatter the Armada's first

venture in May off Finisterre and accompany its remnants on the
hard journey back to Santander.

None of this was put to the test because early in February the
Marquis of Santa Cruz died in Lisbon. In many respects this ablest
of Spanish sailors, hero of Lepanto, victor of Terceira, was most
fortunate of all in his end. His bluff of an armada had been called
but he was never made personally answerable: that fate was reserved for his luckless successor, a man of blameless life who had
projected no great schemes, desired no glittering command, but had
acted with modest competence as the King's Captain General of
Andalusia, "among his orange trees" in Drake's contemptuous
phrase.

Don Alonso de Guzmán el Bueno, Duke of Medina Sidonia, had
never served at sea. Conscripted into command of the greatest
enterprise ever dreamed of in terms of sailing ships, his reactions
were both frank and horrified. His letter to Philip's secretary
Idiaquez on learning of his projected appointment remains the
most famous and unique response ever made to the honors of high
command.* Plaintively he begged to be spared, citing his own
lack of experience of war, his proneness to be seasick and catch
cold, and even his enormous debts:

The force is so great and the undertaking so important that it would
not be right for a person like myself, possessing no experience of sea-
faring or of war, to take charge of it. . . . I possess neither aptitude,
ability, health nor fortune for the expedition. . . . So, sir, you will see
that my reasons for declining are so strong and convincing in his
Majesty's own interests, that I cannot attempt a task of which I have
no doubt I should give a bad account. . . . His Majesty has other subjects who can serve him in this matter, with the necessary experience;
and if it depended upon me I should confer the command upon the
Adelontado-major of Castile. . . . I am certain that the Adelontado will
have the help of God, for he is a very good Christian and a very just
man, besides which he has great knowledge of the sea and has seen
naval warfare. . . .

All this was heartfelt and honest, for Medina Sidonia was also
a good Christian. As is now recognized, he was not being cowardly
or evasive but was sincerely setting out his faults as he saw them.

* Though Requesens had pleaded his own incompetence almost as hard when
ordered to Brussels.

But he must also have known that quite apart from the trust the King felt in him as the son-in-law of the dead favorite Ruy Gómez, Prince of Eboli, there was another reason behind this surprising appointment—the need for someone of his social eminence in the supreme command now that the one outstanding seaman was gone—and he accepted his fate with loyal resignation:

Since your Majesty commands me to serve, and now that I have confessed my limitations and come to terms with my conscience, I pray that God will help me to carry out His will.

Unlike others involved in the Armada's destiny, he was not, in the words of one of them, buoyed up "in confident hope of a miracle." But he would do his best.

As to the value of his services, contemporaries were not kind. To his dying day the good Duke was to endure the popular contempt for his failure. And for centuries this was also the sober judgment of historians. Only in recent times has the full nature of his problem come to be understood and the strength of his reserved and conscientious spirit recognized.

In many ways he performed marvels. Few more depressing situations have faced a commander than those he found in Lisbon that February when with anxious care he entered into his inheritance. Stoically he set himself to sort out the mess: to inspect ships, condemn the unseaworthy, repair and commission others, scour the country for guns and crews, order up stores of small arms, cannon balls and powder, form a staff, draw up sailing instructions in accordance with the flood of orders descending on him from the King.

For a modern view of this labor of Hercules one should turn to the late Professor Mattingly in his brilliant book *The Defeat of the Spanish Armada,* which is also compulsive reading on the great events to follow. Clearly certain things were beyond the power of man to remedy at so late an hour—a serious lack of trained seamen, trained gunners, guns of the right caliber, the sluggishness of many of the ships themselves—yet nevertheless within a matter of weeks the ill-found squadrons which the dying Santa Cruz had managed to assemble had become a fleet whose power was deeply to impress the enemy. The small handful of galleons of the winter had swollen to twenty, including the eight fine ships of the Indies treasure guard which the King had agreed to release for service against England. Four Neapolitan galleasses (galleons in size but also equipped with oars), forty-four armed merchantmen and four galleys made up the rest of the fighting line, supported by store-ships (*urcas*), frigates and other auxiliary craft to a grand total of one hundred and thirty sail, carrying in all thirty thousand men, of whom not quite a quarter were sailors. Medina Sidonia was rightly proud of his part in the creation of this force. As he wrote to Philip on May 14, 1588:

It is now two months ago to-day since I came to Lisbon, and I leave it to others to tell your Majesty how much has been done. The bringing together of so great a force without disorder or dispute, but with all quietude and conformity, is the work of the Lord, through your Majesty's holy zeal. . . .

As to the fire power of the Duke's command when compared with that of the rival fleet awaiting it in the Channel, opinions are still varied after nearly four hundred years. Mattingly seems to accept earlier estimates and implies that the English were richer in ship-killing guns, the Spaniards in man-killing ones, as would be natural for a navy trained in Mediterranean galley tactics of grappling and boarding. More recently however the expert in this field, Michael Lewis,* gives to the Spaniards the heavier guns but with a shorter range to them, so that in effect each fleet would find itself handicapped in the coming battle—the Spaniards being unable to bring their weight of shot to bear on a mobile opponent who kept his distance, and the English being able to pepper but not to sink the heavily timbered galleons of Portugal and Spain.

Whatever its armament, this vast force, christened by popular acclaim the "Invincible Armada"—a name gleefully borrowed by its enemies after its defeat—was seen by its master as defensive. If driven to fight, the instructions given to it by the King were explicit:

Above all you must not forget that the enemy's aim will be to en-gage you at a distance, because they have an advantage in long-range

* *The Spanish Armada* (1960).

guns. . . . Our aim must be to board them, and you will bend every effort to achieve this.

But battle must only be offered if Parma could be got ashore in England in no other way. "If it can be done without fighting," wrote Philip, "either by drawing the enemy off by a diversion or otherwise, it will be better to do it that way and keep your force intact." His concern for the Armada was all-embracing. Dire warnings were issued to its commander to steer well clear of the shoals off the coasts of France and Flanders, and concentration points were carefully laid down in case it should be dispersed by storms in Biscay or off Land's End. Of course spiritual needs were not forgotten, for this was a crusade, even though the Pope seemed very reluctant to advance a ducat.* The Duke's own sailing orders to his command make this clear:

From highest to lowest you are to understand the object of our expedition, which is to regain countries to the Church now oppressed by the enemies of the true faith. I therefore beseech you to remember your calling, so that God will be with us in what we do. I charge you one and all to abstain from profane oaths dishonouring to the names of our Lord, our Lady, and the Saints. . . . Each morning at sunrise the ships' boys, according to custom, shall sing "Good morrow" at the foot of the mainmast, and at sunset the "Ave Maria." Since bad weather may disrupt communications, a watchword is laid down for each day of the week:—Sunday, Jesus; the succeeding days, The Holy Ghost, The Holy Trinity, St. James, All Angels, All Saints, and our Lady.

To secure these provisions nearly two hundred friars were aboard —there is no evidence to suggest that their presence was regarded by the troops as in any way abnormal or unwelcome, for in Spain Church and people were one. It was between kneeling lines of soldiery, all of whom had confessed and communicated and to whom Papal absolution was now granted, that the holy standard of the expedition which the Duke had ceremonially taken from the altar of Lisbon Cathedral was borne in solemn procession through the streets. "Arise, O God, and vindicate thy cause"—the inscrip-

---

* The Spanish ambassador in Rome reported to Philip of His Holiness: "Since the 28th of March, when he learned that the affair was really in earnest and that the moment was approaching when he would have to disgorge his million, his extreme and extraordinary perturbation is evident to everyone."

tion is the perfect complement of Elizabeth's Armada medal: "God blew with His winds and they were scattered." On both sides it was a holy war.

A month passed—a month of foul Atlantic weather—before on May 30 the great fleet cleared from the Tagus and stood out to sea. By the nineteenth of June it had got no further than Corunna off the northwesterly tip of Spain, and there it was decided to put in for water. Early next morning a tremendous gale scattered all those ships that had not made harbor, and another full month went by before they were all reunited.

The hand of God? The Duke evidently thought so; and from Corunna, surrounded by the wreckage of the storm, he wrote to plead with Philip for peace with England or at least a postponement of the enterprise. Though it was June the weather was as wild as in December, which he found strange in view of how fervently the plan had been "commended and devoted to God." After pointing out how he had tried to refuse the task of leading the Armada he went on:

Nevertheless matters reached a point when your Majesty ordered me to sail, which I did, and we have now arrived at this port scattered and maltreated in such a way that we are much inferior in strength to the enemy, according to the opinion of all those who are competent to judge. Many of our largest ships are still missing, as well as two of the galleasses; whilst on the ships that are here there are many sick, whose number will increase in consequence of the bad provisions. These are not only very bad, as I have constantly reported, but they are so scanty that they cannot be more than sufficient to last two months. By this your Majesty may judge whether we can proceed on the voyage, on the success of which so much depends. Your Majesty has embarked in this expedition all your resources both in ships and warlike stores, but I can see no means whatever of redressing any disaster that may befall us. . . . To undertake so great a task with equal forces to those of the enemy would be inadvisable, but to do so with an inferior force, as ours is now, with our men lacking in experience, would be still more unwise. I am bound to confess that I see very few, or hardly any, of those on the Armada with any knowledge of or ability to perform the duties entrusted to them. I have tested and watched this point very carefully, and your Majesty may believe me when I assure you that we are very weak. Do not, your Majesty, allow yourself to be deceived by anyone who may wish to persuade you otherwise.

This was plain speaking with a vengeance. But the King remained unmoved. The scattered ships returned. For a while the sun shone. And on July 22 the Armada sailed again.

In the Netherlands the peace envoys from England had arrived and Parma was impressed by their sincerity. Since his main objective all along had been not the Enterprise of England but the subjugation of the remaining rebel provinces, it was natural that he should match this sincerity with his own and press the King to come to terms with Elizabeth and help to end "the misery and calamity" of the "afflicted states." "This will be better," he wrote, "than risking the Armada in an adventure," and he ended his letter with a flattering suggestion that such a peace would glorify the King's "happy" reign and be a testament to his goodness.

For Philip however the negotiations in Flanders were merely a blind, a means of lulling the English into a false sense of security. Parma had to accept this situation. But it was clear to him that secrecy, on which he laid such store, was no longer possible in view of the delays that had followed the death of Santa Cruz, and it was important that the King should understand.

The enemy [he wrote] has thus been dully warned and knows all about our plans; he has made all his defensive preparations. It is therefore clear that this enterprise, which once promised to be easy and successful, will now prove infinitely more difficult and will cost us much more blood. . . . I am sure that your Majesty has taken care to make the striking force as strong and efficient as is necessary for the task. I am sure also that your Majesty has taken all the necessary steps for my protection on the Channel crossing, so that not the smallest hitch shall occur in a matter of such vital importance.

At this point he returned to the solemn note of warning he had been sounding ever since his change of heart at the year's end:

Failing this and the due co-operation of the Duke with me, both before and during the landing, as well as afterwards, I can hardly succeed as I desire in your Majesty's service.

"Co-operation" was a neutral word that could mean anything. That co-operation before the landing was being demanded was more pointed. But in the phrase "I am sure also that your Majesty has taken all the necessary steps for my protection on the Channel crossing" Parma was once more serving notice in the most explicit terms that he was expecting a fleet that was ready to protect him *in all phases* of the operation from loading to landing and particularly during the vital hours of the sea crossing in the straits.

If we are to believe the historian Luis Cabrera de Córdoba, one of the envoys whom Parma had sent to Spain in April, the impossibility of the Netherlands barges getting to sea unaided through the enemy screen and of the Armada being able to help them in the shoal water off Dunkirk had been put in the most explicit terms to the King's face by Cabrera himself, and Philip could have been left in no doubt as to how the land lay. Yet if Cabrera was really so outspoken, Philip seems to have ignored his message, just as he ignored the implications of Parma's letter. It is true that in his sailing instructions to Medina Sidonia he referred to the chance that Parma might not manage to come out, and suggested in that case that an attack might be mounted on the Isle of Wight*—the revival of an old dream which was to be another fruitful source of misunderstanding in the days ahead. It is true also that his instructions to the Armada do come some way to meet what Parma was demanding: a system of convoy and protection.

You will sail with the whole of the Armada and go straight to the English Channel, which you will ascend as far as Cape Margate where you will join hands with the Duke of Parma, my nephew, and hold the passage for his crossing. . . .

But that some measure of delusion still persisted in Philip's mind is shown in the passage in these same sailing orders where he warns Medina Sidonia to avoid the French and Flemish coasts. Obviously he had not fully gathered either from verbal warnings or from Parma's letters that it was precisely *there* that the Armada's presence would be most needed. Perhaps he willfully blinded himself to a truth he did not wish to recognize: at all events the misapprehension remained.

Between the Governor General and the Armada's new commander the disharmony was total from the start. In April Parma

* An attack on the Wight on the *eastward* run was specifically forbidden by the King.

had sent a personal envoy to the Duke, a Captain Moresini, to urge
the need for his active help during the embarkation from Flanders
and for the rapid transfer of the six thousand Spanish reinforcements which the fleet would bring. On June 22 Moresini was back
in Brussels with the reply. Medina Sidonia had begun to doubt
whether the transfer of the six thousand would be feasible in the
presence of undefeated English ships. But the messenger had
brought from the Duke a still more disquieting letter which assumed not only that Parma could come out with his "fleet" on
call, but actually suggested that he should *run ahead of the Armada*
as in the King's first plan, long since amended.

At the moment when Parma received this letter his main sally-
port of Dunkirk was blockaded by forty English warships, and not
unnaturally he protested warmly to his master:

These things cannot be. . . . The Duke will learn clearly from my
letters that I cannot depart in the slightest degree from the plan laid
down or from your Majesty's express orders. . . . With regard to any
going out to join him, he will plainly see that with these little low flat
boats, built for the rivers and not for the sea, I cannot diverge from the
short, direct passage across.

Otherwise, if he attempted to go out and meet the Duke and came
across the enemy, they could easily destroy him.

This was one of the principal reasons which moved your Majesty to lay
down the precise and prudent orders you did, insisting that your
Spanish fleet should assure us the passage across, as it was perfectly
clear that these boats of ours could not contend with big ships, much
less stand the sea, for they will not weather the slightest storm.

"God grant that no embarrassment may come from this," the
King noted in the margin of this letter. But he did nothing about
it.

On July 22 the Armada got to sea again out of Corunna on a
dying south wind—the tail end of the same wind which had driven
back a strong English squadron sent to repeat Drake's Cádiz raid
of the previous year. Froude in his *History of England* has a fine
passage describing the scene:

It was a treacherous interval of real summer. The early sun was lighting the long chain of the Gallician mountains, marking with shadows the cleft defiles, and shining softly on the white walls and vineyards of Corunna. The wind was light and falling towards a calm; the great galleons drifted slowly with the tide on the purple water, the long streamers trailing from the trucks, the red crosses, the emblem of the crusade, showing bright upon the hanging sails. The fruit boats were bringing off the last fresh supplies, and the pinnaces hastening to the ships with the last loiterers on shore. Out of thirty thousand men who that morning stood upon the decks of the proud Armada, twenty thousand and more were never again to see the hills of Spain. Of the remnant who in two short months crept back ragged and torn, all but a few hundred returned only to die.

At sea, in the treacherous waters off Ushant at the southern entrance to the Channel, the "Most Fortunate Armada," ill-starred from first to last, was struck by another storm and scattered, to be reunited (less one capital ship and all four of its galleys) on the twenty-ninth between the Scillies and Land's End.

Next morning off the Lizard, the most southerly point of the English mainland, Medina Sidonia held a council of war aboard his flagship the *San Martín.* According to one account, there was talk of an attempt to seize Plymouth, where Drake with the western squadron was reportedly at anchor, but this was rejected—fortunately, perhaps, since not only Drake but the bulk of the main English fleet under the Lord Admiral, Howard of Effingham, had warped out of the Sound on the ebb the previous night and were waiting in the shelter of Rame Head.

It was the thirty-fourth anniversary of the King's landing in England to marry Mary Tudor, whose soul would have been perplexed indeed at this sign of God's inscrutable purpose. A hundred and twenty-five ships were advancing against the kingdom which she and Philip had ruled. They came from almost every quarter of the King's vast empire: galleasses from Naples, large merchantmen from the Levant squadron, the royal galleons of Portugal and the Castilian ships of the Indies Guard, with a vast array of storeships and light craft. Of these 125, 68 were fighting ships: 4 galleasses, 24 galleons and 40 converted merchantmen with new superstructures and a new armory of guns.

The formation in which they sailed remains something of an enigma. Some English eyewitnesses at the time and artists afterward pictured it as a crescent with the horns drawn back down-Channel to the west, perhaps the "crescent moon" of Shakespeare's sonnet. But the great authority on the Armada, Laughton,* followed by Michael Lewis in his recent authoritative book, suggests that though this formation may well have had the appearance of a crescent to the English fleet and to the bystanders on the cliffs, its true form was more subtle: two leading wings consisting of the fighting galleons of Castile and Portugal with three galleasses in support; a mass of supply vessels (hulks) tucked in behind the flagship at the center of the line; then stepped back in echelon behind them to either side four squadrons of ten ships apiece, the Andalusian and Biscayan of the rear guard under the rear admiral, Don Juan Martínez de Recalde, on the landward side, and the Guipuzcoan and Levant squadrons of the vanguard to seaward under Don Alonso de Leyva, the Bayard of Spain, whom Philip had secretly appointed to command the expedition if anything happened to the Duke.

Aboard the fleet were nearly nineteen thousand of the most formidable soldiers in the world. The sailors were not of the same quality, but their commanders were the most experienced in the Spanish service, three of them—Recalde, Don Pedro de Valdez and Ocquendo—having taken part in Santa Cruz's great victories in the Azores. There was also aboard one Lope de Vega, gentleman adventurer. It was rather as though Shakespeare himself had been there, but alas the future author of fifteen hundred plays spared the Armada no more than a hymn in honor of its sacred mission.†

In number of galleons and large armed merchantmen the English were to be by no means outmatched, even at the outset of the battle before reinforcements came up, while in long-range guns, in crews, in weatherliness and speed, they had a decided advantage. Nevertheless the sheer weight and pomp of the Armada made an indelible impression on all who saw it—the forest of masts, the banners, the huge, towering superstructures of the galleons, and "great ships" built for boarding an enemy.

It is this visual, stately quality so well shown in contemporary illustrations, the sense of formal drama being played out in front

* J. K. Laughton. *State Papers Relating to the Defeat of the Spanish Armada* (Navy Records Society, 1895).
† Lope composed an eleven-thousand-line poem in the course of the journey. See Gerald Brenan's *The Literature of the Spanish People*.

of an audience on a vast stage, which gives the story of the Armada its special place. To say that the eyes of Europe were on the struggle would be trite but true, for the fate of Protestantism and of many kingdoms was bound up with that of the ships maneuvering in the gray waters of the Channel. Yet it was more directly personal than that. For the next few days watchers on the coast, coming in their hundreds out of Plymouth, Weymouth and the small towns and villages from Cornwall to the Isle of Wight, could clearly see the great mass of the Armada as it lumbered up the Channel, pursued by the ragged lines of the English, and hear the roll of gunfire moving slowly east, while from their decks the Spaniards could watch the landmarks fall astern—the long arm of the Lizard, Berry Head, the hump of Portland Bill above the pencil line of the Chesil Beach, the jagged white teeth of The Needles at the entrance to The Solent.

The setting was grandiose: the battle that followed belongs in tradition to a heroic age. Yet in the first seven days of the running fight up-Channel, from Start Point to Calais Roads, of the two hundred and more ships engaged, not one on either side was sunk by enemy action. When its first phase was over, neither side had the least notion whether it had won or lost.

During the night of Saturday July 30/Sunday 31 the main body of the English out of Plymouth, which had been to leeward of the Armada, weathered it out to sea and reappeared at dawn to windward.

The dexterous speed of this maneuver was so astonishing to the sailing masters of the lumbering galleons of Portugal and the Indies Guard that it was not at first believed that these could be the same ships that had been glimpsed at sundown well up-Channel: certainly its revolutionary daring was not grasped at all. Revolutionary indeed it was. For instead of standing as a land army would have done—and as fleets in the past would have done —to try to bar the Armada's path toward the straits, Howard had deliberately uncovered it, leaving the whole southern coastline open to the Spaniards, whose landing force, it should be remembered, was nearly nineteen thousand strong.

No one in England had put in writing the theory behind this move: many years were to pass before Sir Walter Raleigh (who was present in the later stages of the Armada battle) first set down sailing instructions for a fleet in action in the classic style that was to be followed by all the great English admirals till Nelson brought it to perfection at the Nile. Nevertheless, in the untidy way in which great discoveries are so often made, the English had stumbled on the proper use of that mystical phrase "sea power": a very different concept from that of ships as floating forts or platforms for infantry, the old land-bound notion which had previously been the rule. In his Cádiz raid Drake had shown how the new method could be used against a fleet at anchor by gobbling up its ships in turn: this was now to be extended to the treatment of an enemy fleet at sea, by use of the windward station and attacks in line or in bunches against its tail—"plucking their feathers one by one" in Howard's words. Tactics and strategy were nearly perfect. Only the guns were defective at the range first chosen: the size and velocity of shot had not been properly worked out.

The unfortunate Armada had no innovations to offer beyond the strong defensive formation it took up and the skill, like that of a well-drilled army, with which it kept to it in the light winds which prevailed for the first few days. It had learned some of the lessons of Drake's raid. Small guns had been taken out of the main armament of its ships and larger ones put in: it had been made as near a replica of the rival fleet as knowledge and last-minute ingenuity could devise. Nevertheless it was a cumbersome, unwieldly weapon. Instructed to grapple and board its enemy, it had no means of catching him. Its guns, though more powerful than the English long-range culverins and demi-culverins, were seldom within range, and when they were the gunnery was abysmal. It was simply not good enough for its mission.

And those aboard it were fully aware of this—none more so than its dispirited commander. A profound pessimism bred of past adversities, the sense of a forlorn mission in strange seas, filled the minds of even the bravest of its captains and prevented them from seizing the great and unlooked-for chance that had come their way, the "advantage of time and place" in Drake's famous phrase, which they had gained by their sudden arrival off the enemy coast with a west wind filling their sails and an undefended shore ahead.

This defeatist note can be detected right from the start, before the nimbleness of the English and their own impotence was brought home to them. Even that first morning off the Lizard the message sent back to the Escurial was strangely cautious and defensive for a force which had apparently achieved complete tactical surprise of its enemy a few miles to windward of one of his major ports. "I have decided," wrote the Duke, "to anchor off the Isle of Wight until I learn Parma's situation." Not thus had Drake reported from the waters off Cádiz in '87—he had sailed into the roadstead, hardly bothering to brief his own vice-admiral or his captains on what they should do or expect; and given the Armada's situation, there can be little doubt that he would have come down, if not on Plymouth, at least on Torbay with its eastward-facing anchorage, immune from fire ships in the prevailing wind, where William the Silent's great-grandson was to go ashore exactly a century later, or in The Solent, which had figured largely in Spanish plans and where the English themselves believed the first blow would fall.

The Armada under its inept leadership simply continued to advance. For the details of that strange drifting battle one should go to John Knox Laughton's classic study, to Julian Corbett's *Drake and the Tudor Navy* and the brilliant modern reconstructions by Garrett Mattingly and Michael Lewis. Light westerly winds, backing at times to south or southeast with intervals of calm, dictated the day-to-day activities of two fleets that seemed to lack the power to wound one another mortally. It was a shapeless, episodic, untidy battle. But from the outset the basic motif was made plain: one force achieved a moral dominance over the other. After the first scuffling off Plymouth on Sunday July 31 Medina Sidonia reported in his *Relation,* his report which was later forwarded to the King:

The Duke collected his fleet, being unable to do anything more, because the enemy had recovered the wind and their ships were so mobile and their steerage so good that they did what they wished with them.

Of course this English superiority in ships and crews had long been feared in Spain, as Philip's own sailing instructions show, but the extent of it was profoundly shocking, and certainly from that moment the initiative was never again to lie with the Spaniards and no attempts were made to seize a haven along that Arcadian and almost unguarded coast. The English drove them like a flock of sheep, one Dutchman aboard the Armada reported. "I did not order my fleet or my Council of War to flee and flee," the King was to protest weeks afterward when the whole sorry tale was told. But by the inflexibility of his thinking he *had* ordered it as surely as if he had been on the *San Martín's* decks.

July 31 and August 1 were days of increasing English pressure. On the second, off Portland, a change of wind gave the Spaniards the weather gauge and they indulged in some ineffective chasing and pounding before it veered again and dropped. August 3 was a day of flat calm. On the fourth the fleets were off the Isle of Wight— this was the crucial day, the last on which the Spaniards might have won their battle if they had disregarded the King's orders *not* to attack the island on the eastward run and had gone boldly for shore. The Duke sent to Parma for cannon balls and powder, which both fleets had been expending at a prodigal rate, if to little visible effect. For days his thoughts had been directed to the approaching meeting with his partner, to whom he had already sent off a string of messengers, one from Ushant before even entering the Channel; and now by the hand of Captain Pedro de León he added this reminder:

I beg your Excellency to be ready to come out immediately to meet me when the wind brings me to the coast of Flanders.

This is a very important letter, for taken in conjunction with another sent off to Parma next day telling him to be ready to come out as soon as the Armada is off Dunkirk, it shows that very belatedly, *but at last,* Medina Sidonia had realized that the whole point of his mission was to cover the Channel crossing for Parma's barges. Admittedly the Duke was later to go back on this duty by proposing not to stir beyond Calais Roads, but it certainly seems that on August 4 and 5 he had reached substantial agreement with Parma's plans.

For one illusion that had vanished, however, another one was immediately substituted, and in a letter sent off with the pilot Domingo de Ochoa, alongside lamentations of slow progress and inability to board the enemy, we find the Duke demanding the loan from Parma of "forty or fifty flyboats," the light craft used in harbors and shoal waters along the Zeeland coast, though these were in fact a Beggar monopoly.

Send them to me immediately, because with such boats I am sure we can inflict serious damage on the enemy fleet, the essential condition for the success of our enterprise.

That was on Friday the fifth of August. Next morning the French coast near Boulogne was sighted and by four in the afternoon the Armada was off Calais, where the pilots urged the Duke to anchor, since ahead lay only the North Sea and the inhospitable Nether-lands shore.

In impeccable order on the edge of the shoal water the Armada came to rest, less than thirty miles from Dunkirk, two weeks and a day after its sailing from Corunna and nearly ten weeks out of Lisbon. Its constant shadow, Howard's fleet, dropped anchor just farther out, within long-range shot of it. And that night at dusk a second and very powerful English squadron under Lord Seymour, which had lain in The Downs off the Thames estuary on guard against the Flemish barges, sailed into the roadstead and squatted down to wait. The Duke thought they were thirty-six sail. There was still no word from Parma.

For his enemies later, when all was over, this silence on the Governor General's part was taken as just one more proof of his treacherous refusal to help the Armada in its need or to play an honest part in the great plan. Among the survivors of the disaster and among the Castilian grandees, jealous of the glittering com-mand in Brussels which the King had entrusted to an Italian princeling, this feeling of betrayal was widely held. It was said that Parma had misled his master; that he had never intended to come out or made any preparations to do so; that all his activities were a sham and his real aim, with English collusion, had been to use the King's reinforcements of men and money to further his own ambitions—very grand ambitions, which had included the setting up of his own sovereignty in the provinces independent of Spain.

In this as in most libels there was an element of truth. It was even true that the English, through one of Walsingham's agents, had suggested to him just such an independent sovereignty, with the tempting bait of the Queen's recognition thrown in. It was also true that Parma had never liked the Enterprise of England. Its basic improbability had not escaped that keen, logistical mind, and it conflicted also with his own deep emotional commitment to the Netherlands, his mother's country, where his imperial grandfather had been born, where he himself had been married, and to whose governorship he had succeeded after the almost unbearable frustrations of his father's small Italian duchy.

To a man of immense dedication, struggling with a task which had broken three predecessors but which he seemed on the verge of bringing to a triumphant end, any distraction would have been unwelcome, and this one particularly so. The Enterprise was grossly irrelevant to the reconquest of the provinces and their restoration to the state existing in the Duchess Margaret's time—the proper aim, as he saw it, of Spanish policy in Europe. For like all recent governors of the Netherlands he was the inheritor of the centuries-old tradition of friendship, not enmity, with England, and in the course of his conferences with the Queen's envoys at Bourbourg he had become convinced that a highly advantageous peace could be had for the asking, which would get her troops out of the rebel provinces and clear the board either for a reconquest or a general settlement with the north.

His attitude toward the Armada was therefore bound to be equivocal. In most respects it was an unmitigated nuisance, and worse. But it was not something he could ignore. Servants of King Philip did not resign or argue: they obeyed. Faced with orders, he had no choice but to set about complying with them: moving his army toward the coast; providing it with barges; and cutting a canal between Sluys and Nieuport at a prodigious cost in labor. It would have been untrue to complain—though many did— that nothing in reality had been done. Yet none of these preparations—except perhaps the canal—bore the same stamp of energy with which he had taken Maastricht and astonished Europe with his capture of Antwerp. He carried out the King's plan as far as it lay in his power, but he did it with a kind of resignation, without belief in it and therefore without thoroughness or even a spark of his inventive genius. Perhaps he hoped for a miracle: for a lifting of the rebel blockade and a few days of calm weather in the straits. Certainly nothing he did was equal to the event when it fell upon him that August with its sudden call for action, for the performance of promises, where he could only excuse and explain.

The extreme slowness of communications at the time was to blame for much of what followed: it magnified all his faults.

Rumors galore were flying about Europe but it was not till August 2, when the Armada was actually off Portland within a hundred and fifty miles of him, that Parma in Bruges received the messenger, Captain Rodrigo Tello de Guzmán, whom the admiral had sent off to him on July 25 from the coast of Brittany, and knew for certain that the Armada was at sea. Orders were immediately given for the barges to be brought in-shore ready for embarkation at the ports, and on the sixth Parma wrote to his deputy, the elder Mansfeld, summoning him to Bruges to take over command in the Netherlands during his absence.

Should he have done more and been already on the invasion coast? He lay just behind it, in a fair central position, and it was not till the sixth that he received any definite intelligence that the Armada was even in the Channel. No doubt there were many excuses for him—and in the weeks ahead he used them all—yet a doubt remains: an impression of drift, of indecision, highly uncharacteristic of this brilliant and self-confident man.

On Sunday the seventh more messengers from the Armada came in to him at Bruges—first the pilot Domingo de Ochoa, who had been sent off on the fifth with the request for flyboats. Needless to say, Parma had none to spare; he had precious few of his own and they were blockaded. He had an army and a number of canal barges at the mercy of the elements and the enemy, as he at once sat down to remind the King in a letter full of unanswerable but self-righteous logic. If the Armada would only come within reach he would co-operate at once. If the Channel happened to be free of enemy ships he would lose no time. But the admiral still seemed to be insisting that he could come out to join him, and this was simply not feasible. As he once more pointed out:

Most of our boats are only built for rivers and are unable to weather the least sea. It is quite as much as they can do to carry the men in perfectly fair weather, but as for fighting as well, it is evident they cannot do it. . . .

Of course he had been saying all this for months, apart from the odd boast he had left fall in his correspondence to suggest to the impressionable that he might be able to get out to sea by himself. Certainly the King had at last come to understand the real position. But there had been a time when Parma had suggested a sortie all on his own across the straits, and though he had long since given the notion a decent burial it was one which had died hard and whose ghost still walked, certainly on the *San Martín*'s decks. It was late in the day to try to lay it. Yet even at this hour Parma was still unaware how urgent the matter was and that the Armada had reached Calais, almost on his doorstep.

That same Sunday, August 7, the Armada lay at its anchorage off the town while its pinnaces shuttled backward and forward, bringing supplies of fruit and vegetables and urbane compliments from the French governor, Monsieur de Gourdan, who had driven out with his wife in his carriage on the off-chance of watching a battle. No supplies of shot or powder, however, for France was neutral and the wind had made it impossible for Parma to send them, or so he said.

It was a day of rest, almost a reflection of the peaceful scene of the sailing from Corunna, yet the whole spirit of the enterprise had changed and one survivor later remembered "a great presentiment of evil" and fear of what might befall at the hands of the English "that devilish people and their arts." The Armada had an anchorage, a reasonably good one in fair weather and handy for its task, but on a lee shore—hardly a place to linger in that deplorable summer, as the Governor of Calais did not hesitate to point out in his eagerness to see the last of his dangerous visitors, Spanish and English alike. And the Duke had more definite causes for anxiety than mere presentiment. At dawn Captain Rodrigo Tello de Guzmán had returned aboard the flagship to report that as late as the previous evening there had been no signs of Parma at Dunkirk; while toward nightfall another messenger arrived, this time from Secretary Arceo (a Job's comforter if there ever was one), reporting—again from Dunkirk—that no men or munitions were being loaded on the barges and it was Arceo's opinion that nothing would be ready for a fortnight.

Seeing the crisis approach, the Duke did his best to rise to it. The crowded anchorage seemed a natural target for fire ships such as his own Spaniards in Cádiz had used against Drake in the previous year, so at sunset he sent around the fleet to warn his captains to have boats ready to tow any assaulting vessels clear and himself provided a duty pinnace.

The Duke's worst fears had a way of being realized. Sure enough, as he reports in his *Relation:*

At midnight two fires were seen kindled in the English fleet, which increased to eight; and suddenly eight ships with sails set and fair wind and tide came straight towards our *capitana* [flagship] and the rest of the fleet, all burning fiercely. The Duke, seeing them approach, and that our men did not hinder them, and fearing that they were explosion ships, gave orders to weigh, and also for the rest of the armada to do the same, intending when the fires had passed to return to the same anchorage.

On came the enemy, spurting fire and their ordnance shooting, which one observer found "a horror to see in the night." In fact, in spite of appearances, they were simple fire ships which "did no harm," as another eyewitness wrote pathetically, "except to dislodge our fleet." "Except" is the operative word. To dislodge them had been the English intention. A scene of fantastic confusion followed as the Spaniards, primed with tales of Giambelli's "hell-burners" or "devil ships" which had been launched against Parma's bridge at Antwerp, cut their cables in panic and struggled out to sea, where dawn found them scattered over a wide area, many of them well to leeward with no hope at all of regaining Calais, and only the flagship and a few faithful attendants still hove-to in the straits.

Hoping to reunite his squadrons, the Duke ran down the coast eastward, then rounded to give fight, and there that Monday morning off Gravelines, where Egmont had won his great victory, the combined English fleets fell upon him, closing the range to deadly effect and pounding the small rear guard of ships which had once been the Armada almost without reply.

This time it was no inconclusive battle. From nine in the morning till six at night the deadly work went on—fast, weatherly ships with magazines newly primed against slow, lumbering ones which could hardly defend themselves but which fought on with desperate courage, even regaining formation and facing their enemy in the crescent shape which the English had seen or imagined in the running fight in the Channel.

Off Calais in the shambles of the night the flagship of the galleasses had run aground, right under the walls of the town.

Now two of the Portuguese royal galleons went onto the shoals. The crew of one were taken off by a Spanish pinnace from Nieuport; the other was captured with all hands by Beggar ships from Flushing, its captain held to ransom, the rest thrown overboard to perish. Two smaller ships went down at sea. Few were in much better shape. One of the large carracks was seen plunging into action, blood flowing from its scuppers, its decks a battlefield of dead and dying men; another, "a pitiful sight, riddled with shot like a sieve" as it rolled in the rising wind. "The navy that remained after the last fight," one enemy observer wrote, "were marvellously beaten and shot through."

Yet the Armada survived. In the evening a sudden squall parted the fleets: the broken Spanish lines reformed and sailed on through the night to face new perils—the shoal water off the Zeeland coast which Tuesday's dawn showed straight ahead of them, directly on the only course the wind allowed them. "It was the most fearful day in the world," wrote one of the friars aboard the fleet, "for all our people were now in utter despair of a happy issue and stood waiting for death."

That every ship in the Armada did not strike on the Zeeland banks that morning is the strangest thing in the whole astonishing story. The Spaniards saw the hand of God extended over them: a miracle at last. "From this desperate peril," wrote the Duke, "in only six and a half fathoms of water, we were saved by the wind shifting by God's mercy to the south west." This was the universal reaction of piety and gratitude. "God succoured us in our distress as He always does," wrote Pedro Coco Calderón, chief purser of the fleet, "and changed the wind in our favour, so that our flagship got free of the banks and left the enemy behind."

So the Armada drew clear, but in full flight toward the north. It was the eve of St. Lawrence's Day, in whose memory and in gratitude for the victory of St. Quentin the Escurial had been built.

And what meanwhile of Parma?

Bad communications still dogged his steps. Not at the earliest till the evening of Sunday August 7 could he have learned from secretary Arceo that the Armada had reached Calais; not till Monday the eighth does he tell the King what he has heard:

I have news that the Duke with the Armada has arrived in Calais Roads. God be praised for this.

He still had not the least notion that it had cut and run. And only that afternoon, while it was being battered in its last flight off Gravelines, did he set off for the coast,* having taken time off to write to Philip answering in detail the various complaints about his unpreparedness which were being bandied around by the disgruntled envoys from the Duke, explaining why it had not been possible to preload his army on open barges so small that there was barely room to turn around and where troops if cooped up too long would surely "fall ill, rot and die."

This sluggishness, like the preparations themselves, or lack of them, was to draw down upon him a hot critical fire which has never quite ceased. The army was ready, but were the boats? Critics—and there were many of them—said one thing and Parma said the other, both at wearisome length, and after the passing of so many years proof either way is lacking. Perhaps, as Parma said in a letter to Philip, the boats were ready *for the task they had to effect,* namely to take the men across, while the Duke's observers were honestly expecting much larger and more powerful craft. Or it could be that the boats *were* in poor shape, and that the real villains of the piece were not Parma and his staff but the local contractors in the ports, who, in the words of one indignant Spaniard, "openly and undisguisedly directed their energies not to serve his Majesty, for that was not their aim, but to waste his substance and lengthen the duration of the war. . . ." That seems to strike a realistic and contemporary note. But it does not answer the wider question whether there was ever a serious intention to "come out" or only a face-saving pretense of one. In these vital days was Parma really doing his best to get his invasion force to sea, or was it all a ploy to impress the doubters and satisfy his own and the national sense of honor with proof that man's intentions had been abrogated by the will of God?

For at sea the wind had risen and by Tuesday morning it was blowing a half gale along the Flanders coast—weather in which it was impossible for any light craft to stir. If we accept his move-

* These timings have been disputed. For those interested I have discussed the matter in an appendix.

ments* as he described them to Philip two days later, he was at Nieuport on the Monday night, where the loading of sixteen thousand men was all but complete, and pushing on to Dunkirk, which he reached at dawn on Tuesday, he found everything ready for embarkation and the men waiting on the quay. He was still there when at half past ten in the morning Don Jorge Manrique, the Armada's inspector general, found him with letters from the Duke.

Into the tragic story there now intruded the broad elements of farce. Manrique had been sent off on the Saturday night, the last of the messengers from Calais, but had missed Parma on the road. The request he brought was for an immediate departure to engage the enemy off Calais or to join the Armada in seizing the Isle of Wight. So there at Dunkirk, with the sea boiling outside the harbor and while the Armada was in the last extremity of danger off the Zeeland shoals, the whole lunatic scheme was solemnly debated for the last time and Parma called in his native pilots to try to bring some common sense to bear. It could not have been easy. "Don Jorge Manrique is here, and it is quite pitiable to see how he goes on," wrote one observer. According to another, high words passed, almost flaring into violence. But as the day wore on sobering news reached them from the coast—a group from the Armada, including the King's natural son, the Prince of Ascoli, arrived to tell of the night flight from Calais and of the English pursuit to the north. With those winds there could be no doubt what had happened. The embarkation was suspended—as a temporary measure, it was said—and on the tenth of August Parma sat down to send Philip his formal message of condolence:

God knows how grieved I am at this news, at a time when I hoped to send your Majesty my congratulations at having successfully carried through your intentions. But I am sure that your Majesty knows me to be one of your humblest and devoted servants who has laboured hard in the business and that you will recognise that no one could be more grieved than I am. I will only say therefore that this must come from the hand of the Lord, who knows well what He does and can redress it all, rewarding your Majesty with many victories and the full fruition of your desires in His good time. We should therefore give Him thanks for all things.

* See Appendix for a discussion of these movements and timings.

Was this a hint between the lines that God had shown himself a sound strategist and that the looked-for victories could and should be in the Netherlands, the proper place for them, if only the wherewithal were supplied without delay? He ended:

But above all I beseech your Majesty to recollect that I am without money and know not where or how to obtain any.

It was the one consistent cry of every governor of the Netherlands.

Throughout that Wednesday, the tenth, the Armada fled north on a wind from the southwest, with the English close behind them putting on a "brag countenance," though there was no ammunition left in either fleet. At a council of war aboard the *San Martín* on the afternoon of the ninth, after clearing the Zeeland banks, the Spanish leaders had unanimously declared for a return to the straits and a rendezvous with Parma as soon as the wind changed. This it obligingly did on Friday the twelfth when the fleets were off Newcastle, and the English turned away with it and ran back to the Thames to refit. The Spaniards sailed on northward past the Forth and the Aberdeenshire coast, through the dangerous sound between the Orkneys and Fair Isle and out into the Atlantic beyond the Outer Hebrides, with a thousand miles of turbulent ocean between them and their homeland. It seemed a smaller hazard than Howard's fleet.

The saga of that journey has been told many times, though all its details will never be known. Somewhere in the huge arc of waters between Norway and the Faroes ships foundered without trace, without witnesses even to speak to where they lie. Others have a known grave, marked by bones and spars and flotsam washed ashore over the years on Irish beaches, from the Giant's Causeway to Great Blasket Island south of the estuary of the Shannon.

Of the men shipwrecked on that coast or who anchored off it and came ashore for food and water, only a handful made their way back to Spain—mostly the well to do worth preserving for the ransom money. The rest were either butchered by Irish peasants or shot or hanged out of hand by the military by order of the English

Governor and his scarcely less bloodthirsty deputy in Connaught. Only those ships seaworthy enough, with crews hardy enough, to brave the course in mid-Atlantic which the Duke's pilots had advised and the Duke himself commanded, ever returned to Spain. About seventy of the one hundred and thirty that had left Corunna in July got back, some of them after months of wandering. Of thirty thousand men, two thirds were dead of wounds, disease, starvation and thirst, of Irish cudgels and English rope and the gray-green seas of Galway and Connemara. Many of the survivors died of their privations in the ports and hospitals of Galicia. "The troubles and miseries we have suffered," wrote the Duke, who himself was broken by them, "cannot be described to your Majesty. They have been greater than have ever been seen in any voyage before, and on board some of the ships that have come in there was not one drop of water for a fortnight. On the flagship 180 died of sickness, three out of the four pilots aboard having succumbed, and all the rest of the people are ill, many of typhus and other contagious maladies. All the men of my household, to the number of 60, have either died or fallen sick, and only two have remained able to serve me."

This ship, the *San Martín*, was more fortunate than most. Only one of the senior commanders in the Enterprise lived to serve again against the English. Perhaps of the whole complement of the Armada only five thousand fully recovered from their ordeal. It was a calamity beyond reason, beyond the national power to accept, for this had been a crusade and Spaniards were conditioned by their history to success. For many weeks, long after the truth should have become clear, reports continued to come in of great victories off the Scottish coast, which only the King treated with the polite disenchantment of a man who perhaps from the beginning had feared a bad outcome. In defeat he showed himself a stoic and a compassionate man, far more careful of the shattered lives of his unfortunates than Elizabeth of her own seamen, who were allowed to rot and die in their hundreds aboard the victorious fleet without even the benefit of their pay. He reproached no one, except the adviser whom he had placed at the Duke's side on the *San Martín*. It was God's will. He could accept disaster unflinchingly, and profit by it, as the future was to show, in the building of a fleet more formidable and modern in design than the one he had forced out of Lisbon in '88.

But among his people the damage had been done and the scar of defeat was never quite to heal. The full story of the Armada was not published in its time. In England a vast literature grew up to record and glorify the national triumph: we catch its echoes in Shakespeare's plays and in the vast overseas expansion to come. In Spain the Armada's losses were listed and buried among the archives. Few wanted to remember what had happened. But something of what it must have meant to contemporaries, and still means, is shown in a passage by the Spanish essayist who wrote under the name of Azorín*—written just before the still greater disaster of the Spanish Civil War—in which he pictures a messenger from the north crossing the vast central plain and the sierras on his way to the Escurial, while

on foreign shores, among green seaweeds above the sand, rocking to the sound of the hoarse sea, are planks, hemp, coils and masts, remains of ships which shall be called, in irony by the enemy, "invincible." Wherever the messenger passes he leaves a track of sadness. Soon all Spain will be full of the fatal news. In the Escorial, or in Madrid, an aged man will go down on his knees before a little statue of the Virgin. . . . For a decisive hour will have struck for Spain. Will history open out another perspective for Spain? No one can tell the exact hour which divides two epochs of history. . . . The messenger travels swiftly over plains and mountains: his feet hardly touch the ground. If that which he bore in his knapsack were joy, perchance he could not go so fast. Misfortune journeys with greater speed; hardly has the catastrophe happened, and lo! the news is flying into the farthest corners of Spain.

* José Martínez Ruiz. The extract is from An Hour of Spain, translated by Alice Raleigh.

18

THE PROBLEM OF FRANCE. 1588–89.

Morally, then, the defeat of the Armada was a decisive event.

But militarily it was no more than an episode which settled nothing beyond the fact that vast sea-borne expeditions were liable to failure as much at the hands of winds and tides as of the enemy. In this sense perhaps the Enterprise of England could never have amounted to more than a raid in force even if Medina Sidonia had swept the Channel clear for Parma's barges and there had been no English fleets at sea or Beggar flyboats off the Zeeland coast. Weather and logistics would have had the last word.

The Armada battles did not see the end of Spanish sea power, which was actually on the *increase* during the next two decades both in Europe and the Caribbean. Still less did it signal the world domination of the English navy, for if we except Essex's raid on Cádiz in 1596—admittedly a great feat of arms and highly damaging to Philip's prestige and financial credit—English forays into Spanish waters had a high failure rate. We have only to think of Drake's *débâcle* against Lisbon in '89, his own death and that of John Hawkins on their last disastrous journey to the Americas, and the complete fiasco of Essex's expedition to the Azores in 1597 at a time when another Spanish Armada was at sea.

No: if we leave out the moral factor, it was not in the context of English rise or Spanish fall but in its wider and indeed chance effects on the balance of power in Europe that the Armada was significant and left a lasting mark.

To appreciate this we must glance for a moment at the condition of France, always intimately bound up with that of her neighbors on either side: Spain and the Spanish Netherlands. Her king, Henry III, was the last of the male Valois: a man much abused by Motley for sternly moral and Protestant reasons and equally by French historians in thrall to the Bourbon *gloire* of his successors. A more imaginative but perhaps more truthful picture is preserved by Dumas in *Chicot the Jester*, which shows us the crowned hedonist with his *mignons* and baskets of puppy dogs: a man of peace who could be goaded into crime but who at least tried to spare his countrymen—even the thankless citizens of Paris —the horrors of a bestial and futile civil war. In this he failed, partly because the times were out of joint for men of sensibility and France was hopelessly divided into the warring parties of the Huguenots under Navarre and the ultra-, pro-Spanish Catholics of the League, led by the disloyal princes of the house of Guise.*

With firm handling this second faction could have been brought to heel, and indeed in the months before the Armada Henry had an excellent chance to do it when he filled Paris with his mercenaries and could have crushed the presumptuous rivals who had thrown themselves with incredible rashness into his hands. All that was needed was a brisk skirmish and perhaps a salutary sack of the town. Honorably, humanely, he shrank from such an enterprise against his own subjects, and through lack of orders the royal troops were reduced to the same state of impotence which two hundred years later was to cost Louis XVI Paris on the eve of the storming of the Bastille.

On the "Day of the Barricades" the city rose, the dejected soldiery fraternized with the mob and the Valois fled for his life with a small group of courtiers, leaving Paris to its "King," the Duke of Guise,† and its Spanish paymaster, ambassador Bernardino de Mendoza.

This operation had been a necessary preliminary to the Armada by freeing Parma's army in the Netherlands from the danger of French intervention on its flank. As such it was the only well-mounted event in that whole sorry and disastrous story, reflecting Mendoza's truly brilliant gifts as *agent provocateur* and puppet-master. But when the great Enterprise of England failed, even the poor fugitive king took heart. That winter, as the last remnants of the beaten fleet limped home into the Biscayan ports, Henry summoned his States General to Blois on the Loire, and with them came the Balafré,§ the Duke of Guise, full of arrogant contempt for the weakling whom he had outfaced in his own capital and seemed

* There was also a third party of moderates called *Politiques* balancing between the other two.
† This was the son of the victor of Calais.
§ *Balafrer*: to gash or scar. The Duke had a prominent cheek wound.

about to drive from the throne. And there one December morning, in a room of the royal castle near the head of the great spiral staircase which is one of the marvels of France, the Balafré was struck down by the bravoes of the royal guard. He had been warned of his danger but had thought Henry incapable even of a crime. When the Duke's brother, the Cardinal of Lorraine, had been butchered in turn and the young heir to the dukedom imprisoned, Henry believed himself to be at last the king of France, the victor of a new humanist St. Bartholomew's Day which had rid him of thirty years of Guise ambitions. His mother, Catherine de Medici, knew better, took to her bed and died.

In fact he had signed his own death warrant. A third Guise brother had escaped the trap—Mayenne: a fat, indolent man but a capable intriguer, with Paris and all outraged Catholic France to work on. After the Day of the Barricades the king had been a fugitive, but after Blois he was an outcast, without a friend or an apologist. A born trimmer who had always tried to keep the "options" open, he found himself left with only one possible course —to throw in his lot with Navarre and the Huguenots whom his own mother and elder brother had tried to destroy in the great holocaust of '72 and whom he himself had defeated in the palmy days at Jarnac and Moncontour. Perhaps the dagger of the fantastic Jacques Clément, which put an end to him within a year, came almost as a relief to this able but unlucky man whose somber, hooded eyes look out at us from the Louvre portrait with their suggestion of wasted talent, of badly requited affections, of majesty slighted and deprived.

These two deaths—of Guise and the last Valois—were of crucial importance, not only to France but also to Philip and the Netherlands. "The King of Spain has lost a good captain," the Pope remarked when he heard of the December's work at Blois, but this, if true up to a point, was gross undervaluation of the Balafré's role as mischief-maker and Spanish tool. Deprived of his energy and prestige with the Paris merchants and mobs, the Catholic League was soon to find itself hard-pressed by Navarre and his Huguenots, who in the spring of 1590 won a great victory over Mayenne at Ivry in Normandy and threatened the capital itself.

Navarre's position had been immensely strengthened. As self-proclaimed Henry IV, with the sanction of the late king's solemn deathbed recognition of him as lawful heir to France, he was a much more attractive proposition than the landless fighter who had had little to depend on but the power of his own genial personality. The new "King" recognized by the League, his uncle the aged Cardinal Bourbon, was a prisoner in his hands. On the old man's death, which soon occurred, the only other possible claimants were Mayenne and the young Duke of Guise (foreign Lorrainers by descent and themselves in deadly rivalry with one another) and the children of the two elder sisters of Henry III— Philip's own daughter by Elizabeth of Valois, the Infanta Isabella Clara Eugenia, and the Marquis of Pons, son of Duchess Claude of Lorraine—both of whose rights were debarred by the so-called Salic Law which prevented the succession of a woman to the throne of France and the transmission of her claims to her progeny.

"A chimera," Philip was to call this peculiar doctrine, "a mere invention," and so it was, for the rule against women which had been customary to the tribe of the Salic Franks in the dim mists of time had been resurrected in the fourteenth century, purely as a convenience, to avoid petticoat rule and to bar the accession of a French princess whose legitimacy had been in some doubt since her mother had been taken in flagrant adultery. It was ultimately through this unsavory piece of jobbery that the first Valois king had come to the throne in the person of Philip VI, whose incompetence had led to the humiliating French rout at Crécy, and it was certainly ironical that the same doctrine should have been invoked to deal with the succession problem when the last male Valois died. In common reason, if not by antediluvian tribal custom, the Infanta had as good a right to the throne as anyone. Alas, she was Spanish: her claim was hardly more appealing to sixteenth-century Frenchmen than that of a suspected bastard had seemed to those of the fourteenth.

Only his Protestantism now stood between Navarre and the crown. The King of Spain was no longer faced with a penniless adventurer but with a serious threat to the safety of the Spanish Netherlands, which would find a bad neighbor in a resurgent and Protestant France. His attempts to ward off this danger were now to embroil him, two years after the Armada, in another war beyond his means.

PARMA'S LAST CAMPAIGN. 1589–92.

The rebel provinces of the Union of Utrecht, lying to the north of the great rivers, had so far managed with a modicum of English help to preserve their independence and even to create a kind of commonwealth for themselves. But it was a very fragmented one. Right from the outset two irreconcilable factions had been struggling for mastery of this miniscule territory. On the one side were the conservative and "libertinist" forces of the city oligarchs and small country nobility which found their expression through the local "estates" and States General: on the other, the middle classes in the towns and the Calvinist ideologues who desired not only victory over Spain but over their less-committed fellow citizens.

In all conscience this should have provided enough division for an embryo republic. But it went further. Each signatory at Utrecht knew itself to be sovereign and felt a sovereign distrust of its partners. All were jealous of Holland, the leader and paymaster of the alliance. And indeed for all her virtues, Holland was not the easiest of bedfellows. Under the guidance of her dynamic Advocate, John of Oldenbarneveldt, not only were the extremist preachers curbed and a measure of religious toleration allowed, but a brisk and profitable trade was carried on with Spain as the only means of financing the struggle against her.

If this has a peculiar sound in modern ears, one must admit that this was a peculiar war, and hard economic facts were entirely on the Advocate's side. Such dealings with anti-Christ, which kept Holland eminently prosperous and the Amsterdam merchants happy, could not however be expected to appeal to more rigid Protestants in the other states of the Union or to the numerous refugees from Brabant and Flanders who had brought their grievances and fanaticisms with them into exile. Deeply resentful of

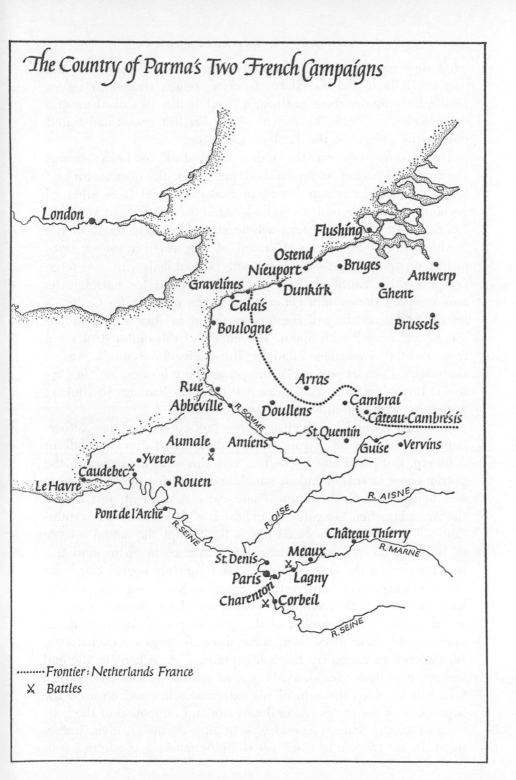

The Country of Parma's Two French Campaigns

London
Flushing
Ostend
Nieuport   • Bruges
Gravelines   Antwerp
• Dunkirk   Ghent
Calais
Boulogne   Brussels

Rue
Abbeville   Arras
R. SOMME   Doullens   Cambrai
Câteau-Cambrésis
Aumale   Amiens   St. Quentin
Yvetot   Guise   • Vervins
Caudebec
Le Havre   • Rouen
R. AISNE
Pont de l'Arche
R. SEINE   R. OISE
Château Thierry
R. MARNE
St. Denis   Meaux
Paris   Lagny
Charenton   Corbeil
R. SEINE

·········· Frontier: Netherlands France
✗   Battles

what they regarded as gross and treacherous materialism on the part of Holland and the States General, which tended to reflect Hollander opinion, these enthusiasts had naturally looked around for a leader, and with the arrival of the English troops had found one in the person of the Earl of Leicester.

This in some ways was the oddest thing of all, for Leicester was the complete magnifico, an unlikely patron for the doctrinaire and leveling preachers whom his royal mistress would have silenced without compunction if they had dared to raise their voice in London. But then Leicester's whole status was odd. Sent to the Netherlands as Lieutenant General of the English forces, with orders on no account to let himself be saddled with sovereign power (which Elizabeth had carefully declined for herself), he had accepted the captain generalship at the rebel States General's hands, to the vast fury of the Queen, intent as always on avoiding a complete breach with Spain. The effects of this outburst of royal rage created anomalies enough. But Leicester himself was a thoroughly devious person: "a dangerous *faux bonhomme*" in Professor Rowse's words; a grandee with radical leanings; a lifelong underling with ambitions to dictate and rule.

Militarily he and his English troops probably saved the Netherlands by holding off Parma in the dark days after the fall of Antwerp. But politically his regime was almost as damaging to the patriot cause as that of Anjou, which had also tried to subvert what was being painfully built up. There came a moment, just before the Armada, when Leicester, in collusion with his extremist Protestant allies in Utrecht, seemed about to attempt the actual seizure of Holland, the powerhouse of rebel resistance to Spain—and this at a time when the Queen's agents were actively negotiating with Parma's delegates at Bourbourg in Flanders. The danger to Netherlands liberties might have been very acute if the Armada had not sailed and destroyed the last of the Queen's pacific illusions: much more might have been lost than three fortresses treacherously surrendered to Parma by English captains. Yet perhaps in the end the result of Leicester's meddling was salutary, since by its very failure it involved the ruin of his extremist allies and ensured the supremacy of the States General and Holland's direction of the war.

Not that the States General was by any means an ideal instrument. In his *History of the United Netherlands,* a continuation of

his classic *Rise of the Dutch Republic,* John Lothrop Motley explains
the limitations of this oligarchic body:

The supreme power, after the deposition of Philip, and the refusal by
France and England to accept the sovereignty of the provinces, was
definitely lodged in the States-General. But the States-General did not
technically represent the people. Its members were not elected by the
people. It was a body composed of delegates from each provincial assembly, of which there were now five—Holland, Zeeland, Friesland,
Utrecht, and Gelderland. Each provincial assembly consisted again of
delegates, not from the inhabitants of the provinces, but from the
magistracies of the cities. Those magistracies, again, were not elected
by the citizens. They elected themselves by renewing their own va-
cancies, and were, in short, immortal corporations. Thus, in final analysis,
the supreme power was distributed and localised among the mayors
and aldermen of a large number of cities, all independent alike of the
people below and of any central power above.

The embryo of more efficient and centralized machinery had
existed in the Council of State, the rebel version of the royalist
body of the same name which had advised the Duchess Margaret,
but this had become identified with Leicester's dubious intrigues
and had lost caste along with him, even before his final departure
from the Netherlands and death in the autumn of Armada year.
For better or for worse, the government of the rebel territories, in
Motley's words, had been "stamped almost at birth with a narrow
provincialism." Yet there was nothing narrow or provincial in the
maritime and commercial growth which was to turn the United
Provinces under the leadership of Holland into the foremost trading
society of its time. Here Motley breaks once more into superlatives:

At least three thousand vessels of between one hundred and four hundred tons, besides innumerable doggers, busses, cromstevens, and similar
craft used on the river and in fisheries, were to be found . . . and one
thousand, it was estimated, were annually built. They traded to the
Baltic regions for honey, wax, tallow, lumber, iron, turpentine, hemp.
They brought from furthest Indies and from America all the fabrics
of ancient civilisation, all the newly discovered products of a virgin soil,
and distributed them among the less industrious nations of the earth.
Enterprise, led on and accompanied by science, was already planning

the boldest flights into the unknown yet made by mankind . . . those famous arctic voyages made by Hollanders in pursuit of the north-west passage to Cathay. . . .

And again on the social front:

The industrial population had flowed from the southern provinces into the north, in obedience to an irresistible law. The workers in iron, paper, silk, linen, lace, the makers of brocade, tapestry, and satin, as well as all the coarser fabrics, had fled from the land of oppression to the land of liberty. Never in the history of civilisation had there been a more rapid development of human industry than in Holland during these years of bloodiest warfare. The towns were filled to overflowing. Amsterdam multiplied in wealth and population as fast as Antwerp shrank. Almost as much might be said of Middelburg, Enkuyzen, Horn, and many other cities. It is the epoch to which the greatest expansion of municipal architecture is traced. Warehouses, palaces, docks, arsenals, fortifications, dykes, splendid streets and suburbs, were constructed on every side. . . .

Not for the first or the last time, in fact, a people had begun to thrive on a war economy—based in this instance on a maritime thrust which was to pay sensational dividends in the years ahead with the foundation of the Dutch East India Company and the creation of a vast empire in the Java Sea.

Far different was the state of the provinces south of the rivers which Parma had reconquered or coaxed back into the Spanish fold. The great port of Antwerp was blockaded by rebel cruisers and by the English garrison in Flushing which commanded the entrance to the Scheldt. The same political and geographical causes which had brought about the defeat of the Armada, by denying it a port in the narrows, now ensured that the provinces still loyal to Philip should find their trade life line cut. "Even as six years before, wolves littered their whelps in deserted farm-houses," writes Motley, "cane-brake and thicket usurped the place of cornfield and orchard, robbers swarmed on the highways once thronged by a most thriving population, nobles begged their bread in streets of cities whose merchants once entertained emperors and whose wealth and traffic were the wonder of the world. . . ."

Perhaps we can do without the indigent nobles, for in the sequel to his great book the master did sometimes tend to embellish his theme, but there is still plenty of reliable contemporary evidence to show that perpetual warfare, banditry on an ever-increasing scale and the exactions of Spanish garrisons had brought much of Flanders and Brabant to a condition of semi-desert. The economic pendulum had swung very far in favor of the north and against the loyalist south, whose Governor General in his letters to the King was constantly harping on the chronic condition of the country and the danger of some new outbreak against Spanish rule.

Militarily one might have expected it to be another matter, for the failure of Medina Sidonia's fleet had brought no corresponding losses to the *tercios* who had been garrisoned along the invasion coast and had perhaps always been earmarked by their commander for a move northward against a more vulnerable enemy. As late as September 3 Philip continued to entertain wild hopes that Parma might still manage a descent on England, but as a more realistic alternative we find him turning also to thoughts of an attack on the isle of Walcheren, so that the year might not end without the consolation of some substantial success. Thus even the King now seemed to see a vigorous prosecution of the war against the rebels as the first priority for Spanish arms. Unfortunately for him this decision had been left too late; for the discouragement stemming from the *débâcle* of the Armada had already affected the morale of the troops and their commander. There were to be no consolations in Walcheren and precious few anywhere else in the Netherlands in the remaining years of the reign or in the half century the war had still to run.

This trend declared itself at once in the unsuccessful siege of Bergen-op-Zoom to which Parma turned his attention once his Armada commitment was wound up. His biographer Van Essen makes no bones about admitting that the Governor General never pressed this attack on the threshold of Zeeland with a fraction of the energy he had shown in far more testing circumstances at Antwerp; and even the compensation of the treacherous surrender by its English garrison of the fortress of Geertruidenberg, within striking distance of the rebel bases in southwestern Holland, was never put to profitable use. This was partly because the capture of Geertruidenberg in April 1589 was followed in the next month by Parma's retirement to take the waters at Spa, a sick man suffering from the first symptoms of dropsy, and partly because of serious mutinies in the "old *tercio*" of Sancho de Leyva. But it was also due to the much wider events we have already noted on the European scene—the assassination of Henry III of France and Navarre's dangerous accession of strength and prestige which took him to the gates of Paris.

Thus Philip was brought face to face with one of the crucial decisions of the reign. Was he to allow the continuation of Parma's offensive against the Netherlands rebels, at the risk of finding a resurgent and perhaps Protestant France on the vulnerable flank within a few days' march of Brussels? Or should he try to cut down the heretical tree at its root by destroying Navarre and the Huguenots, leaving the Hollanders till the larger account was settled? It was a problem of the utmost delicacy, and though in the result Philip was universally blamed—by the Protestants for his ambition and by the Catholics for his failure—who shall say for sure that any other policy would have paid him better dividends, in the Netherlands or in Paris?

The King's decision in fact to intervene in France was rational on the basis of *Weltpolitik* as seen from Madrid. But of course as seen by Parma from his parochial viewpoint in Brussels it was calamitous. It was only step by reluctant step that the Governor General suffered himself to be drawn into the maelstrom. As early as March 1589 the King had been writing that the affair of France was of prime importance. In April and May 1590 these commands were followed with others, insisting that Parma must enter France as rapidly as possible. On June 20 Philip renewed his imperative instructions: four days later he ended a letter with a postscript in his own hand: "I cannot find words to use about an affair which I have so often ordered, and I neither ask nor desire words but actions, that is what I want of you."

The tone of royal exasperation is unmistakable, and in all conscience as one reads Parma's endlessly prevaricating replies, week in, week out, while the crisis mounts in France, one must agree that the King had had his fill of arguments. Yet *a whole month later* we find Parma writing to say that he is still unable to leave the Netherlands without risking their loss, and citing the supporting opinions of his commanders. This in itself would have been enough to harden Philip's heart even if reports had not been reaching him as early as February 1590 from sources unfriendly to Parma to suggest that this disobedience was deliberate, springing from treason and ambition; nor did the chorus slacken when in March the first fruits of reluctant compliance in the shape of an advance of eighteen hundred royalist Netherlands cavalry under Count Philip of Egmont,* the son of Alva's victim, were cut down in Mayenne's defeat at Ivry, a major disaster for Catholic arms, since Navarre, free from the threat of a League field army in Normandy, now set up a close blockade of Paris by seizing the bridges across the Seine and Marne.

By midsummer of 1590 the sufferings of the city had reached horrifying proportions:

Men [writes Motley] devoured such dead vermin as could be found lying in the streets. They crowded greedily around stalls in the public squares where the skin, bones, and offal of such dogs, cats and unclean beasts as still remained were sold to the populace. . . . Men stood in archways and narrow passages lying in wait for whatever stray dogs still remained at large, noosed them, strangled them, and like savage beasts of prey tore them to pieces and devoured them alive. And it sometimes happened, too, that the equally hungry dog proved the more successful in the foul encounter, and fed upon the man. . . . The Spanish ambassador, Mendoza, advised recourse to an article of diet which had been used in some of the oriental sieges. The counsel at first was rejected as coming from the agent of Spain, who wished at all hazards to save the capital from falling out of the hands of his master into those of the heretic. But dire necessity prevailed, and the bones of the dead were taken in considerable quantities from the cemeteries, ground into flour, baked into bread, and consumed. It was called Madame Montpensier's cake, because the duchess earnestly proclaimed its merits to the poor Parisians. "She was never known to taste it herself, however," bitterly observed one who lived in Paris through that horrible summer. She was right to abstain, for all who ate of it died, and the Montpensier flour fell into disuse.

Even worse stories were told and believed. The fanatical spirit of the city under the inspiration of its religious leaders was extreme, and the danger of its fall, which now engaged Philip to the exclusion of all other thoughts, drove him to correspondingly stern ex-

* It is ironic that the heirs of the two most famous patriot leaders should both have gone over to the enemy, for Orange's eldest son, kidnapped from his studies at Louvain, had for long been a Spanish pensioner.

hortations to his Governor General, whom he could hardly believe
was not already at the post of duty in France.

How the priorities were regarded in Brussels is very plain from
the Governor General's reply, couched in terms of resigned despair,
yet still pleading the vital importance of the Belgic provinces, on
whose safety depended the security of a great part if not all of
Philip's dominions.

Since your Majesty repeatedly orders me to go to France with my army
and to save Paris I will do it, because I was born to obey. But I regret
it infinitely and am heart-broken to see that your Majesty supposes,
orders and desires that I should carry out the impossible—I say impossible, because only God can perform miracles. Can your Majesty really
suppose that with the small subsidies you have sent me I can at one
and the same time garrison the Low Countries, pay the mutinous
Spanish Troops and Don Juan Manrique's Germans, sustain Mayenne
and the League, pay retaining fees to the German *Reiters* for the protection of these provinces, keep control of the ports and satisfy the half-
mutinous garrisons in Friesland? Misery and famine have made such inroads here that, not counting the reinforcements already sent to Mayenne
—5,200 men—I have only four thousand left to defend the Low Countries between the Meuse and the Rhine. How can I carry out your
Majesty's orders to invade France with an army of 20,000 men? How
can I supply such an army? Can I have any confidence in the French
nobles, who have so often shown themselves hostile to your Majesty
and the house of Burgundy? In the Netherlands the people are in despair,
believing themselves abandoned by their sovereign. Your Majesty wishes
us to stand on the defensive here, but can one do it when our frontiers
stretch from Luxemburg to Gravelines and from Gravelines to Groningen?
The enemy, having control of the rivers and the sea, can strike within
twenty-four hours wherever he chooses.

This last was palpably true, since in a surprise coup of the utmost
daring and ingenuity patriot forces had just seized Breda, where
Orange had once had his estates and from which raids could be
mounted deep into loyalist territory in Brabant. Without any doubt
all Parma's objections to abandoning the Netherlands in pursuit of
what he regarded as a will-o'-the-wisp were abundantly justified in
terms of his Brussels commitment which it was his duty and his
passion to protect. As he pointed out, the situation in what was left
of the loyalist northeast, at the end of a long line of communications, was dangerously unsound and vulnerable to rebel attack,

while even in Flanders he judged that an army corps was needed to safeguard Bruges and Ghent. Nor was this only a personal opinion. His council of war unanimously supported him, while his deputy, old Count Charles of Mansfeld, whose jealousy makes him a reliable witness on this occasion, had forecast with remarkable prescience in December 1589 that if Philip intervened in France, the Catholic League would nevertheless end by making terms with Henry of Navarre and that Spain would be the only loser by the adventure.

Why then did the King override these objections, which were based on good evidence (if with an element of special pleading about them)? He seems at one stage to have had some doubts in the matter, which were echoed among his closest advisers in Madrid, but the fact was that the pressing danger of a Huguenot takeover in France, combined with his ambitions to see his daughter on the French throne, had made the adventure virtually inevitable. Even Parma himself was aware that there were two sides to the argument. "If I go [to France]," he had written to his master, "the Low Countries could be lost. If I don't go the French will hold me to blame for the fall of Paris and for everything which might follow." These last words sum up Philip's dilemma.

So to France the Governor General went, and with him the bulk of the Netherlands command, including a substantial number of Walloons—"as if there were not graves enough in their own small territories," exclaims Motley with indignant scorn. It was a historic moment, for never before, even in the Emperor's day or after St. Quentin, had a Spanish Army had the run of Northeastern France up to the Paris approaches. In spite of his pessimistic forecasts it was a sizable body that Parma had managed to collect—about twenty thousand men, once he had made his junction with the League's forces at Meaux, and much on a par with what the enemy could bring against him, though weaker in cavalry, as was usual in the Spanish service where infantry was the master arm. Yet it was not as an invader or agent of Spain that he chose to present himself to the Chauvinistic French but as a servant of the true faith who had come to save Catholic lives in Paris and the Catholic succession from the grasp of the heretic "Béarnais."* This was prudent. The religious card was the only one to play against

* The self-declared Henry IV of France was always in Spanish eyes "the prince of Béarn."

Navarre and against Mayenne, who had his own ambitions. In fact in the three-handed game which was to develop—four-handed if one included Philip—the ostensible Huguenot enemy was by far the easiest to deal with. He posed only a strategic problem.

To an invader coming from the east—as France's invaders since the end of the Hundred Years War have tended to come—the direct route to Paris lies along the right or north bank of the Marne to its junction with the Seine at Charenton. Between these two rivers and the Aisne and Oise, whose east-west courses run parallel to the Marne some thirty miles to the north of it, lies a tongue of land aimed like an arrowhead at the capital and devoid of natural obstacles to an army. Some of the fiercest of First World War battles were to be fought in this interriverine strip, whose strategic importance brought Parma to his concentration point with Mayenne at Meaux and Navarre's army to meet him on the right bank of the Marne a few miles west of Lagny, where bridge and fortress were in Huguenot hands.

Obviously Navarre expected the enemy attack near the monastery of Challes in the open country between the armies; his thoughts were not on Lagny on the left bank of the Marne or on the Seine beyond it. But then though Motley, on the evidence of his victories of Coutras and Ivry, sees this contest as a duel between "the two great captains of the age," the Béarnais, as Parma himself was to remark with professional disapproval, was less a general than a dashing leader of light horse, more concerned with skirmishing and chivalrous gestures than with the serious business of soldiering. Faced at Challes with a formal invitation to battle, Parma replied with disdain that it was his habit to engage the enemy on his own terms when the occasion suited him. This was no more than the sober truth. After days of cautious sparring behind his field defenses, he emerged to make a feint attack on the main enemy position, under cover of which he moved rapidly to a flank, threw his pontoons over the Marne, covered the bridge of Lagny with his artillery, and stormed the town on the far bank before Navarre was even aware of what was happening.

With the capture of Lagny went control of the course of the Marne, and food supplies began to reach the starving capital. A swift pounce followed on Charenton at the confluence with the Seine, and as Navarre's army began to disintegrate under the moral effect of these blows, Parma cleared the southern approaches

to Paris, revictualed it, then turned southwest to Corbeil, whose
capture after a month's siege opened the whole course of the Seine
above the city.

The military task which he had declared impossible had thus
been triumphantly carried out at a minimal cost in Catholic lives.
No other commander in Philip's service could have done so much
with such economy or could have resisted the lure of a victor's
entry into the liberated city, which Parma tactfully left to Mayenne
and the captains of the League.

He had other concerns. What should be the future of France in
the new situation he had brought about? He had little faith in the
prospect of imposing a Spanish Infanta or indeed any foreigner on
the French, though this seemed to be the way royal policy was
tending. He knew too much about French susceptibilities and pride
to imagine that they could be compelled—or even bribed—to accept something so repugnant to their deepest instincts. Yet his own
solution, which he advanced to Philip from his camp at Corbeil,
was to say the least disingenuous: a standing army of Spaniards to
be retained in France—the League was demanding a minimum of
ten thousand—and support for Mayenne as a compromise king
who would be "entirely dependent" on Spanish aid. Philip, who
regarded Mayenne as lacking in suppleness and unfit to be anything
beyond "the second personage in France," immediately vetoed the
idea. Parma's view looks suspiciously like a misjudgment, unless it
was the disinterest of a man who only longs to return home and
be quit of an intolerable burden.

Up to this moment the Governor General had shown a loyal if
rather dilatory obedience to the whims and oddities of royal policies
which were dictated hundreds of miles from the battlefields and
conference chambers where they had to be carried out. And one
will do less than justice to the strains imposed by these policies if
one forgets that at the height of the Armada preparations the
King had been bothering his Governor General about a genealog-
ical table of the Burgundian dukes which some indigent scholar
required money to print, and that at a later time of general chaos
and alarm in the Netherlands he was concerning himself—and his
servants—with the authenticity or otherwise of a head of St.
Lawrence (or part of it) which was reputedly in a monastery at
Gladbach in the German state of Cleves and which the King
particularly desired to add to his collection of relics at the Escurial.

Years later it was at last determined that St. Lawrence's bones *were* authentic—but what about an alleged head of John the Baptist at Arnhem?

Similar problems had afflicted Parma throughout his Herculean labors and no doubt they had their cumulative effect. He was to remain loyal to the end and marvelously efficient. We shall nevertheless note in him certain symptoms of the despair which had afflicted Don John and so many of Philip's servants, even down to the ironhearted Alva and Santa Cruz. In what other light should we regard his extraordinary action that autumn in taking his army back to the Netherlands with its task only half done and in the face of Mayenne's pleas and the King's manifest wishes that he should remain in France?

There were colorable excuses in the condition of the troops after an arduous campaign, the hostility shown them by the peasants when they went foraging, and the usual lack of funds. But as one examines the details of that retreat, in itself a masterpiece of war, carried out in impeccable order without loss in the presence of a cloud of Huguenot cavalry under Navarre himself, the impression remains of a much tried man reverting to the simplicities of a soldier's life as he had known it in the carefree days of Gembloux—indeed through French eyes we catch an intimate glimpse of him which perfectly bears this out: of a horseman wearing a felt hat, a furred jacket and large Spanish ruff, galloping up and down the ranks, brandishing his sword and shouting orders.

By December he was back in Brussels. "He had magnificently accomplished his difficult retreat," writes his biographer Van Essen, and so indeed he had. But Spanish policy in France was not one of retreat but of aggression. It depended for its success on unwavering attack. Deprived of their powerful ally, the forces of the League relapsed into impotence, and Lagny and Corbeil were soon back in Huguenot hands. A superior Canute, the Duke of Parma had not succeeded in reversing the tide for long. It was now to engulf him from an unexpected quarter, from the Netherlands.

With Orange's passing the leadership of the rebel provinces had devolved on Holland and her most forceful statesman, the Advocate, John of Oldenbarneveldt, in whom many of the dead man's policies and much of his genius lived on. But in the climate of the sixteenth

century even the most bourgeois society had to look for aristocratic
connections, and this rule had been preserved by promoting the
hero's second son, Prince Maurice of Nassau, to his father's old
stadtholderates in Holland and Zeeland and to the captain generalship of their armies; powers soon to be extended to Gelderland,
Utrecht and Overyssel, leaving only Friesland outside his scope—
and Friesland had for its stadtholder his friend and cousin Lewis
William, son of Orange's brother John of Nassau.

Behind the scenes the States General and Oldenbarneveldt continued to provide the political direction of affairs and to negotiate
with their English and Huguenot allies, but the prestige of the
Nassau name and the concentration of military power in the cousins'
hands was soon to raise them, and particularly Maurice, to a pre-
eminence in the small coalition of republics which Orange himself
had seldom enjoyed. "Spade in hand, with his head full of Roman
castrametation and geometrical problems," writes Motley, "a prince,
scarce emerged from boyhood, presents himself on that stage where
grizzled Mansfelds, drunken Hohenlos and truculent Verdugos
have been so long enacting that artless military drama which con-
sists of hard knocks and wholesale massacres."

Perhaps these familiar by-blows of war had not entirely vanished from the scene, as Motley himself acknowledges in the very
next paragraph, where he remarks that man's bellicose nature has
not changed much since he "first began to walk up and down the
earth and destroy his fellow creatures." But—if only for a while—a
milder or at least more ordered age was dawning. Maurice was to
perpetrate no Naardens or massacres of the kind which even Parma
had allowed at Sichem. He was the model of the scientific soldier,
well versed in mathematics, with something of the textbook warrior about him, as drawn from the best classical sources which
were the passion of Lewis William's life.

The fruits of this antiquarianism, though much derided at
the time, were to prove remarkably successful. Nor did the cousins
fail to provide their own military innovations. Under their direction,
not only were the armies drilled, but they were actually paid—a
very startling innovation indeed by the standards ruling elsewhere.
By a long overdue reform, the striking power of their companies
was raised by an increase in the ratio of musketeers and arquebusiers to pikemen and by a similar reform in the cavalry where the
pistol began to supplant the lance. But it was in the insistence

that an army should not be a predator but a servant of the state, and a servant not only prepared to die but to work for its bread, that Maurice's conceptions were so revolutionary. "Spade in hand" —Motley's puzzling phrase for him—has a simple explanation. His troops were expected to dig: hitherto considered a most degrading and unwar-like task. And as the sieges which were his specialty followed one another with prosaic and almost unvarying success, the charms of the method and its increased sophistication began to draw its acolytes and imitators from all over Europe, till the stadtholder's camp became a true academy of war.

But this is to anticipate, for at first the results were not particularly happy or inspiring. The arrival of Leicester and his English army may have saved the embryo republic but it was a profound embarrassment to those of its leaders—among them the Nassaus and Oldenbarneveldt—who were moderate in their religious outlook and oligarchic in their political ideas. Nor had the deplorably irresolute attempts to relieve Sluys in '87, which Leicester and Maurice mismanaged between them, been much better auguries for the future. The turning point in what might otherwise have been a disastrous story was of course the shift in Spanish policy brought about by the Armada's failure and the need to shore up Catholicism in France which took Parma to Paris and left the patriot forces free to strike at any point they chose against the Spanish-held fortresses along the Waal and Yssel, on which depended the few remaining royalist towns of the northeast.

As early as February 1590, before Parma had even taken himself off to France, the first patriot blow of the campaign was struck against Breda in north Brabant. A picked body of seventy men under a Captain de Heraugière, a Walloon noble who had gone over to the rebellion, was embarked by night on a canal barge carrying turfs for the castle's fuel supply. As an illustration of how times had changed since Alva's gibe at the "men of butter," the exploit deserves to be remembered in Motley's words:

On Monday night, the 26th of February, the seventy went on board the vessel, which was apparently filled with blocks of turf, and packed themselves closely in the hold. They moved slowly during a little time on their perilous voyage; for the winter wind, thick with fog and sleet, blew directly down the river, bringing along with it huge blocks of ice and scooping the water out of the dangerous shallows, so as to render the vessel at any moment liable to be stranded. At last the navigation became impossible and they came to a standstill. From Monday night till Thursday morning those seventy Hollanders lay packed like herrings in the hold of their little vessel, suffering from hunger, thirst and deadly cold. . . . Even when the third morning dawned there was no better prospect of proceeding; for the remorseless east wind still blew a gale against them, and the shoals which beset their path had become more dangerous than ever. . . . In all secrecy they went ashore at a lonely castle called Nordam, where they remained to refresh themselves until about eleven at night, when one of the boatmen came to them with the intelligence that the wind had changed and was now blowing freshly from the sea. Yet the voyage of a few leagues, on which they embarked, lasted nearly two whole days longer. On Saturday afternoon they passed through the last sluice, and at about three o'clock the last boom was shut behind them.

Now, inside the first ring of defenses, in the outer harbor, an officer of the garrison came aboard and entered the small ship's cabin where he was separated only by a sliding trap door from Heraugière and his seventy, who could hear his every movement. Then on the way to the water gate the vessel sprang a leak, soaking the unfortunate human cargo to the skin before it anchored near the guardhouse of the castle.

The winter nights had been long and fearfully cold, and there was almost a dearth of fuel both in town and fortress. A gang of labourers set to work discharging the turf from the vessel with such rapidity that the departing daylight began to shine in upon the prisoners much sooner than they wished. Moreover the thorough wetting, to which after all their other inconveniences they had just been exposed in their narrow escape from foundering, had set the whole party sneezing and coughing. Never was a catarrh so sudden, so universal, or so ill-timed. Lieutenant Held, unable to control the violence of his cough, drew his dagger and earnestly implored his next neighbour to stab him to the heart. . . . But the calm and wary skipper who stood on the deck instantly commanded his companion to work at the pump with as much clatter as possible, assuring the persons present that the hold was nearly full of water. By this means the noise of the coughing was effectively drowned. . . . At last, when the case seemed also desperate, he loudly declared that sufficient had been unladen for that evening and that it was too dark and he too tired for further work. So, giving a handful of stivers among the workmen, he bade them go ashore at once and have some beer and come next morning for the rest of the cargo. Fortunately they accepted his honourable proposition and took their departure. Only the servant of the captain of the guard lingered behind, complaining that the turf was not as good as usual and that his master would never be satisfied with it. "Ah," returned the cool skipper, "the best part of the cargo is underneath. This is expressly reserved for the captain. He is sure to get enough of it to-morrow."

Just before midnight the seventy were at last ashore.

Heraugière marched straight to the guard-house.
"Who goes there?" cried a sentinel, hearing some movement in the darkness.
"A friend," replied the captain, seizing him by the throat, and commanding him, if he valued his life, to keep silence except when addressed and then to speak in a whisper.
Quietly as they had made their approach, there was nevertheless a stir in the guard-house. The captain of the watch sprang into the courtyard. "Who goes there?" he demanded in his turn.
"A friend," again replied Heraugière, striking him dead with a single blow as he spoke.

This is sterling stuff. The characters in the hands of the master storyteller seem as invulnerable and immortal as those in an old Fairbanks film—when the last shot has been taken, Captain Heraugière and his fellow actors, including the forty slain of the garrison he has surprised, will surely get up and go peacefully home to bed. Yet Breda, with its six companies of Italian regulars, undoubtedly fell to this small band of desperadoes and their support troops outside the town: the first triumphal heralds, after a decade of defeat, of the great rebel offensive which was in preparation and soon to astonish Europe.

Maurice's strategy had two objectives: to destroy the last vestiges of Spanish power on his southern front along the Waal, essentially a clearing operation, of which the capture of Breda had been part; and to win control of the north-south course of the Yssel which divided patriot west from royalist east, by pinching out the Spanish-held towns along its length, on which depended Parma's far-northern base of Groningen.

Zutphen, where Sir Philip Sidney had died, was the first link in this chain. Fortress and town fell within a week, though this had

been one of the most bitterly contested strong points in the Netherlands. Nor did its near neighbor Deventer, the state capital of
Overyssel, resist much longer. Maurice's powerful artillery blew
vast gaps in its defenses, and within a fortnight he was on the
march to Groningen, the greatest prize of all, whose capture would
bring the entire northeast under patriot control.

Parma, who had returned from his relief of Paris, reacted to
the threat by moving north against Knodsenberg, the rebel fort
which had been built to harass his principal base of Nymegen on the
Waal, a few miles downstream from the parting of its waters from
the parent stream of the Rhine. But his assault on Knodsenberg
failed, and he was now to find himself on the far bank of an
unbridged, unfordable river in the presence of Prince Maurice's
army which had come hurrying down from Groningen to face him.
Throughout Parma's military career runs this thread of the use of
waterways. Maastricht, Sluys and Antwerp had all been taken
by skillful denial of their courses to the enemy; Paris had been
saved by his brilliant coup against the Bridge of Lagny; and in
his coming campaign in Normandy we shall see the method given
a new use in his mastery of the serpentine windings of the Seine.
On the Waal, with only a losing hand to play, he could do no
more than demonstrate the art of disengagement from an enemy
by crossing his pontoon bridges under strong artillery cover to
the safety of the south bank.

It was a reverse—the first of his career as a commander, but one
which could have been redeemed if he had been allowed to remain
on the Waal with his fortress screen behind him and the strong
point of Nymegen to cover his front. But at Knodsenberg he had
received final and peremptory orders from his master to return to
France where Mayenne and the League were once more in urgent
need of him. In fact for over six months he had been subjected to an
unrelenting pressure from Madrid which he had tried his best to
dodge with a variety of excuses and arguments, mostly founded
on the deplorable state of the loyalist provinces and armed forces.
Thus in March 1591, little more than three months after his return
to Brussels from the Seine, he was pleading "distrust" of his infantry, the "disorder" of his cavalry and his fears that the artillery
was the worst of all. In May, with German *Reiters* and Walloons
to be recruited, he declared himself penniless, "without a *real*": a
complaint to be echoed by every luckless successor.

Inexorably the orders from Spain overtook and submerged these pleas and appeals for help. On May 22, while Maurice's armies were concentrating against Zutphen, Philip was urging his Governor General's immediate return to France with promises of six hundred thousand ducats, which must however be used to pay off the mutinous *tercios* and *not* for the settlement of old debts. Creditors must have patience, noted the King with ineffable smugness.

In July, with Zutphen and Deventer lost, the harassed Governor General was still arguing the absurdity of the French enterprise, which on his estimate would require thirty thousand infantry and ten thousand horse, plus twenty-two thousand men for the defense of the Netherlands and half a million ducats a month in hard cash. Beyond these figures, which were fanciful and which he knew to be fanciful, we sense and indeed may read in Parma's correspondence his deep concern for his adopted homeland—an enemy had already dubbed him "the man of Flanders." His own grip on the machinery of the state and provincial councils and even on the army was weakening: this too comes out very clearly from his letters. Yet at Nymegen in July, in the presence of the enemy, he finds himself summoned away. In fact in a letter of August 4 the King was to show himself even more adamant, adding a postscript in his own hand, perhaps the most impassioned in the whole enormously protracted correspondence: "You know what I want. I have opened my heart to you. To satisfy me you must leave for France, and you will see how grateful I shall be."

How the promise was kept the future was to show. The direct results of this intransigence were the collapse of Spanish power in the northeast Netherlands and Parma's last campaign.

On that same fourth of August 1591 the Governor General reached Spa from Knodsenberg to take the cure and prepare himself for his mission. He was already a very sick man, yet the letters that went out to Madrid that autumn were less concerned with his personal troubles than with the tragic state of the provinces he was leaving behind him at the mercy of the growing enemy strength in the north and incompetent subordinates at home.

These fears were well founded. With no Spanish field army in being, Prince Maurice had given a formidable demonstration of his mobility by switching his forces westward down-river to capture Hulst, at the sea apex of a triangle which enclosed both Antwerp and Ghent, and then moving rapidly back to Nymegen which fell on October 21, thus removing the linchpin which had held together the Spanish positions beyond the Waal.

Nor was the domestic situation in the supposedly "safe" territories of Flanders and Brabant much more reassuring, for it is evident from Parma's own words that there was a growing ground swell of discontent all too reminiscent of the troubles at the time of the wedding celebrations in Brussels in '65. Both the high and the low, he wrote to Philip, considered themselves ruined, destitute, deprived of their rights and pillaged by friend and foe. They had all but given up hope of things improving but regarded themselves as abandoned by their King to the mercy of rebels and heretics.

That he himself was to blame for this state of affairs never really seems to have crossed his mind, though he was prepared to admit to certain "mistakes," and his Council of State and Privy Council were soon to be more outspoken in their reports to Madrid of the confusion and malpractices of his regime and even of its "abominable delinquencies and crimes." Most of these complaints were made in response to the King's own prompting at a slightly later time when it was plain that the Governor General was falling, and may to some extent be discounted as the work of men saying what their master wanted to be said.

Yet no one can read Parma's dispatches in the triumphant days of his reconquest of Flanders and Brabant and then his letters from 1589 onward without being struck, if not with his failing powers, at least with his failing grip over a rapidly deteriorating situation. The fact that his successors fared no better is only half an argument. Intent on his unceasing military cares, he had given too little thought to the civil government of the provinces: corruption was rife at every level, and the mutual jealousies of Spanish colonels, ambitious Flemish nobles and Italian placemen, in whom he put too much trust, had brought about a situation where even loyalists implacably opposed to heresy had begun to compare their lot unfavorably with the more ordered world existing in the rebel provinces. Perhaps it is a miracle that things were not even worse. Harassed by contradictory orders, always in want of money, living from hand to mouth among semi-mutinous troops, a restless population and disloyal nobles, and with a major enemy power ranged along his northern frontiers, the Governor General was still able to raise an army for France and to leave garrisons and some sort of a viable state behind him. His deputy in the provinces, old Count Peter Mansfeld, and Mansfeld's son Charles, one of his own generals, were busily intriguing against him: he was walking on the quicksands of the King's vanishing favor, as friendless and forlorn as Don John in his camp at Bouges and at heart as despairing, but still the indispensable man on whom everyone relied, even the master who was about to betray him.

Philip's attentions were now no longer directed to the Netherlands except as a base, though it was one which he expected to be defended with resources which he had failed to provide. Informed by Parma of the true situation in the provinces, his reaction had been of the coolest—"I am grieved that your affairs are not as they should be, but nevertheless the true remedy lies in a solid re-establishment of the situation in France." And on the long-range view of his responsibilities he may well have been right. To make Catholic France into a good neighbor and ally against heresy had been one of the aims of the treaty of Câteau-Cambrésis in '59 and it was increasingly important now that England had turned into an active enemy and the Utrecht provinces had defected. The way to a settlement of his problems still lay through France, but it must be a France that was willing to be embraced—what was needed was a marriage, not a rape.

At first the King had recognized this truth and had played the dangerous situation which had followed Henry III's assassination with some delicacy and tact. Thus his first candidate had been the aged Cardinal Bourbon, who not only had some colorable rights to the throne but was unlikely ever to sit on it, since he was a prisoner of the Huguenots. This had left time and room for maneuver. But Bourbon was now dead, and though Philip still paid lip service to French aspirations and to the choice of some mutually acceptable candidate—the young Duke of Guise seemed indicated—it is clear that he had already begun to play for the highest stakes and desired nothing less than his daughter's succession as *Reine Propriétaire* or at least as joint ruler with a husband of his own choosing.

This was not only to fly in the face of the Salic Law and two hundred years if not two millennia of history, but also it was an affront to French pride which not even the most fervent Catholic would swallow without the most careful and diplomatic management, a large army of occupation and bribes on an astronomical scale. At one stage agreement seemed to be near on a basis of a down payment of a million *écus* plus an expeditionary force of twenty thousand men, and Parma himself wrote to Philip commending the deal. But how realistic this was, and how much Parma believed in it, is another matter. For one thing, he knew the King would never pay the price in hard cash. And for another, his own earlier favorable view of Mayenne was changing into distrust and fear that some arrangement with Navarre at Spain's expense might come about at any moment.

The results of these doubts were to prove highly unfortunate in the campaign ahead, for they turned the Governor General, who held the purse strings, into the virtual prisoner of Mayenne. For once, his brilliant diplomatic gifts had led him into the misreading of a situation, for though the time was to come when the chiefs of the League were to make their peace with the Béarnais, they were very unlikely to do it with a man as yet unreconciled with Rome. If Philip's ambitions were pitched too high, Parma's touch was too pliant, and this was to cause him trouble not only on the diplomatic front but in the field, where important strategic decisions were to be dictated not by the commander in chief but by the whims of the League. The marvel is that with so many vexations to plague him—an exacting master, a disloyal ally, lack of money, above all lack of money, which brought from him the despairing cry that rather than be left in such straits he would retire to the forest to live on roots—he was still able to carry out his instructions to the letter.

The objective this time was Rouen, the League's main base in Normandy, where the garrison under de Villars was besieged by the Marshal de Biron and Navarre's covering force east of the Seine valley. After his junction with Mayenne the Governor General's strength was in the region of twenty-five thousand but the usual wasting sickness common to all armies soon took its toll, and by the time he had reached Aumale on the borders of Normandy his reports to the King had once more assumed their habitual pessimistic and complaining tone.

Near Aumale an incident occurred which could have had important consequences—in a cavalry skirmish Navarre was wounded and nearly taken. No doubt it would have gone worse with him than in his previous captivity after St. Bartholomew's Day. The opportunity passed; but clearly Parma's line of march, which was organized on the most uncompromising "hedgehog" principle, was impervious to a mere cavalry attack, and Navarre judged it prudent to retreat westward to join de Biron before Rouen, leaving a strong point at Neuchâtel-en-Braye to amuse the enemy.

Parma followed him at the same leisurely pace that had marked his advance, taking Neuchâtel in his stride in February. But here his progress was halted by the news that de Villars in Rouen had smashed Biron's besieging ring in a daring sortie, and no longer needed Spanish help. Mayenne and the League, who had been hot for action, now pressed for a retreat, probably because they had no desire to see a Spanish garrison in Rouen to supplement the one which had already established itself in Paris. Parma complied: sending only token reinforcements into the city before recrossing the Somme to sit down before the small Huguenot fortress of Rue which lay on the flank of his communications between Brussels and Amiens, though otherwise its relevance to his mission was obscure. He too had irons in the fire—he was halfway back to the Netherlands where his abiding interests lay, also his fears.

For throughout his Norman campaign we should remember that he was constantly looking over his shoulder at events in the provinces and at the activities of his deputy Count Peter Mansfeld, in whom advanced age had not blunted a hearty appetite for intrigue and self-advancement. Thus on March 5, at a critical point in Parma's military operations, we find Mansfeld writing to the King with the sour complaint that he has received no instructions from the absentee Governor General for eleven days. On March 8 Parma is lamenting to the King that he has not heard a word from Mansfeld for six weeks! If the result of this mutual recrimination had not been the tragic misgovernment of the Netherlands it would certainly have been comical. The French Leaguers and *their* intrigues fade for the moment into the background, only to re-emerge larger and more menacing than ever in the Governor General's endless round of correspondence with superiors and subordinates who alike no longer listen. "Everyone is out for himself and no one thinks of the communal good," he wrote to Philip from his camp in France. "The Duke of Mayenne is very put out because we have checked his personal ambitions. Since we cannot do without him and he has the power to ruin everything, I try to satisfy him as far as I can."

The dangers of this quaint captivity were to be strikingly revealed, for no sooner had Parma's army retreated out of Normandy than Navarre and Biron redrew their lines around Rouen, and a message now reached the Governor General from de Villars informing him that unless the city were relieved within eight days it would fall: At Neuchâtel Parma had been within close range of his objective; at Rue he was far away on the wrong side of the Somme in a countryside where many of the roads were impassable because of floods, and with some units of his army in open mutiny. The poor fellows as usual had not been paid. But without hesitation he answered the call, crossing the tidal estuary* under cover of a living dam formed by his cavalry and coming down by forced marches on Rouen from the northeast.

Navarre immediately raised the siege and retreated up-river toward Pont de l'Arche, his nearest bridgehead across the Seine. If we are to believe contemporary accounts, the Spaniards were all for a pursuit and an engagement with the enemy which would either destroy him or force him across the river out of eastern Normandy. In this most baffling of campaigns every move, every motive is suspect, and so are the rationalizations of commentators at the time and historians afterward. Whether Parma, who had become increasingly cautious and defensive-minded, ever seriously intended to force a major action against an army now larger than his own must be doubted: certainly on Mayenne's insistence he chose instead to turn directly away from Navarre and move downstream to besiege the enemy town of Caudebec to clear communications between Rouen and the League's base of Le Havre at the river's mouth. And there, while supervising the placing of his guns, he was struck in the right arm by a musket shot. It was a small enough wound; he paid it no attention and only his pallor and the blood seeping through his clothes alerted those around him to what had happened; but the operation to extract the ball put too great a strain on the enfeebled body and fever set in.

Around the sickbed clustered the staffs and the chiefs of the League, clamorous for advice which they would certainly not take. Caudebec had fallen, but Navarre had cut the communications of

* By the ford of Blanchetache where Edward III had crossed the river on the campaign that ended at Crécy.

the invading army with the east and the situation which might have arisen at Pont de l'Arche had been neatly reversed, with the Spaniards in the net. Parma recommended retreat down-river through Lillebonne toward Le Havre. Mayenne preferred they should go to Yvetot, a road communication center well clear of the river valley but lying in a bowl of hills, along whose crests Navarre's much stronger cavalry was soon threatening to outflank the allied line.

The resulting crisis brought Parma from his sickbed to devise one of those felicitous deceptions which sometimes grace the brutal squalors of war. Agents were dispatched to Rouen to drum up every boat and pontoon they could lay their hands on, and on the seventeenth of May, taking advantage of a night of pouring rain, he slipped away from his camp to a better-protected site at Caudebec and then sent his pioneers across the river in small craft to build a fort on the left bank where he planned to lay his bridge. Thirty-six hours later the complete structure was in place and his army, with all its baggage and artillery, was crossing a river nearly a quarter of a mile wide in the short hours of darkness of an early summer's night, under cover of a screen of a few hundred infantry and horse which could have been broken up in one resolute charge if anyone in Navarre's camp had even dreamed such a crossing was possible. When dawn broke, the rear guard under Parma's son, Prince Ranuccio, also crossed the river. Hardly a man was lost; and here is the measure of Parma's genius and of the quality of the men whom he commanded. "No other general, and no technical staff, could have conceived or attempted such a *tour de force* as to take 15,000 men across the Lower Seine in a single night" is Sir Charles Oman's verdict in his classic *History of the Art of War in the Sixteenth Century*. Indeed it was the model withdrawal battle, which raised Parma's prestige to quite unexampled heights in his own time and has never quite lost its power to intrigue admirers.

"Yet after all, what had he accomplished?"—in Motley's carping words. Was he no more than a Mrs. Partington with her mop trying to sweep back "the great current of events" that were "washing away the system and the personages seeking to resist its power"? Not a Protestant current, presumably, since France was fated to remain Catholic.

And here perhaps is the key to a true accomplishment. Though his brilliant retreat across the Seine has the appearance of a small-

scale Dunkirk—no victory, as Churchill had to remind us—Parma's
last campaign in France relieved Navarre's pressure in the north for
some time to come and played its part in convincing that supreme
realist that Paris was "worth a Mass" and indeed could be won in
no other way than by a return to Rome. Thus France was kept from
the Huguenot embrace, as had been the aim of Spanish diplomacy,
and Parma could rightly claim some of the credit in advance. "As
for me," he wrote to Philip from Château Thierry on the road back
to the Netherlands, "wounded and sick though I am, I think I
carried things through in such a way that I can set these services
of mine as among the most important I have ever rendered your
Majesty."

Though he did not know it—was never to know it—the order for
his dismissal was already on its way from Spain.

By the mere fact of his appointment to the governor generalship
of the Netherlands Parma had invited the attention of the Furies
who presided over the fates of almost all the ablest servants of
Spanish imperialism. The list is a long one, from the "Great Captain" in Ferdinand and Isabella's day, through Cortés and the
Pizarros, Don John and Parma, to Ambrogio Spinola and the
"Conde Duque" of Olivares under Philip's degenerate successors
—not one died biblically full of years and honors in the confidence of the master he had served. Not only revolutions devour
their own children.

Like Don John, Parma was vulnerable: a man of semi-royal birth
but wholly dependent on the King's favor. Worse still, he was a
foreigner, an Italian, at a time when Spanish attitudes to Italy
were much on a par with those of later-day Germans toward their
Axis partners. Yet until the shock of the Armada broke the almost
magic aura of success which had attended him, Parma had seemed
unassailable. Again we see the Enterprise of England as a watershed, for once it was over, and the barges which were to have
carried the *tercios* to victory across the Channel were dispersed
along the Flemish canals, the jealousies and hatreds which had
been nursed in silence in the days of prosperity broke through to
the surface, gaining in strength and venom with the failure before
Bergen-op-Zoom and the upsurge of rebel power which followed.

While the Armada was still at the mercy of the northern gales,

rumors that Parma had betrayed it by his lack of spirit and preparation were already being bandied about Europe and soon had the
victim lamenting to Philip "the malice of the world" which made
"the most devoted servants also the most persecuted." One of the
earliest of these talebearers was a Commander Moreo who in
January 1590 was informing the King's powerful secretary Idiaquez
that Parma was hostile to the policy of intervention in France and
had said that the whole world could go hang so long as the
Netherlands were safe. By June Moreo had improved on these
accusations. If Parma had only been executed, he wrote—this time
not to Idiaquez but to the King direct—Catholicism would without
doubt already have been saved in France. Help for Paris would
arrive too late, if it ever started at all: and it is clear from the letter
that Spain's ambassador in the French capital, Mendoza, was saying similar things.

Indeed by this time, in the summer of 1590, a whole chorus of
stridently hostile voices had begun to sound and resound at every
level of government, ranging from those like Medina Sidonia, who
had really suffered in the Armada's defeat, to professional trouble-
makers, disappointed soldiers and the jealous and ambitious
grandees who hoped to use it and the deplorable state of the loyalist
provinces as levers against their Governor. It was a chain reaction,
encouraged by Parma's long absences from Brussels to take the
waters of Spa. The high nobility in Flanders and Brabant—always
grasping and venal—had only been waiting for their opportunity.
Parma's deputy, Count Peter Ernest Mansfeld, was already disaffected, and so was his son Charles, who made the bullets which
the aged parent was encouraged to fire. So was Granvelle's brother
Champagney, who had played a hero's part in Antwerp on the
day of the Spanish Fury but had been turned into an implacable
foe by Parma's choice of another man—Colonel Mondragon—as
commander of its citadel.

The lies and calumnies covered the whole field of Parma's activities in France and the Netherlands. They were known to him
and drew from him an impassioned outburst to the King—"But
what is most wounding is that your Majesty has listened to them
without making the protest which my services merit, and has not
informed me of them, though they affect my reputation and honour.
People have taken more account of these libels than of my actions
performed on the stage of the world."

Such is the way of the world and always has been. Yet the Mansfelds were provincial nobles dependent on the royal favor; Champagney was a cipher who could be exiled with impunity; all the hallooing was so much noise unless the King could be induced to join in the hunt.

It was a gradual process. Van Essen dates the decline in Philip's confidence from the defeat of the Armada, but the seeds of suspicion had been there much earlier—self-sown out of the King's mortal dread of overmighty subjects. Five Netherlands provinces had defected under the leadership of a man—Orange—who had been one of his father's protégés and whom he himself had appointed to high office. Might not the others similarly go astray under an Italian governor who kept too many Italian servants and troops about him? Was it for instance true that English agents had offered Parma the sovereignty of the Low Countries as a satellite kingdom? It was: and Parma had indignantly rejected it.

Yet from Madrid it seemed self-evident that affairs in the Netherlands were deteriorating from day to day. Parma's own letters revealed it. Incessant mutinies; constant complaints and demands for more and more money which seemed to buy less and less in the way of results—it all added up to a government and a society rapidly sliding into chaos. That the King had largely brought this about by placing impossible burdens on his servant was naturally not appreciated in the closed circle of monarch and secretaries. What struck *them* was not the absurdity of the orders but the fact that they were not being obeyed. Instead of compliance there was argument. Parma had not hesitated to express his distaste for his master's French policy, and though in the end he had gone to Paris, he had taken the first opportunity of returning to Spa in defiance of orders. "The King," remarks Van Essen, "did not care for servants who not only allowed themselves to differ from him but told him so without evasion. The Duke of Parma was too independent for his taste." With his morbid suspiciousness the King had also no doubt remembered that Parma's son, Prince Ranuccio, had a claim of sorts to the throne of Portugal through his Portuguese mother which had been aired in certain quarters inimical to Spain at the time of the Spanish rape of that country, and that this same Ranuccio now commanded the cavalry in his father's armies.

By 1592, even those at court who had been well disposed toward the Governor General were busy at the game of picking possible replacements. The King was soon to choose his man—his nephew the Archduke Ernest, one of the brood of Austrian Hapsburgs which had already provided one incompetent puppet ruler of the Netherlands in the person of Matthias in Orange's time. While Parma was actually on the march to the relief of Rouen Philip had sat down to write him what was really a letter of dismissal, though wrapped up in the form of an urgent invitation to come to Spain for consultations—the spider's welcome to the fly. In a covering letter to the bearer of this summons, the Marquis Cerralvo, the King set out precise instructions as to the course to be followed if the victim proved refractory or evasive—in effect, the moment his work in France was done, he was to be got to Spain, either of his own free will or by force.

A benevolent providence—benevolent at least to Parma—interfered somewhat with this plan. Cerralvo died in the course of his journey. The letter to Parma was therefore redated and Cerralvo's instructions were passed on to a new messenger, the Count of Fuentes. In the meantime the King plied the Governor General with reassuring testimonials of his esteem, sending particular congratulations on the relief of Rouen. "Nothing will ever make me change in my attitude towards you," he wrote when Fuentes was actually about to arrive in Brussels.

There is no need to labor our condemnation of Philip: his own words do it. Yet to blame him absolutely and to label him a villain is to forget that in his own mind at least he had a grievance, and to forget also the heritage of distrust which the Emperor had left him and which Orange's defection and the shock of the Armada defeat must have magnified out of reason. It is even possible to make out a case for Philip on the grounds of his servant's very evident failure to safeguard the Netherlands, both externally and internally, and to obey the orders for intervention in France without endless argument and delay. The truth was that Parma had outlived his usefulness to Spain and possibly to the Netherlands also. Nor is there any certainty or even much likelihood that he would have ended like Montigny in Simancas with a rope around his neck. Imprisonment was more probable, or the kind of retirement to the country which had been imposed on Alva till the Portuguese adventure recalled him to the stage.

As it happened, no such situation arose, because when Fuentes

reached Brussels with his infamous commission the intended victim was no longer there but in obedience to his master's orders
had once more set out on the road to France on the interminable
business of the Infanta's election to the throne. He had not got very
far, but at least beyond Fuentes' clutches, in the midst of his army
and in the Walloon country around Arras where he had first made
his diplomatic mark. The ravages of disease had made such inroads
into his strength that when leaving Brussels he had had to be supported in the saddle by his attendants, yet he still managed to
doff his fine hat to the people as elegantly as in the days when the
Antwerp guilds had compared him in their tableaux with that other
Alexander of Macedon. "Everyone regarded it as a miracle that
he was still alive," wrote one observer. "The general opinion is that
he can't go far, since he is nothing but bones and eyes and his own
indomitable spirit."

At the abbey of St. Vaast the journey ended. The dying man's
political testament was already written in a letter to his son—a somber document which set out the state of the loyal provinces and the
one hope of regeneration, as he saw it, which must lie in a massive
offensive against the rebel north: in a continuation, in fact, of his
own lifework which he knew must now pass to another. The King
was more fortunate in his servants than he deserved. Egmont had
prayed for him on his way to the scaffold. And now another victim—
more eminent and as deeply wronged—could write of him (to
Ranuccio):

Such are the reflections on government which I want you in your own
right to present to his Majesty. I have chosen you for the task because
you will have the opportunity of explaining everything to the King,
who is so good, and of assuring him of your desire, like mine, to
sacrifice yourself and all you possess in his royal service—the thing
I most care for in this world.

In fact he had nearly done with worldy things. "I am finished,"
he told one of his old servants at St. Vaast who had caught a
glimpse of his swollen body as he undressed—it was the first day
of December, seven months after his wounding at Caudebec.
"There is no cure for my disease." Indeed there was none, and in
the small hours of the morning of December 3 he died. "This night
at one o'clock," reported his doctor to Prince Ranuccio, "his High-

ness passed away in the prime of life"—he was forty-seven—"having greatly suffered for twenty-eight hours. . . ."

The King paid the event even less attention than he had devoted to Don John, whose mortal remains (except the heart and entrails) had at least been brought back to Spain and laid to rest in the Escurial. Parma was returned to his joke dukedom in Italy. It was left to his enemies in England and Holland to remark that he had been a great man.

20

FAILURE IN FRANCE. REGIMES OF MANSFELD, THE ARCHDUKE ERNEST AND FUENTES. 1593–96.

In the interregnum which followed this death the government in Brussels was exercised in uneasy partnership between Parma's deputy and Acting Governor, Count Peter Ernest Mansfeld, and Philip's commissioner, the Count of Fuentes.

By now, a quarter of a century after Alva, most of those who had been in power at the outbreak of the Netherlands rebellion had passed away. But if the dramatis personae had changed, and changed on the whole for the worse, so had the King of Spain's problem. A small-scale revolt in two remote provinces had drawn him first into war with England and then by inevitable progression into an attempt to dominate his French neighbor, basically stronger than himself. In the course of these troubles his priorities had become muddled. Means had become ends. What had been defensive had turned into aggression. Only in the very last year of his reign was his sanity, like Don Quixote's, to return and allow him to recognize a whole decade of misplaced effort. In 1592, at the time of Parma's death, the prospects of a triumph in France had become his first consideration.

And for a while the mirage beckoned and the thing seemed possible. Under Spanish pressure Mayenne was at last induced to convoke the French States General. What Philip hoped from it is set out in one of the most fascinating and revealing papers he ever wrote.

First comes the preamble, in which his disinterested motives are extolled:

The King much desires that the affairs of France should be given the attention necessary for the preservation of the Catholic cause, the well-being and peace of the inhabitants of that kingdom, because he is touched by the sufferings they now endure.

He then turns to the problem:

The right to the French crown, since the last king, Henry, died without issue, belongs without the least doubt to the Infanta, the lady Isabella, in the right of her mother Queen Elizabeth, eldest sister of the said Henry. . . .

To the objection which could be raised to this, on the ground that the Salic Law excludes women from the succession to the throne, it will suffice to reply that, as the French themselves admit, the Salic Law is a chimera without foundation or reason.

Since the crown of France belongs to the Infanta by right of blood, we must bend every effort to make the States General declare her Queen Proprietress of France. If this truth is hard for them to swallow and they prefer to proceed by election, they ought to give her their votes, which is her due, that is to say to name her their Queen.

To succeed in this, one must on the one hand demonstrate the validity of the Infanta's rights, and on the other show the French that the remedy for their ills and the specific for their safety and peace all depend on the declaration or election. . . . But in the negotiations, everything must be done to persuade and not offend them.

If it should become clear that the French are intent on remaining in their present miserable state, instead of recognising the Infanta as their queen, as they ought, we would consider the election of a king, provided their choice is entirely acceptable to His Majesty. . . .

If this point is reached, the best course for them will be to leave the choice entirely to His Majesty. . . . To bring them to elect a king who will satisfy His Majesty entirely, they must be given to understand that in no other way would he consent to his daughter's marriage to the elected nominee, and that only thus can they count on the continuing help they need. To show them more clearly the error they would commit by failing to elect to His Majesty's satisfaction, one might add that in such case not only would all assistance cease, but His Majesty would also be obliged to uphold his daughter's rights and act as he thought fit.

If in spite of all these above mentioned arguments the French want to make the election of a king themselves, the next best thing that could be done to surmount the pretensions of rival claimants would be to call to the throne one of His Majesty's nephews, a brother of the Emperor, and that one of them whom His Majesty will himself select. If the French, out of excessive attachment to their own tongue, obstinately insist on electing one of their own princes, one should . . . use every means and influence in favour of the Duke of Guise, since he appears to be generally acceptable. . . .

If it becomes clear that the election of the Duke of Guise raises difficulties, and that perhaps the States would prefer the Cardinal of
Lorraine, which hardly seems possible, we would permit even this, so
long as the States do not break up without having made an election.
But this point is not to be reached except as a last resort, and it must
be kept absolutely secret, so that no one knows of it or gets the least
wind of it.

So the options are six in number, in diminishing order of importance—the Infanta as *Reine Propriétaire;* the Infanta as elected
queen; a king to be chosen by Philip; an Austrian archduke; the
Duke of Guise; and the Cardinal of Lorraine at the bottom of the
pile.

We can only marvel at Philip's gross insensitivity to French national pride and at his ignorance of what was possible. In this
fatuous document everything is considered and nothing is understood. Admittedly it was drafted a full year before it formed the
brief delivered to Count Feria, Philip's ambassador to the States
General in the spring of 1593, but the refusal to modify it or to
keep pace with changing events was all too typical. If at the meeting
of the States the King through Feria had simply proposed a marriage between his daughter and the League's best candidate, the
Duke of Guise, he might just conceivably have got for her the kind
of joint sovereignty which a hundred years later was to settle a
similar succession problem in England in the persons of William
and Mary. Unfortunately for himself, he had begun to concentrate
on his fourth alternative, a Hapsburg succession out of Austria,
certainly the most ridiculous of all his proposals and the most
offensive in French eyes,* so that by the time the inept and tactless Feria had fallen back on the Guise marriage, his fifth and almost last line of defense, a sudden shift of the political spectrum in
France had made even this position untenable—a powerful section
of opinion among the Leaguers had begun to make common cause
with the moderate Catholics, the *Politiques,* who for years had
been seeking a middle way out of France's troubles.

Such a marriage of minds was not easily achieved, and indeed
many ultra-Catholics were long to remain opposed to any compromise, but once the process had begun and a consensus of Catholic opinion was in the making, the only possible losers had to be the

* The King had in mind the Archduke Ernest, later his Governor General in the
Netherlands.

Huguenots and the King of Spain. This was inevitable if only because of the nature of the chief claimant to the throne. Navarre had
been raised a Protestant. After St. Bartholomew's he had turned
Catholic for the good of his health, but once he had escaped from
court and was back in a Protestant ambience, with a Huguenot
army behind him, he had turned his coat again: only to ally himself after the murders at Blois with the Catholic Henry III, who
had something to offer him of value in his blessing. Personally he
was quite devoid of religious feeling: a hedonist and self-seeker,
with the virtues as well as the vices which go to make up the
breed. No one except the Vicar of Bray ever changed his religious
allegiances more often. But certainly no one was truer to France
and to the French people, who passionately wanted an end to the
war and their sufferings; which is no doubt why, two centuries
later, his statue was left untouched on the Pont Neuf when all the
rest of the "Capets" were carted off into the Revolutionary junk
yard.

Faced now with a choice between the Huguenots and the throne,
he hesitated hardly at all. The lamentations and reproaches of his
old comrades in arms and of the Queen of England—who in similar
circumstances would have turned Jesuit—did not trouble him in the
least, if by "instruction" at the hands of a few priests he could win
Paris and throw out the Spaniards. In May 1593 he gave notice of
his intended conversion. In July, in a two-day ceremony at St. Denis
in the presence of Leaguer and *Politique* bishops, he underwent
it, reporting gaily to his mistress:

I arrived here last evening, and was importuned with "God save you"
till bedtime. I am beginning to-morrow to talk to the bishops, besides
those I told you about yesterday. At the moment of writing I have a
hundred of these importunates on my back, who will make me hate St.
Denis as much as you hate Mantes. To-morrow I perform the somer-
sault. A thousand times I kiss my angel's beautiful hands and the mouth
of my dear mistress.

Next day, in solemn ceremony in the great church, he had re-
verted to his public role of penitent as he knelt before the high
altar in the presence of a vast congregation, many of whom had
flocked out of Spanish-held Paris for the occasion. "Very great
devotion was noticed in his Majesty," one simpleton observed.

"Throughout the consecration and the elevation of the Host he had his hands clasped, his eyes adored the Eucharist, and he beat his breast three times as the chalice was raised."

Poor Philip: How could he foresee or combat maneuvers so utterly foreign to his own pious nature? The comedy at St. Denis was one of the most cynical, most disgraceful and most successful acts of state on record. Yet Philip's own cynicism cannot be ignored. All his fine precepts for the well-being of the French people and the Catholic religion which he had set out in the preamble to his letter of 1592 had now been handsomely met, but he did not show himself grateful. On the contrary, every resource of Spanish diplomacy was set to work to prevent the Pope from accepting the purified heretic into the true Roman fold, no matter what the French (Gallican) Church had done. Two more years were to pass before the ill-advised petulance and threats of the Spanish ambassador to the Holy See rebounded, to drive the Pope to recognize the force of what had happened and to turn the freethinker into the "Most Christian King."

What the Papacy did was always of importance, even to those who most resisted its pretensions. The recognition of 1595 would not have been worked for so ardently by Navarre's agents or opposed by Philip's if this had not been so. But since the French as a race had been lukewarm about the Papacy ever since the Popes had escaped from their clutches in Avignon in 1377, the key event in the crisis had really been the well-staged mummery in St. Denis which had made a good Gallican of Navarre if not a good Catholic. It remained to get him crowned: but here there were difficulties, since not only were there still Spanish troops in Brittany and the Ile de France, but even Rheims, where the holy oil of St. Remy for the anointing of French kings was kept, happened to be in the hands of Leaguers still unsympathetic to the cause. Motley, unregenerate Low Churchman that he was, has a very Protestant passage which explains how this little obstacle was surmounted:

. . . it was discovered that there was a chrism in existence still more efficacious than the famous oil of St. Remy. One hundred and twelve years before the baptism of Clovis, St. Martin had accidentally tumbled downstairs, and lay desperately bruised and at the point of death. But,

according to Sulpicius Severus, an angel had straightway descended
from heaven, and with a miraculous balsam had annointed the contusions
of the saint, who next day felt no further inconveniences from his fall.
The balsam had ever since been preserved in the church of Marmoutier
near Tours. Here, then, was the most potent of ungents bought directly
from heaven. . . .
Accompanied by a strong military escort provided by Giles de Souvry,
governor of Tourraine, a deputation of friars brought the phial to
Chartres, where the consecration was to take place. Prayers were offered up without ceasing in the monastery during their absence that no
mishap should befall the sacred treasure. When the monks arrived at
Chartres, four young barons of the first nobility were assigned to them
as hostages for the safe restoration of the phial, which was then borne
in triumph to the cathedral, the streets through which it was carried
being covered with tapestry. There was a great ceremony, a splendid
consecration; six bishops with mitres on their heads and in gala robes
officiating; after which the king knelt before the altar and took the
customary oath.

Under these hammer blows of a cunning and brilliant propaganda the Spanish position in France began to crumble. It had
always heavily depended on two things—bribery and prestige—
and what in today's jargon would be called a credibility gap had
opened between what Philip threatened and what he seemed likely
to achieve. He still had armies in being—indeed we must remember
that Parma's invasions from the east had been only part of a much
wider offensive, and that elsewhere around France's borders, and
particularly in Brittany, Spanish and Leaguer forces were still at
large. This general picture was not destroyed all at once by Henry's
conversion or coronation, for Spanish money was still good and the
more extreme Catholics had a long journey to make before they
could salve their delicate consciences by recognizing a heretic in
advance of the Pope.
    But to the waverers and those with an eye to the main chance,
the tide was evidently on the turn, and what in Parma's day had
seemed an irresistible force was being visibly resisted and pushed
back—more by moral persuasion than by physical effort, if one can
use morality in the context of Henry's activities at St. Denis and
Chartres. How far the rot had set in, both in the minds of the more
venal Frenchmen and among the Spaniards themselves, was now
to be shown in the most startling and dramatic fashion in the heart

of the League's citadel, in Paris itself, held by strong forces of Spanish troops.

In 1590 Henry had besieged the city at an appalling cost in human suffering: in 1594 he bought it for the modest price of three hundred thousand livres, an annuity and a marshal's baton for the League's Deputy Governor, de Brissac, in return for the opening of one of the gates by night. In Bernardino de Mendoza's time both purchaser and traitor would probably have paid for their audacity with their lives, but the currency of loyalty and intelligence had become debased, and the *tercios*, taken at a hopeless disadvantage, were rounded up without a fight. Basing himself on the report of an eyewitness, Motley records the scene:

Through the wind and the rain came trampling along the dark streets of the capital a body of four thousand troopers and lansquenettes. Many torch-bearers attended on the procession, whose flambeaux threw a lurid light upon the scene. There, surrounded by the swart and grizzly bearded visages of these strange men-at-arms, who were discharging their arquebuses, as they advanced upon any bystanders likely to oppose their progress; in the very midst of this sea of helmed heads, the envoy was enabled to recognise the martial figure of the Prince of Béarn. Armed to the teeth, with sword in hand and dagger at side, the hero of Ivry rode at last through the barriers which had so long kept him from his capital.

To prevent this, Parma had twice invaded France and forgone his hopes of reuniting the Netherlands; vast sums of Spanish gold had been poured out; thousands of Parisians had died of starvation and perhaps a few from Madame de Montpensier's "cake." All in vain. In his French policy Philip had been in pursuit of the improbable, as Parma had told him often enough. And when a few days after the *coup* his helpless garrison marched out of Paris with their colors flying on the road to Brussels the point of the lesson was clear to everyone. "Commend me to your master," Henry called out to them from a window in the Porte St. Denis as they went by—"Commend me to your master: but don't come back."

In the Netherlands the tide had set against Philip rather earlier. Hulst near Antwerp and Nymegen on the Waal had fallen to Prince Maurice before Parma had even left the provinces to the relief of Rouen, and in the weeks before his death at Arras the rebel offensive had switched to the northeast to overrun Steenwyk near the Frisian border and Koevorden on the main line of royalist communications with Groningen. In the spring of 1593 it was suddenly switched south against Geertruidenberg at the mouth of the Meuse, the last Spanish stronghold in territory now occupied by patriot forces.

To find Geertruidenberg on the map today one has to search hard along the roads between Breda and Utrecht, but in its time it was famous far beyond the borders of the Netherlands as the testing ground of new developments in siege warfare. Prince Maurice had ringed Geertruidenberg with a vast camp, half fortress, half market town, which was the wonder of Europe. Against these lines the elderly Count Mansfeld spent himself in unrewarding skirmishes which Motley has worked up into one of his most charming passages:

In vain he plunged about among the caltrops and man-traps. In vain he knocked at the fortifications of Hohenlo on the east and Maurice on the west. He found them impracticable, impregnable, obdurate. It was Maurice's intention to take his town at as small sacrifice of life as possible. A trumpeter was sent on some trifling business to Mansfeld. . . .
"Why does your master," said the choleric veteran to the trumpeter, "why does Prince Maurice, being a lusty young commander, as he is, not come out of his trenches into the open field and fight me like a man, where honour and fame await him?"
"Because my master," answered the trumpeter, "means to live to be a lusty old commander like your Excellency."

Obviously the courtesies of war had become more refined since Alva's time. But the rebel pressure on the town was not to be denied: in the midsummer of 1593 Geertruidenberg surrendered and the line of the great rivers had been cleared of Spanish troops. It was a month before Navarre's "instruction" at St. Denis—the interrelation between events in France and in the provinces should constantly be borne in mind, since it was their joint pressure that was reducing the Spanish field of choice and maneuver. But what also affected that choice was the deplorable duality of government which now existed in Brussels and inhibited any centralized direction of affairs.

This duality, which had first made its appearance in the seventies when Philip had tried to divide supreme control in the Netherlands between the Duchess Margaret and her son, had been revived in the last year of Parma's life after his return from Rouen to Spa, when Mansfeld, from his perch of deputy in Brussels, had made a take-over bid for the governor generalship by affecting to believe that the incumbent had deserted his post. Long and fierce had been the duels between the protagonists for the favor of the King. Throughout that summer both had been bombarding Madrid and each other with furious complaints. Mansfeld, wrote Parma, must change his "style"; he must not argue with his superior but obey him. Parma, wrote Mansfeld, must either govern or get out. Would he ever return from Spa to his duty or would he remain a perpetual absentee? And even after the final return which was to end at Arras, Mansfeld was still writing his personal complaints to Philip and was being listened to, since it suited the King's purpose to listen to every calumny against the man whom he had already decided to replace.

With Parma's death and in the absence of a new Governor General with overriding powers, this duality of control grew in scope and developed into a ludicrous tug of war between old Peter Mansfeld, the man in possession of the civil machine of government, and Fuentes, who carried the King's commission as commander of the armies, though even this had been wrapped up in a ridiculous ambivalence.

Fuentes was a Spaniard of Spaniards, a relative of Alva's and recognizably out of the same mold, as can be gathered from his boast that he intended to enter Paradise sword in hand. He found Count Mansfeld "aged and decrepit." Not too decrepit however to outwit him and seize the reins by a skillful use of the powers of the Netherlands Council of State. Civil and military government were thus divided, and at a desperately critical time, with dangers looming on every front.

Naturally both men were soon launched on a campaign of impassioned and non-stop abuse of each other's conduct and complaints of the deplorable condition both of the provinces and the army. "So many officers and so few men," Mansfeld laments in January 1593, as war leaders have lamented so often since. But that Fuentes should command even this mutinous rump of a once great force struck him as a derogation from his supreme authority,

though he was prepared to concede command of the field army
destined for France. As for Fuentes, his opinions of his rival became
steadily more frantic as their disagreements grew. By April 1593 we
find him wondering aloud whether his assignment to the Netherlands is not a mark of royal disfavor, a punishment, not a promotion: by September he is prepared to agree with the popular
view that Parma was a martyr.

What the world thought of this extraordinary regime of Tweedle-
dum and Tweedledee was vigorously expressed. One anonymous
letter writer judged Fuentes full of hauteur and intolerance, much
given to womanizing—perhaps the one charge which could not be
laid at Count Mansfeld's door, though the old man's capacity for
mischief was otherwise unique. Don Esteban de Ibarra, a spy whom
Philip had planted in the Netherlands administration, found them
both impossible. Nor could much be expected of the Council of
State as adviser or referee, since we have Ibarra's candid estimate
of that body also. Councilor Assonleville is faithful but old. Richardot (Parma's favorite) Ibarra would rather see in Granada or
Valladolid than in Brussels. Morailles is a republican.

Such was the governmental system of provinces, themselves sunk
in apathy, threatened by rebel attack and soon to be consigned to
the King's Hapsburg nephew, the Archduke Ernest, a middle-aged
valetudinarian with little but his debts to distinguish him. And it
is a symptom of how far things had sunk that the arrival in Brussels
of this singularly inept person was greeted by the public and the
pageant masters with the most fabulous "Joyous Entry" for years.
Motley sneers at this enthusiasm but it was probably heartfelt.
Anything was better than Count Peter Mansfeld—or such at least
was the opinion for a week or two.

Then the complaints began, led by the Archduke in person. His
first official letter to Philip from Brussels was a request for money:
a theme he was to develop at least as eloquently as any predecessor or successor.

Up to this moment the principal grievance of the south Netherlanders had been the all-pervasiveness of Spanish influence in
their affairs. But with the arrival of Ernest the tune changes. It is
now the Spaniards who are heard deploring the influence of German counselors in the archducal household. Don Esteban de Ibarra

(a man prepared to complain of *everyone* with equal zest) denounced this weakness of the new incumbent from the start. By
November 1594, after nine months' experience of the regime, he
had concluded that things were never worse and was referring to
the Archduke tartly as "that man." Soon he varied this. It was not a
matter of morals, he explained to Philip, since Ernest lived "like
an angel." The evil sprang from the German favorites and from the
Archduke's incapacity for affairs, his poor health and lack of martial
talents.

All these undoubted failings should have been known to Philip,
whose intelligence service was after all reckoned supreme in his
age, and it was at the very least an unjustifiable risk to appoint an
untried man of sedentary habits to what was already the cockpit
of Europe. But whom should he have trusted? To whom could he
have turned? The imperial siblings in the shape of Don John and
Parma had only brought him trouble in the end. Perhaps nephews
in the legitimate line would be safer and would carry more social
weight than genius which was liable to be cursed with too much
independence of mind. Philip's choice of the Archduke was not
quite as absurd as appears at first sight.

But his instructions were inexcusable. Having appointed the man
to a post which had killed off three governors in a row, the King
was not even prepared to leave him to salvage what was left of the
royalist position in the Netherlands, but was insistent that the
French burden must be shouldered as a priority, no matter what
had happened in recent months to shipwreck the League and
Spanish policies. "Although recent happenings in France have
brought things to their present pass," he wrote to his nephew in
June 1594, "it is not the less necessary to intervene there; on the
contrary, we must busy ourselves all the more, since the danger to
religion which has always been my chief care has increased. The
remedy for our present troubles in France lies either in a 'good' war
or in some peace treaty; and since such a treaty could at the moment
only be a snare and detrimental to religion, I am determined not to
abandon my defence of the faith, trusting in God, whose cause it
is. . . ."

It is impossible to withhold some admiration from a man who in
the face of such reverses remains so constant to his principles,
however mistaken they may be. The King still had some hope that
by Spartan attitudes he could prevent the Papacy from sliding into

an accommodation with the enemy, and for a year and more he succeeded. But of course in the Netherlands, where the war he had forgotten was rising to a new climax, this concentration on France was bound to be disastrous. Less than two months after this letter was sent off, the great city of Groningen in the far northeast of the provinces surrendered to Prince Maurice, and with it collapsed the whole royalist position between the Ems and the Rhine. Alva must surely have turned in his grave, for it was in this countryside that he had chastised the first outbreak of rebellion at Jemmingen. Simultaneously, widespread mutinies of Spanish, Italian and Walloon troops were raging in loyalist territory south of the rivers, exposing the whole of Parma's reconquests to the danger of a rebel thrust into Brabant.

These mutinies were not to be fully cleared up till December, only weeks before the Archduke Ernest's death after holding office for just a year. "He had accomplished nothing," is Motley's epitaph on this sad and undistinguished man.

He was very indolent, enormously fat, very chaste, very expensive, fond of fine liveries and fine clothes, so solemn and stately as never to be known to laugh, but utterly without capacity either as a statesman or a soldier. He would have shone as a portly abbot ruling over peaceful friars, but he was not born to ride a revolutionary whirlwind, nor to evoke order out of chaos. Past and present were contending with each other in fierce elemental strife within his domain. A world was in dying agony, another world was coming, fully armed, into existence within the handbreadth of time and of space where he played his little part, but he dreamed not of it. He passed away like a shadow, and was soon forgotten.

By the "Past," Motley of course meant reactionary, Catholic, Inquisitorial Spain: the new world he saw coming into existence lay elsewhere, but above all in the expansionist maritime powers of England and the Dutch Republic—and of course in the long view of what was to follow, this was a valid enough judgment.

But this is only a partial one. If the glories of the coming age included the arts and the graces of living, then they were Spanish in inspiration and practice. Cervantes, Lope de Vega, Calderón, Góngora and Velázquez are sufficient answer in themselves to any hasty dismissal of the "Past," whose *mores* and etiquettes were to permeate the future for at least another half century to come. And though it is probably true that Spain as a world power was already in decline—my own theme as much as Motley's—it would be an error to ignore the extraordinary resilience which was to enable her to survive immense humiliations and still remain a force to be reckoned with in a changing world.

Nothing shows this more clearly than the events which followed the Archduke's death and the succession to the interim governorship of Count Fuentes by personal direction of the deceased. At the time of his reluctant partnership with old Count Peter Ernest Mansfeld (still alive and semi-active in Luxemburg) Fuentes had done little to suggest that he had the stuff of leadership in him.

But sole responsibility is a wonderful restorative. His inheritance was a mutinous army, a bankrupt estate and war on two fronts. As though this were not enough, it was his aim to impose a tight Spanish control on the loyalist provinces, even at the cost of antagonizing the local interests which Parma had always respected, had perhaps respected too well. Fuentes' mere appointment to office had outraged the provincial worthies, to the extent of driving some of them into exile—the Duke of Aerschot to end his days prosaically in Venice; the younger Mansfeld to die of a fever in the service of the Emperor against the Turk—but these were very expendable people, whose absence went some way to strengthening the Brussels government for the next stage of the duel with France which Philip was still demanding and which Fuentes, unlike Parma, was eager to carry out.

His great predecessor had avoided pitched battles; Fuentes sought them. Advancing into Picardy he occupied Le Catelet, and outside Doullens routed a French army commanded by that same de Villars who had once defended Rouen for the League. The new regime had a short way with traitors. De Villars was taken in the field, and while his captors were disputing their share of the ransom money, which was likely to be large, the Spanish Commissary General of cavalry arrived on the scene to order the man's execution on the spot, which was carried out by an arquebus ball through the head. The victory was followed by the capture of Doullens itself, where the French garrison was butchered in retaliation for similar French excesses in the neighboring town of Ham; after which Fuentes marched on to Cambrai, which fell to him in the autumn of 1595.

Meanwhile in the Netherlands another stalwart from Alva's time had likewise been active. Colonel Mondragon, Governor of Antwerp citadel, had been an old man in the heyday of the Blood Council, and though now over ninety was still as ardent an adventurer as on the night in '72 when he had led his army across the mud flats of the Scheldt to the relief of Ter Goes in perhaps the greatest single exploit of the war. Learning that Prince Maurice had advanced on the royalist fortress of Grol (or Groenlo), he determined to forestall him; which was the more remarkable because Grol was almost on the German border, a far cry from Antwerp where he had been tranquilly living out his days.

Collecting a small but highly efficient and mobile force, Mondragon set out at once for the Rhine, crossed it in spite of the earnest dissuasions of his lieutenants and marched north to its confluence with the Lippe near Wesel, where his mere presence was enough to bring Maurice hurrying from his unfinished business at Grol to cut him off. In a game of catch-as-catch-can as fascinating as any in military annals, the veteran decisively outpointed his young opponent and disrupted all the carefully laid schemes for a summer offensive which had been planned by that scientific but limited commander. Even Motley forgets his prejudices on this occasion to give us an unforgettable cameo of the victor:

This was Mondragon's last feat of arms. Less than three months afterwards, in Antwerp citadel, as the veteran was washing his hands previously to going to the dinner table, he sat down and died. Strange to say, this man—who had spent almost a century on the battle-field, who had been a soldier in nearly every war that had been waged in any part of Europe during that most belligerent age, who had come an old man to the Netherlands before Alva's arrival, and had ever since been constantly and personally engaged in the vast Flemish tragedy which had now lasted well nigh thirty years—had never himself lost a drop of blood. His battlefields had been on land and water, on ice, in fire, and at the bottom of the sea, but he had never received a wound. Nay, more: he had been blown up in a fortress—the castle of Danvilliers in Luxemburg, of which he was governor—where all perished save his wife and himself, and, when they came to dig among the ruins, they excavated at last the ancient couple, protected by the framework of a window in the embrasure of which they had been seated, without a scratch or a bruise. He was a Biscayan by descent, but born in Medina del Campo. A strict disciplinarian, very resolute and pertinacious, he had the good fortune to be beloved by his inferior, his equals, and his superiors. He was called the father of his soldiers, the good Mondragon, and his name was unstained by any of those deeds of ferocity which make the chronicles of the time resemble rather the history of wolves than of men. To a married daughter, mother of several children, he left a considerable fortune.

Of course Mondragon was a phenomenon, a Methuselah, whose life span went back to within little more than a decade of the capture of Granada which had sparked off the huge explosion of Spanish power in Europe and the Americas; indeed his life may be said to have been almost exactly contemporaneous with its zenith and ended as the slow decline began. Since he was an original, it would be unfair to use him as a yardstick by which to measure others, but certainly his toughness and resolution, his imperturbability and endurance, were widely mirrored among his contemporaries and were among the agencies which had taken Spain to the mastery of half the known world.

It is tempting to see in the caution of his subordinates at the Rhine crossing on his last campaign a living proof of the difference between a generation which took the miraculous for granted and one which through the pages of Cervantes was soon to learn to laugh at it. Mondragon and Fuentes, who both left the stage in 1595, one for the grave, the other for a minor role in Italy, were not the last of their kind, for the Spanish Army was to remain for another half century the most potent in Europe, at least in the eyes of opponents dazzled by a legend of almost uninterrupted victory. But deep down an age was ending. There had been a surfeit of great and terrible events and of men of outsize talents for good and evil. With the advent of Fuentes' successor in the governor generalship in Brussels—another of Philip's Austrian nephews, the Cardinal Archduke Albert, who had been his viceroy in Portugal —we enter another era of more pliable persons, more doubtful of themselves, the inheritors of imperialism but no longer its advocates or even believers. The King himself at the end of his life conforms to this same pattern. It is time to return to him.

21

TROUBLES IN ARAGON. 1590–92.
THE DARKENING SCENE. FINANCIAL PROBLEMS.
THE SETTLEMENT. 1595–98.

Since the last embers of the Morisco revolt in the Alpujarras had been stamped out in 1571 metropolitan Spain had given its ruler no anxiety, seeming to be one of the few peaceful areas in a distracted Europe which had the Calvinists battering at one door and the Turks at the other. Suddenly in 1591, at the height of the dual crisis in France and the Netherlands, this prosperous and apparently stable society began to break apart under the impulse of one of its main components—Aragon.

The three units of the "Crown of Aragon" had always been a potential source of trouble, if only because of their agelong antipathy to Castile. In the next century, in the time of Philip's grandson and his minister Olivares, the jealous particularism of Catalonia and its reluctance to bear its share of the burdens of empire were to spell the final collapse of Spanish power. In 1591 Aragon itself rose to protect a scoundrel who had claimed the protection of its *fueros*, its civil liberties, which the ruler was suspected of trying to subvert.

The germs of all this lie in some of the strangest byways of Spanish history. A volume would be needed to tell how Antonio Pérez, an illegitimate sprig probably of *converso* stock, rose to succeed his father as one of the King's secretaries of state; of his enormous peculations; his scandalous sale of offices; his liaison with the widow of his patron the Prince of Eboli; and of the mysterious murder in Madrid in 1572 of Don John of Austria's faithful secretary and shadow, Juan de Escovedo, which finally brought him down. Perhaps a historical novel would be a better medium to make the most of these engaging monsters—Pérez himself, and his mistress, the Princess Eboli, whose favor Philip was also rumored to enjoy, though she was a matriarch with a quiverful of children and wore a Nelsonic black patch over one eye.

Why Escovedo died at the hands of hired ruffians in a Madrid street, and the ratio of guilt between Pérez, his undoubted executioner, and the King must always remain obscure. Perhaps Escovedo had learned too much about corruption at court and had become a threat to Pérez, who turned the tables by displaying him to the King as an agent of Don John's supposedly treasonable ambitions. All that is certain is that the crime was never forgotten and that by 1579, when the rape of Portugal was brewing, Philip had tired of his corrupt, compromising and dangerous servant.

The method used to get rid of him was an almost exact repetition of the way Egmont had been snared by Alva in '67 and a preview of the treatment to be meted out to Parma. The King had been full of praise for his victim's services and had worked with him in cabinet to within an hour or two of the man's arrest. But thereafter, in typically Spanish fashion, an endless series of delays set in. Not for another six years was Pérez sentenced for his peculations to two years imprisonment, perpetual banishment and a swingeing fine; not for another five—which brings matters down to 1590—was he accused of Escovedo's murder and put to the torture. Without more ado he confessed. And almost exactly two months later, with the help of his wife Juana—one of those heroines of humor and fidelity who seem to be attracted to thoroughly bad men—he escaped, wearing her cloak, and fled across the Ebro into Aragon. Juana remained behind and was clapped into prison with her children.

This was the beginning of a greater drama, for the national party in the Aragonese capital of Saragossa had long been looking for a pretext for rebellion. Philip's agents were in hot pursuit of the fugitive, charged with the duty of taking him dead or alive, but the Saragossans, to whose "liberties" Pérez had appealed, were beforehand in snatching him from under the agents' noses and lodging him in the Justicia's jail,* where he was safe from all but the due processes of the law. Charged in the Justicia's court by the too legalistic King, Pérez repeated his confession to Escovedo's murder, but now alleged that he had acted under the royal orders, producing documents to prove it.

---

* The Justicia was a high functionary, a kind of Chief Justice, also traditionally the guardian of the rights and liberties of every Aragonese citizen.

The sensation when this leaked out was naturally immense, and became ungovernable when under Philip's urging the Inquisition in Saragossa interested itself in the affair and transferred the accused from the Justicia's jail into its own dungeons on a specious charge of heresy. In Castile this would have worked admirably, and no doubt Pérez would duly have been burned at the stake in person as he was later to be burned in effigy. In Aragon it brought out the mob. Philip's representatives were baited, reviled, manhandled in the streets, while amidst scenes of revolutionary enthusiasm Pérez was delivered from the Inquisition and carried back in triumph, like the ark of the convenant, to safety in the Justicia's jail.

If this had been the temper of the other cities of Aragon, or if Catalonia or Valencia had stirred, Philip would have been faced with a situation beyond his power to put down. Fortunately for him there was a general reluctance to follow the capital's lead and even a certain sympathy for his cause which was echoed in Saragossa itself among the well to do and the magistrates. But at this point, in September 1592, the Justicia died, and his son, who succeeded to the office, became a tool in extremist hands. Another attempt to transfer Pérez to the Holy Office brought on more savage rioting, and when the King's troops from Castile at last approached the city there was actually an attempt to lead out local forces to resist them. Very few, however, obeyed the summons, and those who did turned tail without a fight. Four days later the royal troops entered Saragossa unopposed. Pérez himself had escaped across the Pyrenees, but the unfortunate young Justicia was beheaded for his part in the affair and throughout the following year there were executions, culminating in a grand *auto-da-fé*.

Now this Rake's Progress, the most romantic story to come out of a cruel and unforgiving age, had seemed to end as the best tales never should, with the triumph of the tyrant. It was as though the Sheriff of Nottingham had driven Robin Hood, Maid Marian and all their merry men out of the glades of Sherwood Forest. For sad to relate, the delinquent but fascinating Pérez was never again to see his home or his devoted and ill-used wife but became a wanderer on the face of the earth, an agent of his country's enemies, the author of scurrilous memoirs of his old master which were worked up into a book and had a considerable propaganda success in Europe.

But the story is still more remarkable and instructive when one turns to the part played in it by the "tyrant," "the royal criminal called Philip," to borrow Motley's words. Outraged at being presented to the world as Escovedo's murderer, he hired relays of assassins in attempts to murder his tormentor! Yet toward Aragon, once the executions of the guilty were over, he showed an extraordinary clemency. He could have destroyed all her cherished *fueros,* but he did not. Faced with a chance of modernizing an archaic system and extending his own arbitrary power across the Ebro, he chose instead to content himself with reforms which clipped Aragon's wings but left her identity and obstructive power intact, much as he had done with Portugal when she too had lain at his mercy. One sees that for all his temptations he was no Louis XIV or Bonaparte but a sincere believer in provincial and traditional rights, more moderate in this respect than other rulers of his time, and in his insistence on uniformity of religious belief within his borders no more exacting or fanatical than the Queen of England or their "High Mightinesses" in The Hague who could have had "liberties" by the sackful if they had consented to return to Rome.

By a singular mischance, however, this creditable but rather outdated attitude of mind, which deprived Spain of the benefits of any central direction of affairs and pooling of effort, was taking place in a Europe where Spain's enemies were drawing together into a hostile coalition fired by a common hatred of her pretensions. In January 1595 Henry IV formally declared war on her—a propaganda exercise to demonstrate to doubters that his cause was now as national as Francis I's campaigns against the Emperor. In the spring of the next year an Anglo-French treaty was signed in London, to which the rebel provinces of the Netherlands adhered, thus bringing into being the triple alliance which had long been the nightmare of Spanish diplomacy.

It was an alliance without a heart. The Hollanders (or Dutch as they were now coming to be called) disliked the English, remembering Leicester's intrigues with abhorrence. They were also grieved at the French king's translation into a Papist. Queen Elizabeth thoroughly disliked the Dutch. They had been very rude to Leicester and were constantly demanding money—the ultimate crime in her eyes. She too had been pained by the mere thought of

Henry's conversion and had written him one of her most pungent and characteristic letters:

Ah! what grief; ah! what regrets; ah! what groans have I felt in my soul. . . . My God! Is it possible that any worldly respect can efface the terror of divine wrath? Can we by reason ever expect a good sequel from such iniquitous acts? . . . 'Tis bad to do evil that good may come of it. Meantime I shall not cease to put you in the first rank of my devotions, in order that the hand of Esau may not spoil the blessings of Jacob. As to your promises to me of friendship and fidelity, I confess to have dearly deserved them, nor do I repent, provided you do not change your Father—otherwise I shall be your bastard sister by the father's side—for I shall ever love a natural better than an adopted one. I desire that God may guide you in a straight road and a better path. Your most sincere sister in the old fashion. As to the new, I have nothing to do with it.

Elizabeth R.

What really troubled her, however, was less the danger to Henry's soul than her own inbred suspicions of France, natural enough in the ruler of a country which still bitterly mourned the loss of its old possessions across the Channel. When Calais fell in 1596 to a brilliant and unexpected Spanish thrust, her reaction was to inform her French brother that she would help him recapture it, provided she might thereafter keep it! Even the checkered history of coalitions shows little to equal this for gall, except perhaps the cheerful alacrity with which Henry himself was to desert her and his Dutch friends the first moment it suited him.

Yet in Madrid this gathering together of mutually jealous forces was regarded with dismay. The success at Calais, which caused consternation in France and England and threw a fine apple of discord between them, could not hide the unpalatable truth that the war was being lost, nor was the King himself any longer the vigorous man in the prime of life whom we met in the famous letters from Portugal. In 1580 his fourth wife had died; in 1582 his eldest surviving son. We catch echoes of the tragedy in the letters to the Infantas and in the sad resignation of his words when he decreed that there should be no court mourning for a prince for whom God must have appointed a kingdom of His own. Few men can have suffered more bereavements or accepted them more stoically as the will of a divine providence which he tried to serve. But the cost was immense, even to one so gifted with faith, and by 1595 the King was an old and ailing man who knew that his burdens must soon pass to the last of his sons—the future Philip III—whose indolence and lack of spirit were already painfully clear to him.

Deprived of any sure hope of the future, he had few comforts or joys beyond his tender love for his children. When his younger daughter Catherine had been married in 1585 at Saragossa to the Duke of Savoy, and the King went on to Barcelona to see her off on her way to Turin, observers noted the affecting nature of this parting—that he had roused himself to overcome his distaste for travel to venture so far from the Escurial is just one small proof of his devotion. The real apple of his eye was the elder sister, the Infanta Isabella Clara Eugenia, whom the Venetian ambassador in 1595 noted as a confidante with whom he shared even the greatest problems of state. The closeness of the bonds uniting the family and their retainers can be seen in a number of paintings in the Prado which are among the most charming and touching memorials of the reign: one of the Infantas as children, solemn as statues in their stiff brocade dresses and ornate little caps; another of Isabella with her favorite companion, that same Madalena whose taste for the bottle had so teased the King in Portugal; a third, of Isabella again, holding a miniature of her father in her hand.

These affections, these intimacies with those he loved, played a diminishing part in Philip's life. Immured at his desk, tormented by his problems, a sufferer from arthritis, gout, weakness of the eyes (the fruit of his midnight labors) and a serious blood infection, he had become the prisoner of a system only to be borne by one who thought of himself as God's regent. There was much in this that was admirable and was duly admired by contemporaries.

But Spain herself was also a victim of this immense and inordinate devotion which tried to shoulder every burden and prevented any devolution of powers or proper harnessing of the genius of the nation. The list of her ills is even longer than that of the King's infirmities—crippling taxation; bad harvests; the decay of farming and industry; a galloping inflation fed by the flow of treasure from the Indies; an adverse balance of trade; serious outbreaks of plague which caused a labor shortage and forced up wages and costs; an ever-growing class of entrepreneurs and unproductive middlemen; a ruinously costly war on three fronts; a moral disintegration spreading from the top, where offices were for sale and were bought by

the less deserving. Forty years later, in an age when all these failings had been magnified, a harassed minister of the Crown would
wonder aloud: "Where are the leaders?" No one would have
needed to ask such a question in the time of Alva, of Requesens,
Parma, Santa Cruz or García de Toledo. But in the last years of
Philip's reign the question could have been asked and could not
have been answered, for those who were closest to the King would
have proved the point—a committe of secretaries, of faceless men,
who merely reflected the moods of their royal master and his talent
for endless procrastination. A system which raised such men to high
office and kept them there was giving too many hostages to fortune.
And in 1596 retribution began.

It began at Cádiz, where a large Anglo-Dutch fleet under the
Lord Admiral Howard, Raleigh, and Leicester's successor in the
Queen's affections, the Earl of Essex, swept into the roadstead, cut
up the shipping and landed a raiding force which stormed and
sacked the town. Though in the Caribbean fine new fortifications
were being erected, nothing whatever had been done to protect
one of the major ports of metropolitan Spain, which, incredible
though it may seem, remained for over a fortnight in English hands
without counterattack from the forces of a nation reckoned to be
the most powerful in the world. But the consequences were more
damaging than the sack of a town, for by an unfortunate chance
the *Flota,* the treasure fleet which should have been on its way to
Vera Cruz, was caught at its anchorage, looted and destroyed.

To the King's bankers abroad this was worse than any defeat: it
was a raid on Ali Baba's cave. In every finance house in Europe
there was a hurried reappraisal of credit risks, while in Spain itself
the sense of shock and outrage was translated into an urgent call
for revenge against the English which was not confined to one
class but embraced the court, the clergy, provincial nobles, merchants and even peasants and the riffraff of the towns. Drake's
raid of '87 had caused nothing like it, for Spain in those days had
been a self-confident nation, not hagridden with a sense of unmerited defeat. The great Armada of 1588 had taken years to prepare: but now in the late summer of 1596 a successor was fitted
out in a matter of weeks as a result of unparalleled exertions in
which even the King joined with a show of energy which aston-

ished his familiars. Money came flooding in: from the royal treasury, from the Church, from the Cortes of Castile: nearly a hundred ships were assembled in Lisbon and nearly half as many more were ordered up from Andalusia and El Ferrol to rendezvous with the fleet off Corunna. Even the strategic plan was more sensible than in '88, for the large expeditionary force aboard was to be directed not against the well-protected and distant estuary of the Thames, but against Catholic Ireland where there was a ready-made political and military situation to exploit.

And in one day of storm off Finisterre all these fine hopes were blown away. A third of the ships went down; perhaps as many as five thousand men were drowned; and of the survivors, many died, like their predecessors in Medina Sidonia's time, of their privations and the plague in Spanish ports.

Philip himself remained undaunted by the disaster, turning at once to the thought of new armadas. But where was the money to come from? Almost the last resources of the Crown had been poured into the equipment of the fleet, and under the double blow of its loss and the destruction of the Indies squadron at Cádiz his ambitions and his means had finally parted company; his credit had collapsed; no more loans were available from bankers who had read the signs of the times. The result was the third state bankruptcy of the reign, declared in November 1596, in one of the most interesting and barefaced state papers ever to come out of the royal secretariat.

In his preamble the King sets out the causes of the crisis as he sees them, citing first of all his numerous burdens as the standard-bearer of Catholicism in its struggle with heresy, and then going on to list the "grievous charges, discounts and interests" which he was unfairly expected to pay on his borrowings. "Thus all our domains, taxes, revenues, and all ordinary and extraordinary reserves stand burdened and covered with obligations in the hands of merchants," he exlaims with an aristocratic scorn which overlooks his own and his father's part in the growth of the system of state bonds (*juros*) which had financed his wars and mortgaged his future.

And now the said merchants [he continues] who hitherto have given on bills of exchange such moneys as were necessary to provide for the protection of our royal state and to carry on the war which we are waging for these righteous and special reasons, refuse to do this any longer and make difficulties in further dealings with us, seeing that they have in their own hands and power all the royal revenues by means of the said pledges, certificates and transfers.

As one reads this abject confession it requires an effort to remember that its author was absolute ruler of a kingdom which owned the American mines and a virtual monopoly of the world's supply of precious metals. How could such a situation have come about?

The King thought he saw one answer in

. . . financiering and unhallowed practices with bills of exchange which have been introduced and become spread abroad among so many people, who in order to follow such pursuits have abandoned agriculture, cattle raising and mechanical works, and embarked in trade, finding therein gain and profit to the disservice of the Lord God and of us, with great injury to our kingdom. . . .

He saw another in the flight of American treasure out of Spain into the hands of "rebels and foes of Christianity." This was largely true; but who was to blame? The care of farming and industry was surely the government's concern, yet nothing had been done to stop the drift of landless peasants to the towns: indeed one must suspect that their presence as a pool of rootless and mobile labor which could be enlisted in the armies or exported to help colonize the Indies was actively *desired*. As for the traders and moneylenders, a man who had had recourse to them for forty years could hardly complain of the results; while to lament the flight of specie out of the kingdom was to plead guilty to gross mismanagement of a gold mine.

To say so much, however, is not to acquit the King's bankers, whose own ambitions had been exorbitant and whose greed for interest had outrun discretion: indeed it is almost with a sneaking feeling of respect that one turns to Philip's *Diktat*, with its singular display of the advantages enjoyed by royal bankrupts over less exalted ones in the complicated game of getting even with one's creditors.

First the carrot, with which the King encourages a proper spirit of compromise in his bankers by announcing that he will "meditate" on ways and means of paying them what may seem to him "properly due."

And then the big stick, wielded with gusto:

We have now given command to devise some means of restoring order and of accomplishing in the best possible way that which we are so highly and legally bound to do . . . and we have found no other remedy than to call in and disburthen our royal incomes, liberating the same from the unjust damages put upon them through this financiering and bills of exchange. . . . Accordingly we suspend and declare suspended all such assignations made by us in any manner whatsoever since September 1st 1575 and December 1st 1577 unto this date, to the said merchants and traders, whether of taxes, gifts, domains, rents, or any other property or revenues whatsoever, on account of such bills of exchange or other advances. And we order the monies coming from such pledged property to be henceforth paid into our royal treasury, for the support of our own necessities, declaring from this day forth all payments otherwise made to be null and void.

As we see from the proviso which the King wrote into his decree, he had not intended a war à outrance on his creditors but more a holding operation as a prelude to a settlement at less ruinous interest rates. However, he had badly miscalculated both his own powers to influence financiers and the effects of this sudden repudiation on investment and trade. At the end of a year the suspension had itself to be suspended in obedience to laws more inexorable than any royal decree, for it was not the foreign bankers but the economy of the nation that had been hurt by a collapse of confidence and credit almost as traumatic in its way as the defeats at sea. Not only God but Mammon seemed to have abandoned Spain. For two years no convoys sailed for the Indies; the great fairs at Medina del Campo closed down; everything was at a standstill except prices.

For some time voices had been protesting—tentatively at first but growing in volume—against the costs of foreign adventures which were eating up all Spain's resources. We must be careful to be selective here, for the two sea-borne Armadas had been popular in a country whose commercial axis had shifted southward to Andalusia, the base of the vital Indies trade which the English were threatening to disrupt. With Elizabeth there could be no peace except on Spanish terms—no one from the King and the court to the most penurious *pícaro* on the streets of Seville desired it. But the campaigns in France and the interminable troubles in the Netherlands which had resulted in a slump in the wool trade and the virtual closure of Antwerp were obviously vexatious and helpful to no one except the heretic English and Dutch.

The nation was still prepared to fight where it felt its vital interests were at stake, but already the war-weariness and disillusion which in the next reign resulted in one of the most craven and perhaps sanest eras in Spanish history were working like a leaven throughout society and in their courses had reached the King. The year 1597 was to see his last attempts to master his problems in the old way, by assertions of aggressive power—a new thrust of his Netherlands army which captured Amiens on the road to Paris; then a third Armada against England, even larger than in '96, which the "Protestant Wind" dispersed off El Ferrol, while it was still hundreds of miles from its objective on the Cornish coast. Worse still, in the Netherlands at Turnhout, that January, a Spanish army had been caught on the march by Prince Maurice's cavalry and destroyed, much as the "States" forces had been routed by Don John and Parma at Gembloux.

This was a portent. If we except Heiligerlee, which was a defeat for her auxiliaries, no Spanish army had been beaten in the open field since Ravenna in 1512. Philip was not to live to see the even greater disaster shortly to befall his nephew the Archduke Albert on the dunes of Nieuport, but Turnhout was unmistakable evidence of his waning powers, and when in the autumn of the same year the French recaptured Amiens the lesson was learned at last. There would have to be peace.

In the Netherlands, in the intervals between his attempts to suppress the rebellion in the northern states, the King had made numerous attempts to lure them back into the fold either by direct approach or through the mediation of Vienna. He had tried this method in Don John's time, in Parma's and again on the appointment of the Archduke Ernest, with varying optimism and good faith but with an invariable lack of success. In these negotiations the King had gradually become the more pliable of the two parties, and toward the end might have been content with a nominal acceptance of his sovereignty coupled with a guarantee of religious freedom for the suppressed Catholics of the north. But nothing could be had on these terms because the Dutch knew themselves to be winning and were finding actual advantages in a struggle which threw open the huge monopoly of the Hispano-Portuguese empire to their increasingly powerful fleets. They had a vested interest in war, like the English, whose depredations in the Indies had provided a natural outlet for forces which might have caused trouble at home. Essex's rebellion against Elizabeth at the end of her reign and the rise of radical Puritanism under the Stuarts once anti-Spanish policies were relaxed are proof enough of the dangers lurking under the surface unity of the Protestant states, which could however be exorcised—as the Dutch showed—by continuing aggression.

But with the French, Philip had much more reason to hope for a *détente*. France was as bankrupt as Spain, without any Indies to turn to. Parts of her territory were still in Spanish hands or were controlled by Leaguer nobles who expected substantial bribes for turning their coats. And in Rome there was a Pope—Clement VIII —who was not intent like so many of his predecessors on playing off France against Spain in the interests of political balance in Europe, but was concerned with the unity of Catholicism in the struggle against heresy and was busily pressing some accommodation on Paris. From Madrid and Brussels similar peace feelers had gone out—not for forty years had France been so courted by other European powers, including the Dutch and English whose protests and appeals against apostasy filled the diplomatic air.

In fact Henry had no intention of making a genuine peace with Spain, but only the appearance of one which would give him a breathing space to put his own house in order by buying off his rapacious Catholic nobility. A deal with the Papacy and with Philip particularly appealed to him at the moment he was about to decree a large measure of religious toleration to his Huguenots by the famous Edict of Nantes, an act of enlightened statesmanship which only an ex-heretic with a Jesuit confessor could have carried off. If Spain and the Papacy could be made to swallow this and still press for peace, he could certainly bear with fortitude the reproaches of his Protestant friends.

The result of this need for a settlement, so widely felt in Catholic Europe, was the Peace of Vervins of 1598. By its terms Philip gave up his new conquests in Picardy and the Pas de Calais, along with other territories occupied by his troops in Brittany; recognized the Béarnais as lawful King of France; and received as a compensation a recognition of his own rights to the old duchy of Burgundy so vague as to be virtually meaningless. This return to the state of affairs existing after Câteau-Cambrésis was a severe diplomatic reverse for Spain after so much effort in so many triumphant campaigns on French soil, but at least it was a peace which recognized realities and in spite of Henry's duplicity was to lead in time to a genuine *détente* and a royal marriage between the Hapsburg and Bourbon dynasties with very fateful and ironic consequences for Europe.*

When this peace was signed Philip had only a few months to live. No doubt he would have been happy to be quit of all his problems, but for him there could be no retirement to Yuste such as his father had chosen at the end of his life. Yet there could be an abdication of a kind, and in the same city of Brussels where the Emperor had laid down his Netherlands inheritance.

Under another dispensation, under a kindlier star, the unborn child of Philip's marriage with Mary Tudor might have come to rule a joint kingdom bridging the narrow seas, independent of Spain though allied with her and part of her system. Too many deaths, too many enmities, had destroyed a conception which could have changed the face of Europe. The germ of the idea remained—a shedding of the load of empire which the Emperor had twice in his life envisaged but had at last rejected, leaving the provinces tied firmly to their incompatible partner, Spain. More resolute than his father, Philip had determined that the separation must be made and the Netherlands handed over to his Hapsburg nephew, the Archduke Albert, and a wife to be provided for him in the person of the Infanta Isabella Clara Eugenia. If they had a child, the Netherlands—including in theory the seven northern states—would pass to that child, not to Philip III: if they died childless the provinces would return to Spain. Rumors current at the time suggested that the King was aware of a certain physical incapacity of the Archduke which made the outcome a certainty, which may be true, though one would imagine that a man who was going to so much trouble to be rid of a millstone would hardly want it back, even round the necks of his descendants.

* Philip's granddaughter, Anne of Austria, was of course the mother of Louis XIV, whose own marriage to another Infanta—Maria Theresa—eventually brought the great-great-grandson of the ex-heretic Henry to the Spanish throne. He was a Philip too—Philip V—and lies in the same vault of the Escurial.

On balance we should perhaps allow Philip at least the credit for a luminous idea which made peace with the Utrecht provinces more possible by removing Spain and her xenophobic feelings from the direct arena of conflict with the heretic. It was a small service after so many mistakes and it was not one that lasted for long, since in the next century the territories returned to Spain. But it was probably during the rule of the "Archdukes," as Albert and Isabella came to be called, that the division between Protestant north and Catholic south grew acceptable to the mass of people. The fact that the boundaries of Belgium and Holland today run much along the lines that existed between the loyalist and Utrecht provinces in 1598 is some small proof of the King's sagacity in the face of a problem which was insoluble in his time and has remained so.

THE BREACH MADE FINAL. DEATH OF PHILIP. 1598.

The war between Spain and her rebellious subjects which had begun with Count Louis's victory at Heiligerlee had now lasted for
thirty years. Including a twelve-year truce it was to last for another
fifty, but already the main issues had been decided, demarcations
of territory laid down.

In the south an economy had been all but destroyed. It was in
those loyalist provinces, in the quadrilateral that enclosed Ghent,
Antwerp, Brussels and the textile centers of Artois and Hainaut,
that the real wealth of the Netherlands had lain. Nature had
abundantly blessed them with rich agricultural land and a river
system which the ingenuity of man had transformed through a
complex of towns, roads and canals into an industrial workshop
where the new capitalist skills could be put through their paces.
Its focal point had been Antwerp on the upper estuary of the
Scheldt. No founding father of this great metropolis which seemed
to dominate the trade routes of a continent can ever have conceived that a few miles of tidal water and the mud flats of the
miserable islands that flanked its exit to the sea might become a
threat to its existence and to that of the provinces lying behind it.
In good Emperor Charles's golden and supranational days such
thoughts would not even have occurred to the jealous minds of
rivals in another aspiring city to the north—Amsterdam.

Antwerp's tragedy was not wholly of her own making. Many of
her sufferings—the iconoclastic riots of 1566, the Spanish and
French Furies and the great siege—were by-products of her own
eminence, which made her possession a matter of critical importance to both the warring factions. She did not even choose the
wrong side: it was chosen for her. An influential minority group
of her citizens had tried to take her into the Calvinist camp, but
with Parma's triumph she had become part of an empire which
controlled one element of her being, the hinterland of Brabant,

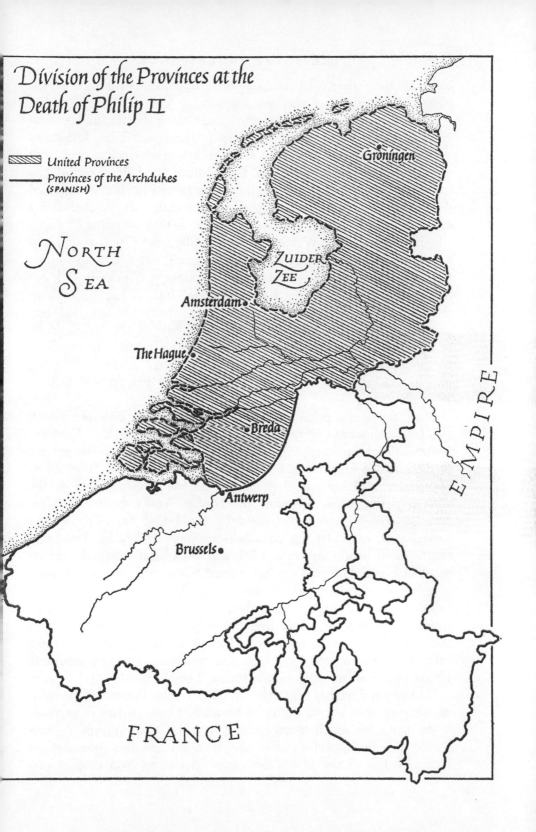

Division of the Provinces at the
Death of Philip II

▨ United Provinces
── Provinces of the Archdukes
(SPANISH)

NORTH
SEA

ZUIDER
ZEE

Gröningen

Amsterdam

The Hague

Breda

Antwerp

Brussels

EMPIRE

FRANCE

but not the other, the estuary of the Scheldt through which passed the trade that was her lifeblood.

Once this was cut off by rebel forts downstream and enemy cruisers based on Flushing, Antwerp became that most forlorn of towns, a seaport without access to the sea. Her decline was very rapid. By 1598 her population had shrunk by half; most of the merchants and bankers who had created or fed on her wealth had decamped; the famous exchange was moribund; only canal craft lay at her wharves. Along the coast of Flanders—that long line of dunes which stretches from Walcheren to the cliffs near Calais—there was no other harbor in Spanish hands which could even pretend to play the same part in the economy of the country. Antwerp did not die. In our own times we have witnessed one of her triumphant resurrections—a phoenix of a city! The provinces that had lain under her wing continued under the mild rule of the "Archdukes" to be one of the most urbane parts of Europe, as we can see from the houses of the time which still line the Gran' Place in Brussels, and in the canvases of Rubens with their joyful appreciation of life's pleasures.

But there was a price to be paid for all this, for civil peace and the free enjoyment of a faith—the living faith of the Counter-Reformation then sweeping Europe. In the debatable lands subject to the raids of northern armies and freebooting bands, large tracts of country had become depopulated as the peasants fled to the shelter of the towns or across the border. And even in the safer areas, a society which had lived by trade had been largely deprived of its markets: the economic windows had been closed and barred both inside and out. With the fall of Antwerp, the movement of population and capital toward the north, which had been a trickle, became a flood. To some Catholic observers—Granvelle's brother, Champagney, among them—Calvinists were better suited to trade than true believers, and certainly the loss of these vigorous and enterprising men, who took their skills and goods with them into exile, was a setback which the southern economy could ill afford and a substantial bonus to the heretic north.

To the comfortable oligarchs of the Utrecht states this invasion of refugees was not an unmixed blessing. Many of the newcomers were men with a grievance looking for a political system to overthrow, and in Leicester's time they had formed the spearhead of forces hostile to the States General and aiming to set up a new theocracy; men of the same nature as those who later in England were to form the "Barebone's Parliament." But at least they had brought with them the priceless gift of energy, and when the effect of their arrival was added to the native thrust of Zeelanders and Hollanders the result was an economic explosion almost unique in history. In 1557 the nucleus of what was to become the United Provinces amounted to a few half-drowned lands on the edge of the North Sea; forty years later they were negotiating on equal terms with France and England; within another ninety they had soundly defeated the heirs of the Armada victory off the Thames itself and had placed a Dutchman on the English throne.

It was a remarkable performance. Amsterdam, a small town at the beginning of the reign, had overtaken Antwerp by the end of it to become the mart for the goods of northern Europe. The society she mirrored was often brash and ostentatious: a world on the make, with foibles of which Motley amusingly reminds us:

During this year and the next the States of Holland . . . raised the duty on imports and all internal taxes by one eighth and laid a fresh impost on such articles of luxury as velvets and satins. . . . Starch too became a source of considerable revenue. With the fast-rising prosperity of the country luxury had likewise risen, and as in all ages and countries of the world of which there is record, woman's dress signalised itself by extravagant and very often tasteless conceptions. . . . The honest burgher's vrow of Middelburg or Enkhuyzen claimed the right to make herself as grotesque as Queen Elizabeth in all her glory. . . . Formerly starch had been made of the refuse part of corn, but now the manufacturers of that article made use of the bloom of the wheat and consumed as much of it as would have fed great cities. In the little village of Wormer the starch-makers used between three and four thousand bushels a week. Thus a substantial gentlewoman in fashionable array might bear the food of a parish upon her ample bosom. . . .
"May God preserve us," exclaimed a contemporary chronicler, unreasonably excited on the starch question, "from farther luxury and wantonness, and abuse of His blessings and good gifts, that the punishment of Jeroboam, which followed upon Solomon's fortunate reign and the gold ships of Ophir, may not come upon us."
The states of Holland not confounding—as so often has been the case—the precepts of moral philosophy with those of political economy, did not, out of fear of the doom of Jeroboam, forbid the use of starch. They simply laid a tax of a stiver a pound on the commodity, or about six

percent ad valorem. . . . Meanwhile the preachers were left to thunder from their pulpits upon the sinfulness of starched ruffles and ornamental top-knots, and to threaten their fair hearers with the wrath to come, with as much success as usually attends such eloquence.

This is a heartening reminder that even the most Puritan concepts have to give way to women's whims and the average man's inclination to enjoy them. The inordinate use of starch by these good ladies in their attempts to impress their husbands or the neighbors was not the least significant of the trends of the times, and we see the same influence at work in those groups of civic dignitaries who hang in their sober, and sometimes inebriated, glory on the walls of the Rijksmuseum and the Frans Hals house in Haarlem. The burgher and the burgher's wife were bursting out of the strait jacket which the old social system had imposed on them. Naturally they had no desire that artisans and suchlike should join in. These second-generation revolutionaries were of the least revolutionary caliber ever seen on earth, and from the conflict between their ingrained conservatism and the radicalism of the refugees and Calvinist divines dangerous new tensions were to grow.

For the time being each fertilized the other. Prosperity at home: expansion abroad—such was the picture presented by this embryo state, which was not one but seven, plagued with mutual jealousies and with a large Catholic element which was either neutral or actively subversive.* With such support, and in the midst of a war with the world's most powerful empire, these provincials were embarking on projects of breath-taking daring and naïveté. In 1598 two expeditions set out from Amsterdam to find the northeast passage to China. That of Barents—whose name still finds a place on the maps, and rightly, since he died in these wastes—reached a point in latitude 76 degrees north before being imprisoned for one whole ghastly year in the pack ice off Nova Zembla.

This was a freak, an excess of initiative, like a similar attempt at the far side of the globe in Antarctic waters, but it symbolized an attitude of mind widely held among a people whose dreams of commercial gain had no limits, real or imaginary. These wildly unpractical expeditions into the unknown were balanced by the

* Particularly in Groningen which remained in a state of chronic unrest.

appearance of Dutch shipping off the coasts of South America and in the Spice Islands of the East Indies, where in the years to come a great empire was to be founded which survived Spain's for more than a century.

The sea is a radical element and since the days of the Argonauts has always carried souls as restless and ungovernable as itself—protesters against governments, adventurers, pirates, explorers, and traders in search of a good profit or an empire on the cheap. From the point of view of the merchants in Amsterdam and her satellite ports the war against Spain was a desirable war, the only entrance card to territories from which in peacetime all non-Spaniards were excluded.

But on land it was another matter. There, there was little to be won, because the physical features of mere and river and fortified town which had checked Alva and Requesens on their northward march were just as effective obstacles in reverse when the States General turned to the offensive against Brabant. In a terrain which favored defensive war, warfare had no apparent purpose. This had long been realized. After the failure of the Armada Parma had made no sustained attempt to drive north across the rivers: and similarly Prince Maurice showed an equal caution when urged to advance into Flanders and roll up the royalist position between Brussels and the sea. Battles were to be fought over the old ground —Nieuport, a northern victory; the capture of Dunkirk by Spain's Genoese commander, Ambrogio Spinola—but about these sieges, these movements of great armies, there was increasingly an air of the theater, marvelously portrayed in Velázquez's great picture of the *Surrender of Breda** which breathes the high civilities and exhaustion of an age. A few years more into the future and all this has changed: the victors are not Spaniards or Dutchmen but Condé's Frenchmen, and at Rocroi in 1643 there is no pretty unfurling of banners, no pageant of a surrender of keys, but the grim realities of battle as the last ten thousand of the *tercios* are cut to pieces on the field.

Placed midway between the horrors of Alva's time and those of the Thirty Years War, the campaigns that marked the end of the sixteenth century have almost an agreeable air which mirrored a real yearning among many people on both sides of the border to recognize their brotherhood and return to the state of affairs

* To Spinola in 1625.

that had existed at the Pacification of Ghent: indeed so strong was this feeling, that the all but moribund States General of the obedient provinces was galvanized into life and held meetings with the delegates of the Utrecht states to try and resolve their differences.

But it proved impossible to find a middle way. The religious cleavage had deepened since Orange's time: the north was more Calvinist, the south more fervid in its Catholicism as the tide of the Counter-Reformation rose. Besides, the Brussels States General was no longer a power in its own right but only the pale reflection of the archducal court; while the Utrecht provinces, sure of their liberties after thirty years of struggle, were in no mood to allow the King of Spain or his agents the least say in their affairs—they would not even listen to their old ally the Queen of England when she urged a settlement upon them. Self-confident and prosperous states, firmly planted on the map of Europe, they no longer felt the need for anyone's protection. It was the measure of Philip's failure that his pacific intentions in the last year of his life could not bring them back into even nominal allegiance to his new puppet state. The divorce from Spain which dated from the Abjuration of 1581 had become final.

For some time the King's health had been failing and dire reports of it had gone out in the dispatches of foreign ambassadors who underestimated the tenacity of his hold on life as long as unresolved problems remained to obsess him.

By the summer of 1598 there was peace with France, the settlement of the Netherlands on his daughter and nephew had been arranged, and it only remained to return from Madrid to the Escurial which had always been his refuge. In June he was brought there by litter against the advice of his doctors. The six-day journey, which in health he could comfortably have covered in two, brought on a fever, and by August it was plain that he was dying: plagued with sores that made every movement a torture and with vermin which seemed to horrified observers to be consuming the body of the living man. He uttered no word of complaint, showed a tender consideration for those about him. Even Motley, who judged him a monster, admits that he died like a saint and a hero, and we can sense the writer's astonishment that good and evil should so co-exist.

But souls are more complex than was imagined in the days of a triumphant liberalism. In this deathbed scene, which was closely observed and recorded by many witnesses, we are seeing the true man, who had sent heretics to a fearful death but was humbly pre-pared to suffer in his turn if such were God's will. He was troubled by no feelings of repentance, declaring that he had never wronged anyone in his life, and this deeply held belief goes far to explain, if it certainly does not excuse, his darkest acts: the murders of Montigny and Escovedo, the imprisonment of Don Carlos, the ban against the Prince of Orange, and his more wide-spread tyrannies in the Netherlands and in the suppression of the Moriscos, whose religion his great-grandparents had sworn to protect. All had been done as part of a stewardship which he resigned in touching words: "Having governed my kingdom for forty years, I now hand it back in the seventy-first year of my age to God Almighty to whom it belongs, recommending my soul into His blessed hands, that His Divine Majesty may do what He pleases therewith."

From the moment when he learned from his confessor that his illness was mortal he had concerned himself with preparations for death and with the consequences for himself and for Spain—all at the same measured pace and with the same careful eye for detail that had marked his working days. Nothing was forgotten. A courier was sent to Rome to ask for Papal absolution—and by some miracle of promptness, very unusual in the Spanish service, man-aged to return in time. The order of the funeral procession was laid down; minute provisions were made for the singing of masses and the release of prisoners; and the state coffin was brought to the sickroom for inspection along with a number of the sacred relics for which the Escurial had become one of the leading depositories in Europe.

If this smacks somewhat of the morbid strain inherent in the family, it was also a reflection of a true piety and perhaps of a desire to impress his successor with the majesty and mortality of kings. In these last hours his concern for his son and the in-heritance he was leaving him were obviously paramount in his thoughts, and there is much poignancy in his instructions to the feeble and pious heir to honor God and lead a Christian life.

"Alas, Don Cristóbal, I fear that they will govern him," he had confided to de Moura, who since Eboli's death had been closer to him than anyone except the Infanta: and indeed in the last moments of the reign there seems to have occurred an incident so full of symbolism of what was passing and of what was to come that one almost suspects the gravity of the Fates, as the Prince demands and eventually receives from Don Cristóbal's reluctant hands the keys to a (bankrupt) treasury and straightway hands them to his favorite, the Marquis of Denia, later Duke of Lerma, the first of a line of *Privados*, Mayors of the Palace, who were to rule and ruin Spain.

Apart from this incident, so reminiscent of Shakespeare's Henry IV, all was done with dignity, with that royal sense of occasion which was natural to Philip, that "perfect master in the art of ruling," as one contemporary described him. The death of a king of Spain was a great matter which would be reported for good or ill throughout Europe: therefore a political event, as well as an affirmation of God's purpose and a Christian response to suffering. In particular Philip seems to have been determined to impress his successor with a need for fraternal love for the Infanta Isabella, to whom the Netherlands had been willed away. A contemporary report of the bedside scene records things with admirable simplicity:

Then, speaking to the prince, he said: "Besides all that which I have heretofore spoken to you, I pray you have a great care and regard for your sister; because she was my looking glass and the light of mine eyes. Keep the commonwealth in peace, placing there good governors to reward the good and punish the bad. . . . And so I give my last farewell to my children, commending them to all peace and safety. . . ." Not long after he fell into another fit, whereupon he called for the extreme unction, which was given him by the archbishop. Then he called for a crucifix which had been kept safely in a chest, which was the very same his father held between his hands, when he died; with the which he desired likewise to die. Hereupon his Highness [the Prince] returned to his father; at whose coming Don Christopher [de Moura], upon his knees, presented to him the royal key, which the prince received and gave it to the Marquess of Denia; whereupon the King said to him: "Remember I commend unto you Don Christopher, for the most faithful servant which I ever had; and so have care of all the rest, which I commend unto you." And so he took his leave of him again, embracing him, at which instant his speech failed; and in this sort he continued two days, and died upon Sunday the 13th September, about three of the clock in the morning.

Later that day the Venetian ambassador, Francesco Soranza, reported to his government:

The king is dead. His Majesty expired at the Escurial this morning at daybreak, after having received all the sacraments of the Church with every sign of devoutness, piety and religion. Although change is usually popular, yet nobles and people, rich and poor, universally show great grief. His Majesty lived seventy-one years, three months and twenty-four days; he reigned forty-two years ten months and sixteen days. He was a prince who fought with gold rather than with steel, by his brain rather than his arm. He has acquired more by sitting still, by negotiation, by diplomacy, than his father did by armies and by war. He was one of the richest princes the world has ever seen, yet he has left the revenues of the kingdom and of the crown burdened with about a million of debts. . . . Profoundly religious, he loved peace and quiet. He displayed great calmness, and professed himself unmoved in good or bad fortune alike. . . . On great occasions, in the conduct of wars, in feeding the civil war in France, in the magnificence of his buildings, he never counted the cost; he was no close reckoner but lavished his gold without a thought; but in small matters, in the government of his household, in his presents and rewards, he was more parsimonious than became his station. . . . He held his desires in absolute control and showed an immutable and unalterable temper. He has feigned injuries and feigned not to feel injuries, but he never lost the opportunity to avenge them. He hated vanity and therefore never allowed his life to be written. No one ever saw him in a rage, being always patient, phlegmatic, temperate, melancholy. In short, he has left a glorious memory of his royal name, which may serve as an example, not only unto his posterity and his successors, but unto strangers as well.

Soranza's judgment is of value as showing how Catholic Europe— through the eyes of the ambassador of a state traditionally opposed to Spain—viewed the greatest of Spain's kings. For far more than most rulers, Philip has been the victim of that great gulf between ideas which we call the Reformation and which makes a dispassionate judgment of him difficult even today. To Protestants he was anti-Christ. Of this man of undoubted piety, a devoted husband and father, with the endurance of a Stoic and a deep sense of personal responsibility for his acts, Motley could write:

There have been few men known to history who have been able to accomplish by their own exertions so vast an amount of evil. If Philip possessed a single virtue it has eluded the conscientious research of the writer of these pages. If there are vices—as presumably there are—from which he was exempt, it is because it is not permitted to human nature to attain perfection even in evil.

This view, if perhaps in less thundering form, still has its up-holders, for whom Philip's crimes—as crimes they undoubtedly were—are not excused by the provocations offered him or by his genuine belief in God's approval. Its advocates have a case, and it is only half an answer to point out that in the general collapse of the once united Church into factions, each passionately claiming the empire of Christ, deeds were being done also in Protestant Europe from which it is pleasanter to avert the mind. Barbarities are never to be excused. All the same, it is not helpful to judge one age of faith from the viewpoint of another diametrically opposed to it, as Motley did; and our own more disenchanted period, which has seen even worse horrors for worse causes, no longer shows the same certainty about moral problems and moral condemnations. Criticism of Philip has not ceased but it has changed direction. It is not the King's capacity for wickedness that now excites remark but rather his incapacity as a ruler to deal with the problems of his time.

Yet even here there is no general agreement about him. Far more than the infinitely devious Elizabeth or that miracle of inconstancy, Henry of Navarre, he continues to deny analysis. Was his reign the "disgraceful failure" that Motley dubs it on the strength of the *débâcle* against France and England and the loss of the Protestant Netherlands? His success in resisting Protestant pressure in France, in retaining the larger part of his Burgundian inheritance and the vast enlargement of his empire by the acquisition of Portugal and her colonies and the settlement of the Philippines, suggests quite the opposite. But if the real ills that afflicted Spain lay deeper and were infinitely more disastrous than the loss of seven provinces and three Armadas, was Philip part author of these ills or more the victim of circumstances and forces beyond one man's power to remedy?

We are approaching the great historical mystery of Spain's "decline" which has obsessed almost as many people and produced as wide a variety of theories as the fall of Rome itself. Was there even a decline at all? One eminent Spanish essayist* has denied it, calling in aid his country's abundant gifts in the realms of the spirit, where certainly Don Quixote still rides and Don Juan carries off his ever-willing victims. Let us admit as most Spaniards would that the decline is a manifest fact and had become so by 1600, when a perceptive critic, Gonzalez de Cellerigo, was writing of his countrymen: "It seems as if one had wished to reduce these kingdoms to a republic of the bewitched, living outside the natural order of things."

This is a moral judgment. And as Professor Elliott has pointed out in a recent study, most other judgments on Spain's decline have been on economic grounds. Research has established many of her ills: rural depopulation; inflation; an inequitable tax burden that penalized the poor and the productive; racial intolerance; a labor shortage; the growth of the Indies into a competitor instead of a market for Spain's goods; the decay of commercial enterprise; a contempt for hard work; a swelling ratio of clerks and monks to merchants and farmers; to which one may add Motley's tremendous indictment of the King who presided over everything: "All that breathed or grew belonged to him, and most steadily was their stream of blood and treasure poured through the sieve of his perpetual war."

Yet other nations had been suffering comparable troubles. Endemic warfare and a steep rise in the price of commodities were common to practically every country, while the urban unemployed in the streets of Seville had their counterpart in the hordes of "sturdy beggars" which so alarmed the government of Elizabeth. Were Spain's material ills indeed the cause of a decline which was not matched elsewhere, or were they rather symptoms, outward and visible signs of an inward and spiritual malaise which was to be mirrored in the literature of the next reign? And was that brilliant outburst of talent itself a compensation for something that was felt to have been lost?

One returns to Gonzalez de Cellerigo and his definition. In

* Azorín.

Charles's middle years Spain had certainly not been living "out of the natural order of things," but had been an integral part of Europe, open to the winds of humanist thought and served by scholars of international reputation, her king an emperor with responsibilities stretching from Peru to the Danube. Yet even in those fortunate times there had been forces working the other way to pull Spain back from Europe and inward on herself. Geography and long contact with the Moors had made her people naturally withdrawn and self-sufficient. The Emperor's European prestige had been admired as a national asset but his commitments in Germany and long absences abroad had been resented, and when he died, and the Empire passed elsewhere, the divorce from an alien continent was accepted with relief along with a new king who was entirely Spanish in character and upbringing. There were other factors too which contributed to this isolationism. The Reformation in its Calvinist phase prevented any dialogue between the Catholics and heretics of a kind that had been possible in Luther's time. The Netherlands rebellion accentuated this trend: if it brought Spaniards to the lower Rhine it brought them there as executioners and Inquisitors, no longer as friends or trading partners. Furthermore, as a natural reaction to the spread of heresy, religious intolerance grew within Spain herself and in turn sparked off both the Morisco rising and the savage ill-treatment of England's Protestant seamen at San Juan de Ulúa and in the jails of the *Suprema*.

As a consequence, by the middle of Philip's reign the humanist Spain of the 1530s which had admired Erasmus had become a society closed to speculative thought, indeed to every thought that had not originated in Castile and been cleared by the Inquisition. Even the Indies and the exploitation of their fabulous wealth had only served to make Spain turn her back more firmly on her old associates. Like a fortunate prospector in the Klondike she had sat down on her claim, unwilling to share it, yet unable to develop its potential. The full force of this xenophobia was not to be felt till the next reign, when the expulsion of the entire Morisco population with all its harmful consequences was everywhere greeted as a victory, but long before that time the national hatred of other races and creeds had resulted in the lunatic search for "pure blood" and in a willing acceptance of the rituals of the Holy Office.

These feelings had their roots in an overweening confidence in Spain's power and destiny. It would have been very odd if Spain had *not* had such feelings, for the conquest of the Indies and the stream of treasure which it unlocked seemed to belong more to the realms of fantasy than to anything else and were the strongest meat that could have been fed to a nation which through too much reading of chivalry books was a ready believer in marvels. It became natural to think that a few Spaniards in armor could rout whole empires of savages, and if there were doubts of how the sons of the *Conquistadores* might fare against the more formidable French and Turks, these vanished in the smoke of battle at St. Quentin and Lepanto. There seemed no end to what Spain might achieve as God's secular arm, and when the first challenge came to these beliefs—in the Netherlands rising—heretics seemed no more able to stand against her soldiers than Montezuma's Aztecs at Tenochtitlán.

It was only gradually that these confident feelings became affected by events which perversely did not fit the pattern. The Netherlands rebellion dragged on, defying every effort by force or diplomacy to put it down. To be rejected by so small a client state was a hurtful blow to pride. And soon a chain reaction was seen—English troops came to the Low Countries; English ships began to attack the Indies life line, then Spain herself, apparently with impunity.

Of course these incidents caused no widespread collapse of morale, but their continuance and the sense of growing danger undoubtedly affected those who were engaged in the Indies trade —a substantial part of the population of Andalusia and the Biscayan ports—and bred in them and in the seamen who had fought against the English an impatience for a revenge in whose possibility the avengers only half believed. *Il faut en finir:* there would have to be a reckoning one way or the other. It was in this spirit that the Armada sailed out of Lisbon carrying with it the fears of the few and the uninformed expectations of the many. Its failure was a shattering blow to everyone, and it is from this moment that the questioning begins and soon rises to a crescendo in the deliberations of the Cortes, in learned memoranda, in lampoons and street ballads and the complaints of government officials. What has gone wrong? What is to be Spain's future? What is at the root of troubles which everyone senses and no one can

define? Indeed we ask these questions still, and though much of the
evidence is there in the archives, the answers come no more easily
than they did to the inquiring seekers of Philip's time. If the economic maladies and a few naval and military defeats hardly add up
to catastrophe—to Spain's disappearance by the mid-seventeenth
century from the ranks of the major European powers—what
caused it?

Perhaps a failure of the will, a kind of neurosis. Nations like
individuals suffer them—one has only to instance the example of
France in 1789, of Tsarist Russia in 1917, France again between
the two World Wars, and perhaps—tell it not in Gath—England
today or America tomorrow. The physical ability to act and survive
has nothing to do with it. It is not a matter of what a nation
is but of what it thinks of itself: and probably there has always
been a dark, self-questioning side to Spanish pride, an insistence
on suffering and the need for expiation which we see—vicariously—
in the bull ring on Sunday afternoons and in the great Corpus
Christi processions of hooded penitents, so reminiscent of the
sixteenth-century *auto*.

Whatever she may be today, by 1590 Spain had become a nation
of bewildered and self-questioning zealots. Doubts about her well-
being which could have been faced in the days when she was
outward-looking festered once she had turned in upon herself.
In the course of three decades she had seen a rebellion break
out in a remote province and grow to embroil her with an England
which traditionally had been her ally and a France which at
Câteau-Cambrésis she thought she had tamed. These military
problems and the financial and manpower strain imposed by
them were central to her predicament, just as the Netherlands
revolt was central to the cycle of wars which spiraled out of it.
If there was a material cause for her decay, it was this constant
and ever-growing drain on her resources, now in the Low Countries, now in Italy, in Africa against the Barbary corsairs, in the
Alpujarras, in France, in the Caribbean, and then among the
trading posts in Brazil and the Indian Ocean which she had to
protect on behalf of her resentful Portuguese partner in empire.
All these strains, which did not find their full expression for
another half century, when Spain allowed herself to become embroiled in a major war in Germany as well, were certainly present
before Philip's death. He had brought most of them about by

his mistaken policies. While still the strongest nation in Europe, the Spain of his time had become infected with self-doubt. A kind of dry rot set in. But like a studio prop the façade of the stricken edifice remained very lifelike and impressive to beholders till suddenly, midway through the seventeenth century, it was realized that there was nothing behind.

APPENDIX

PARMA'S MOVEMENTS AT THE HEIGHT OF THE ARMADA CRISIS

On December 30, 1588, Parma wrote to the King's secretary Idiaquez defending himself against allegations of lack of preparedness and zeal during the Armada crisis. He used the following
words:

On 7th August when Secretary Arceo came and I left Bruges I had
already embarked at Nieuport 16,000 foot-soldiers; and when I arrived
at Dunkirk on Tuesday 8th before dawn, the men who were to be
shipped there had arrived and their embarkation was complete.

This recital does not accord with other facts and dates. Parma
says he reached Dunkirk on Tuesday August 8. But Tuesday was
not the eighth; it was the ninth. Arceo's movements are neutral
to the inquiry. He was sent off from Calais on the evening of
Saturday the sixth. He would have been at Dunkirk on the morning
of the seventh, and that night Medina Sidonia received news
from him that nothing was stirring at Dunkirk and that Parma had
not arrived there. He could have seen Parma at Bruges on the
seventh; equally it could have been the eighth. But Parma's other
letters indicate that he did not leave Bruges on the seventh.
He wrote to Philip from there on the eighth, and that *this* was not
a misdating is suggested by the fact that on the seventh he had
told Philip that he planned to leave for the coast next day. Furthermore, on the tenth Parma wrote to Philip setting out his movements. He said that on the eighth he arrived at Nieuport; then
pushed on to Dunkirk (presumably in the small hours of the
ninth) where he found the men waiting on the quays. At 10:30 in
the morning (almost certainly of the ninth) Manrique arrived, followed by the Prince of Ascoli. It is clear from Ascoli's own letter
to Philip that he reached the port on the ninth, and this fits in with
the rest of the timetable.

Parma's letter of December 30 to Idiaquez must therefore be wrong. The simplest explanation is that he updated his movements either by accident or in an attempt to show himself prompter in arrival at Dunkirk than he had actually been.

SOURCES OF QUOTATIONS

Chapter 1

[page 3] Sir John Mason, J. W. Burgon, *Life and Times of Sir Thomas Gresham*. I, 175.

Chapter 3

[page 17] Motley, *Rise of the Dutch Republic*, i, 96. Badovero MS
[page 18] Cabrera, i, 12.
[page 19] Soriano MS.

Chapter 4

[page 27] Quoted in Prescott, *History of Philip II*, 81.
[page 33] Prescott, *op. cit.*, 97.
[page 35] Brantôme, *Oeuvres*.
[page 37] Quoted by Strickland, *Lives of the Queens of England*, iii, 118.
Quoted in Prescott, 114, from *Memorias de la Real* Academia vii, 268.

Chapter 6

[page 56] Groen, *Archives et Correspondances Inédites de la Maison d'Orange-Nassau*, vi, 117.
[page 57] Quoted in Motley, i, 279. *Simancas State Papers*, vi, 175.
[page 60] Gachard, *Correspondance de Philippe II sur les Affaires des Pays Bas*, i, 230.
[page 61] *Papiers d'Etat de Granvelle*, edited by Weiss, vi, 562.
Gachard, *Correspondance (Pays Bas)*, i, 207.
[page 62] Gachard, *Correspondance (Pays Bas)*, i, 284.
[page 63] Gachard, *Correspondance de Guillaume le Taciturne*, ii, 45.
[page 64] *Mémoires de Granvelle*, edited by Dom Prosper Levesque, ii, 53.
[page 65] Quoted in Motley, i, 371.
Gachard, *Correspondance de Guillaume le Taciturne*, ii, 67.
[page 70] Groen, *Archives*, i, 426.
[page 72] Gachard, *Correspondance de Guillaume le Taciturne*, ii, 106.
[page 77] Quoted in Motley, i, 486, from Renom de France MS., i, 18.
[page 85] Prescott, 299.

Chapter 8

[page 107] Gachard, *Correspondance (Pays Bas)*, i, 631.
[page 113] Quoted in Ruth Putnam, *William the Silent*, i, 294, from Groen, *Archives*, iii, 209.
[page 117] *Simancas State Papers*, 539.
Gachard, *Correspondance (Pays Bas)*, ii, 316.
[page 122] Gachard, *Correspondance (Pays Bas)*, ii, 185.
[page 127] Pieter Geyl, *The Revolt of the Netherlands*, 127.
[page 129] Gachard, *Correspondance de Guillaume le Taciturne*, iii.

Chapter 9

[page 139] Quoted in Merriman, *The Rise of the Spanish Empire*, iv, 26.
[page 140 /42] Gachard, *Lettres de Philippe II a ses Filles, les Infantes Isabelle et Catherine*.
[page 150] Groen, *Archives*, iv, 246.
[page 159] Robert Fruin, *Siege and Relief of Leyden 1574*, 134.

Chapter 10

[page 162] Groen, *Archives*, v, 226.
[page 167] Gachard, *Correspondance de Guillaume le Taciturne*, iii, xii (Introduction).

Chapter 11

[page 176] Quoted in Motley, iii, 128.
[page 177] Gachard, *Correspondance de Guillaume le Taciturne*, iii, liii (Introduction).
[page 179] Quoted in Stirling Maxwell, *Don John of Austria*, ii, 490.

Chapter 12

[page 185] Quoted in Motley, iii, 250, from Strada, ix, 466.
[page 187] Lefèvre, *Correspondance de Philippe II sur les Affaires des Pays Bas*, i, 58.
[page 192] Quoted in Stirling Maxwell, *Don John of Austria*, ii, 327 footnote.
Quoted in Stirling Maxwell, *Don John of Austria*, ii, 331–32.
[page 193] Quoted in Stirling Maxwell, *Don John of Austria*, ii, 332.

Chapter 14

[page 216] Quoted in Geyl, 127. *Report* of Van Leyden Burgomaster of Utrecht.

Quoted in Van Essen, *Alexandre Farnese*, ii, 132. A.G.R. *Copies de Simancas*, Vol. 12.

[page 221] Gachard, *Correspondance de Guillaume le Taciturne*, iv, 202.

[page 222] Lefèvre, *Correspondance (Pays Bas)*, ii, 287.

[page 226] Quoted in Strickland, *Queens of England*, iii, from Murdin's *State Papers*.

[page 228] Gachard, *Correspondance de Guillaume le Taciturne*, vi, 106.

[page 230] Van Essen, iii, 115. From A. A. Van Schelven, *Willem van Oranje*, 276.

[page 231] Motley, iii, 506. From Bor, xvii, 349.

Chapter 15

[page 235] Poullet and Piot, *Correspondance de Granvelle*, xi, 19. Quoted in Van Essen, iii, 189.

Correspondance de Granvelle, xi, 18.

[page 236] Paolo Rinaldi, *Liber Relationum*. Van Essen, iii, 207.

Van Essen, iv, 13.

[page 239 Van Essen, iv, 61–62.
/40]

[page 241] Van Essen, iv, 136.

Van Essen, iv, 140. Based on Bor, ii, 606.

Chapter 16

[page 244] Gachard, *Relations des Ambassades Vénitiens*, 218.

Chapter 17

[page 249] A.G.R. *Copies de Simancas*, Vol. 17. Van Essen, v, 166.

[page 252f.] *Calendar of State Papers, Spanish*, iv, Elizabeth 1587/ 1603, 83.

[page 255] *Calendar of State Papers, Spanish*, iv, Eliz., 135.

[page 256] A.G.R. *Copies de Simancas*, Vol. 18. Van Essen, v, 195.

A.G.R. *Copies de Simancas*, Vol. 18. Van Essen, v, 196.

[page 257] A.G.R. *Copies de Simancas*, Vol. 18. Van Essen, v, 200.

A.G.R. *Copies de Simancas*, Vol. 18. Van Essen, v, 201.

[page 258] A.G.R. *Copies de Simancas*, Vol. 18. Van Essen, v, 201.

[page 259] *C. S. P. Spanish*, iv, Eliz., 207.

[page 261] *C. S. P. Spanish*, iv, Eliz., 295.

[page 262] *C. S. P. Spanish*, iv, Eliz., 245.

C. S. P. Spanish, iv, Eliz., 290.

[page 262f.] *C. S. P. Spanish*, iv, Eliz., 233.

[page 263] *C. S. P. Spanish*, iv, Eliz., 318.

[page 264 C. S. P. *Spanish*, iv, Eliz., 261. Van Essen, v, 214.
  /65]
[page 265] C. S. P. *Spanish*, iv, Eliz., 245.
[page 266] C. S. P. *Spanish*, iv, Eliz., 315. Van Essen, v, 220.
[page 266 Froude, *History of England*, Vol. 12, 388.
  /67]
[page 271] C. S. P. *Spanish*, iv, Eliz., 357. Van Essen, v, 222.
             C. S. P. *Spanish*, iv, Eliz., 394.
[page 272] C. S. P. *Spanish*, iv, Eliz., 360. Van Essen, v, 223.
[page 273] A.G.R. *Copies de Simancas*, Vol. 19. Van Essen, v, 224.
[page 275] C. S. P. *Spanish*, iv, Eliz., 365.
[page 277] C. S. P. *Spanish*, iv, Eliz., 400.
[page 278] C. S. P. *Spanish*, iv, Eliz., 439.
[page 279] C. S. P. *Spanish*, iv, Eliz., 366.
[page 280] C. S. P. *Spanish*, iv, Eliz., 370. Van Essen, v, 226.
[page 282] C. S. P. *Spanish*, iv, Eliz., 432.
[page 283] Azorín, *An Hour of Spain*, translated by Alice Raleigh
             (Travellers Library, 1933, 52–53).

Chapter 19

[page 290] A. L. Rowse, *The England of Elizabeth*, Vol. 1, 282.
[page 294] Lefèvre, *Correspondance (Pays Bas)*, iii, 504.
[page 296] Lefèvre, *Correspondance (Pays Bas)*, iii, 315. Van Essen,
             v, 290.
[page 297] Lefèvre, *Correspondance (Pays Bas)*, iii, 512.
[page 306] Lefèvre, *Correspondance (Pays Bas)*, iii, 591.
[page 310] Van Essen, v, 345.
[page 313] Van Essen, v, 355.
             Lefèvre, *Correspondance (Pays Bas)*, iii, 361.
[page 314] Lefèvre, *Correspondance (Pays Bas)*, iii, 531.
[page 315] Van Essen, v, 370.
[page 316] Lefèvre, *Correspondance (Pays Bas)*, iv, 106.
[page 317] *Le Testament Politique d'Alexandre Farnese*, in Bulletins de
             la Commission Royale d'Histoire, Brussels, 1922, Vol. 86, 171.
             Quoted in Van Essen, v, 383.

Chapter 20

[page 319 Appendix 2 to Gachard, *Lettres de Philippe II a ses Filles*, 74.
  /20/21]
[page 322] Quoted in Motley, *History of the United Netherlands*, iii,
             241.
[page 322 Ibid., 240.
  /23]

[page 325] Ibid., 244.
[page 329] Gachard, *Lettres de Philippe II a ses Filles*, Introduction, 45.

Chapter 21

[page 338] Strickland, iii, 475.
[page 341 Espejo, *El Interés de Dinero en los Reinos Españoles*, 502.
/42/43] Motley, *History of the United Netherlands*, iii, 414.

Chapter 22

[page 356] *Harleian Miscellany*, Vol. 2, 395.
[page 357] *Calendar of State Papers, Venetian*, ix, 1592/1603, 342.

Appendix

[page 364] *Calendar of State Papers, Spanish*, iv, Eliz., 502.
         Lefèvre, *Correspondance*, iii, 377.

BIBLIOGRAPHICAL NOTE

For the history of the Netherlands revolt the grandest and most detailed picture is provided in J. L. Motley's *Rise of the Dutch Republic* and its sequel *The History of the United Netherlands*. Modern scholarship however has varied many of Motley's judgments. The best corrective is supplied by Pieter Geyl's *Revolt of the Netherlands*, but one should also consult P. J. Blok's *People of the Netherlands*; H. Pirenne, *Histoire de Belgique*; G. Edmundson, *History of Holland*; Kervyn de Lettenhove, *Les Huguenots et les Gueux*; Burgon, *Life and Times of Sir Thomas Gresham*; and Conyers Read, *Life of Sir Francis Walsingham*.

Most of the earlier sources—Strada, Guiccardini, de Thou, Renon de France, Brantôme, Bor, Meteren—have found their way into the body and footnotes of Motley's books. But the documentary sources of letters of the times are of first-class importance. Foremost among them are the *Correspondance de Philippe II sur les Affaires des Pays Bas* (translated into French by M. Gachard and in the later volumes by J. Lefèvre); *Correspondance de Guillaume le Taciturne* (Gachard); *Correspondance de Marguerite d'Autriche, Duchesse de Parme* (Gachard, Lefèvre); *Archives et Correspondances Inédites de la Maison d'Orange-Nassau* (Groen van Prinsterer); *Relations des Ambassades Vénitiens* (Gachard). One should also consult *Calendar of State Papers* (Foreign), C. S. P. (Venetian), C. S. P. (Spanish).

For a general picture of Spain, two excellent modern authorities are J. H. Elliott, *Imperial Spain, 1469–1716*, also his essay "The Decline of Spain" in *Past and Present*, No. 20, 1961; and John Lynch, *Spain Under the Hapsburgs*, Vol. 1, *Empire and Absolutism, 1516–1598*. Also see Fernand Braudel, *La Méditerranée et le Monde Méditerranéen à l'Époque de Philippe II*; R. B. Merriman, *The Rise of the Spanish Empire*; R. Trevor Davies, *The Golden Century of Spain*; J. B. Trend, *The Civilisation of Spain*; R. Menéndez Pidal, *The Spaniards in Their History*; J. Klein, *The Mesta*. The Spanish "conciliar system" of government is well explained in H. Koenigsberger, *The Government of Sicily Under Philip II*. Political theory is dealt with by Bernice Hamilton in her *Political Thought in Sixteenth-Century Spain*.

For the literature of the period see Gerald Brenan, *The Literature of the Spanish People*. The intellectual background is set in A. F. G. Bell's *Luis de León*. See also W. J. Entwistle, *Cervantes* and Señor Salvador de Madariaga's *Don Quixote* "An Introductory Essay in Psychology."

For Portugal, see H. V. Livermore, *History of Portugal*.

For the Spanish empire in the Indies, the two great classics are of course Prescott's *History of the Conquest of Mexico* and *History of the Conquest of Peru*. For more modern studies see J. H. Parry's *The Spanish Seaborne Empire*, *The Age of Reconnaissance* and *The Spanish Theory of Empire in the Sixteenth Century*. See also Madariaga's *The Rise of the Spanish-American Empire* and *The Fall of the Spanish-American Empire;* C. H. Haring, *The Spanish Empire in America;* and F. A. Kirkpatrick, *The Spanish Conquistadores*.

The main authority for financial details of treasure shipments and trade is Earl J. Hamilton's *American Treasure and the Price Revolution in Spain, 1507–1650*. Hamilton's figures have been reassessed in studies by W. W. Borah, S. F. Cook and L. B. Simpson. See also H. and P. Chaunu, *Seville et l'Atlantique, 1504–1650*, and C. H. Haring, *Trade and Navigation Between Spain and the Indies*.

The Spanish Inquisition is dealt with magisterially and at length by H. C. Lea, *History of the Inquisition of Spain*. Shorter studies may be recommended, in particular Henry Kamen, *The Spanish Inquisition* and A. S. Turberville, *The Spanish Inquisition*.

The Armada battles are dealt with in J. K. Laughton's *State Papers Relating to the Defeat of the Spanish Armada;* J. S. Corbett, *The Spanish War*, also his *Drake and the Tudor Navy;* J. A. Williamson, *The Age of Drake;* and more recently in Garrett Mattingly's *The Defeat of the Spanish Armada* and Michael Lewis's *The Spanish Armada*. See also T. Woodrooffe, *The Enterprise of England*. For the Spanish side, see C. Fernández Duro, *La Armada Invencible*.

Consult Sir Charles Oman's *A History of the Art of War in the Sixteenth Century* for land battles of the period. Robert Fruin's *The Siege of Leyden* is a detailed study of this key incident.

The leading figures of the period have all been described at length and in depth by many writers.

Philip II. One may begin with Prescott's biography, but this is diffuse and incomplete. An interesting article by H. Lapeyre in *Bulletin Hispanique*, 1957, *"Autour de Philippe II,"* should be read as an introduction to both King and biographers. Motley's view is marred by gross bias. J. H. Mariejol's *The Master of the Armada* is a French version which has been translated by W. B. Wells. Sir Charles Petrie's *Philip II* is a recent study (1963). However, Philip is perhaps best seen and understood in his voluminous correspondence in the editions edited by Gachard and Lefèvre and in his letters from Portugal to his daughters, the Infantas (Gachard).

The King's great antagonist William the Silent, Prince of Orange, is the subject of biographies by R. Putnam, C. V. Wedgwood and F. Harrison. He also is however best seen in his own letters under the editing of Gachard and Groen van Prinsterer.

The Emperor Charles V is the subject of an outstanding book by Karl Brandi. See also Royall Tyler, *The Emperor Charles V*.

The Duke of Alva may be glimpsed in *La Correspondance du duc d'Albe sur l'invasion du Comte Louis de Nassau en Frise* (Gachard). Motley does full justice to his despotic nature.

The romantic life of Don John of Austria is displayed in Stirling Maxwell's classic biography. See also G. Slocum.

For Alexander Farnese, later Duke of Parma, see Léon van der Essen. This book and Parma's own correspondence in the Gachard/Lefèvre collections are of great interest and engage one's sympathy for this most brilliant and long-suffering of Philip's servants.

For other notable figures, consult Gregorio Maranon, *Antonio Pérez* (translated by C. D. Ley); the correspondence of *Cardinal Granvelle* (edited by Piot); Agnes Strickland, *Lives of the Queens of England*, Vols. 2 and 3; A. L. Rowse, *The England of Elizabeth;* J. E. Neale, *Queen Elizabeth I* and *The Age of Catherine de Medici;* P. de Vaissièro, *Henri IV;* M. Reinhard, *Henry IV;* L. Pastor, *The History of the Popes from the Close of the Middle Ages; The Life of Saint Teresa* (translated by J. M. Cohen).

INDEX

Abjuration, the (1581), 224–25, 354
Abjurations, Inquisition and, 102, 103
Accord, the, 80–81, 82
Acts of Supremacy and Uniformity, 39
Aerschot, Duke of, 62, 81, 83, 124, 166, 167, 168, 175, 241; exiled, 331; and William of Orange, 183, 184
Africa, 87, 119. *See also* specific places
Aisne River, 298
Albert, Cardinal Archduke, 333, 346–47, 349, 350, 354
Alcabala, 96, 122
Alcantara, battle of, 211
Alcantara, order of, 8, 89
Alcazar-el-Kebir, 208, 209
Alicante, 10
Aljubarrota, 208
Alkmaar, 46, 135; siege of, 136–39, 154
Alost, 167, 169
Alpujarras, 89, 362; revolt of Moriscos in, 119–20
Alva, Fernando Alvarez de Toledo, Duke of, 14, 61, 63, 69, 71, 105–38, 173, 178, 179, 237, 302, 327; and Charles V, 106; conscripts army, 86; described, 105–6, 107–8, 116, 235; Netherlands regime, 105–38, 147–48, 149, 151, 152, 237, 243, 244, 245, 330; and Philip II, 106, 108–9, 111, 115, 118, 122, 123–25, 138, 146, 147–48, 149, 152; and Portugal, 210–11, 316; replaced by Requesens, 148, 149; and war with Papacy, 28–31; and William of Orange, 116–18, 122, 138
America(s). *See* Caribbean Islands; Indies; New World; specific places
Amiens, 344

Amsterdam, 80, 85, 127, 134, 135, 153, 288, 292, 353; Declaration of Independence, 224; described, 46, 351–52; loss of, 190
Anabaptism (Anabaptists), 47–48, 52, 133
Andalusia, 10, 12, 89, 95, 97, 147, 341, 343
Anglican Church, 39
Anjou, Francis of Alençon, Duke of, 178n, 189–91, 214, 222, 223, 225–31, 234, 290; death of, 231–32; described, 225–26, 231–32; and Elizabeth I, 226–27
Anna of Saxony, Princess, 57–58, 73, 162
Anne of Austria (fourth wife of Philip II), 129, 140, 162; death of, 338
Anne of Austria (granddaughter of Philip II), 346
Antonio, Don, 209, 210–11
Antwerp, 56, 68, 76, 83, 84–86, 232; Anjou and, 228, 229–30; and Armada, 256–57, 344; decline of, 348–40, 351; described (1559) 45–46; desecration of Cathedral and churches in, 78–80, 81; Don Juan's attempt on, 178–80; fall of, 169–71; "French Fury," 229–30, 232; Parma's attacks on, 219, 234, 236–42, 243, 348; and rebellion, 111, 123, 124–25, 151–52, 169–71, 234, 236–42, 292, 293, 305, 307; "Spanish Fury," 171, 314
Apologia (William of Orange), 48, 222–24
Aragon, 4, 5, 8, 12, 88, 89, 95, 96; Council of, 93–94; Inquisition, 100; trouble in (1590–92), 334–37

Aranjuez, 141
Arceo (Secretary), 276, 278, 364
"Archdukes," Provinces of the, 347, 349, 350, 354
Aremberg, Count, 49, 81, 113
Armada, Spanish (1588), 2, 15, 91, 92, 97, 240, 246, 247–83, 284, 285, 293, 316, 340, 343, 361; defeat and casualties, 281–83; effects of, 284, 285, 290, 302, 313–14; map of route of, 248; Parma's movements at height of crisis, 314–15
Armada, Spanish (1596), 340–44
Armada, Spanish (1597), 344
Armenteros (secretary of Margaret of Parma), 63, 64
Army, Spanish, 29–38, 43, 54ff., 61; and Armada, 249ff.; expenses, 148, 151, 152; and French campaigns, 293–315; mutinies, 151–52, 155, 166, 168–71, 294, 315, 330, 331; and Netherlands rebellions, 106–38 passim, 148–60 passim, 165–71, 172–94 passim, 218ff., 234–42, 249ff.; 305ff., 325–38, 344; at Rocroi, 353
Arras, 317, 326, 327; Treaty of, 218, 220, 221, 227; Union of, 215, 217–18
Artois, 49, 81, 112, 189, 214, 215, 216, 348
Ascoli, Prince of, 280, 364
Assonleville, Councilor, 74, 328
Asturias, 10
Augsburg, Peace of, 26
Aumale, 309
Austria, 4, 5, 6, 7, 17, 183, 184, 187–88, 220, 316
Autos-da-fé, 87–88, 103, 104, 142, 363
Avila, Sancho d', 169
Azores, 211
Azorín (José Martinez Ruiz), 283, 359
Aztecs, 198, 361

Babington Plot, 251
Badovaro, describes Philip II as timid, 25–26
Balboa, Vasco Núñez de, 197, 199, 313
Balearic Islands, 101
Bands of Ordonnance, 29, 60, 74
Barbary pirates, 119, 120, 362
Barcelona, 12, 97

Barents, Willem, 352
Bayonne, 71
Beauvoir, Lorde de, 84, 85
Bedford, Earl of, 33
Beggars (Beggar party), 73, 74, 81, 85–86, 112, 113, 125, 152–60, 179. See also Sea Beggars
Belgium, 194, 296, 346
Bergen-op-Zoom, 293, 313
Berghen, Count, 74, 111
Berlaymont, Count, 52, 73, 81, 83, 107, 109, 124
Beveren, 236, 238, 241
Beza, Theodore, 39
Bijns, Anna, 47
Biron, Marshal de, 209–10, 311
Biscay, Bay of, 97, 254
Bishoprics, creation of, 48–49, 51, 55–56
Black Death (epidemic), 98–99. See also Plague
Black Prince (son of Edward III, King of England), 254, 311n
Blanchetache, 211n
Blois, 59, 285–86
Blomberg, Barbara (the widow Kegell), 173
Blood Council, 109–10, 111–12, 123, 124, 128, 138, 149, 174
Bohemia, 16
Boisot, Louis de, 155, 156–58, 159–60
Boleyn, Anne, 59
Bommel, 151
Bosch, Hieronymus, 47
Bossu, Count, 128, 129, 138, 190, 191, 240
Bouges, 192
Bourbon, Cardinal, 287, 308
Bourbons, 346. See also specific individuals
Bourbourg, 274, 290
Brabant, 41, 44–45, 46, 49, 55, 58, 182, 183, 288–90, 296, 302, 307, 314, 330, 348, 353; and rebellion (1567–85), 116, 130, 132, 134, 167–68, 169, 190, 191, 224, 234ff.
Braganza, Duchess of, 208
Braganza, Duke of, 141
Brantôme, Pierre de Bourdeilles, Signeur de, 31, 34, 35, 106
Bray, Guy de, 58
Brazil, 13, 211, 362

Breda, 86, 165, 296, 302–4, 353
Brederode, Count, 66, 69, 72, 73–74, 77, 82, 83, 85
Breughel, Peter, 44, 46
Brill, 126, 128, 134, 136, 223
Brissac, de, 325
Brittany, 275, 323, 324
Bronkhorst (Governor of Leyden), 155
Broodhuis (Brussels), 114
Bruges, 44, 67, 234, 235, 236, 275, 297, 364
Brussels, 8, 19, 41n, 56, 66, 69, 71, 73, 80, 184, 185, 326, 346, 348, 350; abdication by Charles V in, 2–9; in Alva's regime, 107, 109, 113–14, 122, 147; described (1559), 44–45; Don John in, 174–78, 184; fall of, 234, 238, 241; Parma in, 296, 300, 316–17; Requesens' regime, 148; Union of, 172–73, 175, 184, 215
Bruxelles, Vicomte de, 3, 239, 240
Buren, Anna van, 118
Buren, Philip William of Orange, Count of, 54, 86, 111, 295
Burghley, William Cecil, Lord, 33, 192, 226, 251
Burgos, 13, 97
Burgundy, 2, 3, 4–5, 8, 25, 41, 42–43, 164, 347, 358

Cabrera de Córdoba, Luis, 18, 265
Cádiz, 203, 252, 254, 270, 284; Anglo-Dutch attack on, 340–41
Calais, 30, 34–38, 273, 276, 277, 280, 338, 345, 364
Calais Roads, 269, 272, 279
Calatrava, order of, 8, 89
Calderón, Pedro Coco, 278
Calderón de la Barca, Pedro, 96, 330
Calificadores, 102
Calvin (John) and Calvinism (Calvinists), 5, 21, 39–41, 58, 107, 182, 360; and Armada, 255; in France (see Huguenots); and Netherlands rebellions, 48, 53, 58, 72–86, 98, 127, 132, 154–60, 212–33, 234–42, 242–46, 288, 350, 352, 354
Cambrai, 49, 69, 226, 331
Campagna, Roman, 30
Canary Islands, 101
Cantabrian Mountains, 10

Cape Verde Islands, 211
Caraffa, Giovanni Pietro. See Paul IV, Pope
Caraffa family, 26, 28
Carande, on expenditures by Charles V, 22
Caribbean islands, 5, 8, 121, 197–207, 234–44, 249, 284, 362. See also Indies
Carinthia, 5
Carlos, Don (Infante), 9, 119; imprisonment and death of, 142–45, 162, 355
Carrera de Indias, 13, 164, 202–4, 269, 341
Cartagena, 203, 206
Casa de la Contratación, 202
Cascais, 211
Castile, 4, 6, 8, 9, 12–16, 20, 23, 24, 27, 146, 163, 164; Cortes, 88; Council of, 93; described, 95; economy, 97; Inquisition, 99, 100; Philip II and, 87, 88, 89, 95; and Portugal, 207–8
Catalans, 12, 88, 95
Catalina (Infanta), 140–42
Catalonia, 5, 100
Câteau-Cambrésis, 38, 39, 48, 58–59, 225, 308, 362
Catherine (daughter of Philip II). See Savoy, Catherine, Duchess of
Catherine of Aragon, 17
Catherine de Medici (French queen), 59–60, 71, 130, 189, 208; death of, 286
Catholicism (Catholics), 4, 5–6, 15–16, 21, 26–30, 39, 87–88, 90–92, 96 (see also Papacy; specific individuals); and Armada, 250–51, 253, 262; and Counter-Reformation (see Counter-Reformation); and France, 286–87ff., 208–18, 219ff.; and Inquisition (see Inquisition); and Netherlands rebellions, 39, 47–50, 51–86, 105–38 passim, 147–70 passim, 172–81, 182–94, 212ff., 234ff., 340–47, 350, 352, 359
Catholic League (the Holy League), 72–75, 77, 81–82, 114, 122, 245, 285, 286–87, 296, 297, 299, 300, 305ff., 219ff., 345

Caudebec, 311, 312, 317
Cavallo, describes Netherlands, 47
Cavalry, Army, 29, 35, 61, 116, 151, 170, 297, 305
Cecil, Lord. *See* Burghley, William Cecil, Lord
Celestina, La (Rojas), 99
Cellerigo, Gonzalez de, 359–60
Censorship, 104. *See also* Index, the
Cercamps, 35, 36, 37
Cerralvo, Marquis, 316
Cervantes Saavedra, Miquel de, 1–2, 15, 95–96, 120, 186, 330, 333
Challes, 298
Champagney (Antwerp governor), 169, 170, 314–15, 350
Chantonay, quoted on Philip II's irresolution, 70
Charenton, 298
Charles V, Emperor (Charles I of Spain), 25, 26, 30, 33, 34, 49, 54, 57, 87, 89, 90, 360; abdication of, 2–9, 54; Alva and, 106; and Antwerp defenses, 236, 237; described, 4–9, 18–20, 38, 43, 54, 143, 238, 360; edicts of, 104, 119, 172, 174; and finances, 22–23, 30; and Indies, 201; and Netherlands, 41, 42, 43, 47–48, 49, 51, 164, 236, 237; and Philip II, 2–9, 17–20, 21, 26, 51, 70, 87, 167, 360; and Portugal, 208; and Protestants, 47–48, 49
Charles IX, King of France, 59, 129, 131, 139
Charles the Bold (of Burgundy), 4, 17
Charlotte de Bourbon, 162, 232
Chartres, 324
Chièvres, M. de, 23, 90
China, 352
Church, Spanish, 15–16, 30, 34; and Armada, 262–63, 341; and Indies, 200–1; and Inquisition, 98–104; Philip II and, 90–92, 96
Churchill, Sir Winston S., 70
Cimaroons, 205–6
Clement, Jacques, 286
Clément VIII, Pope, 345
Cobham, Lord, 191
Coligny, Gaspard de, 32, 38, 118, 130
Cologne, 188; conference, 216–17, 220, 222
Columbus, Christopher, 4, 197, 207

Compromise of the Nobles, 72–75, 111, 167
Condé, Prince of, 33
Connaught, 282
Conquistadores, 5, 12, 197–202, 207, 361
Consejo de la Hacienda (Finance Council), 21, 22–23
Consejo de la Suprema y General Inquisición, 101
Consulado, 202
Consulta, 2, 54, 57, 63, 94
Contarini, describes Philip II, 244
Conversos, 13, 99–100, 104
Corbeil, 299, 300
Corbett, Julian, 271
Cordilleras, 10
Córdoba, 12, 119
Cortes, 12, 88, 96, 341, 361
Cortés, Hernando, 198, 199, 201, 313
Corunna, 51, 263, 266–67, 341
Council of Blood (Council of Troubles or of Tumults), 109–10, 111–12, 123, 124, 128, 138, 149, 174
Councils, royal, 43, 51–52, 93–94, 95. *See also* specific councils
Council of State, 93, 108, 166–67, 291, 328
Counter-Reformation, 29, 52, 67, 90, 96, 213, 350, 354
Courts, 43, 46, 92. *See also* specific courts
Crécy, 287, 311n
Cruzada, 90, 91
Cuba, 197, 200
Culemburg, Count, 72, 73–74
Currency (specie), 14, 21–24, 31, 97, 121, 342
Cuyck, Jan van, 126–27
Cyprus, 120

Darien, 205, 206
"Day of the Barricades," 285, 286
Declaration of Independence (Netherlands provinces) 224–25, 354
Defeat of the Spanish Armada (Mattingly), 260–61
De la Marck, Lumey, 125–26
Delfland, 154, 156
Delft, 46, 80, 127, 135, 155, 160, 232–33
Denia, Marquis of (later Duke of Lerma), 356

Deventer, 115, 256, 305, 306
Diego, Don (Infante), 140, 162
Diest, 234
Dominican friars, 100
Don Quixote (Cervantes), 1–2, 10, 13, 27n, 95–96, 120, 186, 359
Dordt, 127, 128
Doria, Andrea, Admiral, 5, 106, 192
Douai, 214
Doullens, 331
Dover, Strait of, 250
Drake, Sir Francis, 23, 205–7; and Armada, 249, 252–53, 254, 259, 267, 270–71; at Cádiz, 243–44, 249, 271, 276; death of death, 278
Drake and the Tudor Navy (Corbett), 271
Dudley, Robert, 37
Dumas, Chicot the Jester by, 285
Dunkirk, 230, 231, 234, 255, 256, 257, 265, 266, 272, 273, 276, 280; Parma and Armada crisis, 364–65; Spinola captures, 353
Dutch East India Company, 292, 353
Dutch language, 41, 42, 46, 75

East Indies, Dutch, 292, 353
Eboli, Princess of, 334–35
Eboli, Ruy Gómez de Silva, Prince of, 145–46, 147–48, 195, 209, 245, 260, 356
Ebro, 10, 337
Edict of Blood (1550), 47–48
Edicts of Faith, 101
Edicts of Grace, 101
Edward III, King of England, 254, 311n
Egmont, Count (Lamoral, Prince of Gavre), 33, 35, 49, 50, 62, 81; and Alva, 107, 108–9; arrest and execution of, 109–11, 114–15, 317; described, 53; and Philip II, 68–71; and Protestant heresy, 53, 54, 55, 62, 63, 64, 65, 66, 68–69, 71, 72, 74, 81, 82, 83, 86; and William of Orange, 54, 63, 72, 86
Egmont, Countess, 73
Egmont, Philip, Count of, 241, 295
Eindhoven, 234
Electors, imperial, 8, 21
El Greco. See Greco, El
Elizabeth I, Queen of England, 30, 39,

59, 125, 205–6; and Armada, 247, 251–52, 255–56, 263, 264, 273–74, 282; Anjou and, 226–27, 228; described, 37, 226–27; Drake and, 23, 205–6, 251; Essex and, 345; and France, 60, 121–22, 131, 226–27, 243–45, 322, 337–38; and Netherlands, 176, 189–92, 223, 225, 228, 231, 243–46, 255–56, 258, 264, 289, 337–38, 340, 354; and Parma, 251–52, 264, 273–74, 290; and Philip II, 36–38, 205–6, 251, 322; plots against, 121–22, 205–6, 251; and Spain, 36–38, 121–22, 125, 176, 189–92, 205–6, 223, 225, 228, 231, 243–46, 247, 251–52, 255–56, 340, 342–44, 345
Elizabeth Tudor. See Elizabeth I, Queen of England
Elizabeth of Valois, 38, 39, 87–88, 119, 140, 143, 287, 320; death of, 145
Elliott, J. H., 359
Emden, 116, 125
Emperor Charles V, The (Tyler), 22
Ems River, 116
Encabezamiento, 96
Encomiendas, 200, 201
England, 9, 16, 19, 21, 23, 30, 39 (see also Elizabeth I, Queen of England); Acts of Supremacy and Uniformity, 39; and France, 34–38, 121–22, 226–27, 243–45, 285, 337–38, 345; and the Indies, 195, 203, 204ff., 343, 345; and Ireland, 94; and Netherlands, 121–22, 223, 225, 228, 231, 243–46, 249ff., 264, 290–92, 302, 315; and Parma, 251–52, 264, 273–74, 315; and Spain, 87, 95, 121–22, 174, 176, 189–92, 195, 203, 204ff., 217, 223, 225, 231, 243–46, 247–83, 284, 308, 330, 340–45, 362; and Spanish Armada, 240, 246, 247–83, 284, 285
Enkhuizen, 126, 127, 135, 138, 292, 351
Erasmus, Desiderius, 39, 46, 360
Ernest, Archduke, 320, 321n; Netherlands regime of, 316, 319, 328–31, 344; replaces Parma, 316, 319
Escadrille Volant, 59

Escovedo, Juan de, 176, 179, 186, 334, 337, 355
Escurial, the, 34, 49, 91, 92, 96, 140, 146–47, 278; Philip's last days in, 354–57
Essex, Earl of, 345; Cádiz raid (1596) by, 284, 340
Excusado, 91
Eyck, Jan van, 47

Fabritius, 68
Farnese, Alexander. *See* Parma, Alexander Farnese, Duke of
Ferdinand, Don (The Grand Prior), 106, 109, 129
Ferdinand I (Holy Roman Emperor), 7, 8, 20, 54
Ferdinand V, King of Aragon and Castile, 4, 5, 12, 13, 88, 90, 100
Feria, Count, 35, 37
Ferrol, El, 344
Field preaching, 75–76, 77, 80, 82
Finance Council, 43, 51–52, 68, 94
Finisterre, 259, 341
Flanders, 41, 42, 44, 46, 49, 67, 80, 81, 110, 131, 167, 169, 182, 186, 189, 224, 332, 350; Anjou attacks, 229; and Armada, 257, 258, 264, 266, 279; Parma's attacks on, 231, 234; rebellion (1589–92), 288–90, 297, 306, 307, 314
Fleece, Order of. *See* Golden Fleece, Order of the
Flemish language, 46, 186
Flemish mercenaries, 29
Florida, 204
Flotas, 203, 204
Flushing, 50, 83, 84, 126, 134, 136, 227, 292, 350
"Forty," Corporation of the, 155–56
France, 4, 6–7, 16, 21, 23, 39, 117, 284–87; and Armada, 249, 276, 284; and England, 34–38, 121–22, 226–27, 243–45, 285, 337–38, 345; Huguenots (*see* Huguenots); and Indies, 204; and Netherlands rebellion, 41, 42, 48, 107, 112, 117, 121–22, 129, 189–90, 191, 215, 223, 226–33, 284–87, 296, 300–18; and Portugal, 211; religious wars in, 58–60, 88, 117, 118, 130–32, 288–318, 319–31; and Spain, 25–38,

121–22, 130–32, 164, 187, 213, 215, 217, 223, 228–33, 243–45, 284–87, 288–318, 319–25, 331, 332–39, 344–46, 354, 361, 362
Franche Comté, 4. *See also* Burgundy
Francis I, King of France (François of Valois), 6–7, 25, 28, 204, 337
Francis II, King of France, 59
Frankfurt Diet, 62
Frederick (Fadrique), Don, 129, 132–34, 135, 136
"French Fury," 229–30, 232
French mercenaries, 117
Friesland, 42, 49, 80, 112, 113, 127, 215, 224, 291, 296, 301
Froude, *History of England* by, 266–67
Fruin, Robert, 159
Fuentes, Count of, 316–17, 319, 327–28, 331–33
Fueros, 88, 95, 334, 337
Fuggers, 7

Gachard, on Orange's Walcheren attempt, 83
Galeones, 203, 206
Galicia, 10
Gallican Church, 323–24
Gascon infantry, 31, 33
Gascony, 58
Geertruidenberg, 293, 326
Gelderland, 42, 127, 132, 215, 291
Gembloux, 185, 187, 188
Geneva, 39–40, 48, 58, 107
Genoa, 28
Gérard, Balthazar ("Guion"), 232–33
Germania, Valencian, 89
German mercenaries, 29, 31, 33, 34, 82, 117, 134, 149, 151, 154, 169
Germany, 4, 5, 6, 7, 16, 21, 24, 26, 29, 39, 57; Charles V and war in, 360, 362; and Lutheranism, 47; and Netherlands, 41, 42, 47, 48, 112, 113, 115, 118; Philip II and, 87
Geyl, Professor, 127–28
Ghent, 50, 80, 85, 110, 168, 186, 189, 214, 215, 232, 293, 307, 348; fall of, 234, 236, 240; Pacification of, 171, 172–73, 175
Giambelli, floating bombs of, 238–42
Glippers, 154, 155

Goes, 134

Gold, 14, 21, 22–24, 197–98, 201–2, 206, 342

Golden Fleece, Order of the, 3, 8, 46, 49, 60–61, 72, 73, 74, 114

Gombert, N., 47

Góngora y Agorte, Luis de, 96, 330

Gorcum, 127

Gouda, 127, 128

Gourdan, Duke of, 276

Granada, 12, 13, 99, 100, 104, 119

Grandees. See Nobility

Granvelle, Antony Perrenot, Cardinal, 51–52, 54, 55, 56–57, 60–70, 148, 169, 187, 188, 245; and France, 60; and Parma, 222, 235; and Philip II, 52, 56, 57, 60–70, 195, 209–10, 225; and Portugal, 209–10; and Protestants, 56–57, 60, 61, 62–70, 209–10; and William of Orange, 60, 61–64, 228–29

Gravelines, 35, 277, 279

Greco, El, 96, 146

Gregory, St., 33

Gresham, Sir Thomas, 85

Groeneweg, 156–57

Groningen, 41, 42, 49, 80, 115, 182, 224, 304, 305, 326, 330, 352

Guadalquivir, 203

Guadalupe, Sentence of, 88

Guiccardini, Francesco, 44, 45, 46

Guise, Francis of Lorraine, 2nd Duke of, 31, 34, 35

Guise, Henry of Lorraine (the "Bale-fré"), 3rd duke of, 285–86, 308, 320, 321

Guises (house of Guise), 38, 59, 60, 131, 232, 245, 249, 285–86. See also individual members

Gunpowder Plot, 36

Haarlem, 46, 76, 127, 352; capture of, 135, 136, 138, 148, 154; Parma raids, 219

Hague, The, 46, 159, 224, 337

Hainaut, 167, 189, 190, 214, 215, 216, 348

Hals, Frans, 46, 352

Ham (French town), 331

Hammes, Nicholas de, 72

Hapsburgs, 3–4, 5, 7, 17, 35, 48, 143, 208, 209, 318, 346. See also individual members

Haren, Adam van, 126

Hawkins, Sir John, 121, 204–5, 243, 284

"Hedge sermons," 75–76

Heiligerlee, 113, 114, 115, 191, 344

Henry, King-Cardinal of Portugal, 209, 210

Henry II, King of France, 31, 39, 58–59

Henry III, King of France, 284–87, 294, 308, 320, 322

Henry IV, (Henry of Navarre), King of France, 59, 130, 178, 223, 232, 238, 245, 285, 286–87, 294; and Parma's campaigns, 295, 297–300, 209–13, 325; Philip II and, 345–46, 358; and succession to throne, 322–25, 326; and war with Spain, 337–39

Henry V, King of England, 34, 35

Henry VIII, King of England, 50, 243

Henry the Impotent, (Henry IV, King of Castile), 146

Heraugière, Captain, 302–4

Herrera (Spanish artist), 96

Hesse, Landgrave of, 113, 162

Hessels, Councilor, 110, 111

Hèze, Baron, 167

Hidalgos, 90, 97

Hispaniola, 197, 200, 206

Histoire des Troubles aux Pays Bas (Van der Vynckt), 71

History of the Art of War in the Sixteenth Century (Omar), 312

History of the United Netherlands (Motley), 290–92

Holland, 41, 46, 49, 71, 75, 80, 85, 234, 300ff., 347; and Armada, 255; and rebellion (1567–73), 127, 128, 131, 132, 134–36; (1573–74), 149, 153, 154, 160, 161, 163, 167–71; (1576–77), 172–73, 174, 175; 1577–78), 182, 190–91; (1578–84), 213–14, 215, 223, 224, 228; (1589–92), 288ff.; (1598), 351ff.

Holy League. See Catholic League (the Holy League)

Holy Lion, monastery of, 113

Holy Roman Empire, 5, 41, 114, 116

Hoogstraten, Count, 66, 69, 83, 111, 112; killed, 117

Hoorn, 127, 292

Horn, Count, 62, 63, 65, 66, 74, 108–9; arrest and execution of, 110, 111, 114–15

Howard of Effingham, Lord Admiral, 267, 269–70, 273, 281; and Cádiz attack, 340

Huguenots, 39, 58, 59–61, 213, 285–94, 297ff., 308–31 passim (see also France: religious wars in); and Edict of Nantes, 345; and Netherlands rebellion, 112, 118, 129, 130–32

Hulst, 307, 325

Hundredth Penny (tax), 122–25

Ibarra, Esteban de, 328–29

Iberian mountain range, 10

Iberian peninsula, map of (sixteenth century), 11

Idiaquez (secretary to Philip II), 314, 364–65

Incas, 198

Index, the, 39

Indian Ocean, 362

Indian mines, 13, 14, 22, 23, 148, 163, 195–204, 214

Indies, Spanish, 5, 8, 13, 14, 63–64, 88, 89, 95–96, 121, 195–211, 342–43, 345, 359–61; fleet of, 13, 164, 202–4, 269, 341; map of, 196

Indies fleet (Indies Guard), 13, 164, 202–4, 269, 341

Infantry, 29, 31, 297

Inquisition, Italian, 28

Inquisition, Spanish, 13, 15–16, 87, 90, 98–104; abjurations and, 102, 103; Council of, 94, 101; Edicts of Faith, 101; Edicts of Grace, 101; in Netherlands, 55–56, 62, 67–68, 71, 72, 360; punishments, 102–4

Institutes of the Christian Religion (Calvin), 41

Inter Caetera (Papal Bull), 197

Ireland and the Irish, 94, 281–82, 341

Isabella, Empress (Isabella of Portugal, mother of Philip II), 17, 195, 209, 220

Isabella I, Queen of Castile, 4–5, 12, 13, 15, 90, 100

Isabella Clara Eugenia (Infanta), 140–42, 287, 297, 299, 308, 317, 320, 321, 338; closeness to father, Philip II, 339, 355; marriage to Archduke Albert, 345—47; and Netherlands, 346–47, 349, 350, 354, 356

Islam, 12, 15. See also Moors (Moriscos); Moslems

Isthmus of Panama, 4, 7, 30, 203, 205, 206, 207

Italy, 12, 19, 23, 24, 26–31, 36, 96, 313, 315, 362; Council of, 94

Ivry, battle of, 286, 295

Jarnac, 118

Java Sea, 292

Jemmingen, 115–16, 117, 129, 138

Jesuits, 90, 147

Jews, 13, 23, 27, 98–100; Inquisition and, 98–100

Joanna, Queen, 4, 7, 139, 143

John (Juan) of Austria, Don, 119, 137; death of, 193–94, 318; described, 178, 186, 193–94, 313; and Escovedo, 334–35; Netherlands regime of, 173–81, 183–94, 214, 217, 218, 222, 244, 245; and Philip II, 176–77, 186–93 passim

John Casimir, Count Palatine of the Rhine, 188–89, 190, 191, 213, 215, 221

John of the Cross, St., 96

John of Nassau (brother of William the Silent), 150

John of Nassau (son of William the Silent), 301

Joinville, Treaty of, 249

Judería (Jewish ghetto), 99

Julius II, Pope, 28

Juros, 163

Justicia, office of, 335–36

Justin of Nassau (son of William the Silent), 238, 256

Kapelle, 154

Kempis. See Thomas à Kempis

"King's Rock" (or "King's Chair"), 92

Kirklaan road, 158, 159–60

Knights of St. John, 106

Knodsenberg, 305

Knox, John, 39

Koevorden, 326

Kouwenstein dyke, 240, 242

La Fère, 32, 33
Lagny, 298, 300, 305
Lalaing (stadtholder), 189
La Mancha. See Mancha, La
"Land Jubilees," 47
Landscheiding, 154–55, 156, 157
Landsknechts, 29, 31
Languet, Hubert, 148
Langueville, Duke of, 33
Lannen, 159–60
Lasso (de Lattre), Orlando, 47
Laughton, John Knox, 268, 271
Lawrence, St., 34, 278, 299–300
Laws and lawyers, 43, 94, 201
League, Catholic Holy. See Catholic
   League
LeBlas, punished by Inquisition, 67
Le Catelet, 331
Legazpa (envoy of Charles V), 22
Le Havre, 60, 311, 312
Leicester, Earl of, 225, 226, 227, 244,
   246, 249, 255–56, 290, 291, 302,
   350; death of, 291; Dutch dislike
   of, 337
Leipsic, 58
Leon, 8, 10, 95
León, Louis de, 96
León, Pedro de, 272
Lepanto, battle of (1571), 1, 15, 120–
   21, 122, 361
Lewis, Michael, 261, 268, 271
Lewis William of Nassau, 301
Leyden, 80, 127, 135, 149; siege of,
   152–60, 161, 164
Leyderdorp, 158, 159–60
Leyva, Alonso de, 268
Leyva, Sancho de, 294
Lille, 214
Lillebonne, 312
Lima, Peru, 199
Lisbon, 12, 210, 211, 252–53, 259, 260,
   262, 282, 341. See also Portugal
Lizard, the, 267, 270
London, 35; Antwerp compared to, 45
Loos, 117
Lorraine, Louis, 2nd duke de Guise,
   Cardinal of, 286, 321
Lorraine, Duchess of, 57, 287
Los Cobos (secretary to Philip II),
   22–23, 93
Louis XIV, King of France, 91
Louis XVI, King of France, 285

Louis of Nassau, Count, 53, 72, 112,
   113, 115–16, 118, 129, 130, 131–
   32; death of, 149–50
Louise de Coligny, 232–33
Louvain, University of, 47, 86, 111–12,
   175, 176
Low Countries, 2, 11, 39, 60, 111, 121,
   130, 132, 151, 187, 189, 193, 297,
   315, 362. See also specific places
Luther (Martin), and Lutheranism, 5–
   6, 21, 29, 67, 81, 84, 118; and Netherlands, 47–50, 57, 360
Luxemburg, 4, 41, 107, 172–73, 174,
   184

Maastricht, 85, 117, 149–50, 183; fall
   of, 219–20, 221, 235, 305
Machiavelli, Niccolò, 27
Madrid, 92, 111
Magistrates, 92, 126, 127
Malaga, 10
"Malcontents," 214, 216, 221
Mancha, La, 10
Manoel the Fortunate, King of Portugal,
   208, 209
Manrique, Jorge, 280, 364
Mansfeld, Charles, count of, 72, 111,
   241, 275, 297, 308, 310–11, 314–
   15
Mansfeld, Peter Ernest, count of, 72, 81,
   82, 111, 308, 310, 314–15, 331
Maps: division of Netherlands at Philip's
   death, 349; embattled Netherlands
   (1568–98), 137; Iberian peninsula
   (sixteenth century), 40; Netherlands (before rebellion), 40; Parma's
   French campaigns, 289; route of
   Armada of 1588, 248; Spanish empire in Indies, 196
Marche-en-Famine, 175
Margaret, Duchess of Parma, 49, 184–
   85, 186, 187, 188, 200–21; described, 51; and Granvelle, 63,
   64, 66; and Philip II, 51, 63, 65,
   76, 77, 82, 107–8, 220–21; regime
   in Netherlands of (1559–67), 51–
   86, 148; replaced by Alva, 105,
   107–8; signs "Accord," 80–82
Margate Point, 254–55, 265
Marguerite de Valois (Navarre queen),
   130, 178, 225, 228
Marian Fathers, 19

Maria Theresa (French queen), 346n
Marne River, 298
Marnix, John of Tholouse, 53, 72, 84
Marnix, Philip of St. Aldegonde, 53, 72, 128, 150, 237, 240
Martin, St., 323–24
Mary, Duchess of Burgundy, 4
Mary (Mary Stuart), Queen of Scots, 57, 173, 174, 222, 245
Mary I (Mary Tudor), Queen of England, 7, 8–9, 30, 31, 35, 36, 38, 164, 267; childlessness of, 87, 346
Matthias, Archduke, 183–88, 189, 221, 223, 224, 229, 316
Mattingly, Garrett, 260–61, 271
Maurice, Elector-Duke of Saxony, 7, 57
Maurice of Nassau, Prince of Orange, 137, 301–4, 305, 306–7, 325–26, 332, 353; Groningen surrenders to, 353; victory at Turnhout, 344
Mauritshuis, 47
Maximilian I (Holy Roman Emperor), 4, 17
Maximilian II (Holy Roman Emperor), 4, 8, 62, 114, 116, 129, 130, 143–44
Maya Indians, 198
Mayenne, Charles of Guise, duke of, 286, 287, 295, 296, 297–300, 305, 311, 312; convokes States General, 319; distrust of, 309, 310–11
Meaux, 297, 298
Mechlin, 43, 49, 132, 133, 178, 191, 224; archbishopric of, 56
Medenblik, 127
Medici, Giovanni Angelo. See Pius IV, Pope
Medina Celi, Duke of, 136, 148
Medina del Campo, 97, 164, 343
Medina Sidonia, Alonso de Guzmán el Bueno, duke of, 259–64; and Armada, 255, 259–83 passim, 293, 314, 364; Relation of, 271, 277
Mediterranean Sea, 121, 122
Megen (Netherlands grandee), 81
Meghem, Count, 115
Melancthon, Philipp, 6
Memling, Hans, 47
Mendoza, Bernardino de, 116, 146, 285, 325
Mendoza, Pedro de, 192, 252n, 314
Mercedes, 62

Merriman, Professor, 139
Meseta, 10, 14, 15, 120
Mesta, 13, 96
Methodism, 76
Metz, 7, 22; siege of, 106
Meuse River, 115, 153, 154–55, 158, 192, 326
Mexico, 4, 14, 101, 198, 204, 361
Michele, describes Philip II, 25–26
Middelburg, 134, 149, 167, 351
Miguel, Don, 4
Milan, 5, 21, 28
Milliones, 96n
Missionaries, 147, 200–1
Molina, Tirso de, 96
Moluccas (Spice Islands), 211, 353
Moncontour, 118
Mondragon, Colonel, 134, 149, 314, 332–33
Mons, 80, 129, 130, 131–32, 136, 190
Montezuma, 198, 361
Montigny, Count, 61, 62, 74, 111, 316, 355
Montmorency, Constable, 31, 32–33
Montpensier, Duke of, 33
Montpensier, Madame de, 295, 325
Mook, 150, 151, 152
Moors (Moriscos), 12, 14, 15, 27, 89, 94, 104, 119, 147, 355, 360 (see also Moslems); Inquisition and, 99, 104; revolt of, 119–21, 360
Morailles, Councilor, 328
Moreo, Commander, 314
Moresini, Captain, 266
Moriscos. See Moors (Moriscos)
Moselle River, 4
Moslems, 6, 21, 27, 95, 100, 119–21. See also Islam; Moors (Moriscos)
Motley, John L., 2–3, 31, 33–34, 83, 86, 182; on Alva, 105–6, 124; on Anjou, 226; on Antwerp attacks, 169–71, 229–30; on Archduke Ernest, 328, 330; on autos-da-fé and Philip II, 87–88; on Breda attack, 302–4; on Calvinism, 213, 215, 218; on desecration of churches, 78–79; on Don John of Austria, 173, 176, 180; on French campaigns, 295, 297, 298, 312; on Haarlem sieges, 135, 219; on Henry III, 284; on Henry IV, 323–24, 325; on heresy and rebellion edicts, 74–75, 76; on Holland,

291–92, 351–52; on Inquisition, 55; on Leyden siege, 158; on Mansfield, 326; on Mondragon, 332–330; on Montigny, 61; on Naarden battle, 133–34; on Netherlands, 43–45, 55, 127, 148; on Paris siege, 295; on Parma, 212, 295, 297, 298, 312; on Philip II, 18, 87–88, 354–55, 358, 359; on Prince Maurice, 301, 302; on rebellion, 127, 148; on St. Bartholomew's Day massacre, 131; on Sea Beggars, 126; on Spanish army, 168; on States General, 290–91; on Vargas, 110, 123; on warfare, 117; on wedding ceremony of William of Orange, 58; on Zeeland assault, 165–66

Motley, Stirling Maxwell, 119
Moura, Cristóbal de, 146, 209, 210, 355–56
Muhlberg, battle of, 6, 106
Munster, Treaty of, 1

Naarden, 133–34, 135
Namur, 178, 180, 185, 187, 188, 191, 192, 220
Nantes, Edict of, 345
Naples, 5, 7, 21, 27, 28, 31, 94, 101
Napoleon I, 89, 91
Nauton, Sir Robert, 37
Navagero (Venetian ambassador), 27
Navarre, 12; Black Death in, 98–99
Navarre, Henry, King of. See Henry IV (Henry of Navarre), King of France
Nelson, Horatio, 270
Netherlands, 1–9, 39–50, 51–86, 94–95, 96, 281–87, 296, 300–18, 340–47, 348–54 (see also specific battles, individuals, places, religions); Alva's regime in, 105–38, 147–48, 149, 151, 195, 212–33, 243, 244, 245, 330; death of Philip II and, 348–63 passim; description (geography; history), 41–50; Don John's regime in, 182–94; England and (see under England); France and (see under France); language(s), 41, 42, 46, 58; maps of, 40, 137, 349; Margaret of Parma's regime in, 51–86, 105,

107–8, 148; Parma's regime in, 195, 212–33, 234–42, 243–46; regimes of Mansfeld, Archduke Ernest, and Count Fuentes, 319–33; religious edicts, 47–48, 52ff. (see also specific edits); Requesens' regime in, 137, 148–60, 161–71, 173, 193; Spanish Armada and, 249ff., 264–81 passim; Spanish finances and, 20–21, 22, 23, 122–28, 138, 163–65
Neuchâtel-en-Braye, 310, 311
Nevers (French marshal), 33
New Castile, 10, 89
"New Laws" (1543), 201
Newcastle, 281
New World (Americas), 16, 97, 202, 342. See also Caribbean Islands; Indies; specific places
Nieuport, 15, 234, 255, 257, 274, 278, 280, 353, 364
Nobility, Netherlands, 49–50, 52–53, 56, 61, 62–70, 72–73, 74, 77, 80–83, 314
Nobility, Spanish, 89–90, 93–94, 146, 345
Noircarmes, 107, 124, 132
Nombre de Dios, 23, 203, 206
Noordla lake, 157, 158
Norfolk, Duke of, 121
Normandy, 305, 309–12
North Africa, 87, 119
North Foreland, 254–55
North Sea, 41, 273, 351
Nova Zembla, 352
Nymegen, 136, 305, 306, 307, 325

Ochoa, Domingo de, 272, 275
Oise River, 298
Old Castile, 10, 13, 95
Oldenbarneveldt, John of, 288, 300–2
Olivares, Count of, 1, 313, 334
Oman, Sir Charles, 312
Oosterweel, battle of, 84, 85
Oporto, 207, 211
Orange, Prince of. See William the Silent, Count of Nassau and Prince of Orange
Orange, principality of, 53, 54
Orangists, 63, 122–38, 151–60 passim, 164–71 passim, 172–81, 182–94 passim, 214–33, 234–42. See also

William the Silent, Count of Nassau and Prince of Orange
Orchies, 214
Orsoy, 132
Ortiz, Captain, 219
Ottoman Empire. See Turkey and the Turks (Ottoman Empire)
Oudenaarde, 78, 85
Oudewater, 127
Overyssel, 49, 132, 224, 305
Oxenham, John, 207

Pacification of Ghent, 171, 172–73, 175, 177, 188, 214, 215, 216–17, 218, 354
Panama, 4, 7, 30, 203, 205, 206, 207
Papacy (popes), 8, 12, 39, 67 (see also Catholicism; specific events, popes); and France, 329–30; and French succession (1593), 323–24; and Inquisition, 100–4 (see also Inquisition); and Netherlands revolt (1559–67), 51, 55ff.; Philip II and, 90, 96, 345; Spanish war with, 26–38
Paris, 60, 130, 285, 286, 310, 325; siege of, 295–99, 305, 314, 315
Parma, Alexander Farnese, Duke of, 72, 137, 184–87, 190, 191, 193, 208, 234–42, 243, 329; and Antwerp attack, 234, 236–42; death of, 317–18, 319, 326, 327; described, 212–13, 273–74, 312–16, 318, 328, 331; French campaigns (1589–92), 288–318, 325, 331; illness, 293, 306, 317–18; last days of, 307–8, 312–18; Netherlands regime of, 195, 212–13, 234–42, 243, 244, 245, 254–82 passim, 285, 288–318, 325–26, 353; and Philip II, 146, 193, 214, 216, 220, 222, 223, 234, 236, 244, 252, 254–66, 272–76, 278–82, 294ff., 306–18 passim, 325, 364; replaced, 316–18, 327; and Spanish Armada, 249–66, 271–83, 285, 313–15, 353, 364–65; wounded, 311–12, 317
Parma, Charles Farnese, Duke of, 212
Parma, Margaret, Duchess of. See Margaret, Duchess of Parma
Passy, Colloquy of, 59–60
Paul IV, Pope, 26–31, 39
Pavia, 7, 34

Pedro the Cruel (Spanish king), 99
"Peiswillers," 238, 240
Pérez, Antonio, 64, 66, 93, 176, 186, 195, 209; and Aragon trouble, 334–36
Pérez, Gonzalo, 93
Pérez, Juana, 335, 336
Perpetual Edict, 175, 177, 214
Perrenot, Antony, Bishop of Arras. See Granvelle, Antony Perrenot, Cardinal
Perrenot family, 51, 54
Peru, 4, 101, 195–204, 207; silver mines, 13, 14, 22, 23, 195–204
Philip II, King of Spain; accession to throne (background; birth), 2–9, 10–16, 17–24; and Armadas, 247–83 passim, 284, 316; "crimes" of, 355, 358–59; criticism of, 355, 358–63; death of, 354–57; and decline of Spain, 354–63; described (characterized), 8, 17–21, 25–26, 87–88, 91–93, 139–47, 162, 244, 300, 338–40, 354–61; finances (economics; debts; bankruptcies), 2, 7, 14, 17–24, 29, 30, 31, 34, 36, 38, 88, 89–98, 163–65, 203, 214–16, 334–37, 339–47, 357, 359–62; illness, 339–40, 354–57; last years of, 338–47, 354–61; letters to his daughters, 20, 140–42; marriages (children; family), 7, 8–9, 17, 19–20, 24, 30, 39, 87–88, 119, 129, 140–45, 162, 164, 208, 338–39, 346, 355–57, 358 (see also specific individuals); and Netherlands (see Netherlands; specific events, individuals); piety and religion of, 51–86 passim, 87–92, 355; and specific countries, events, individuals (see specific countries, events, individuals)
Philip III, King of Spain, 1, 140, 339, 355–57
Philip V, King of Spain, 346n
Philip VI, King of France, 287
Philip the Fair (Philip IV of France), 4, 5
Philip the Good (Duke of Burgundy), 8
Philip the Handsome (Philip I of Castile), 42
Philippines, 101

Piatti (Spanish agent), 249

Picardy, 31, 36, 331

Pirates (piracy), 119, 120, 121, 125–27, 362; and Indies, 203, 205–7

Pius IV, Pope, 39

Pizarro, Francisco, 198, 199, 201, 313

Pizarros, 199, 201, 313

Plague, 157–58. *See also* Black Death

Plessis-les-Tours, 223, 226

Plymouth, 121, 242, 256, 267, 269, 271

Politiques (party), 285n, 321, 322

Pons, Marquis of, 287

Pont de l'Arche, 311, 312

Poperinghe, 78

Portland, 272, 275

Portugal, 10, 17, 315 (*see also* Lisbon); and Armada, 268, 269; and Indies, 195, 196; Philip II in, 140–42; Spain and, 195, 207–11, 225, 245, 247, 315, 335, 345, 358, 362

Potosí, 23, 202, 203

Preaching, 75–76, 77, 80, 82

Prescott, William H., 26, 28, 31, 33, 85, 86; describes Antwerp, 45

Prinsenhof (convent), 232–33

Privados, office of, 356

Privy Council, 43, 51–52, 68, 74

Protestantism (Protestants), 5–6, 15–16, 26, 29–41, 75ff., 88, 144, 288, 294 (*see also* specific aspects, countries, individuals, sects); Armada and, 269; and Inquisition, 104 (*see also* Inquisition); and Netherlands, 47–50, 52ff., 105–38 passim, 149–60 passim, 161–71, 212ff., 234–42, 345–57; view of Philip II by, 357–58

Provence, 58

Puritanism, rise of, 345

Putnam, Ruth, 113

Pyrenees, 10

Pyrenees, Peace of the, 1

Quemadero, 87, 103

Quentin, St., 33

Raleigh, Sir Walter, 59, 269–70, 340

Ranuccio, Prince, 209, 312, 315, 317

Ravenna, battle of (1512), 344

Real de a ocho ("Piece of Eight"), 14n

Recalde, Juan Martínez de, 268

Reconquista, 12, 15, 120

Reformation, Protestant, 5–6, 15–16, 75ff., 213ff., 357–58, 360. *See also* Protestantism (Protestants); Reformed Church; specific countries, denominations, individuals

Reformed Church, 161, 184, 213ff. *See also* Protestantism (Protestants); Reformation, Protestant; specific countries, denominations, individuals

Regensburg, Diet of, 6

Rembrandt, Harmensz van Rijn, 46

Remy, St., oil of, 232–24

Requesens y Zúñiga, Luis de, 222, 259; described, 148–49; regime in Netherlands of (1573–74), 137, 148–60, (1574–76), 161–71; replaced, 173, 193

Revolt of the Netherlands (Geyl), 127–28

Rheims, 323

Rhine River, 115, 126, 305, 333, 360

Rhynland, 153, 154–55, 156, 158

Richardot, Councilor, 328

Richebourg, Marquis de, 239

Ridolfi Plot, 121–22, 245

Rijksmuseum, 47, 352

Rijnemants, 191

Rise of the Dutch Republic (Motley), 2–3, 234. *See also* Motley, John L.

Roble de Billy, de, 239, 240

Rocroi, battle of, 29n, 353

Roda, de, 167, 171

Roermond, 129, 130

Rojas, Fernando de, 99

Rome (Roman Catholic Church), 28, 30, 90. *See also* Catholicism; Papacy

Romero, Julian, 115, 131

Rotterdam, 46, 127

Rouen, 209–12, 316, 326

Rowse, A. L., 290

Royal councils, 43, 51, 93–94, 95. *See also* specific councils

Rubens, John, 118

Rubens, Peter Paul, 118, 350

Rudolf of Hapsburg, Emperor, 187–88, 191

Rue, fortress of, 310, 311

Ruiz, José Martínez (Azorín), 283, 359

Ruiz, Madalena, 141–42, 339

Sadler, Sir Ralph, 226
Sagres, castle of, 252, 253
St. Aldegonde. *See* Marnix, Philip of
    St. Aldegonde
St. André, Marshal, 33
St. Bartholomew's Day, 58
St. Bartholomew's Massacre, 32, 130–
    32, 228
St. Denis, church of, 322–23
St. Gudule, church of, 54
St. John, Knights of, 106
St. Lawrence's Day, 278
St. Omer, 78
St. Quentin, battle of, 31–34, 35, 69,
    278, 361
St. Trond, 77
St. Vaast, abbey of, 218, 317
Salamanca, 13
Salic law, 287, 308, 320
Sambre River, 192
San Domingo, 206–7
San Juan de Ulúa, 203, 204, 205, 360
San Lorenzo, 92, 96
San Martín (Spanish Armada flagship),
    267, 272, 276, 281
Santa Cruz, Alvaro de Bazán, Marquis
    of, 146, 247–49, 250, 252, 253,
    254, 257–59, 260, 268; death of,
    259, 264
Santander, 255, 259
Santiago, order of, 8, 89
Saragossa, 12–13, 335–36
Savoy, 36
Savoy, Catherine, Duchess of, 339
Savoy, Duke of, 30, 31, 33, 339
Scheldt River, 45, 46, 84, 134, 257,
    236–42, 292, 348–50
Schieland, 157, 158
Schiller, Johann C. F., 143
Schwartzreiters, 29, 33
Scotland, 39; Catholics in, 250, 253
Sea Beggars, 125–27, 132, 134–38, 156–
    60, 165–71, 240 (*See also* Beg-
    gars); and Armada, 272, 278
Sebastian I, King of Portugal, 208, 209
Secretary of State (Spanish), office of,
    93
Segovia, 13, 69, 70; "Wood of," 92
Seine River, 298, 299, 305, 311, 312
Senne River, 44
Sentence of Guadalupe, 88
Serfdom, 88, 200, 201

Sermons, "hedge," 75–76
Servicios, 96
Seville, 13, 95, 104, 164, 202, 203, 359
Seymour, Lord, 273
Shakespeare, William, 283
Sichem, 190, 235, 301
Sicily, 5, 8, 12, 94, 101
Sidney, Sir Philip, 148, 227, 304
Sierra Morena, 10
Sierra Nevada, 10
Silver, 5, 13, 14, 23, 95, 201–4, 347
Simancas, 92, 111n, 316
Sluys, 254, 255, 256, 274, 302, 305
Smet, Christopher de, 68
Soignies, forest of, 44
Solent, The, 254, 269, 271
Somme River, 32, 311
Soranza, Francesco, 357
Soriano (Venetian envoy), 19, 25, 26,
    147
Souvray, Giles de, 324
Spa, 178, 293, 306, 314, 315
Spain, death of Philip II and decline
    of, 348–63; description, geography,
    history, 1–9, 10–16, 87–104, 119–
    21, 334–37 (*see also* specific as-
    pects, events, individuals, loca-
    tions); and England, France,
    Indies, Netherlands, Portugal (*see*
    England; France; Indies; Nether-
    lands; Portugal); government and
    economy (Councils, Church, and
    Inquisition), 87–104 (*see also*
    Armadas, Spanish; Army, Spanish;
    Church, Spanish; Inquisition, Span-
    ish; specific aspects, councils, in-
    dividuals)
Spanish Armada (Lewis), 261n, 268
Spanish Armadas. *See* Armada, Spanish
    (1588); Armada, Spanish (1596),
    Armada, Spanish (1597)
"Spanish Fury," 171, 314
"Spanish Road," 176, 178
Specie. *See* Currency (specie)
Spice Islands. *See* Moluccas (Spice
    Islands)
Spice trade, 24, 207, 353
Spinola, Ambrogio, 313, 353
Spithead, 254
Stadtholders (stadtholderates), 43, 46,
    49, 71, 82

State Council, 43, 51–52, 55, 62, 63–71, 73, 83
States General, French, 285, 319–22
States General, Netherlands, 3, 42, 50, 60, 77, 167, 168, 171–91 passim, 214–31 passim, 245, 288ff., 301, 351–54; and Elizabeth I, 246; and taxes, 122–25
Steenwyk, 326
Strada, de, 86, 117
Stubbs (pamphleteer), 227
Styria, 5
Suleiman the Magnificent, 6
Suprema, 101, 360
Surrender of Breda (painting), 353
Swiss, 107

Tagus River, 254, 258, 263
Tassis, Pedro, 170
Taxes and taxation, 89, 90, 91, 95, 96, 97–98, 122–28, 138, 163, 343, 351. *See also* specific taxes
Tello de Guzmán, Rodrigo, 275, 276
Tenochtitlán, 198, 361
Tenth Penny (tax), 122–25, 127–28, 136, 149, 162
Terceira, 211
Tercius reales, 91
Tercios. See Army, Spanish
Teresa, St., 15, 90–91; *Life*, 96
Termonde, 86
Terra Nova, Duke of, 188, 217
Thames River, 254–55, 256, 281
Theatines (monastic order), 26
Thirty Years War, 16
Thomas à Kempis, 47
Thou, de, 31, 33
Titelman, Peter, 67
Titian, 33, 120, 139
Tocqueville, Alexis de, 123
Toledo, 13; Archbishop of, 90, 91
Toledo, Garcia de, 146
Tongres, 117
Torbay, 271
Tordesillas, Treaty of, 197, 211
Torquemada, Tomás de, 100–1
Touraine, 60, 75, 80, 81
Tournai, 58, 214
Trade, 350–52. *See also* Currency; Indies; specific aspects, items, places
Trent, Council of, 67–68, 70
Tresslong, Bois de, 126

Tunis, 6, 106
Turkey and the Turks (Ottoman Empire), 6, 15, 16, 21, 28, 96, 119, 120, 122, 249, 361
Turnhout, 15, 85, 344
Tuscany, 28
Twentieth Penny (tax), 122–25
Tyler, Royall, 22
Tyrol, 5

Union of Arras, 215, 217–18
Union of Brussels, 172–73, 184
Union of Utrecht, 215–16, 222, 234, 288ff.
United Netherlands. *See* United Provinces (United Netherlands)
United Provinces (United Netherlands), 184, 234, 291–92, 349, 351
Ushant, 267
Utrecht, 41, 42, 49, 80, 123, 126, 128, 136, 347, 350ff., 354; Union of, 215–16, 222, 234, 288ff., 347, 350ff., 354

Valdez, Francisco de, 152, 153, 155, 156, 159–60
Valdez, Pedro de, 268
Valencia, 5, 10, 12, 51, 88, 89, 100
Valenciennes, 68, 80, 83, 85
Valladolid, 13, 17, 97, 104
Valois, French house of, 4, 35, 48, 225, 231–32, 284–87. *See also* specific individuals
Van den Bergh, Count, 132
Van der Does, Jacob, 155–56
Van der Essen, Léon, quoted on Parma, 236, 239, 241, 293, 300, 315
Van der Vynckt, *Histoire des Troubles aux Pays Bas* by, 71
Van der Werf (Leyden burgomaster), 155, 158
Van Ende, 171
Vargas, Juan de, 111, 112, 124, 171; Motley describes, 110, 123, 171
Vaucelles, 25, 36
Veere, 127
Vega, Garcilaso de la, 96
Vega, Lope de, 15, 19, 268, 330
Velázquez, Diego Rodríguez de Silva y, 96, 330, 353
Venta Cruces, 206

Venice (Venetians), 45, 120, 357. *See also* specific individuals
Vera Cruz, 203, 206
Vervins, Peace of, 345–46
Vienna, 6, 8, 183, 184. *See also* Austria
Viglius van Aytta (Frisian jurist), 74, 124
Villalar, 89
Villars, de (French marshal), 309, 310, 311, 331
Voorweg, 156, 157

Waal River, 115, 304, 305, 307, 325
Walcheron, isle of, 83–84, 126, 127, 134, 149, 293
Walloon provinces, 41, 42, 46, 49, 58, 75, 182, 190–91, 213ff., 227ff.; destruction of churches in, 78–80, 81; soldiers, 151, 169–70, 297, 305
Walsingham, Sir Francis, 191–92, 225, 226, 244, 245, 251, 258, 273
Wedgwood, Veronica, 54
Welsers, 7
Wentworth, Earl of, 35
Wesley, Charles, 76
Wesley, John, 76
Wight, Isle of, 253, 254, 265, 269, 272
"Wild Beggars," 112. *See also* Beggars
Wille, Ambrose, 75
Willebroek, 86
William the Silent, Count of Nassau and Prince of Orange, 3, 50, 53, 54, 301 (*see also* Orangists); *Apologia*, 48, 222–24; death of, 228–29, 232–33, 234; described, 53–55, 58, 118, 161–62, 232–33, 234; enters

Antwerp in triumph, 179–81; and Granvelle, 60, 61, 62, 63, 66; and King's Ban against, 222–24, 235; marriages, 57–58, 86, 118, 162, 232–33, 234; and Philip II, 54, 62, 63, 71–74, 129–30, 161, 222–24, 355; and Protestant rebellion in Netherlands, 53–55, 60–86 passim, 118–38 passim, 149–71 passim, 174, 175, 177–81, 214–33 passim, 237, 315; as ruler of Netherlands, 179–81, 182–92, 315
Wittenberg, University of, 5
Wool trade, 13, 44, 344
Wormer, 351

Ypres, 85, 234, 235
Ysel River, 154
Yssel River, 154n, 304
Yuste, 20, 30, 34, 38, 139, 143
Yvetot, 312

Zacatecas, 202
Zeeland, 46, 49, 55, 71, 126, 128, 134, 149, 161, 163, 165–71, 172, 174, 175, 182, 191, 291, 293, 301; and Armada, 255, 256, 272, 278, 280, 281; and rebellion (1578–84), 213–14, 215, 223, 224, 228; and trade, 351
Zeirickzee, 165–66
Zoetermeer lake, 156, 157
Zoeterwoude, 158, 159
Zuider Zee, 126, 127, 135
Zutphen, 133, 190, 234, 304–5, 306